CONTENTS

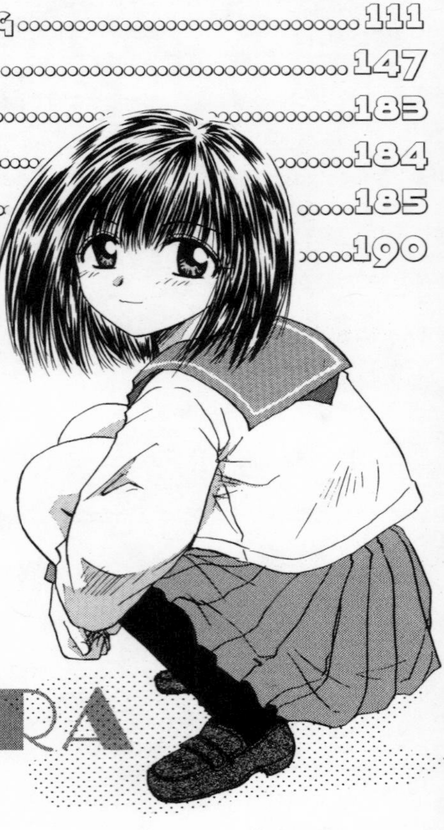

KAGETORA

A Note from the Author

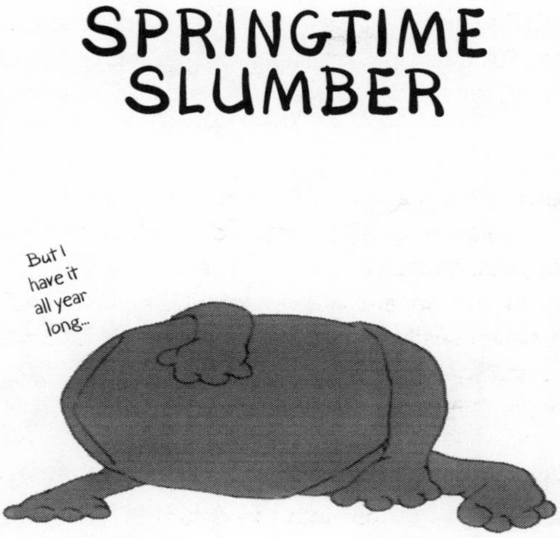
SPRINGTIME
SLUMBER
But I have it all year long...

I got a hold of some good sake, so I'd like to bring it with me and go look at the flowers. Now the problem is my allergies and if I can take any time off of work...Hmm, what should I do?

Segami

Honorifics Explained

Throughout the Del Rey Manga books, you will find Japanese honorifics left intact in the translations. For those not familiar with how the Japanese use honorifics and, more important, how they differ from American honorifics, we present this brief overview.

Politeness has always been a critical facet of Japanese culture. Ever since the feudal era, when Japan was a highly stratified society, use of honorifics—which can be defined as polite speech that indicates relationship or status—has played an essential role in the Japanese language. When addressing someone in Japanese, an honorific usually takes the form of a suffix attached to one's name (example: "Asuna-san"), or as a title at the end of one's name or in place of the name itself (example: "Negi-sensei," or simply "Sensei!").

Honorifics can be expressions of respect or endearment. In the context of manga and anime, honorifics give insight into the nature of the relationship between characters. Many translations into English leave out these important honorifics and therefore distort the "feel" of the original Japanese. Because Japanese honorifics contain nuances that English honorifics lack, it is our policy at Del Rey not to translate them. Here, instead, is a guide to some of the honorifics you may encounter in Del Rey Manga.

-san: This is the most common honorific and is equivalent to Mr., Miss, Ms., or Mrs. It is the all-purpose honorific and can be used in any situation where politeness is required.

-sama: This is one level higher than "-san." It is used to confer great respect.

-dono: This comes from the word "tono," which means "lord." It is an even higher level than "-sama" and confers utmost respect.

-kun: This suffix is used at the end of boys' names to express familiarity or endearment. It is also sometimes used by men among friends, or when addressing someone younger or of a lower station.

-chan: This is used to express endearment, mostly toward girls. It is also used for little boys, pets, and even among lovers. It gives a sense of childish cuteness.

Bozu: This is an informal way to refer to a boy, similar to the English terms "kid" and "squirt."

Sempai/
Senpai: This title suggests that the addressee is one's senior in a group or organization. It is most often used in a school setting, where underclassmen refer to their upperclassmen as "sempai." It can also be used in the workplace, such as when a newer employee addresses an employee who has seniority in the company.

Kohai: This is the opposite of "sempai" and is used toward underclassmen in school or newcomers in the workplace. It connotes that the addressee is of a lower station.

Sensei: Literally meaning "one who has come before," this title is used for teachers, doctors, or masters of any profession or art.

[blank]: This is usually forgotten in these lists, but it is perhaps the most significant difference between Japanese and English. The lack of honorific means that the speaker has permission to address the person in a very intimate way. Usually, only family, spouses, or very close friends have this kind of permission. Known as yobisute, it can be gratifying when someone who has earned the intimacy starts to call one by one's name without an honorific. But when that intimacy hasn't been earned, it can be very insulting.

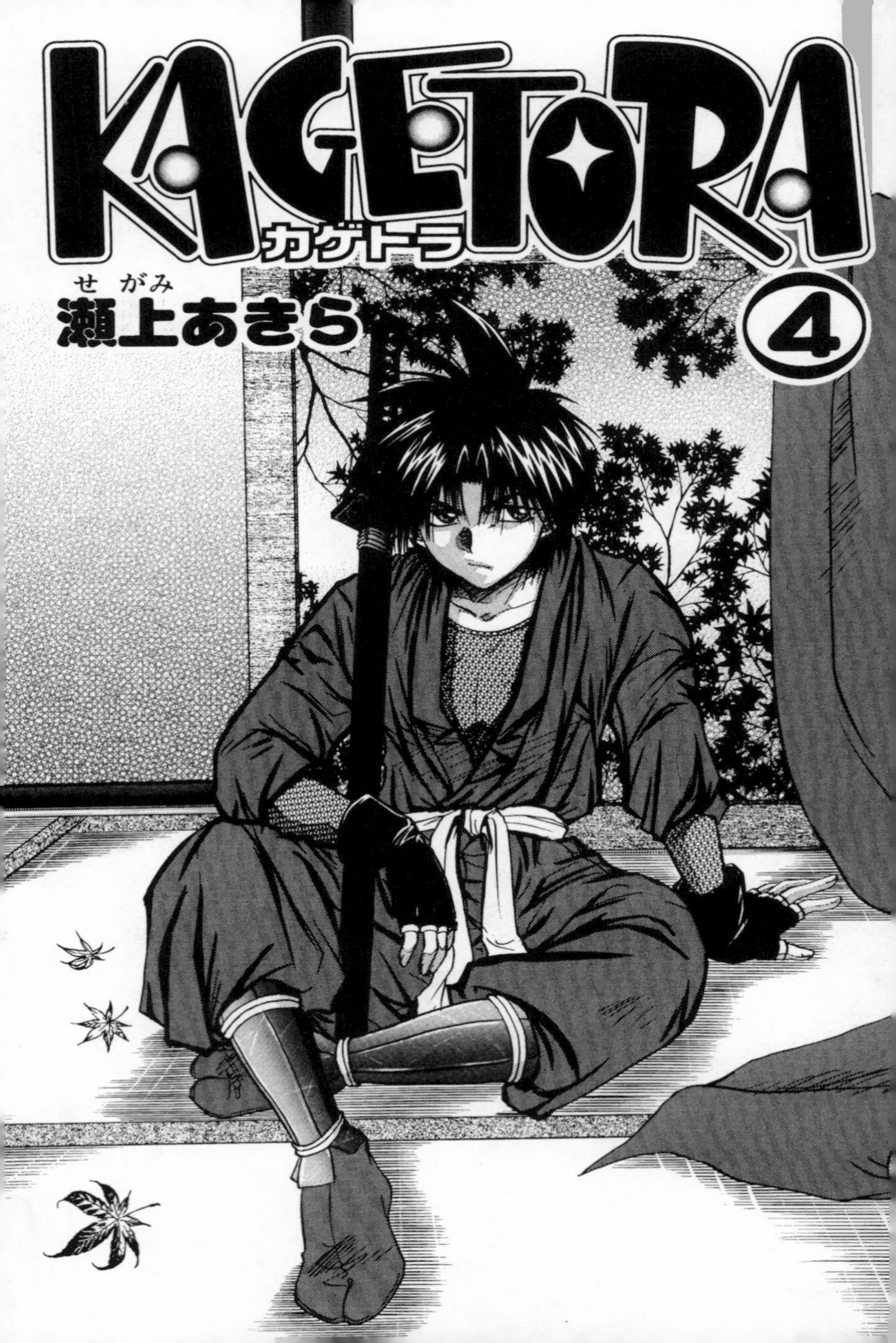
KAGETORA
カゲトラ
せがみ
瀬上あきら
4

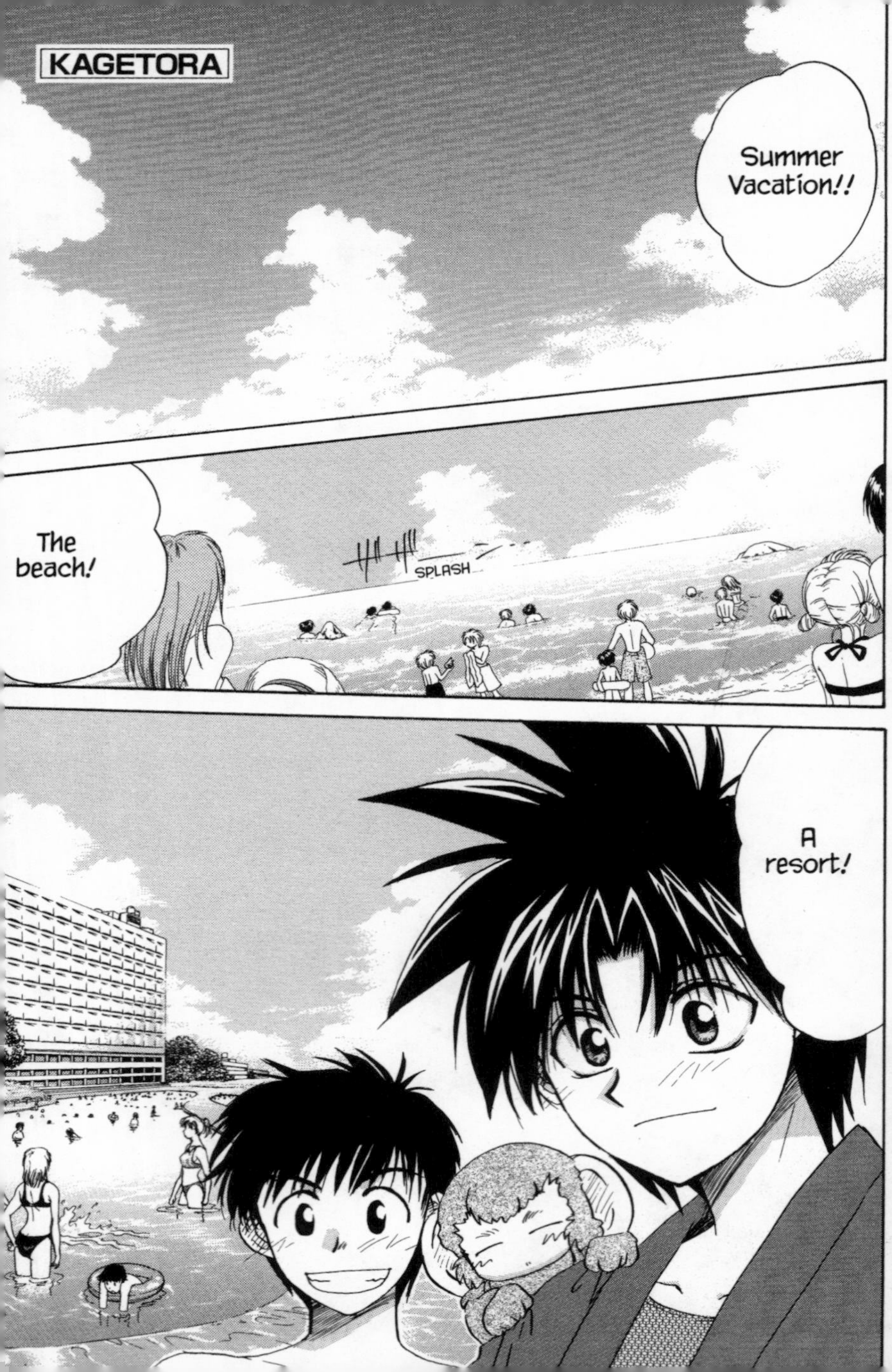
Summer Vacation!!
SPLASH
The beach!
A resort!

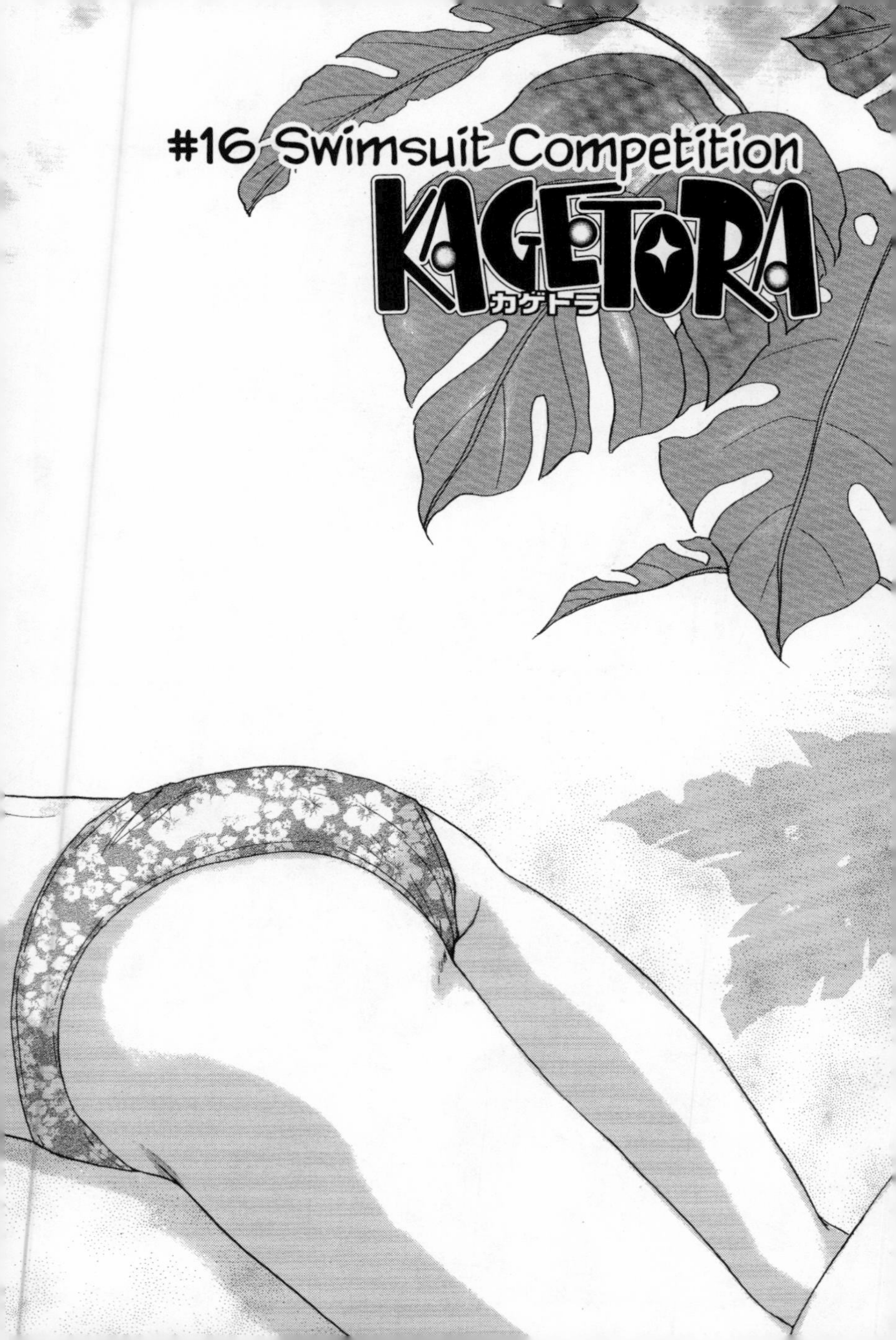
#16 Swimsuit Competition
KAGETORA
カゲトラ

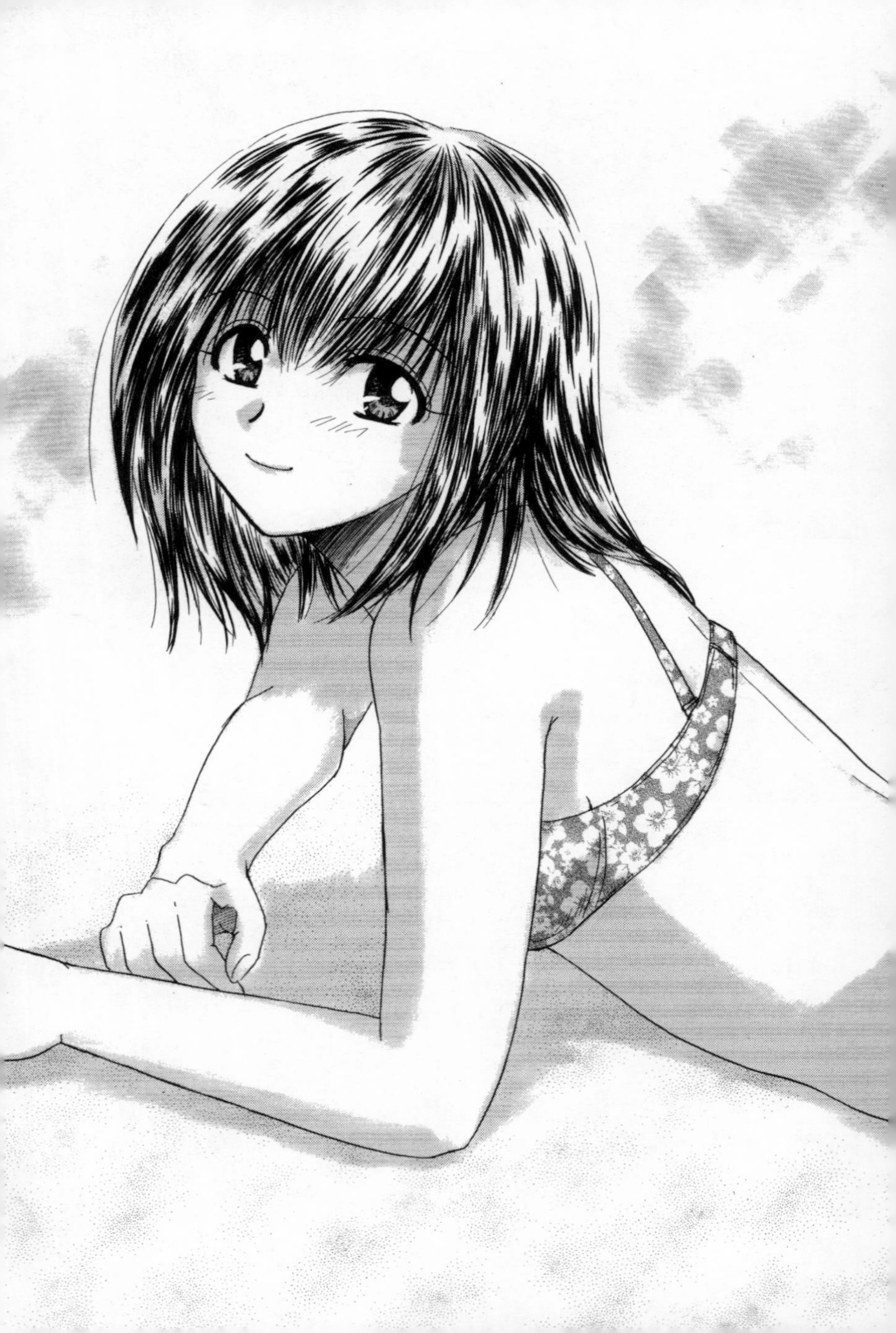

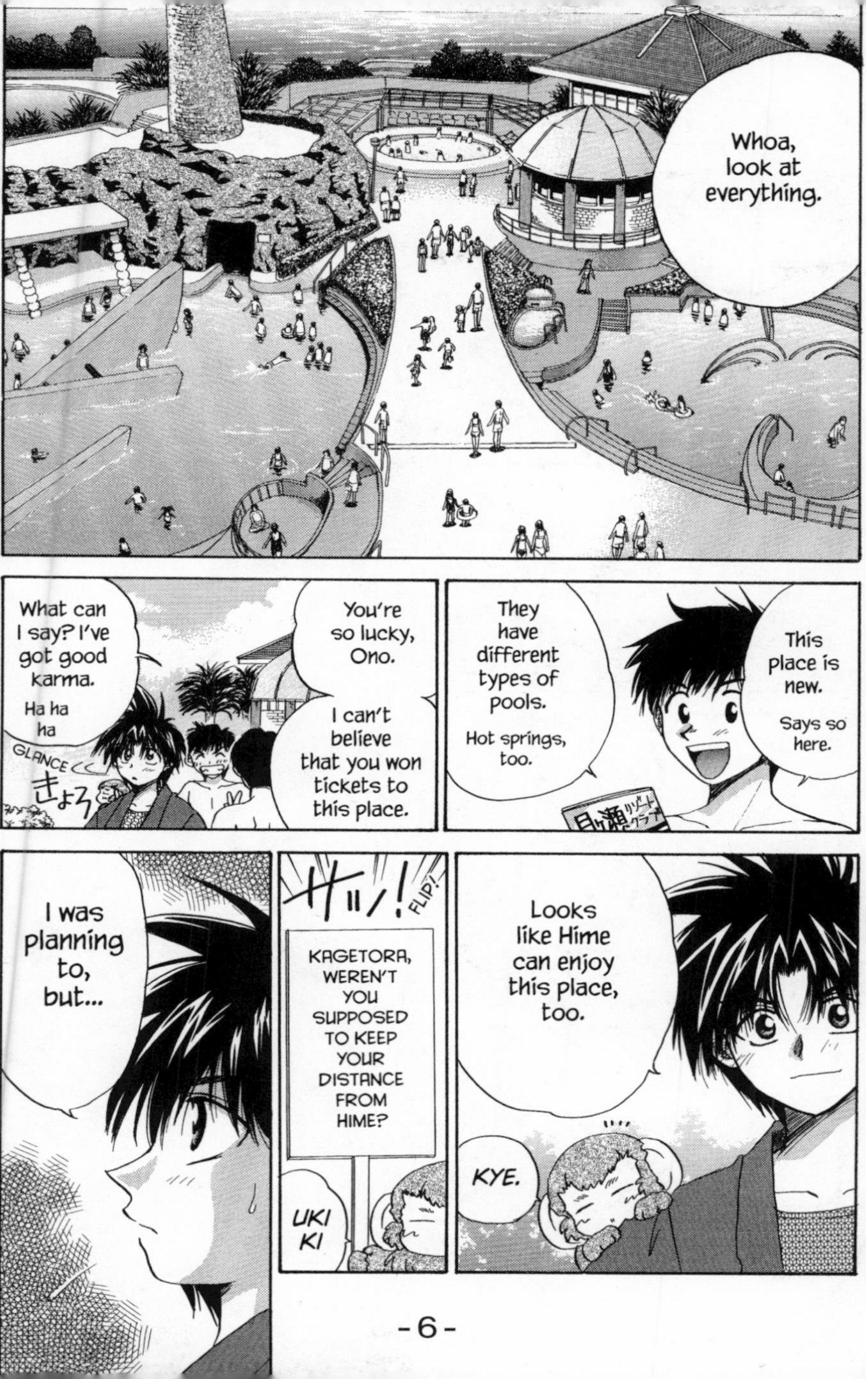
Whoa, look at everything.
This place is new.
Says so here.
They have different types of pools.
Hot springs, too.
You're so lucky, Ono.
I can't believe that you won tickets to this place.
What can I say? I've got good karma.
Ha ha ha
GLANCE
きょろ
Looks like Hime can enjoy this place, too.
KYE.
サッ!
FLIP!
KAGETORA, WEREN'T YOU SUPPOSED TO KEEP YOUR DISTANCE FROM HIME?
UKI KI
I was planning to, but...

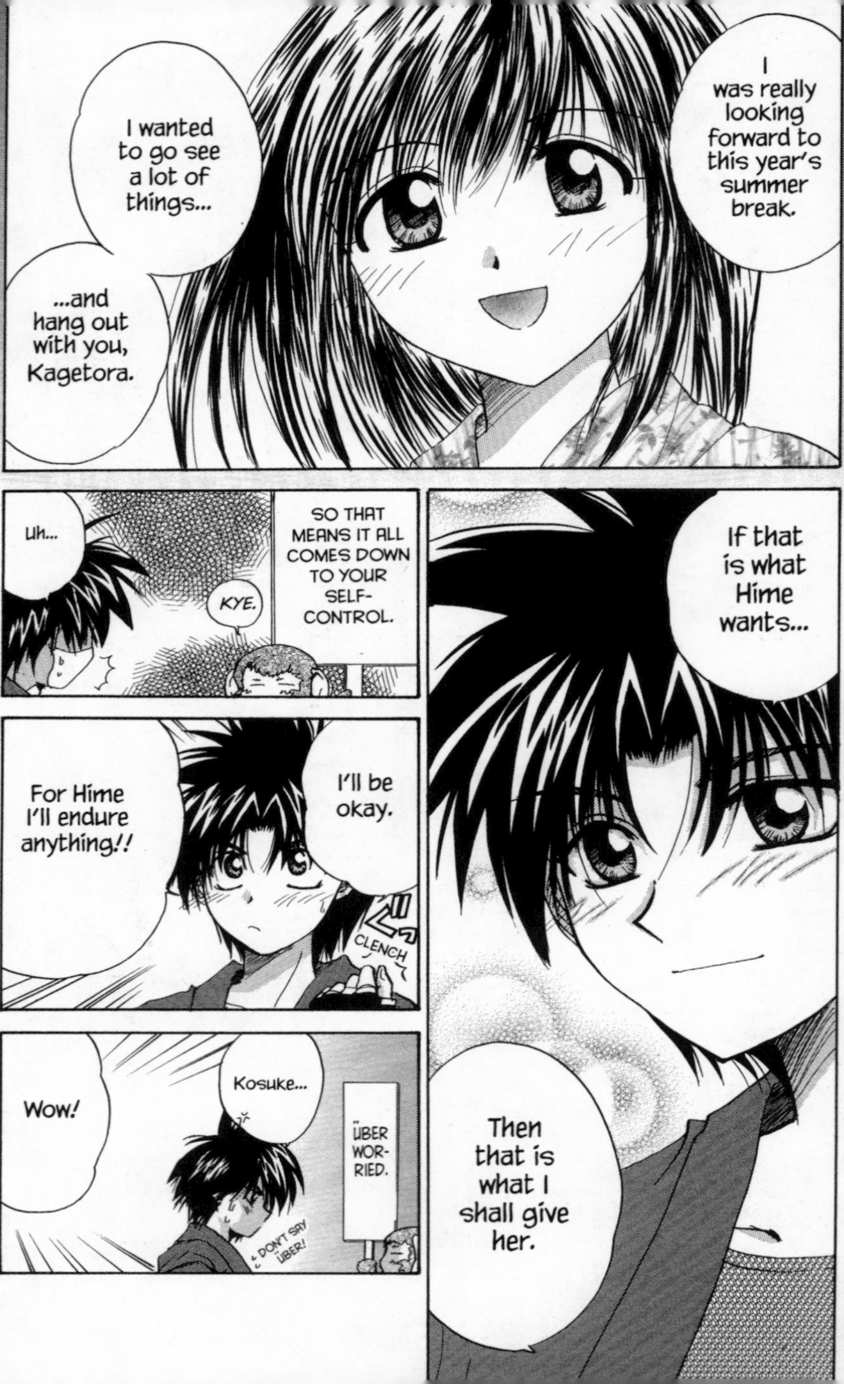
I was really looking forward to this year's summer break.
I wanted to go see a lot of things...
...and hang out with you, Kagetora.
If that is what Hime wants...
Then that is what I shall give her.
SO THAT MEANS IT ALL COMES DOWN TO YOUR SELF-CONTROL.
KYE.
Uh...
I'll be okay.
CLENCH
For Hime I'll endure anything!!
ÜBER WORRIED.
Kosuke...
DON'T SAY ÜBER!
Wow!

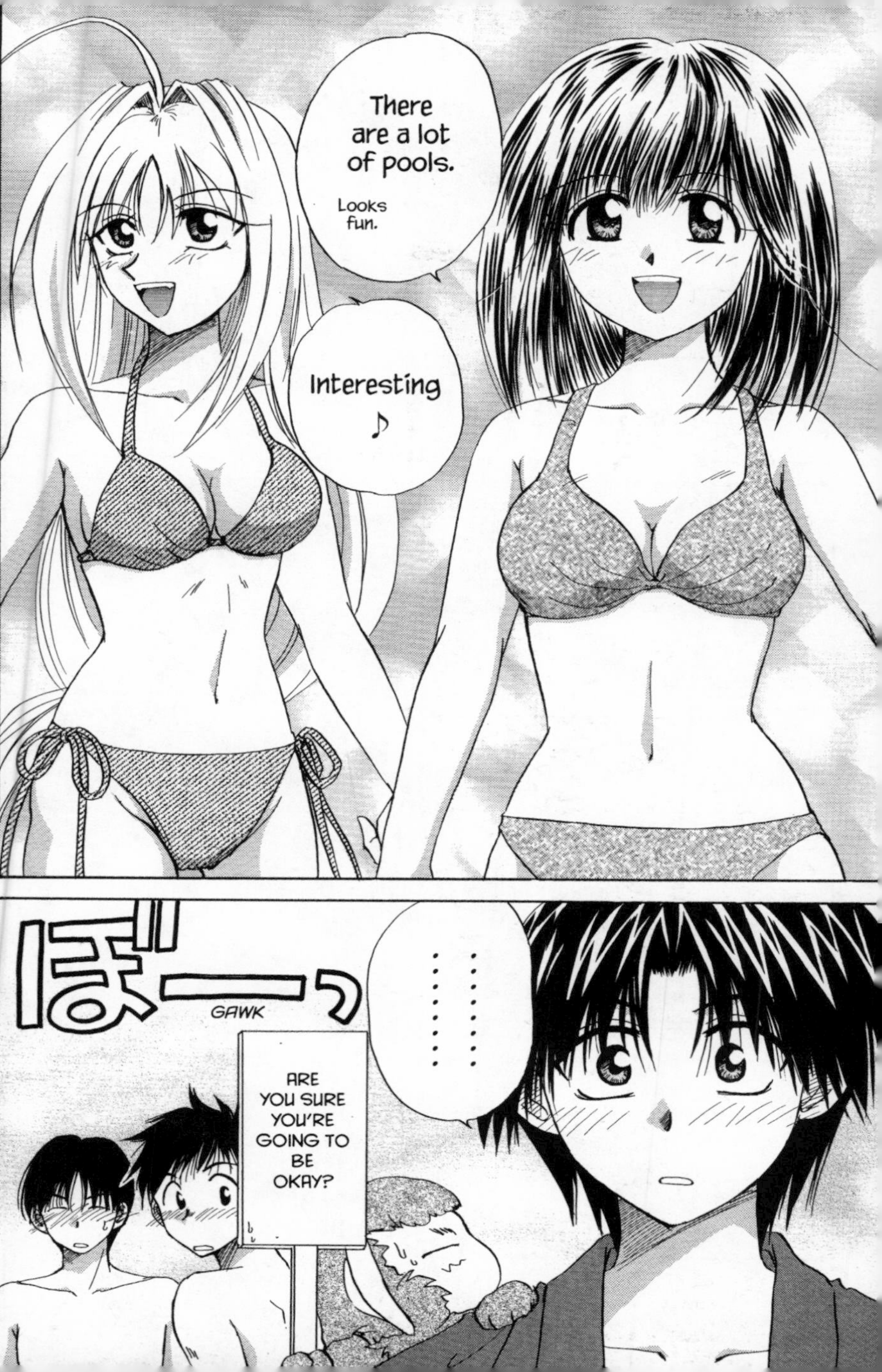
There are a lot of pools.
Looks fun.
Interesting ♪
......
......
ぼーっ
GAWK
ARE YOU SURE YOU'RE GOING TO BE OKAY?

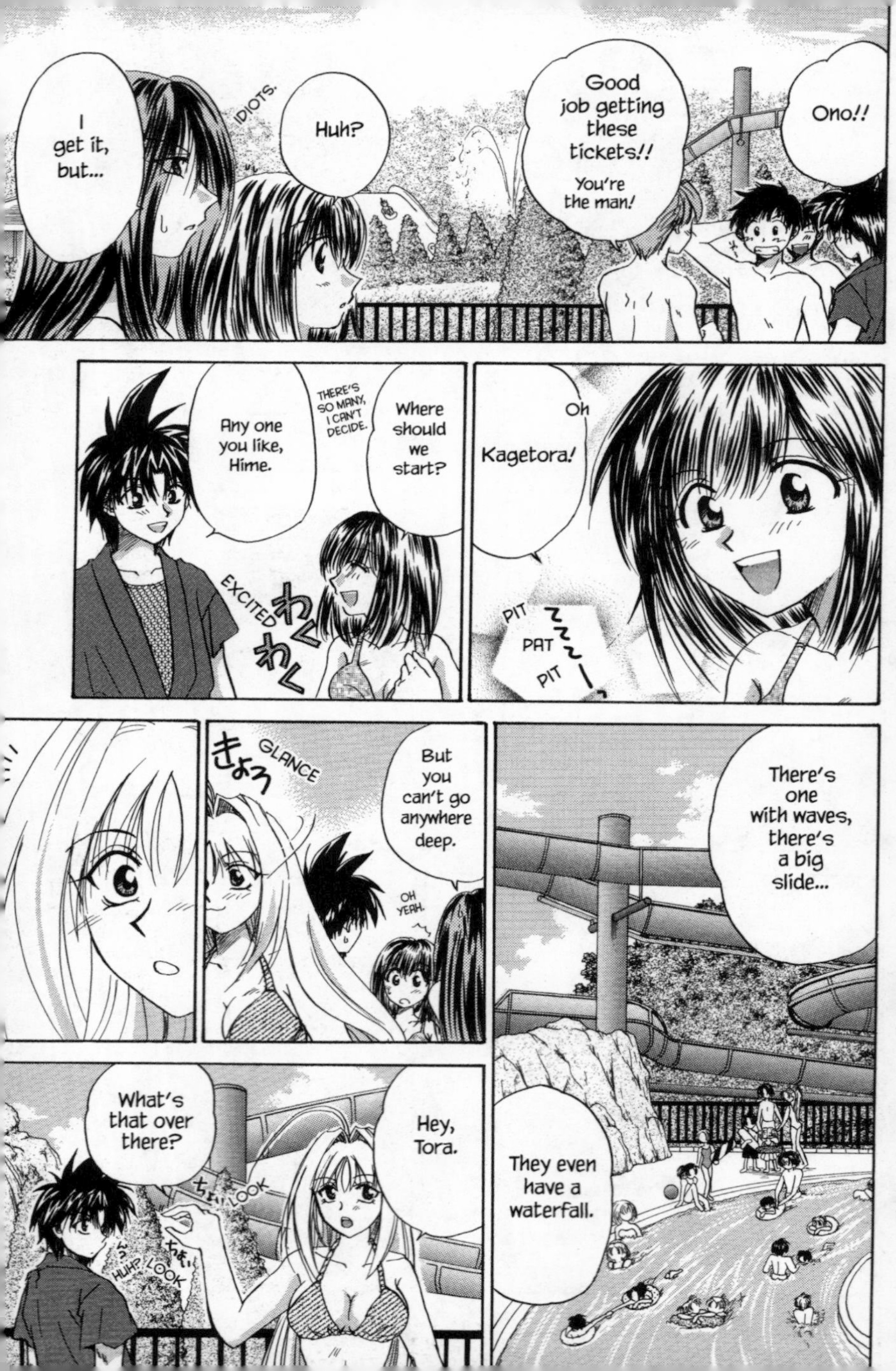

Ono!!
Good job getting these tickets!!
You're the man!
Huh?
IDIOTS.
I get it, but...
Oh
Kagetora!
PIT
PAT
PIT
Where should we start?
THERE'S SO MANY, I CAN'T DECIDE.
Any one you like, Hime.
わくわく
EXCITED
There's one with waves, there's a big slide...
They even have a waterfall.
But you can't go anywhere deep.
きょろ
GLANCE
OH YEAH.
Hey, Tora.
What's that over there?
LOOK
HUH? LOOK

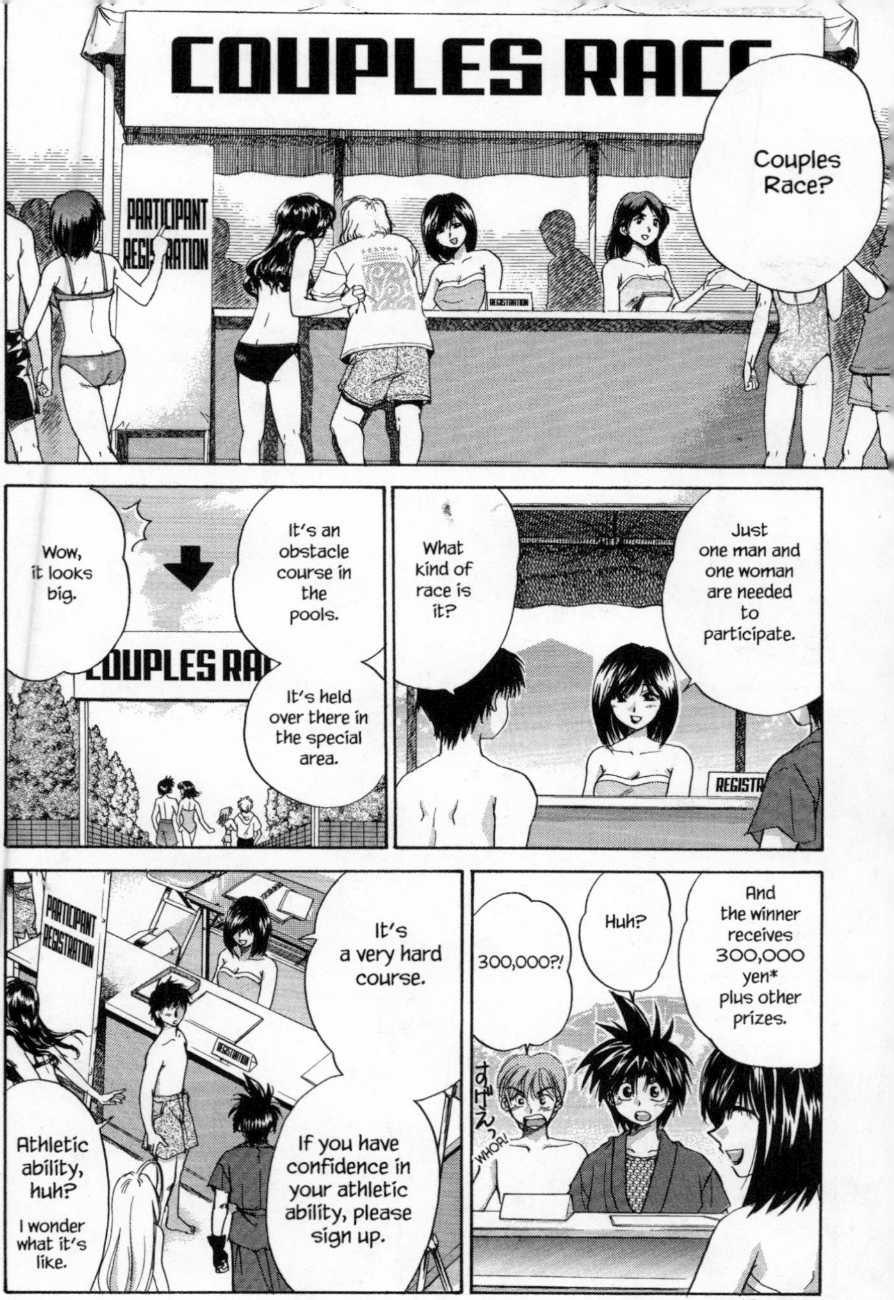
COUPLES RACE
PARTICIPANT REGISTRATION
REGISTRATION
Couples Race?
Just one man and one woman are needed to participate.
What kind of race is it?
REGISTRA
It's an obstacle course in the pools.
It's held over there in the special area.
Wow, it looks big.
COUPLES RA
And the winner receives 300,000 yen* plus other prizes.
Huh?
300,000?!
すげえっ
WHOA!
It's a very hard course.
If you have confidence in your athletic ability, please sign up.
PARTICIPANT REGISTRATION
REGISTRATION
Athletic ability, huh?
I wonder what it's like.

* $3,000

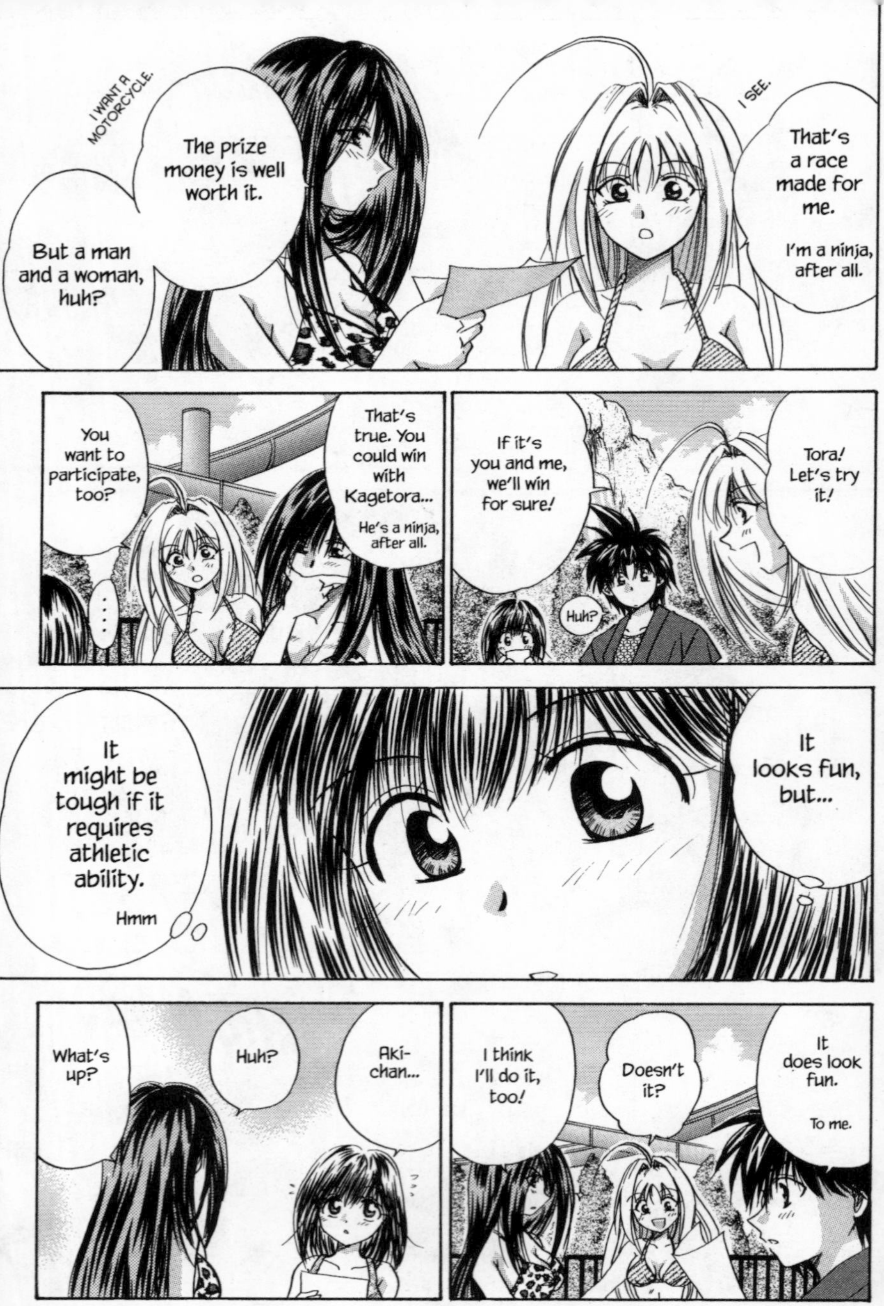
I SEE.
That's a race made for me.
I'm a ninja, after all.
I WANT A MOTORCYCLE.
The prize money is well worth it.
But a man and a woman, huh?
Tora! Let's try it!
If it's you and me, we'll win for sure!
Huh?
That's true. You could win with Kagetora...
He's a ninja, after all.
You want to participate, too?
...
It looks fun, but...
It might be tough if it requires athletic ability.
Hmm
It does look fun.
To me.
Doesn't it?
I think I'll do it, too!
Aki-chan...
Huh?
What's up?

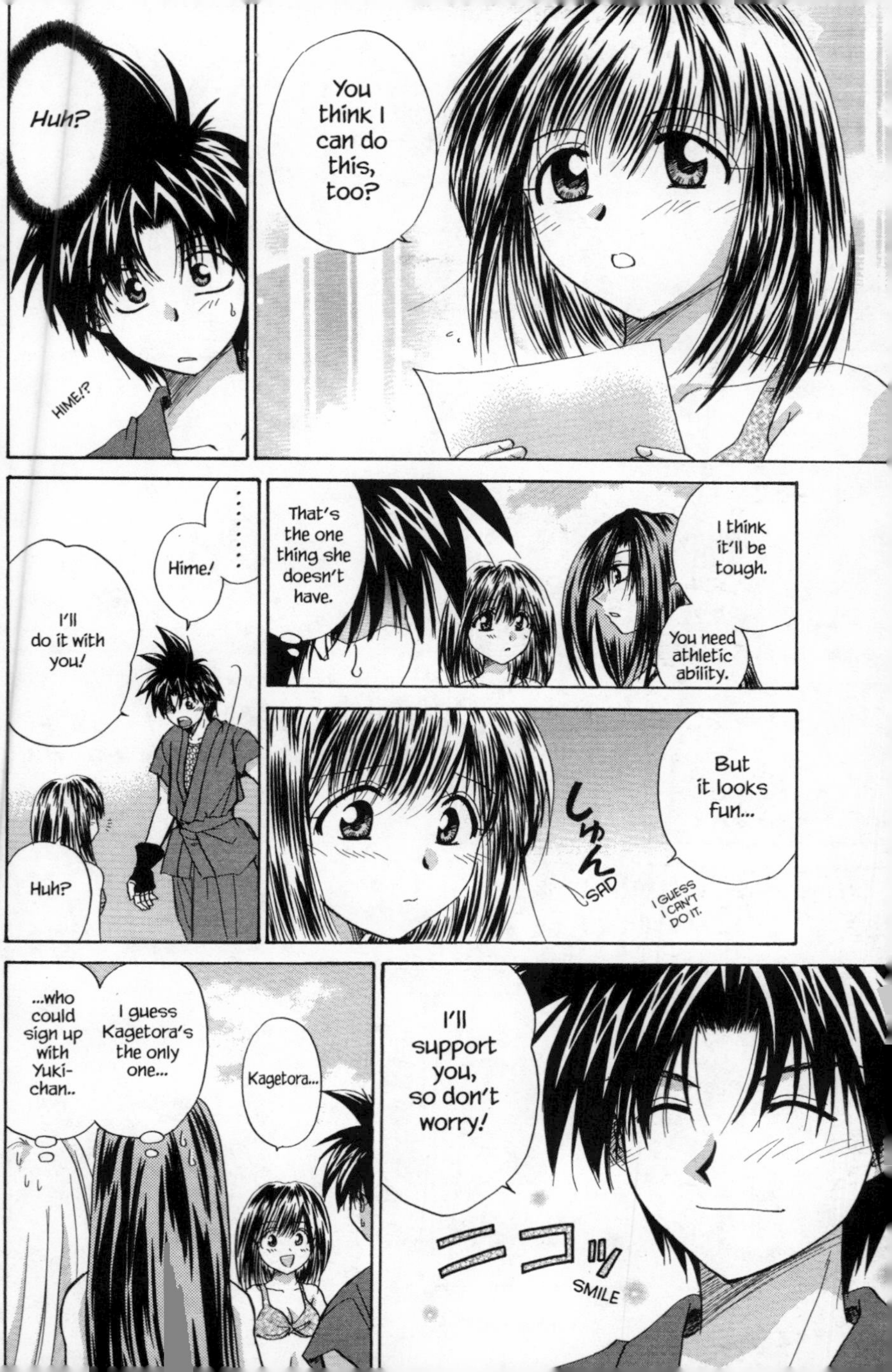
You think I can do this, too?
Huh?
HIME!?
I think it'll be tough.
You need athletic ability.
That's the one thing she doesn't have.
But it looks fun...
しゅん
SAD
I GUESS I CAN'T DO IT.
......
Hime!
I'll do it with you!
Huh?
I'll support you, so don't worry!
ニコッ
SMILE
Kagetora...
I guess Kagetora's the only one...
...who could sign up with Yuki-chan..

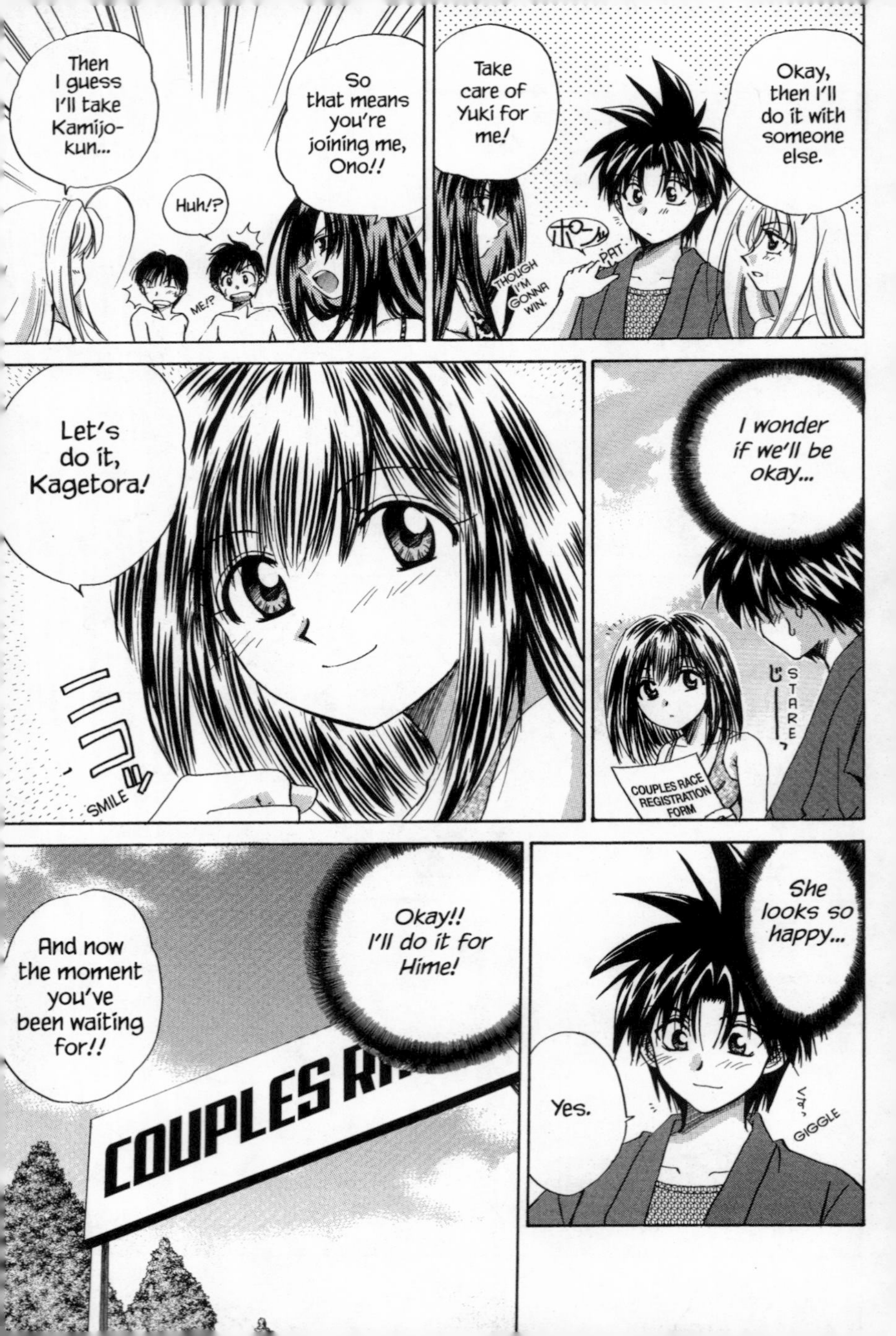
Okay, then I'll do it with someone else.
Take care of Yuki for me!
PAT
THOUGH I'M GONNA WIN.
So that means you're joining me, Ono!!
Then I guess I'll take Kamijo-kun...
Huh!?
ME!?
I wonder if we'll be okay...
STARE
COUPLES RACE REGISTRATION FORM
Let's do it, Kagetora!
SMILE
She looks so happy...
GIGGLE
Yes.
Okay!! I'll do it for Hime!
And now the moment you've been waiting for!!
COUPLES

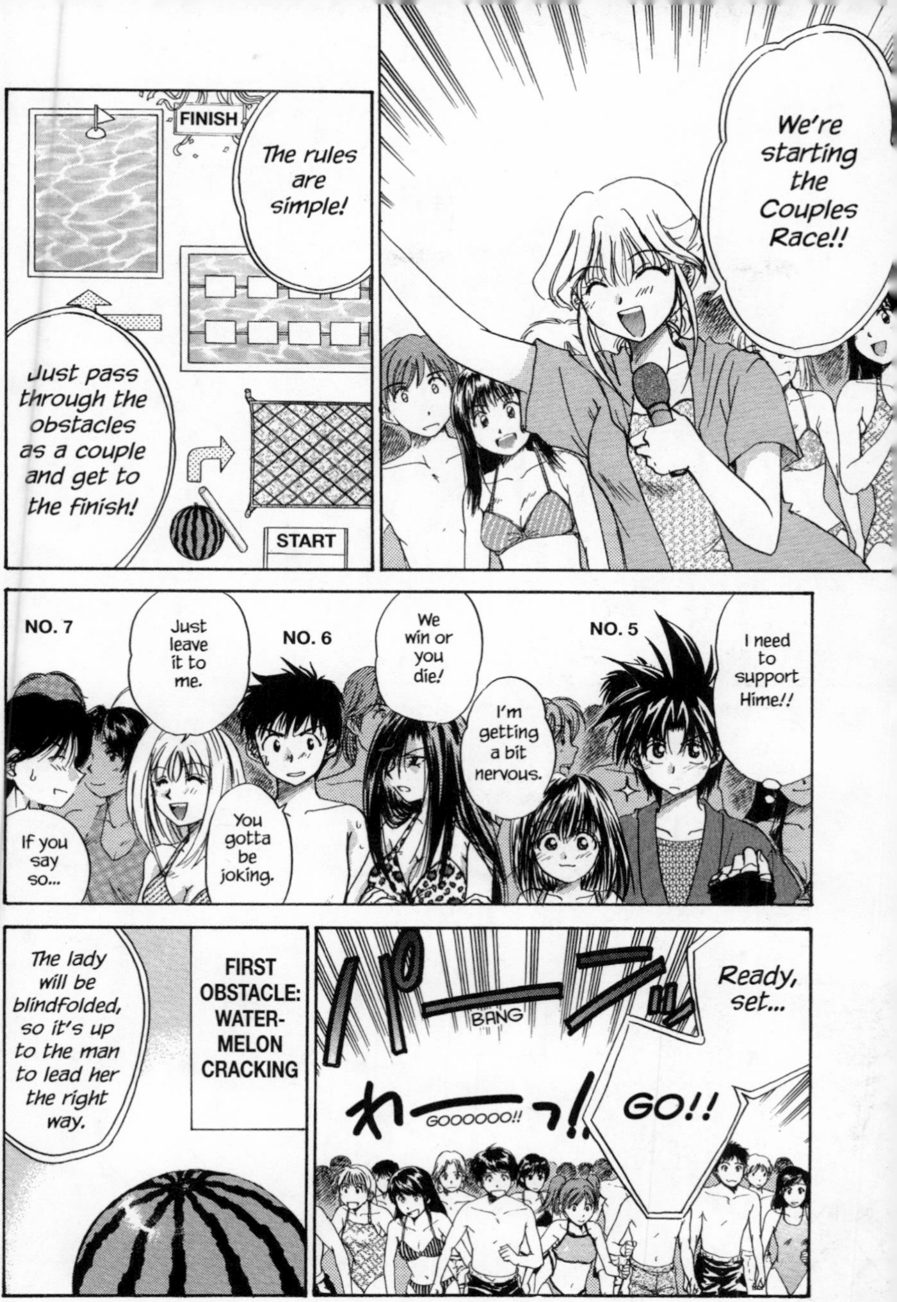
We're starting the Couples Race!!
The rules are simple!
FINISH
Just pass through the obstacles as a couple and get to the finish!
START
NO. 5
I need to support Hime!!
I'm getting a bit nervous.
We win or you die!
NO. 6
You gotta be joking.
Just leave it to me.
NO. 7
If you say so...
Ready, set...
BANG
GO!!
GOOOOOO!!
FIRST OBSTACLE: WATER-MELON CRACKING
The lady will be blindfolded, so it's up to the man to lead her the right way.

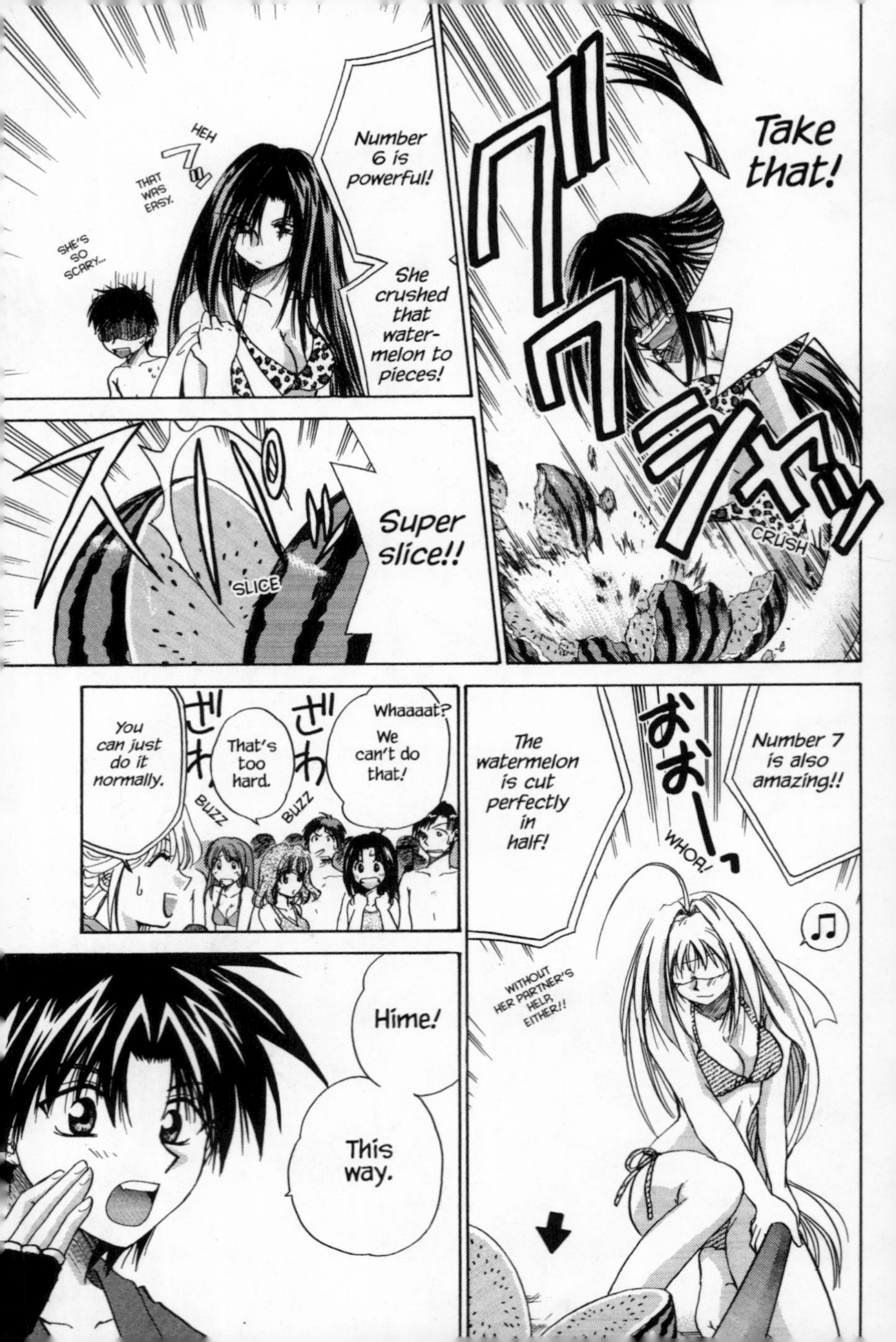
Take that!
グシャッ
CRUSH
Number 6 is powerful!
She crushed that watermelon to pieces!
HEH
THAT WAS EASY.
SHE'S SO SCARY...
スパッ
Super slice!!
SLICE
Number 7 is also amazing!!
おおー
WHOA!
The watermelon is cut perfectly in half!
♫
WITHOUT HER PARTNER'S HELP, EITHER!!
Whaaaat? We can't do that!
ざわ
BUZZ
That's too hard.
ざわ
BUZZ
You can just do it normally.
Hime!
This way.

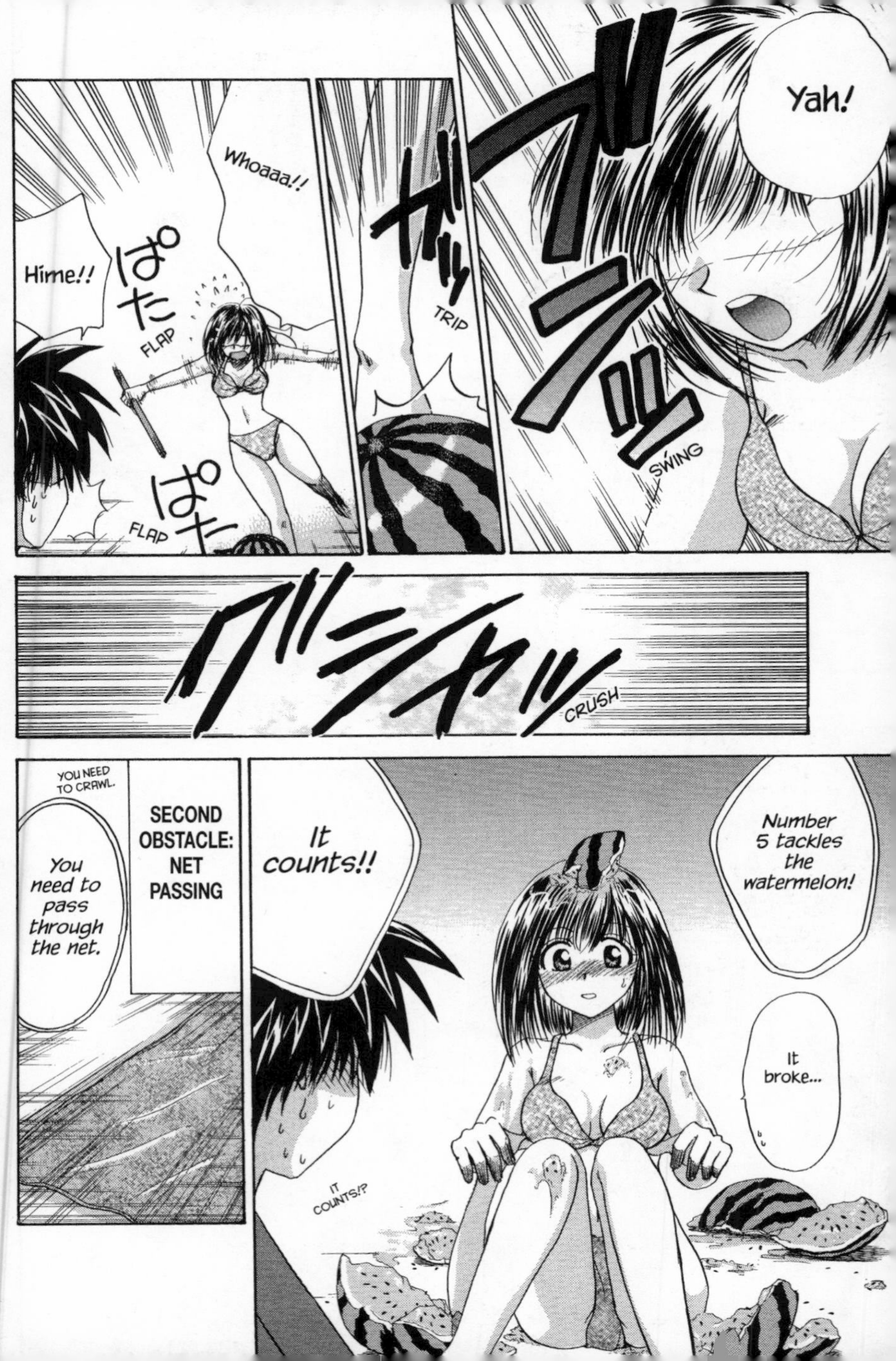
Yah!
ブンッ
SWING
ガッ
TRIP
Whoaaa!!
Hime!!
ぱた
FLAP
ぱた
FLAP
グシャッ
CRUSH
Number 5 tackles the watermelon!
It counts!!
It broke...
IT COUNTS!?
SECOND OBSTACLE: NET PASSING
You need to pass through the net.
YOU NEED TO CRAWL.

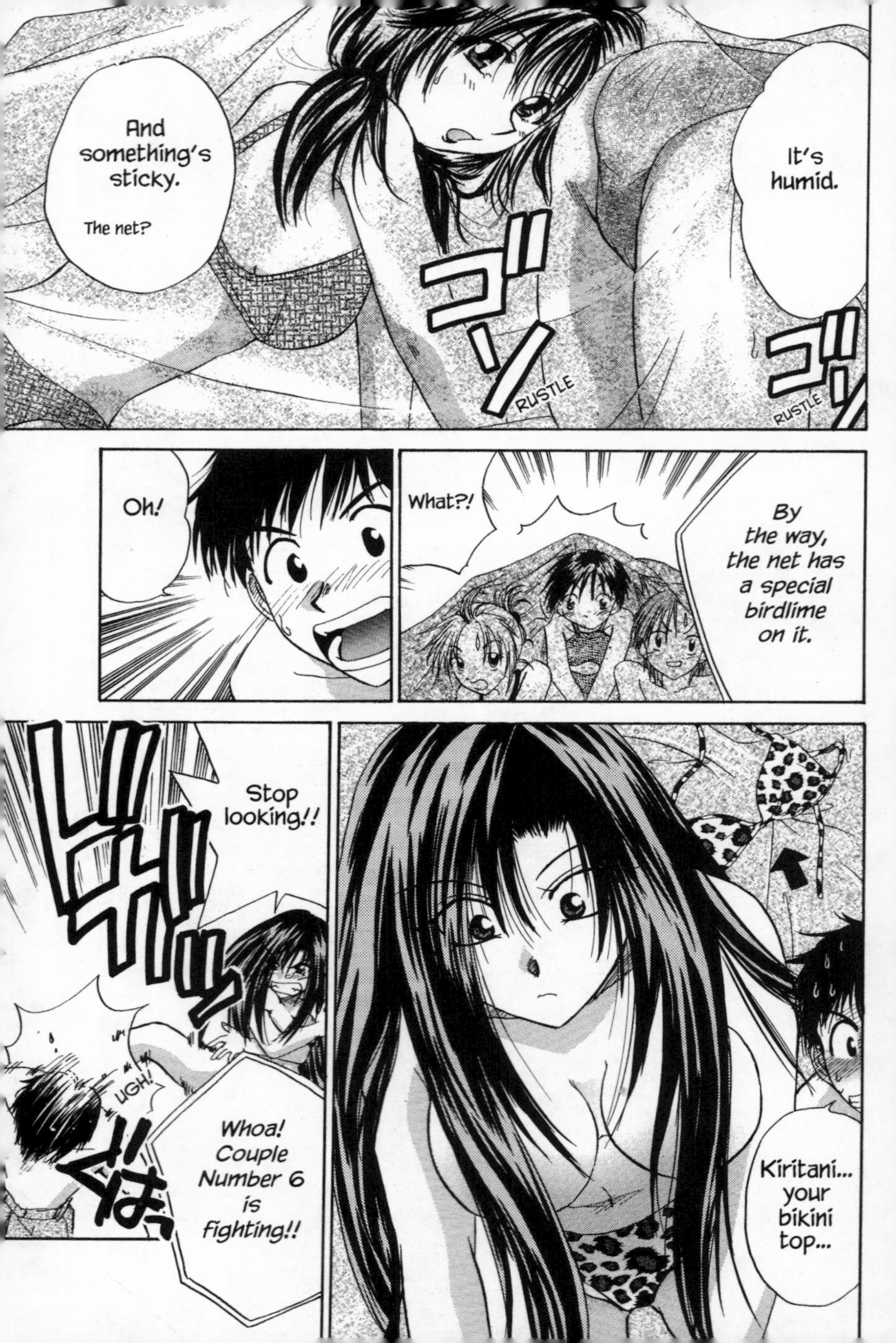
It's humid.
RUSTLE
RUSTLE
And something's sticky.
The net?
By the way, the net has a special birdlime on it.
What?!
Oh!
Kiritani... your bikini top...
Stop looking!!
Whoa! Couple Number 6 is fighting!!
UGH!

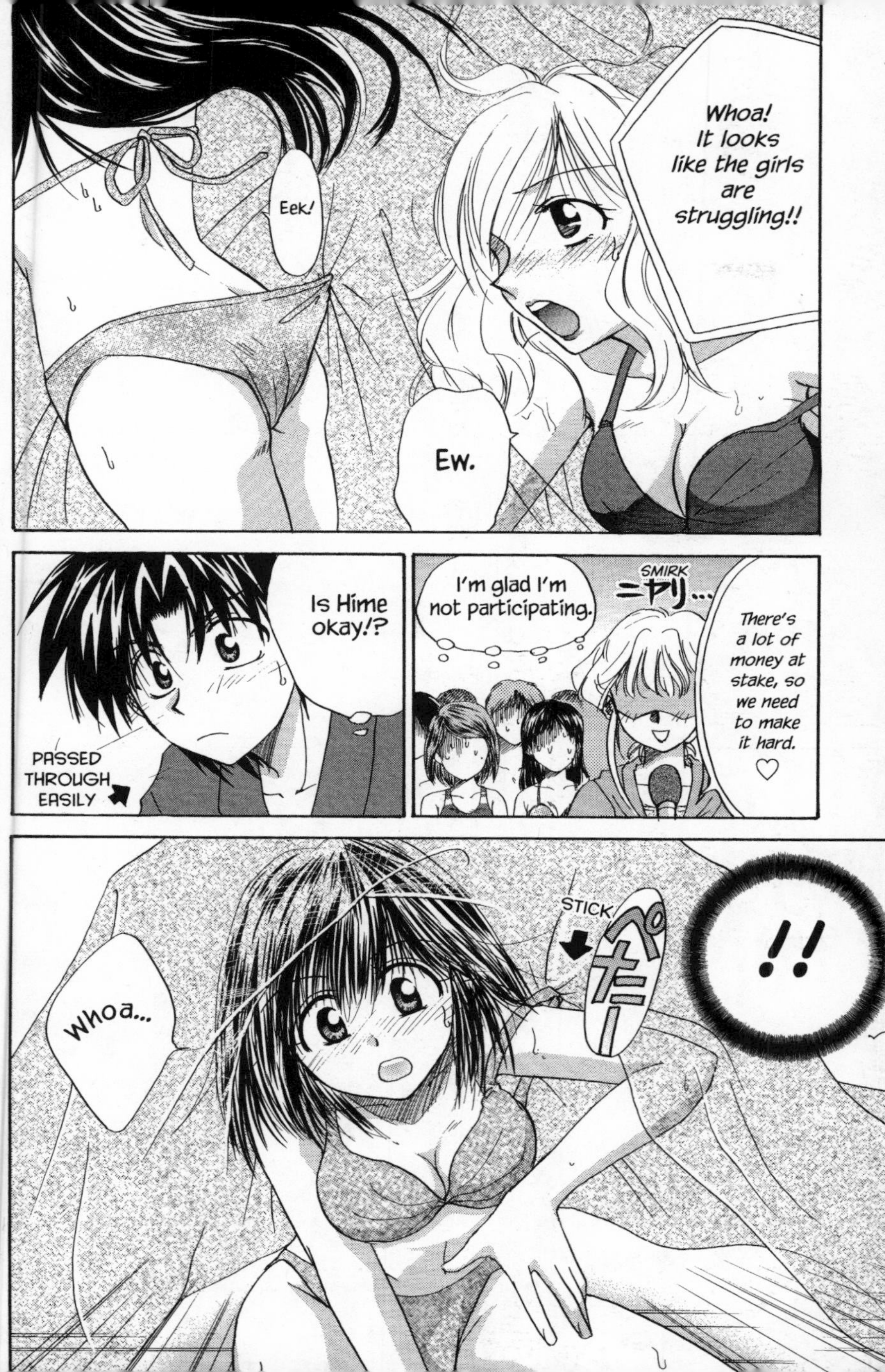
Whoa! It looks like the girls are struggling!!
Eek!
Ew.
There's a lot of money at stake, so we need to make it hard. ♡
ニヤリ…
SMIRK
I'm glad I'm not participating.
Is Hime okay!?
PASSED THROUGH EASILY
!!
ペター
STICK
Whoa...

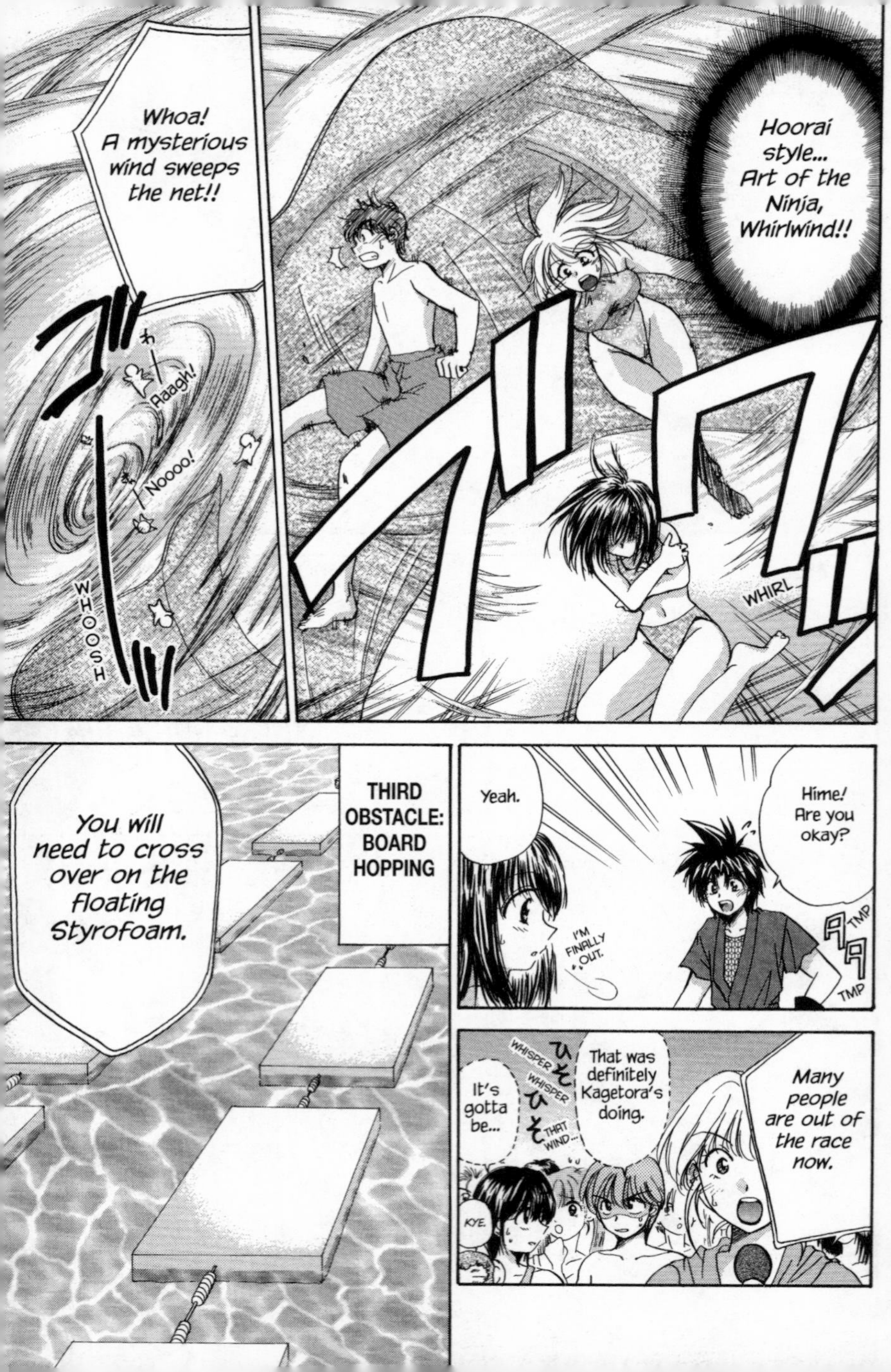
Hoorai style... Art of the Ninja, Whirlwind!!
WHIRL
Whoa! A mysterious wind sweeps the net!!
Raagh!
Noooo!
WHOOSH
Hime! Are you okay?
TMP
TMP
Yeah.
I'M FINALLY OUT.
Many people are out of the race now.
That was definitely Kagetora's doing.
WHISPER
WHISPER
ひそひそ
THAT WIND...
It's gotta be...
KYE.
THIRD OBSTACLE: BOARD HOPPING
You will need to cross over on the floating Styrofoam.

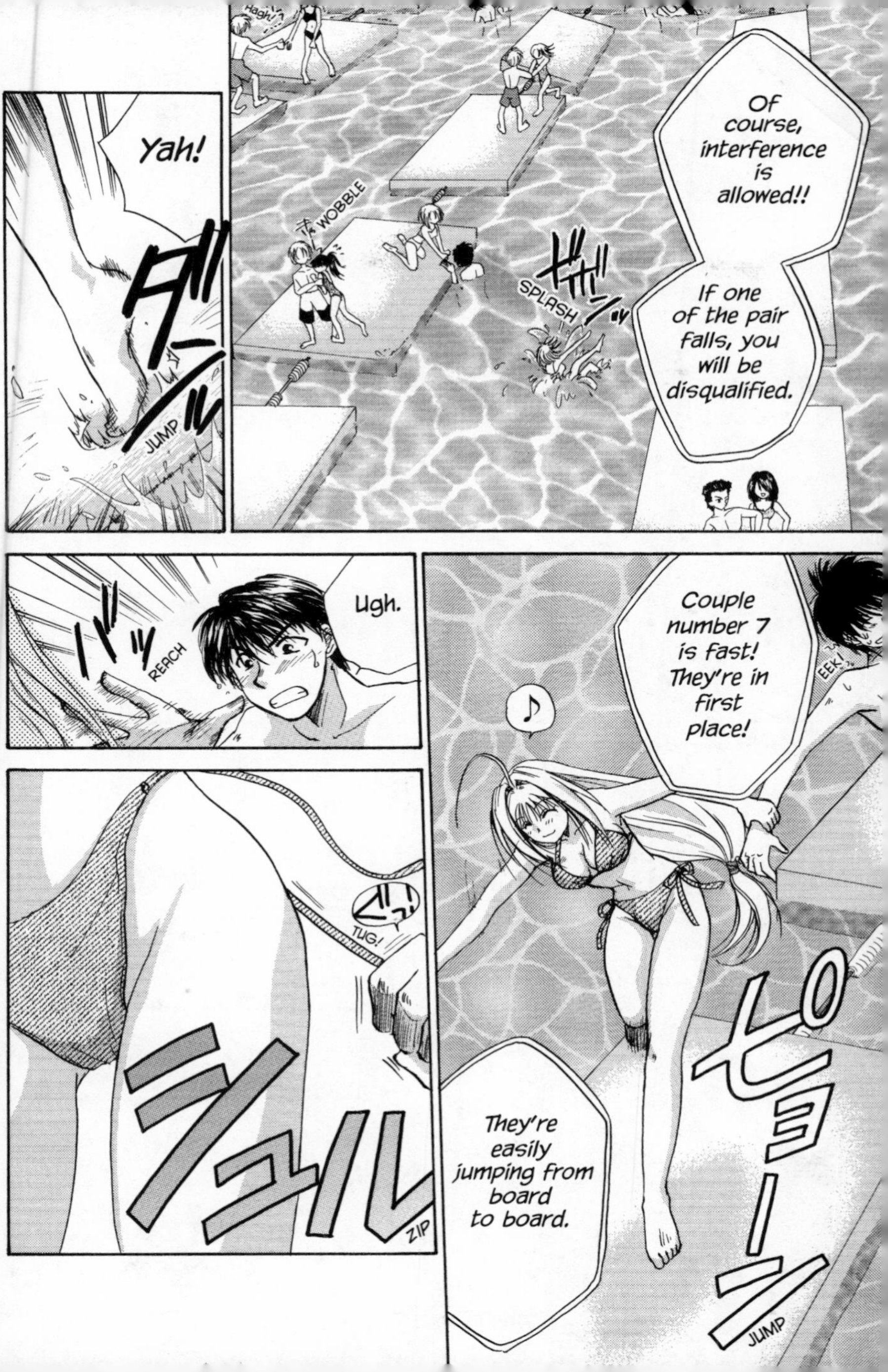

Of course, interference is allowed!!
If one of the pair falls, you will be disqualified.
Hagh!
SPLASH
WOBBLE
Yah!
JUMP
Couple number 7 is fast! They're in first place!
EEK!
♪
JUMP
They're easily jumping from board to board.
Ugh.
REACH
TUG!
ZIP

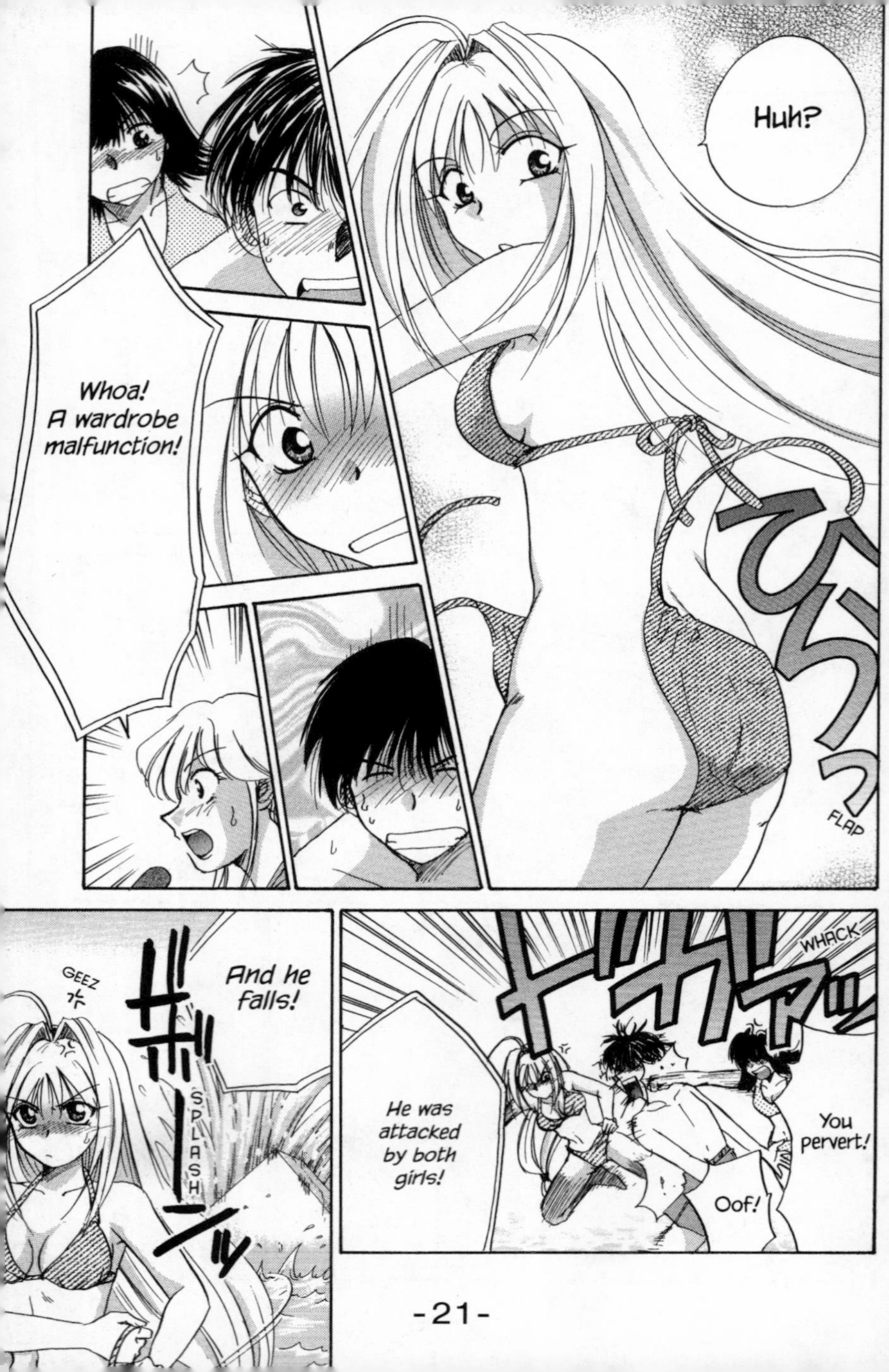
Huh?
FLAP
Whoa! A wardrobe malfunction!
WHACK
He was attacked by both girls!
You pervert!
Oof!
And he falls!
GEEZ
SPLASH

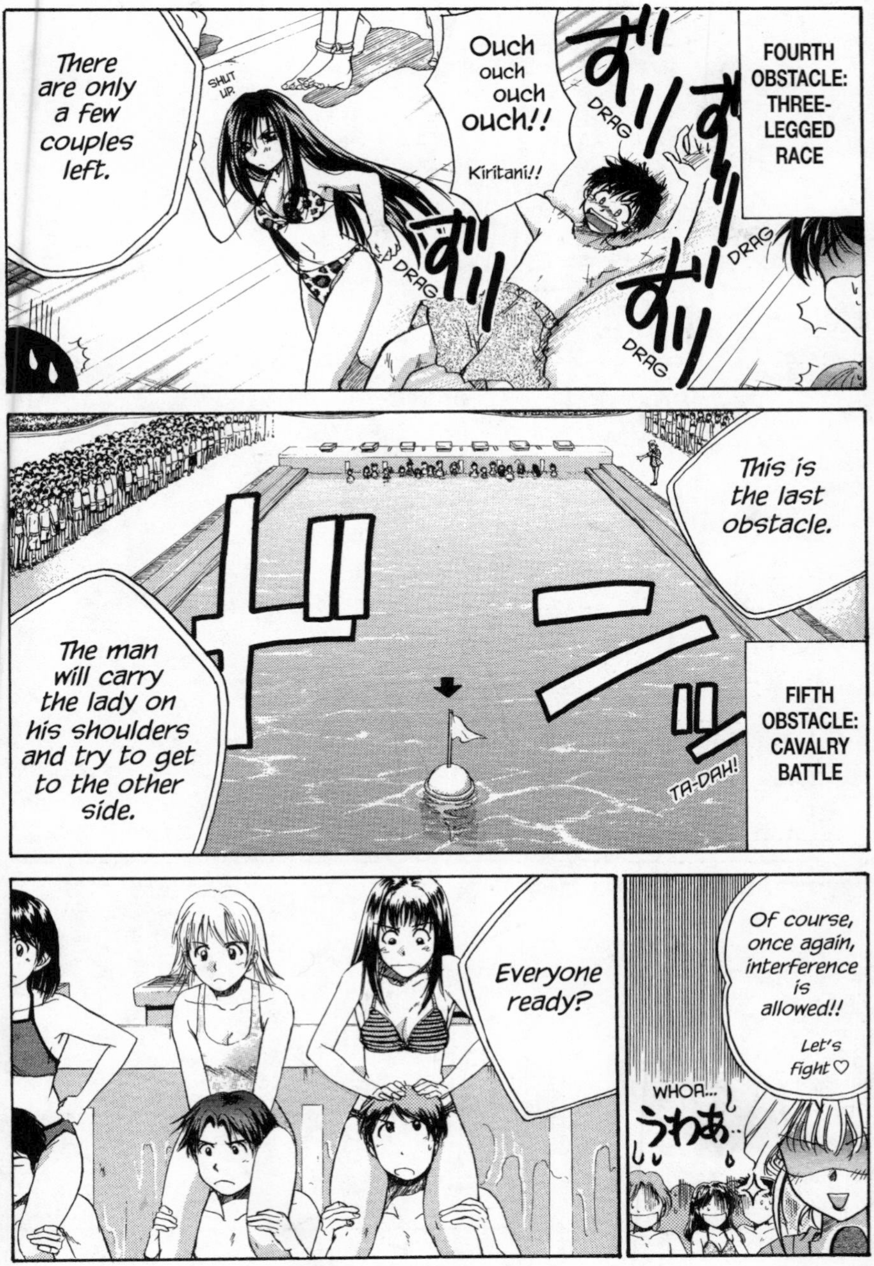
FOURTH OBSTACLE: THREE-LEGGED RACE
ずりずり
DRAG
DRAG
Ouch ouch ouch ouch!!
Kiritani!!
ずり
DRAG
DRAG
SHUT UP.
There are only a few couples left.
FIFTH OBSTACLE: CAVALRY BATTLE
This is the last obstacle.
ドーン
TA-DAH!
The man will carry the lady on his shoulders and try to get to the other side.
Of course, once again, interference is allowed!!
Let's fight ♡
WHOA...
うわあ…
Everyone ready?

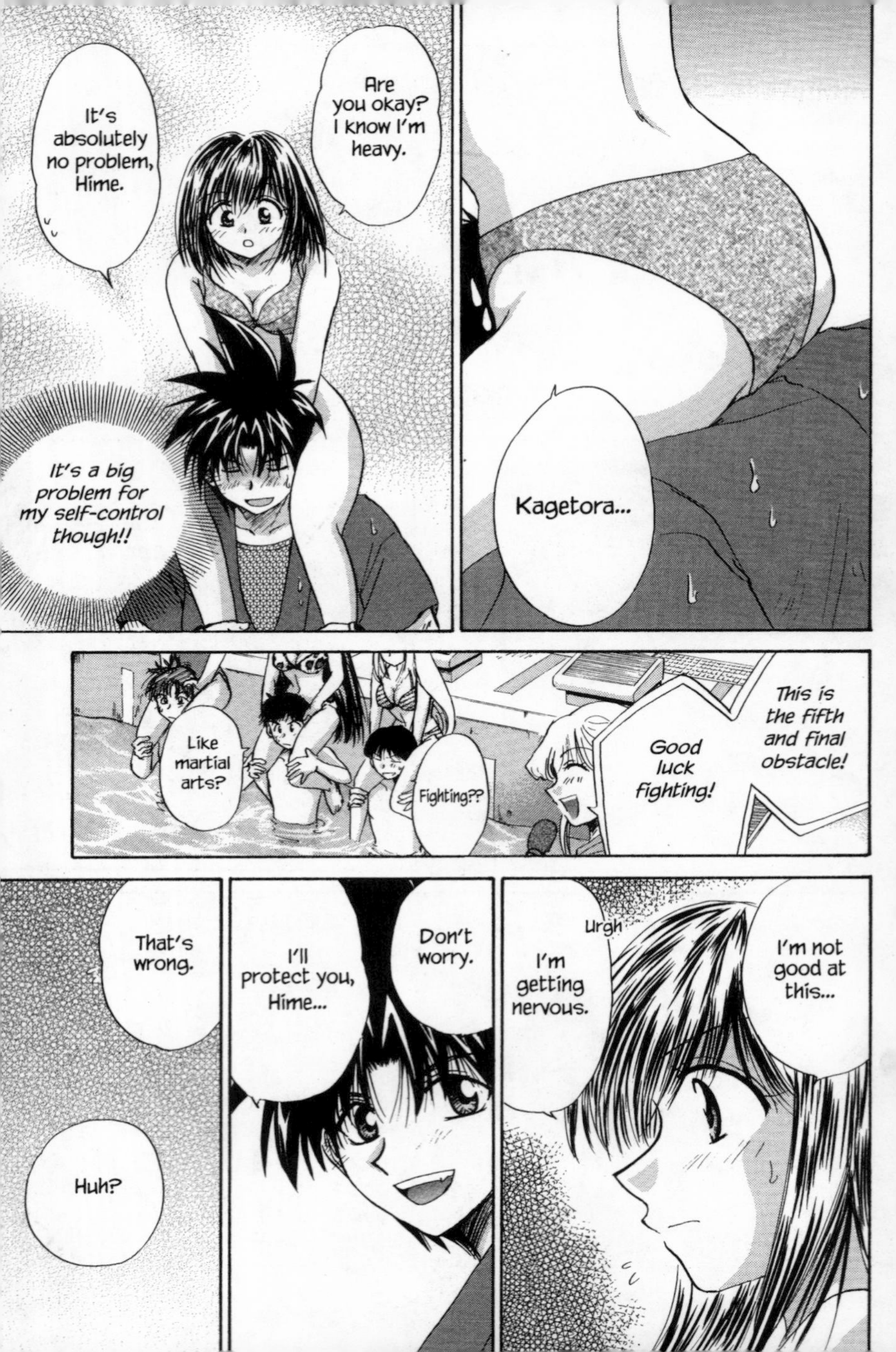
Kagetora...
Are you okay? I know I'm heavy.
It's big absolutely no problem, Hime.
It's a big problem for my self-control though!!
This is the fifth and final obstacle!
Good luck fighting!
Fighting??
Like martial arts?
I'm not good at this...
Urgh
I'm getting nervous.
Don't worry.
I'll protect you, Hime...
That's wrong.
Huh?

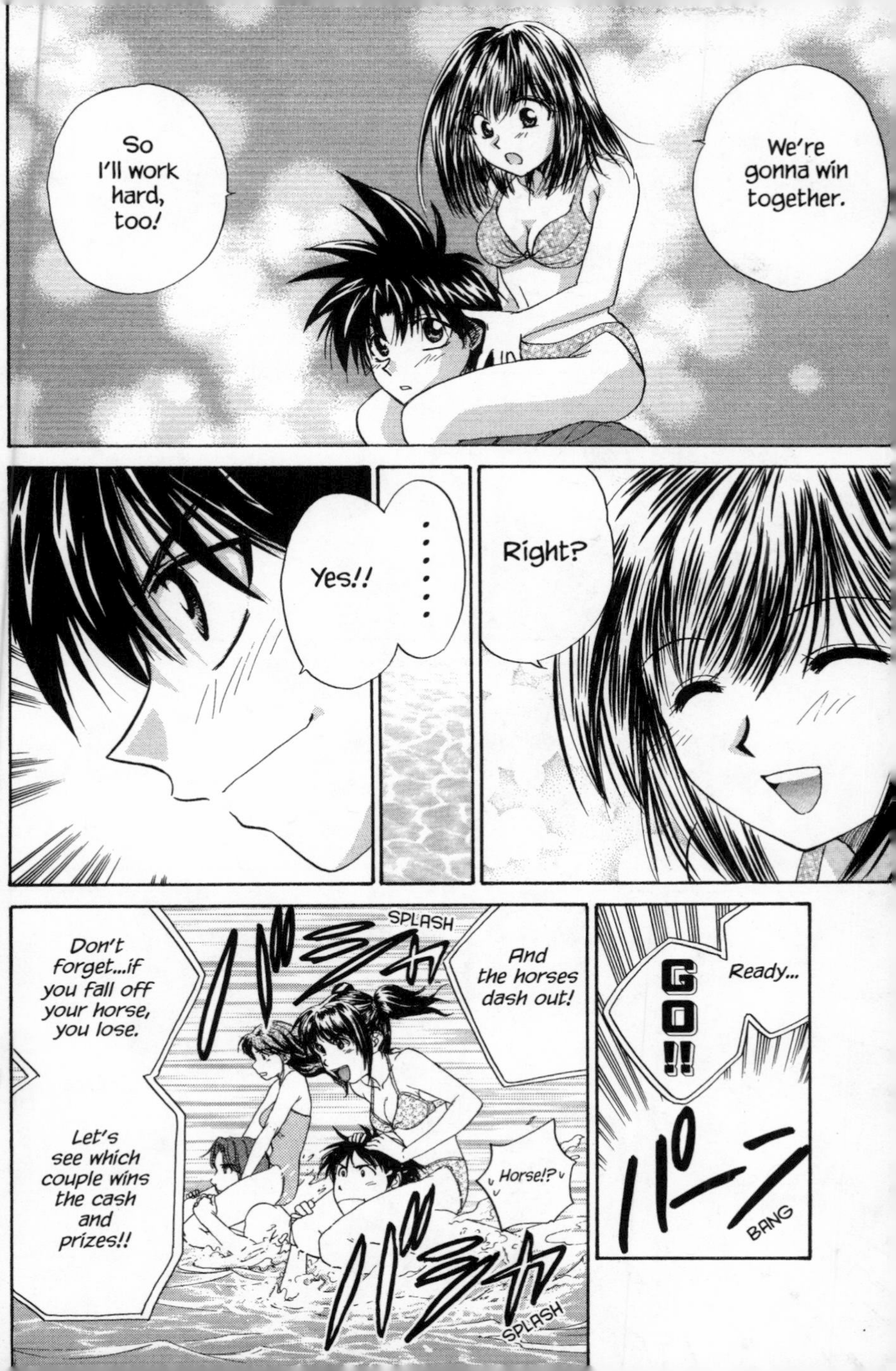
We're gonna win together.
So I'll work hard, too!
Right?
......
Yes!!
Ready...
GO!!
パーン
BANG
SPLASH
And the horses dash out!
Don't forget...if you fall off your horse, you lose.
Horse!?
Let's see which couple wins the cash and prizes!!
SPLASH

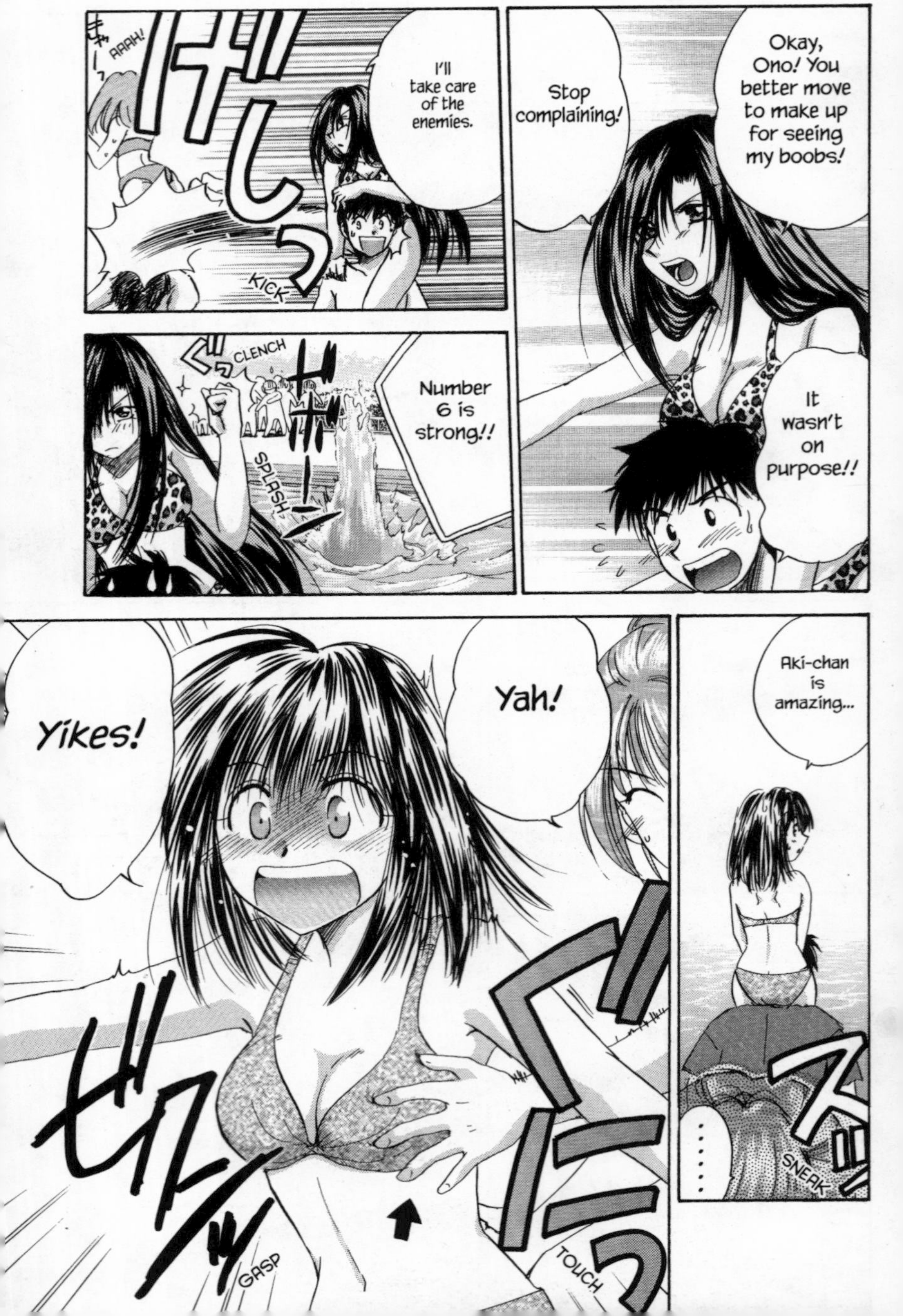
Okay, Ono! You better move to make up for seeing my boobs!
Stop complaining!
It wasn't on purpose!!
I'll take care of the enemies.
KICK
AAAH!
Number 6 is strong!!
CLENCH
SPLASH
Aki-chan is amazing...
......
SNEAK
Yah!
Yikes!
TOUCH
GASP

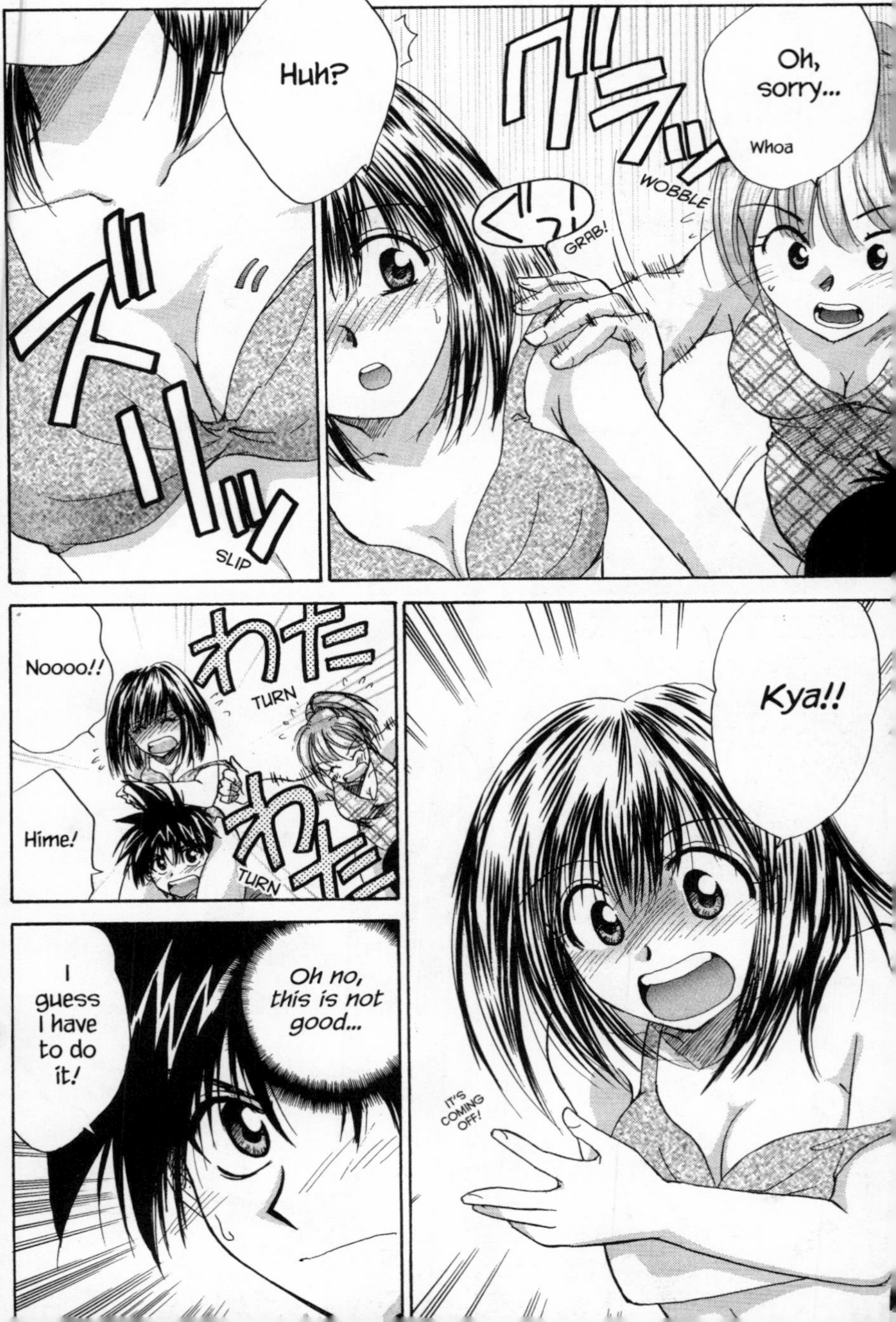

Oh, sorry...
Whoa
WOBBLE
ぐっ!
GRAB!
Huh?
SLIP
Kya!!
IT'S COMING OFF!
Noooo!!
TURN
Hime!
TURN
Oh no, this is not good...
I guess I have to do it!

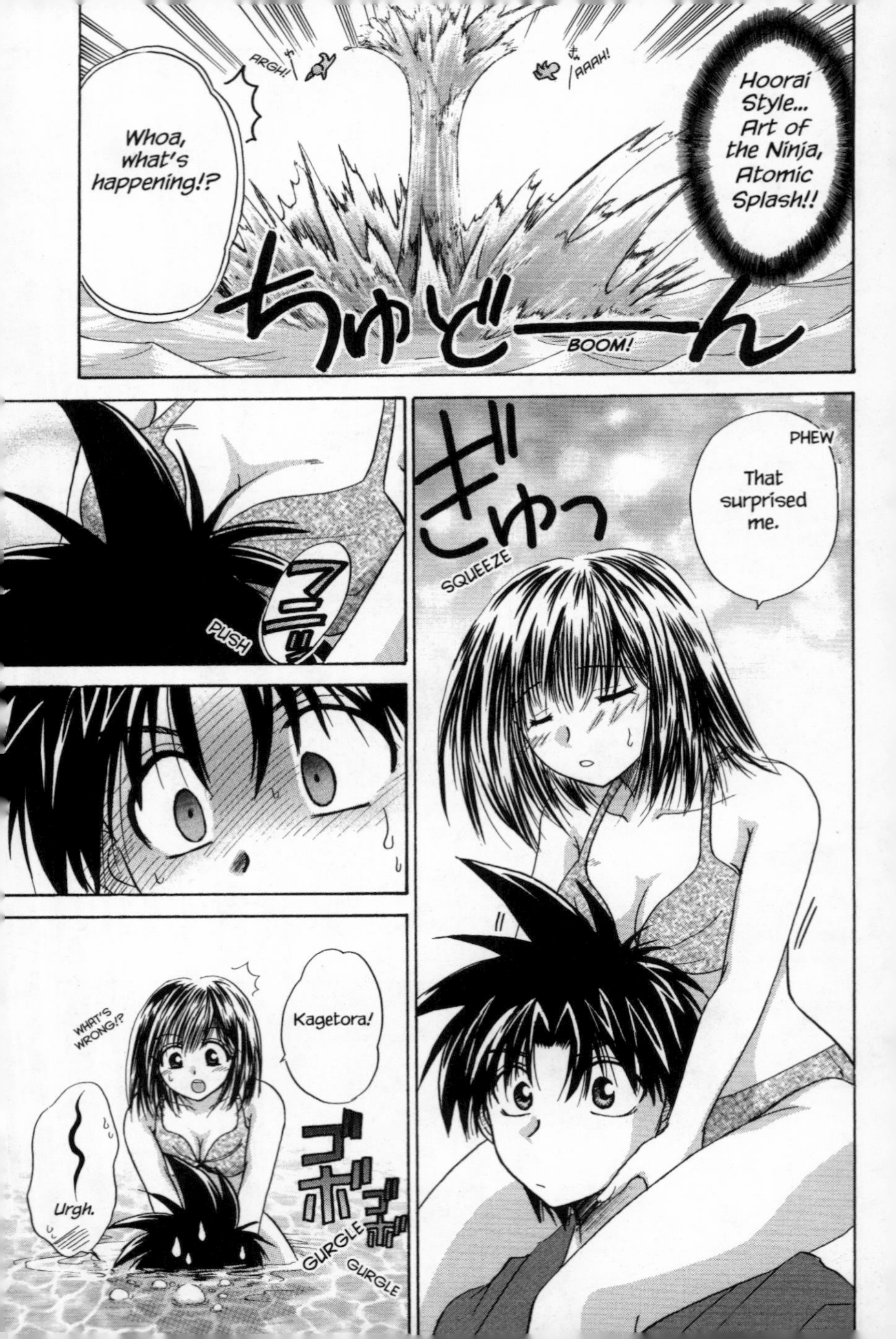
Hoorai Style... Art of the Ninja, Atomic Splash!!
AAAH!
ARGH!
Whoa, what's happening!?
ちゅどーーん
BOOM!
ぎゅっ
SQUEEZE
PHEW
That surprised me.
PUSH
Kagetora!
WHAT'S WRONG!?
Urgh.
GURGLE
GURGLE
GURGLE

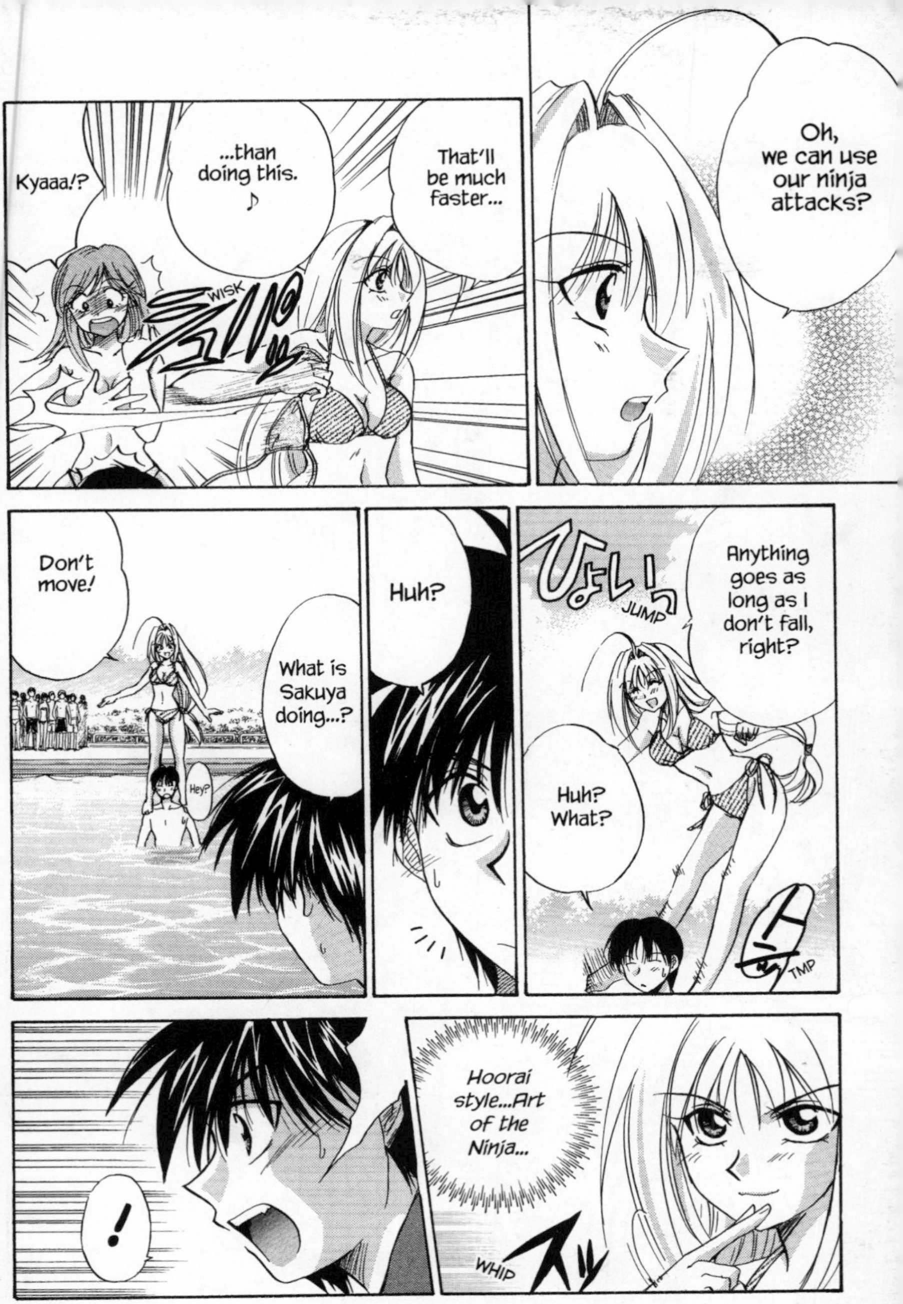
Oh, we can use our ninja attacks?
That'll be much faster...
...than doing this. ♪
WISK
Kyaaa!?
JUMP
Anything goes as long as I don't fall, right?
Huh? What?
TMP
Huh?
What is Sakuya doing...?
Don't move!
Hey?
Hoorai style...Art of the Ninja...
WHIP
!

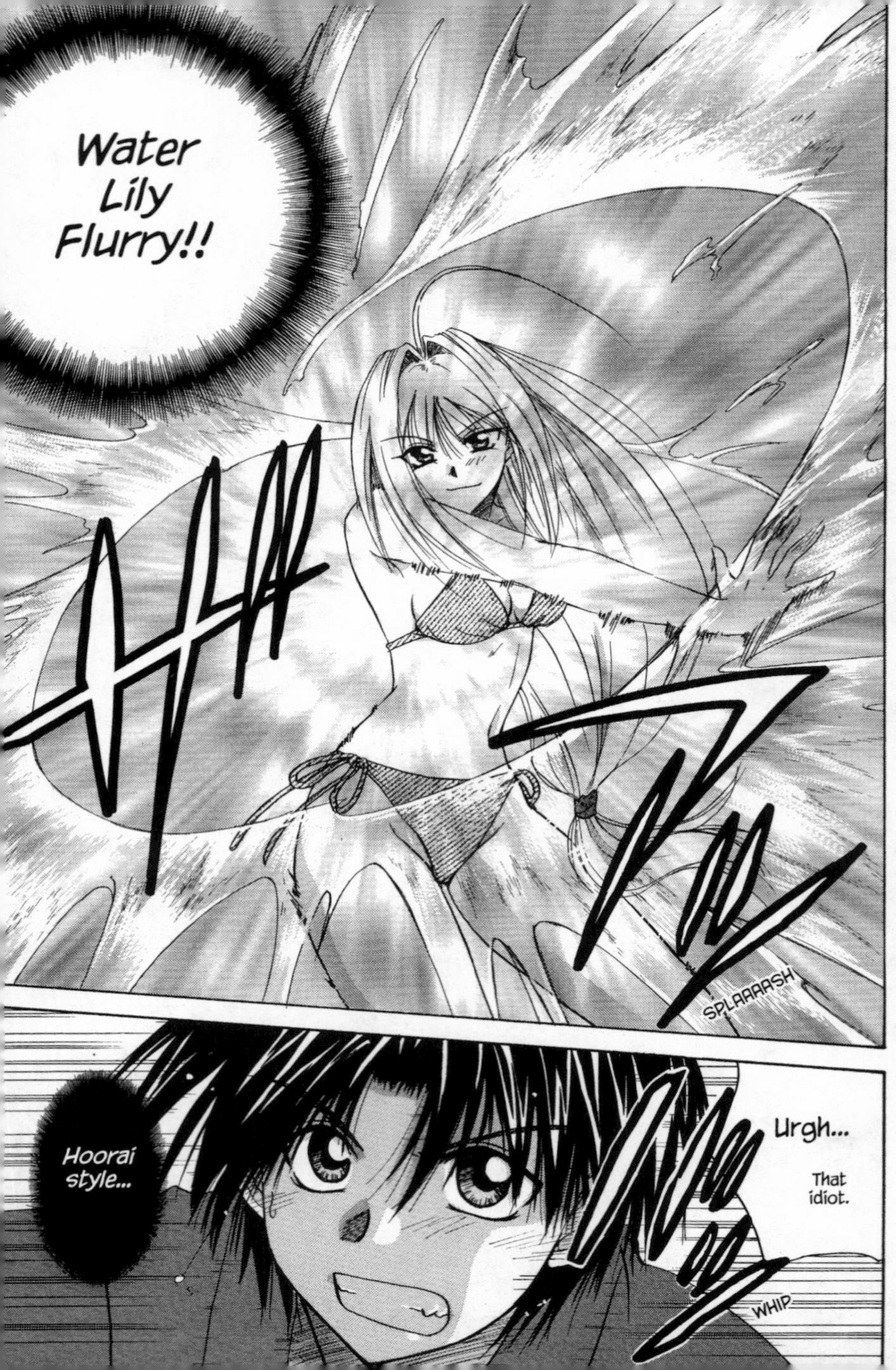
Water Lily Flurry!!
SPLAAAASH
Urgh...
That idiot.
Hoorai style...
WHIP

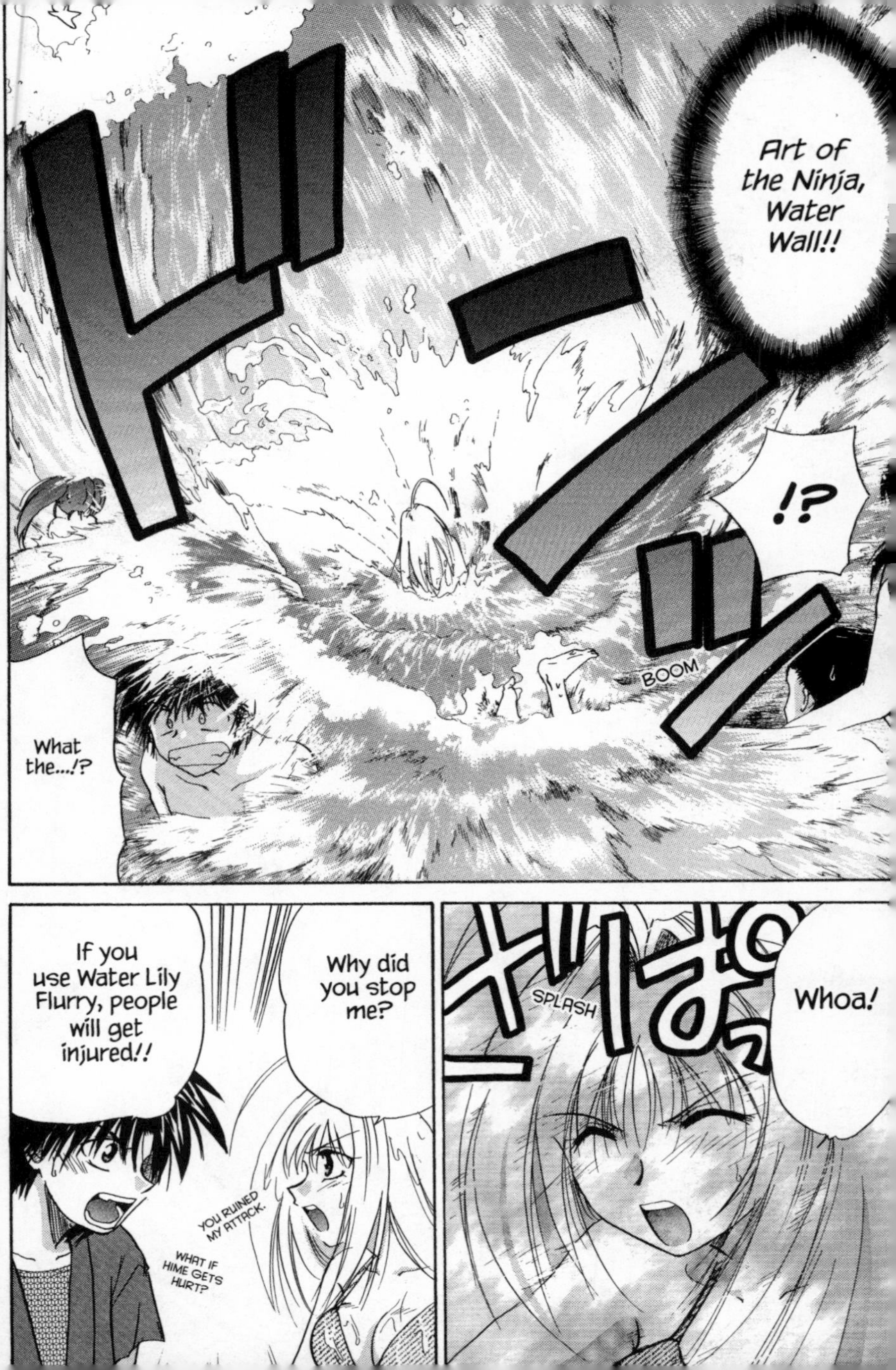
Art of the Ninja, Water Wall!!
!?
BOOM
What the...!?
Whoa!
SPLASH
Why did you stop me?
YOU RUINED MY ATTACK.
If you use Water Lily Flurry, people will get injured!!
WHAT IF HIME GETS HURT?

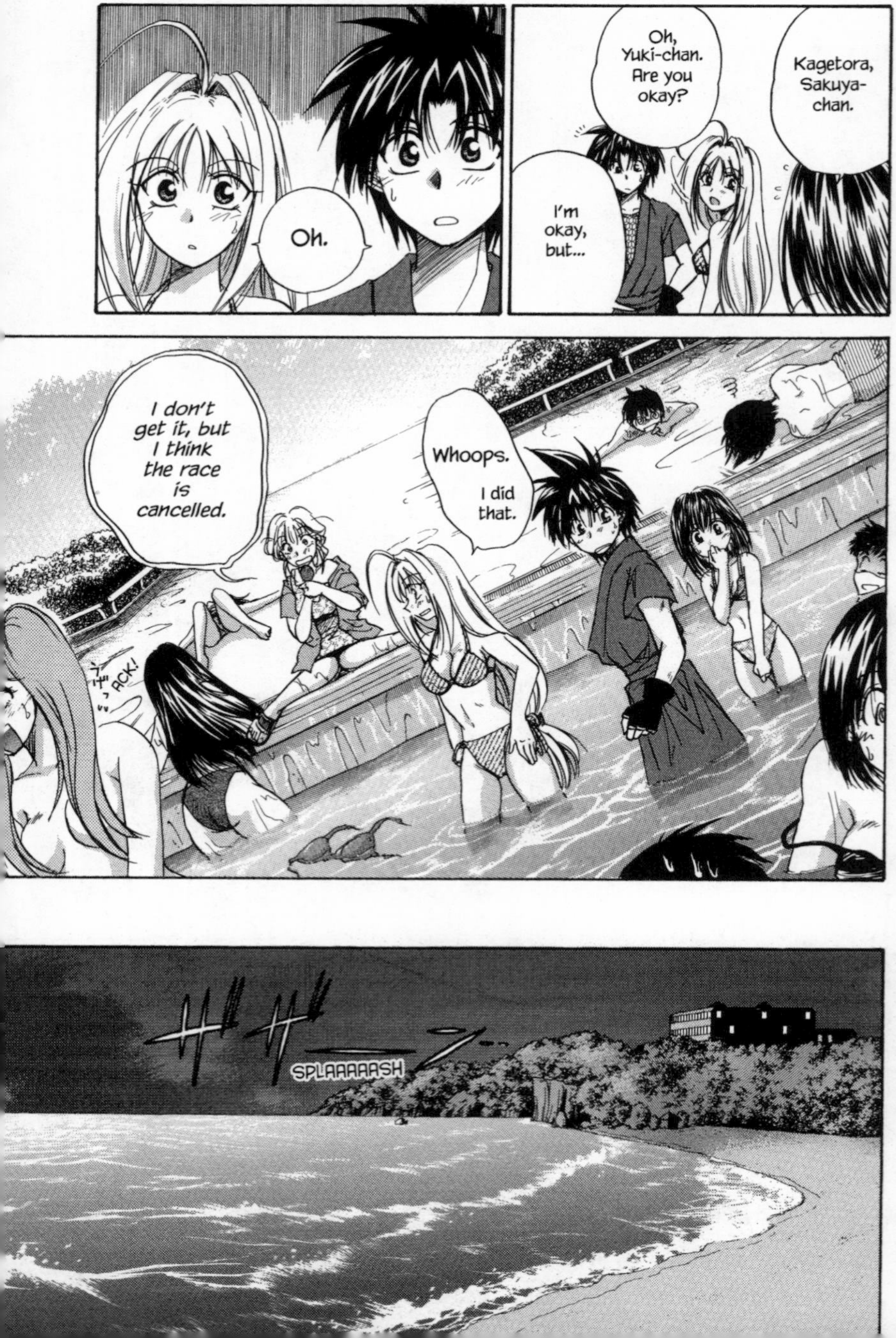
Kagetora, Sakuya-chan.
Oh, Yuki-chan. Are you okay?
I'm okay, but...
Oh.
Whoops.
I did that.
I don't get it, but I think the race is cancelled.
ACK!
SPLAAAAASH

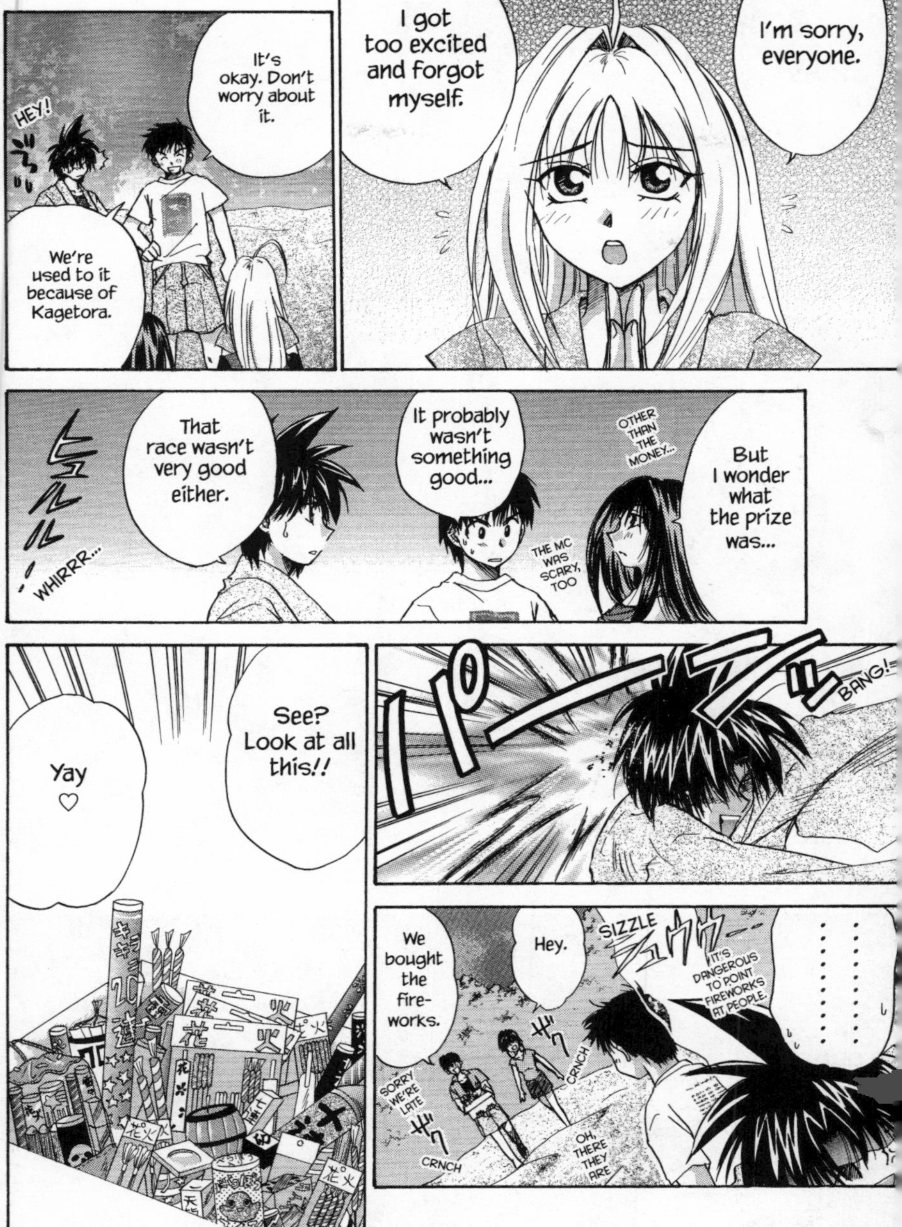
I'm sorry, everyone.
I got too excited and forgot myself.
It's okay. Don't worry about it.
HEY!
We're used to it because of Kagetora.
But I wonder what the prize was...
OTHER THAN THE MONEY...
It probably wasn't something good...
THE MC WAS SCARY, TOO
That race wasn't very good either.
WHIRRR...
BANG!
......
IT'S DANGEROUS TO POINT FIREWORKS AT PEOPLE.
SIZZLE
Hey.
We bought the fire-works.
SORRY WE'RE LATE
CRNCH
OH, THERE THEY ARE
CRNCH
See? Look at all this!!
Yay ♡

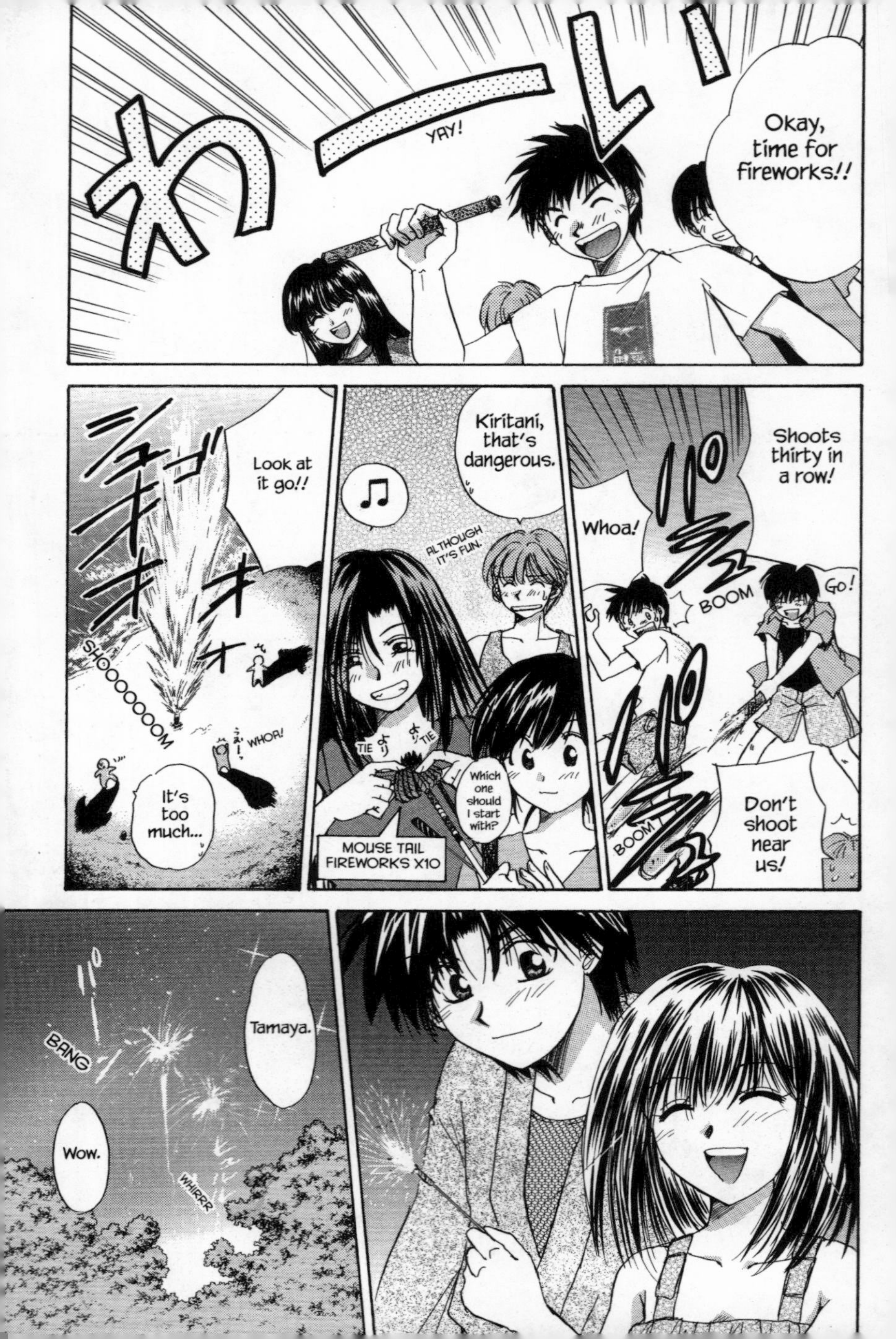
Okay, time for fireworks!!
わーい
YAY!
Shoots thirty in a row!
Go!
Whoa!
BOOM
BOOM
Don't shoot near us!
Kiritani, that's dangerous.
♫
ALTHOUGH IT'S FUN.
TIE
TIE
Which one should I start with?
MOUSE TAIL FIREWORKS X10
Look at it go!!
SHOOOOOOOOM
WHOA!
It's too much...
Tamaya.
BANG
Wow.
WHIRRR

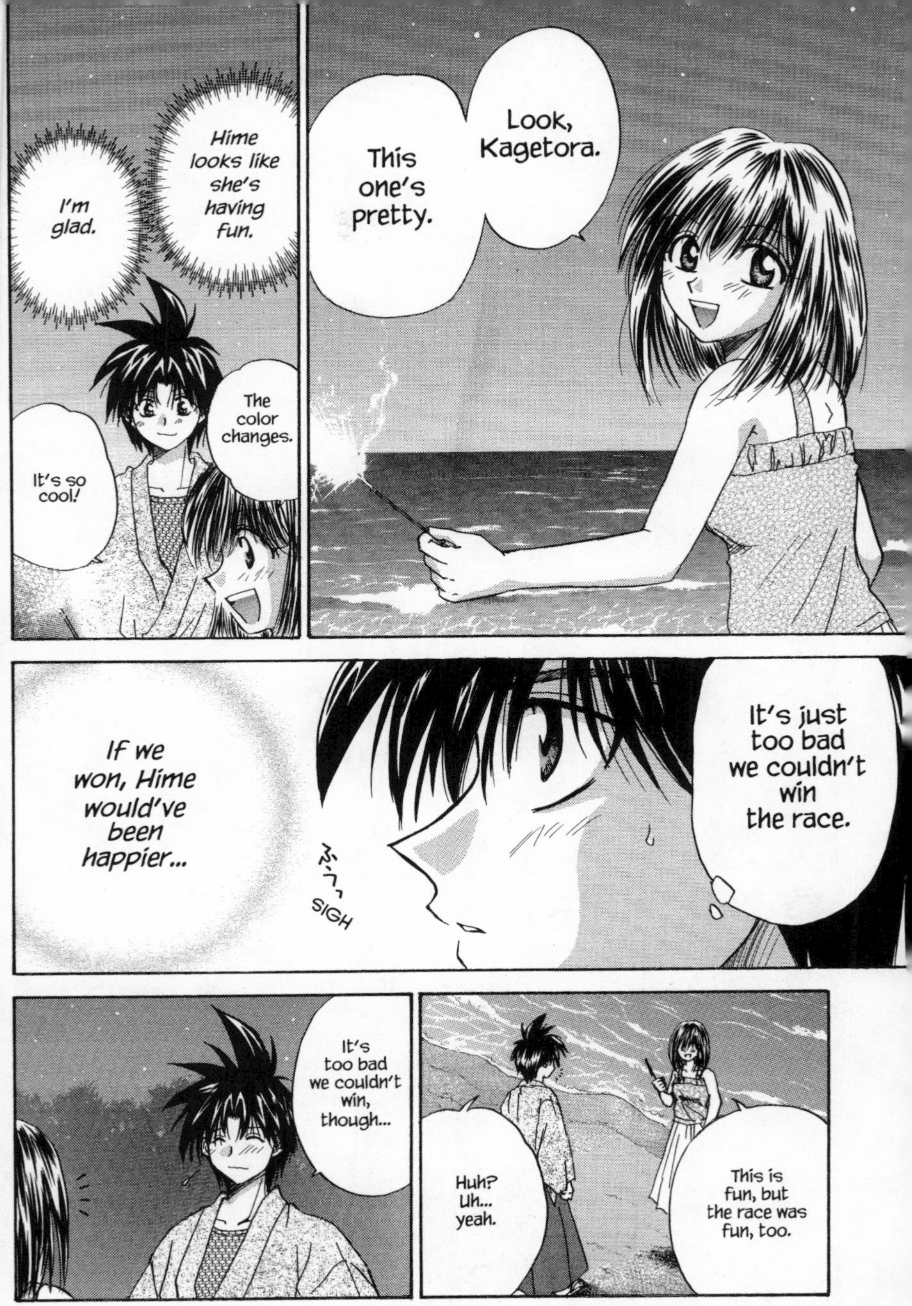

Look, Kagetora.
This one's pretty.
Hime looks like she's having fun.
I'm glad.
The color changes.
It's so cool!
It's just too bad we couldn't win the race.
SIGH
If we won, Hime would've been happier...
This is fun, but the race was fun, too.
Huh? Uh... yeah.
It's too bad we couldn't win, though...

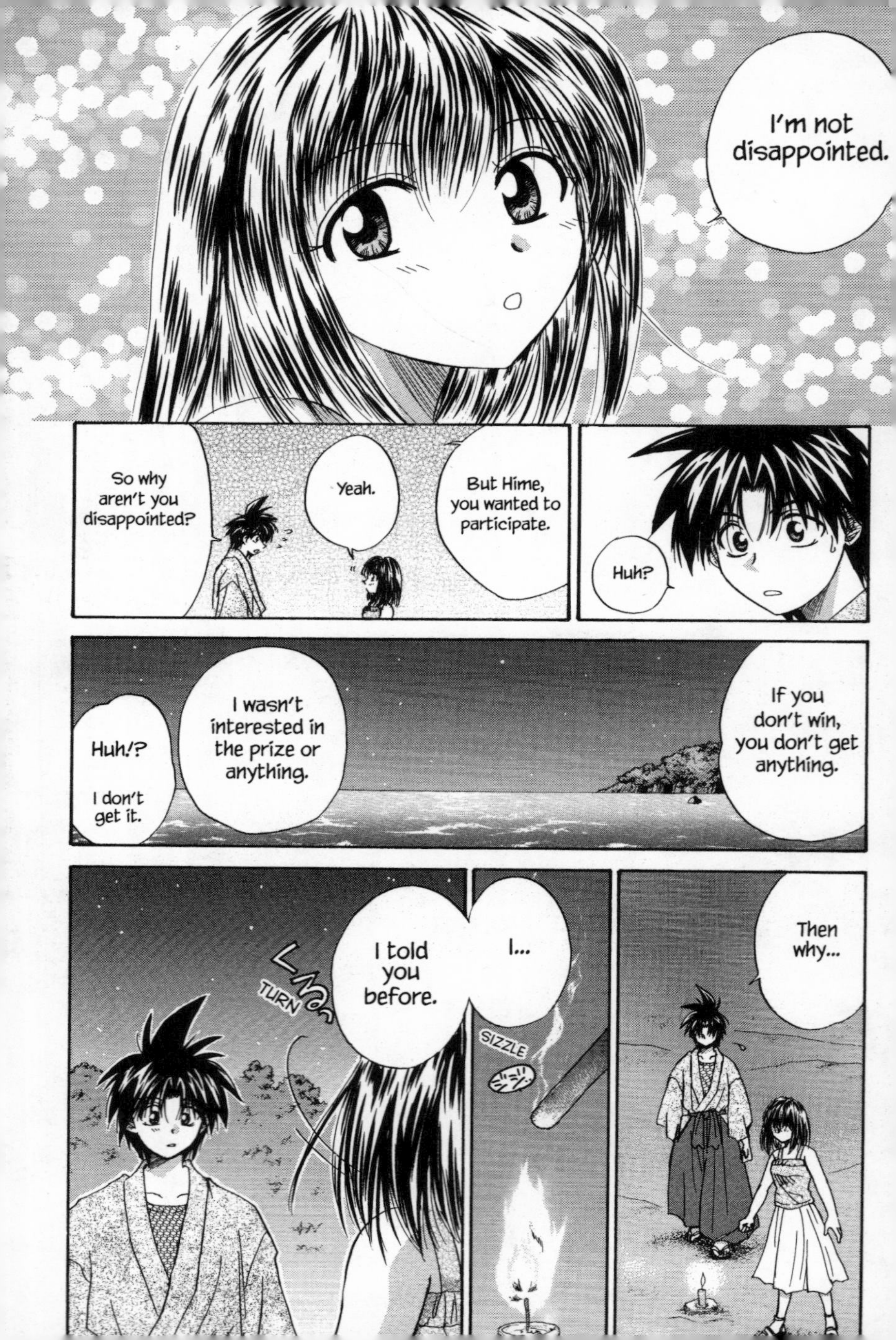
I'm not disappointed.
Huh?
But Hime, you wanted to participate.
Yeah.
So why aren't you disappointed?
If you don't win, you don't get anything.
I wasn't interested in the prize or anything.
Huh!?
I don't get it.
Then why...
I...
SIZZLE
I told you before.
TURN

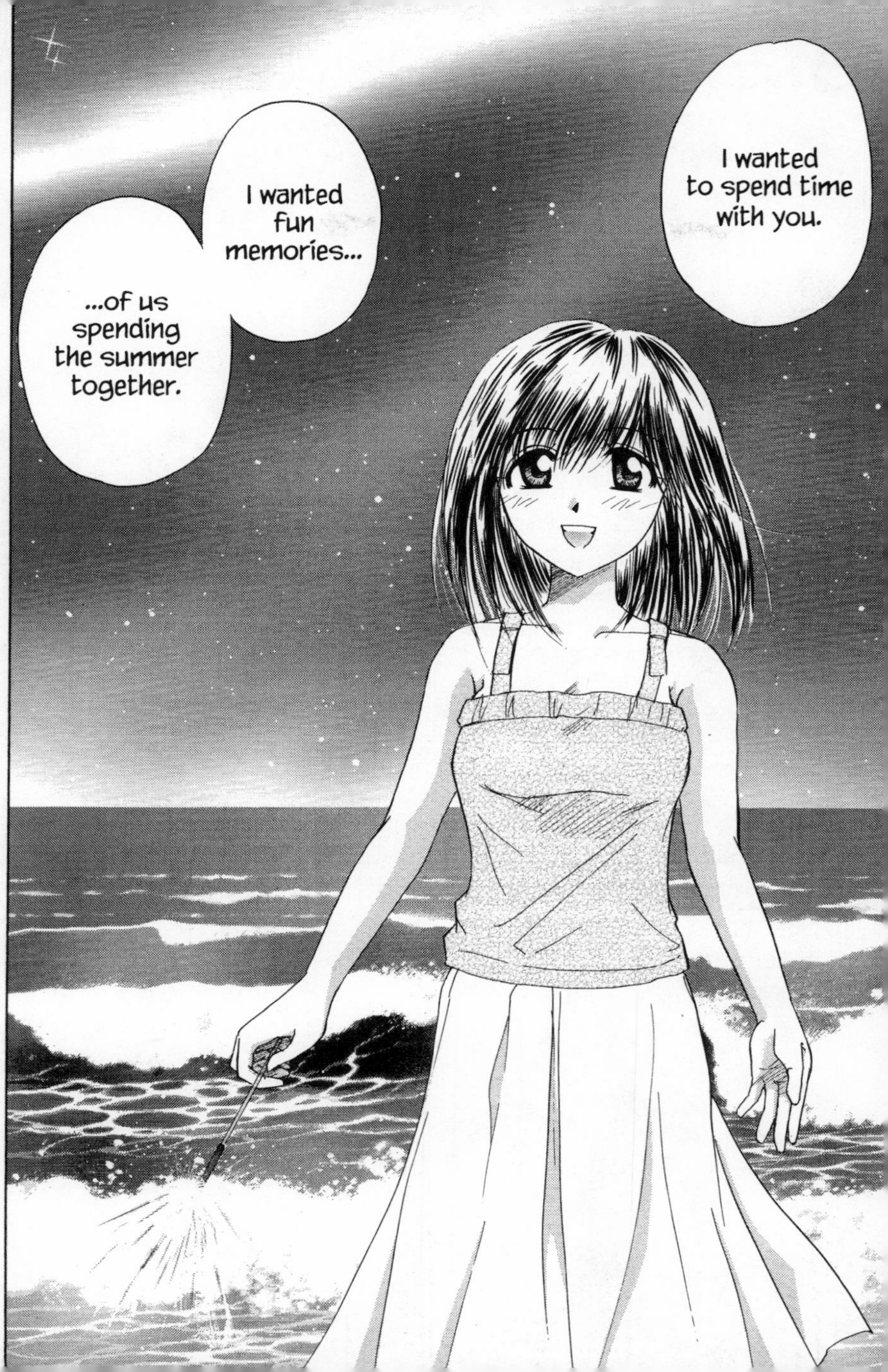
I wanted to spend time with you.
I wanted fun memories...
...of us spending the summer together.

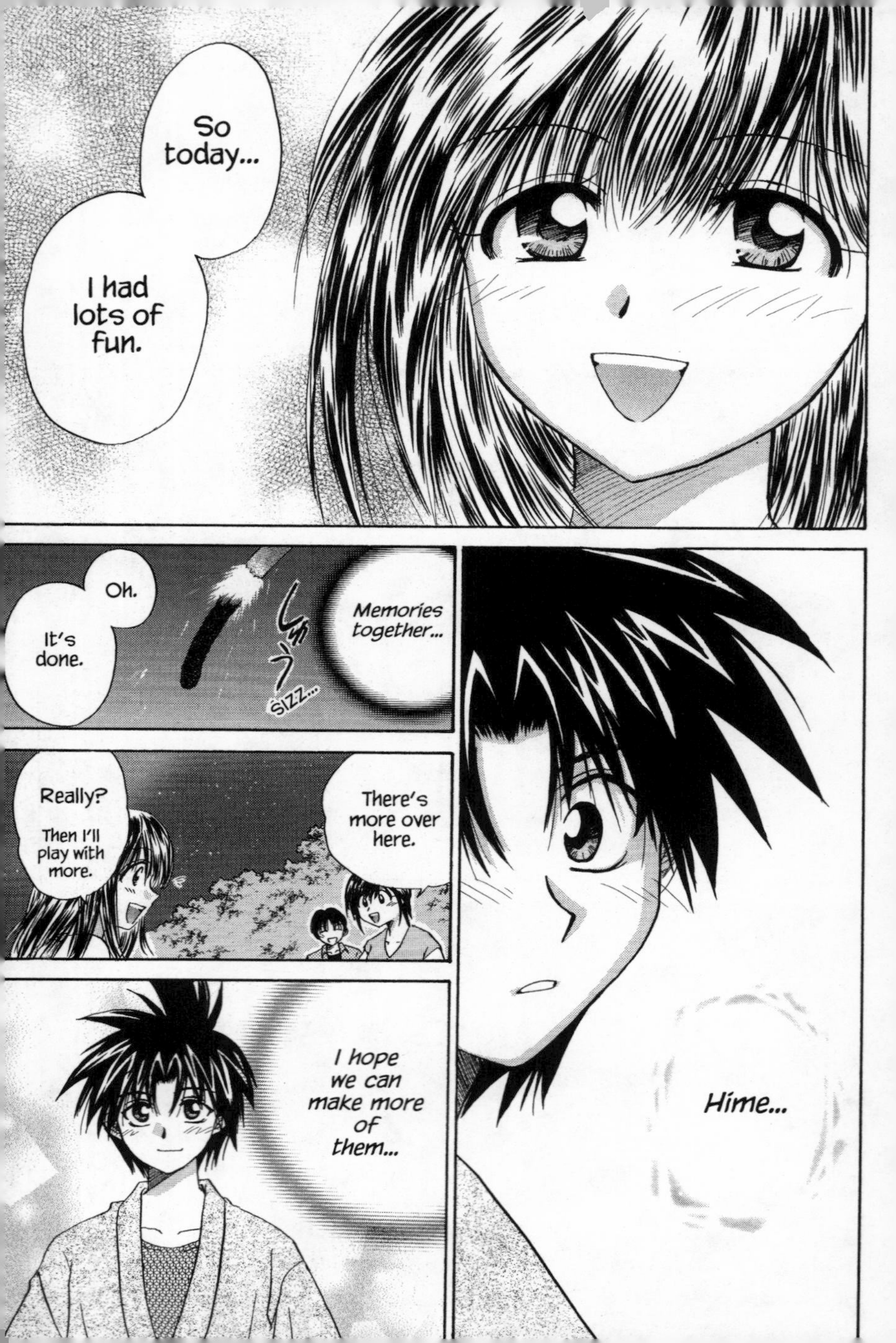
So today...
I had lots of fun.
Hime...
Memories together...
SIZZ...
Oh.
It's done.
There's more over here.
Really?
Then I'll play with more.
I hope we can make more of them...

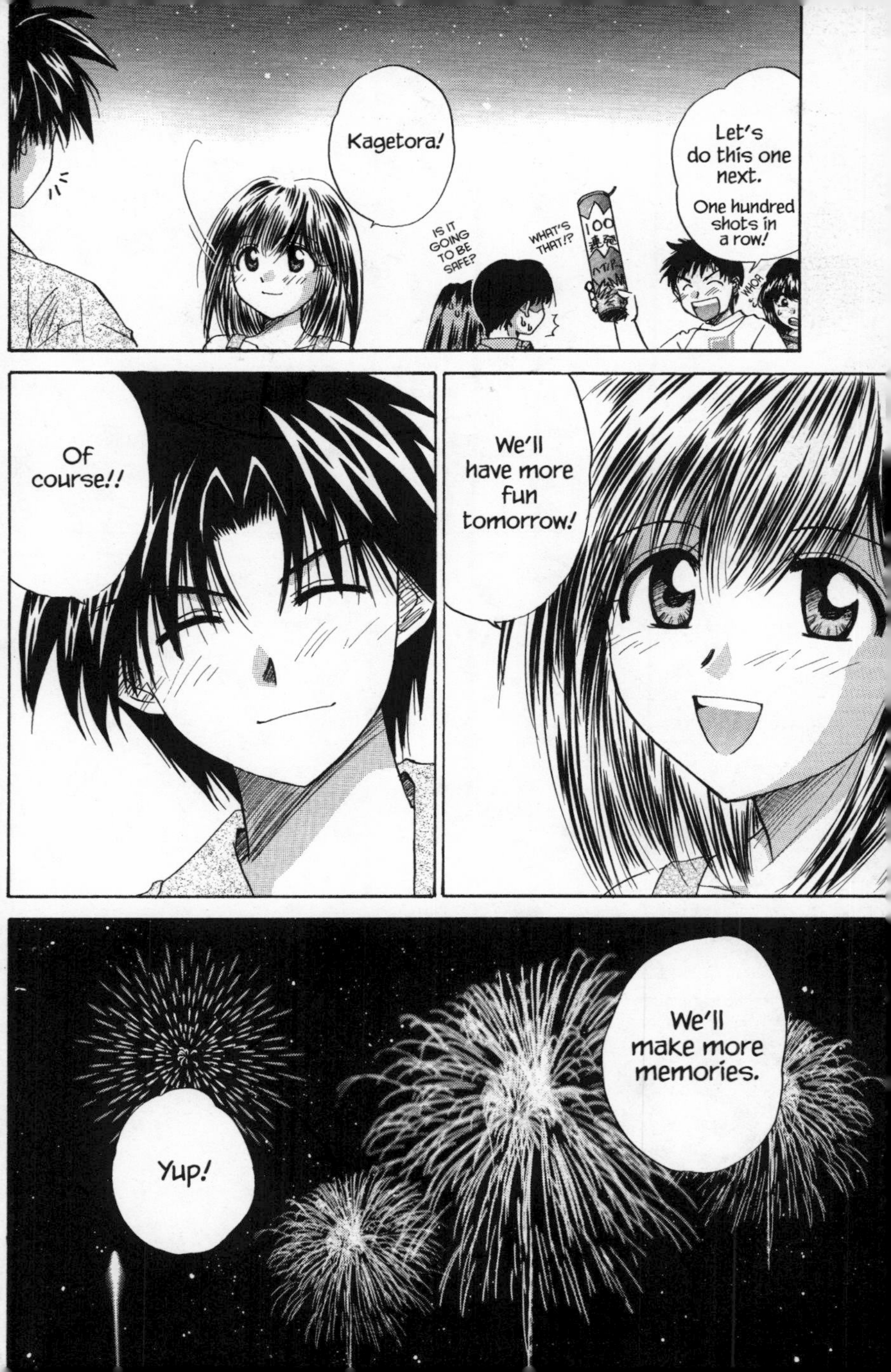
Let's do this one next.
One hundred shots in a row!
WHOA
WHAT'S THAT!?
IS IT GOING TO BE SAFE?
Kagetora!
We'll have more fun tomorrow!
Of course!!
We'll make more memories.
Yup!

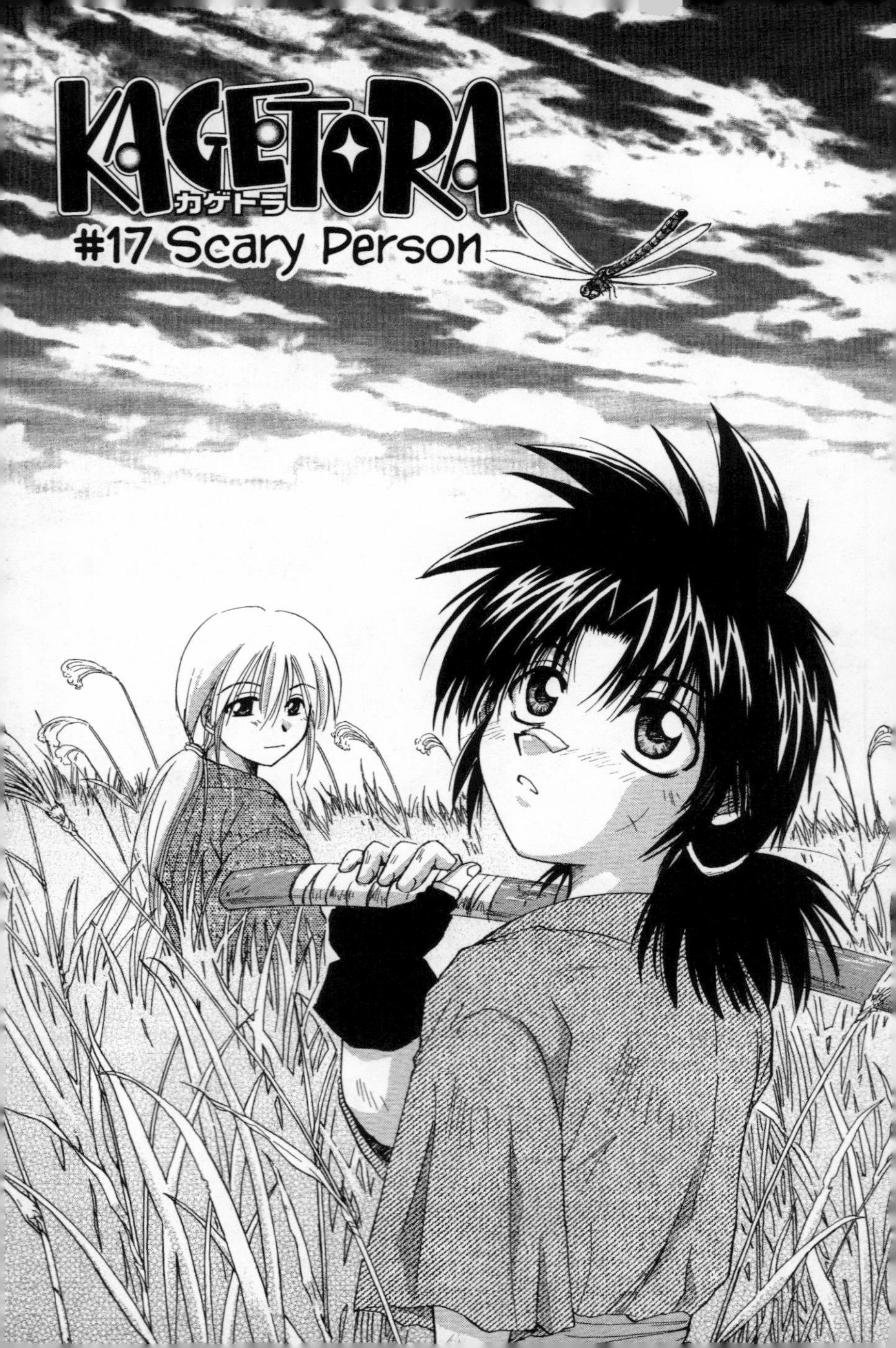
KAGETORA
カゲトラ
#17 Scary Person

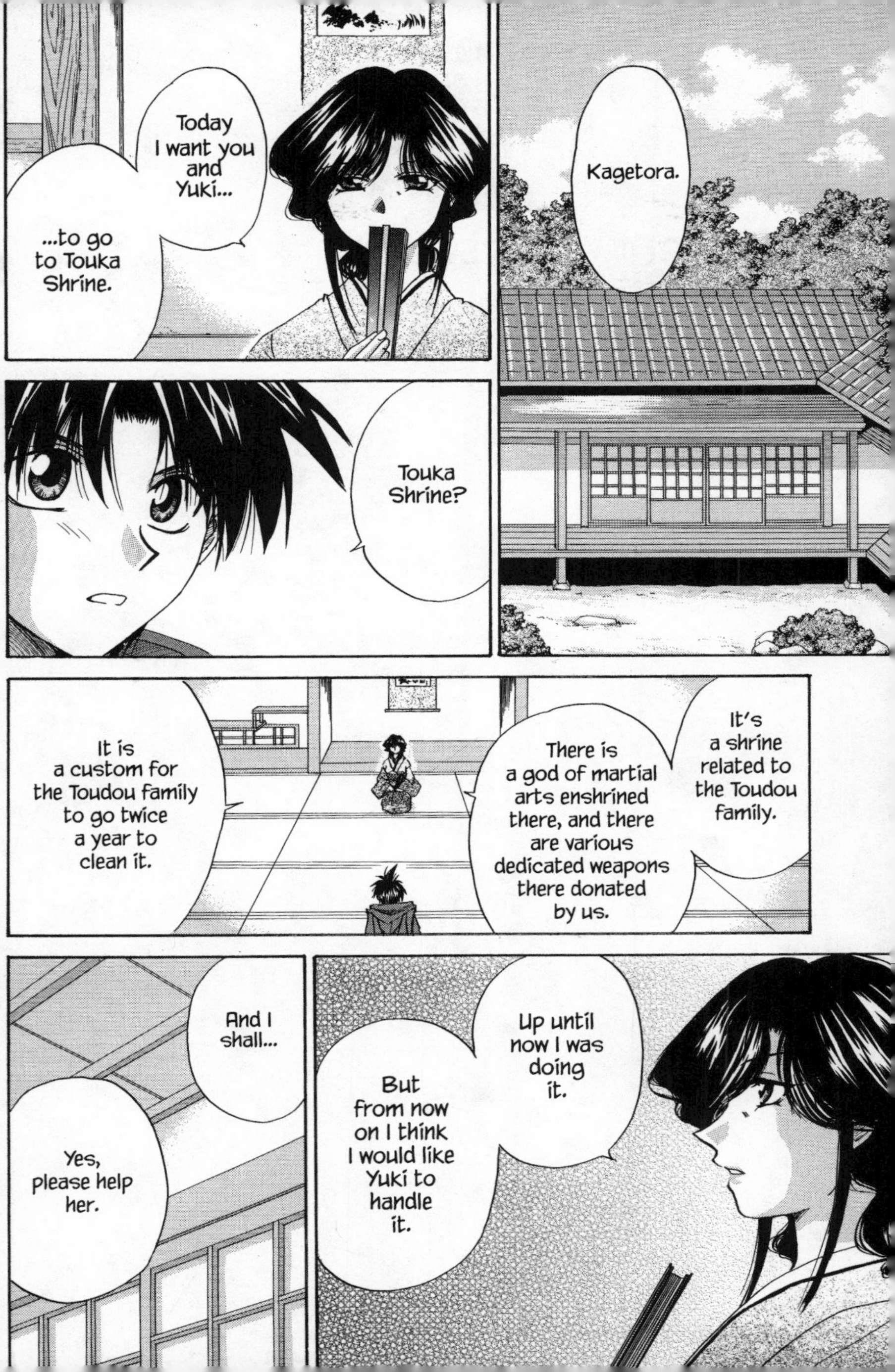
Kagetora.
Today I want you and Yuki...
...to go to Touka Shrine.
Touka Shrine?
It's a shrine related to the Toudou family.
There is a god of martial arts enshrined there, and there are various dedicated weapons there donated by us.
It is a custom for the Toudou family to go twice a year to clean it.
Up until now I was doing it.
But from now on I think I would like Yuki to handle it.
And I shall...
Yes, please help her.

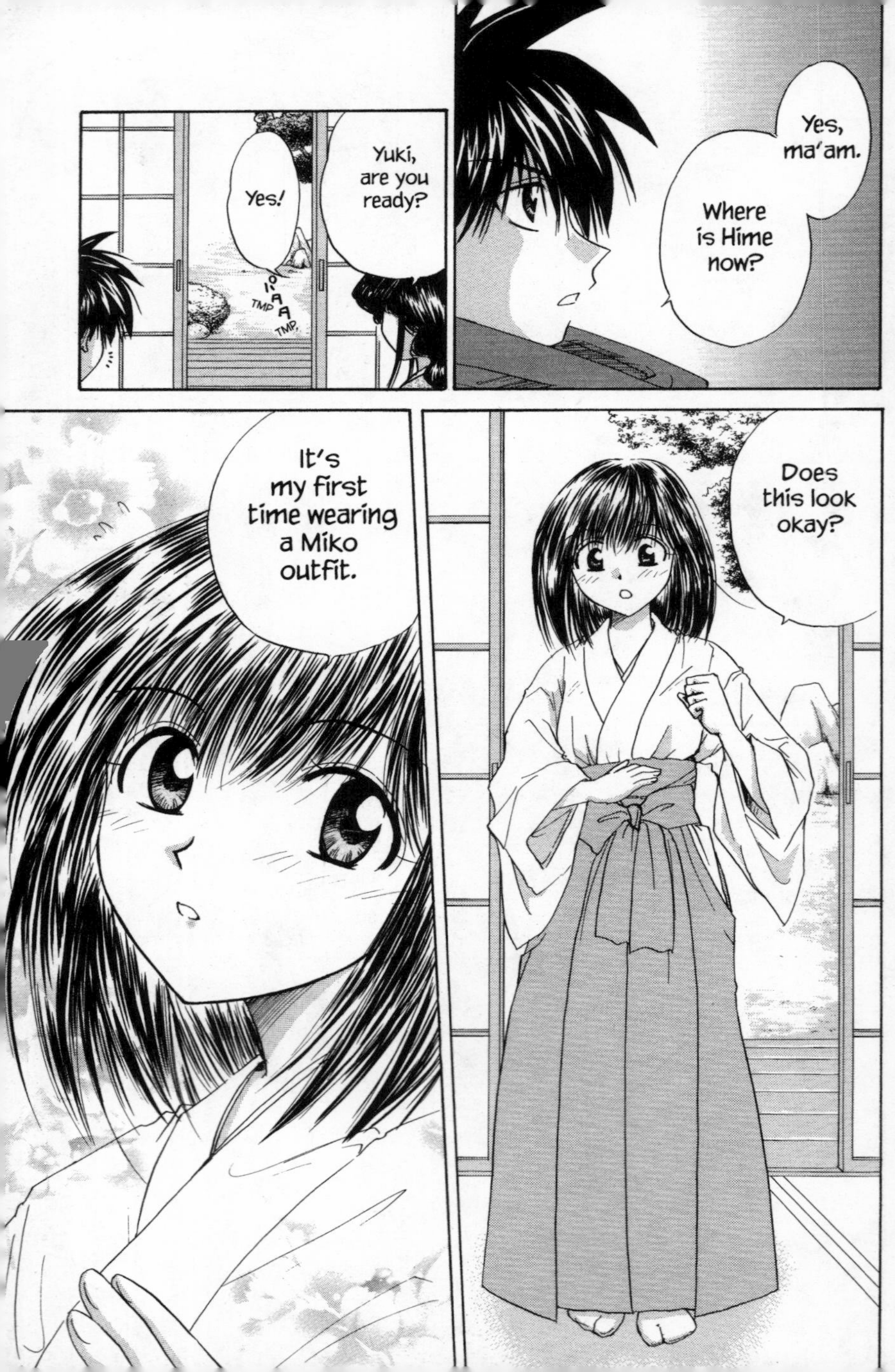
Yes, ma'am.
Where is Hime now?
Yuki, are you ready?
Yes!
TMP TMP
Does this look okay?
It's my first time wearing a Miko outfit.

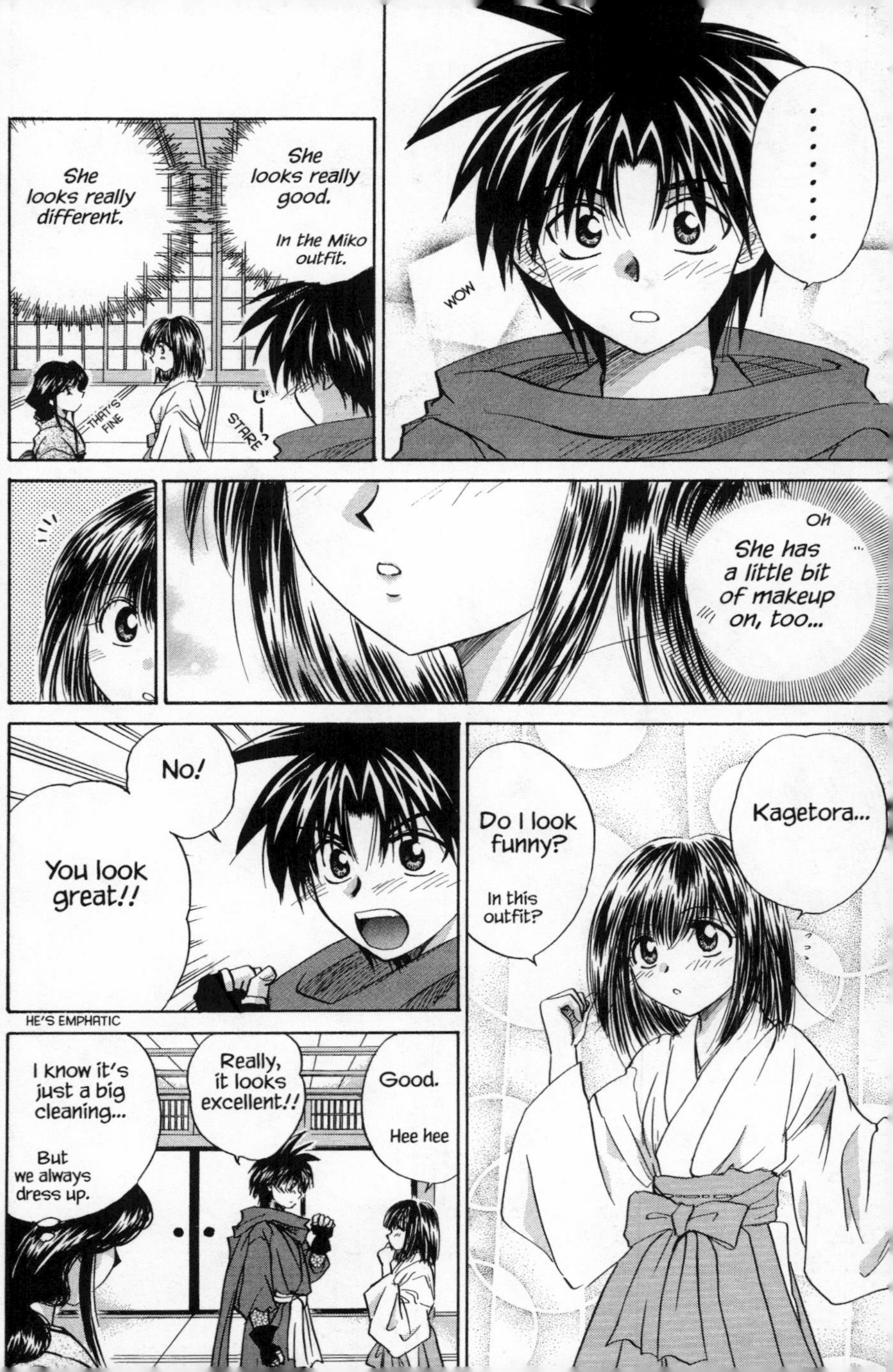
......
WOW
She looks really good.
In the Miko outfit.
She looks really different.
THAT'S FINE
じー
STARE
Oh
She has a little bit of makeup on, too...
Kagetora...
Do I look funny?
In this outfit?
No!
You look great!!
HE'S EMPHATIC
Good.
Hee hee
Really, it looks excellent!!
I know it's just a big cleaning...
But we always dress up.

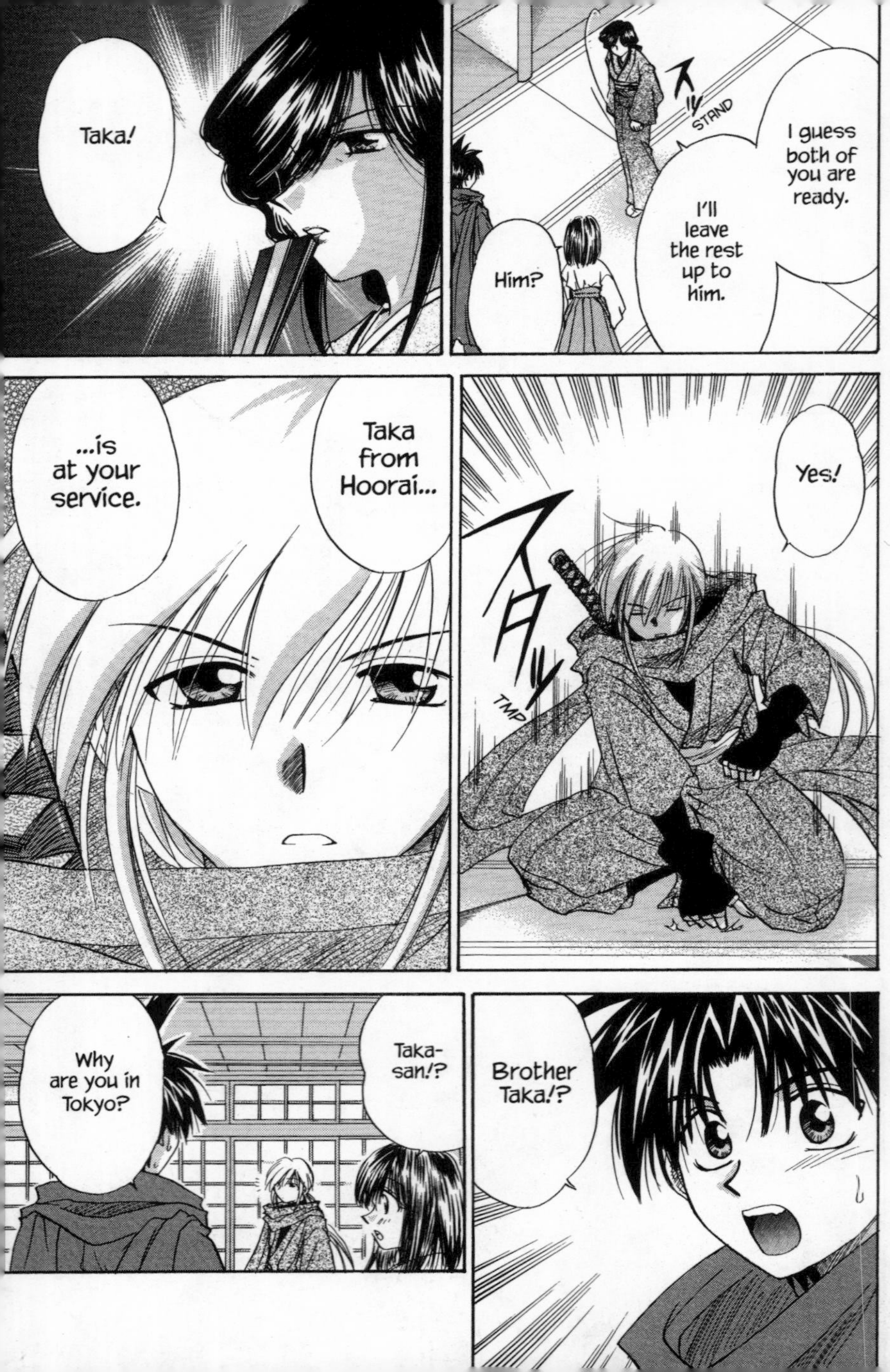
STAND
I guess both of you are ready.
I'll leave the rest up to him.
Him?
Taka!
Yes!
TMP
Taka from Hoorai...
...is at your service.
Brother Taka!?
Taka-san!?
Why are you in Tokyo?

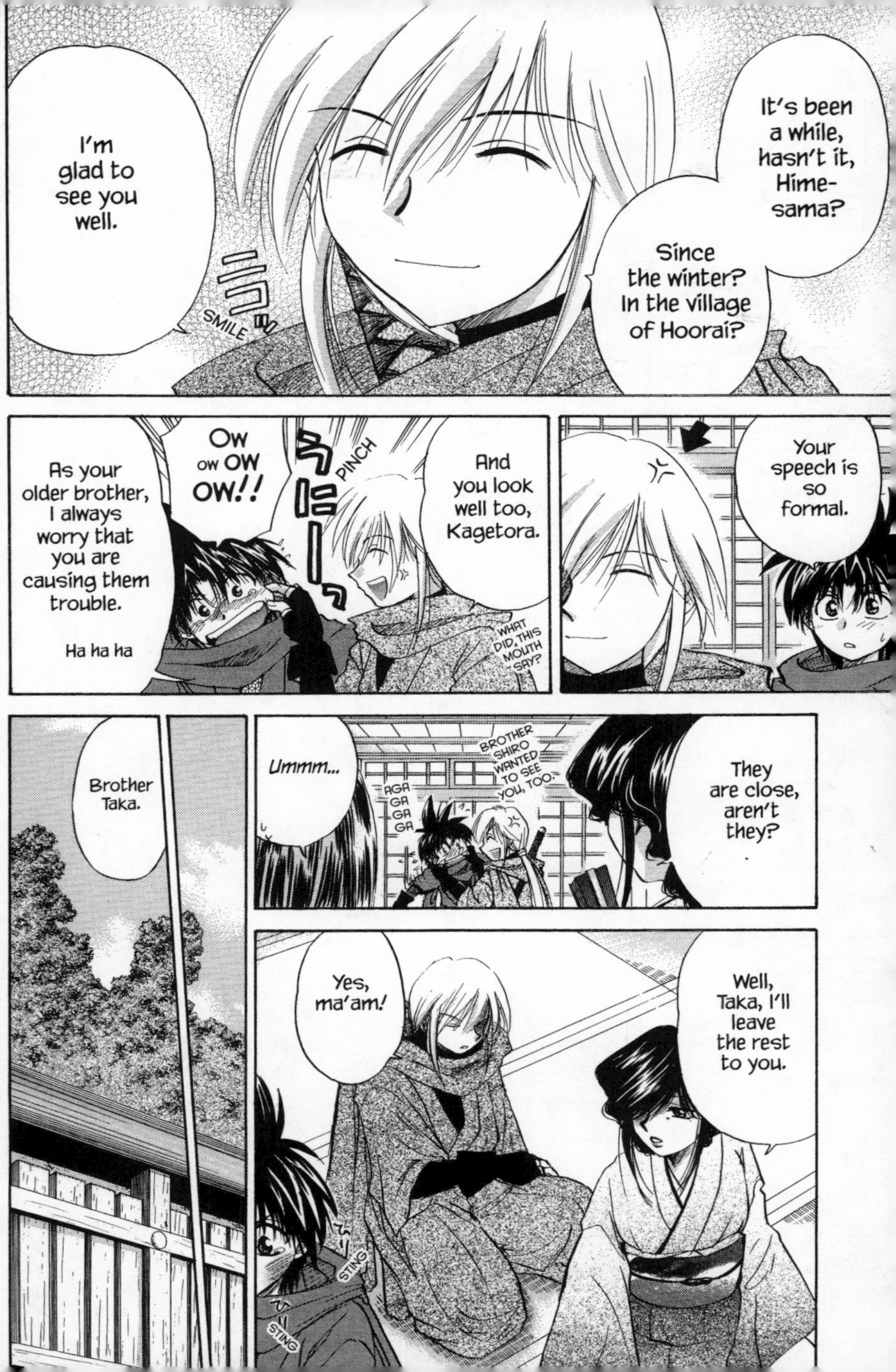
It's been a while, hasn't it, Hime-sama?
Since the winter? In the village of Hoorai?
SMILE
I'm glad to see you well.
Your speech is so formal.
And you look well too, Kagetora.
PINCH
WHAT DID, THIS MOUTH SAY?
Ow ow OW OW!!
As your older brother, I always worry that you are causing them trouble.
Ha ha ha
They are close, aren't they?
BROTHER SHIRO WANTED TO SEE YOU, TOO.
AGA GA GA GA
Ummm...
Well, Taka, I'll leave the rest to you.
Yes, ma'am!
STING
STING
Brother Taka.

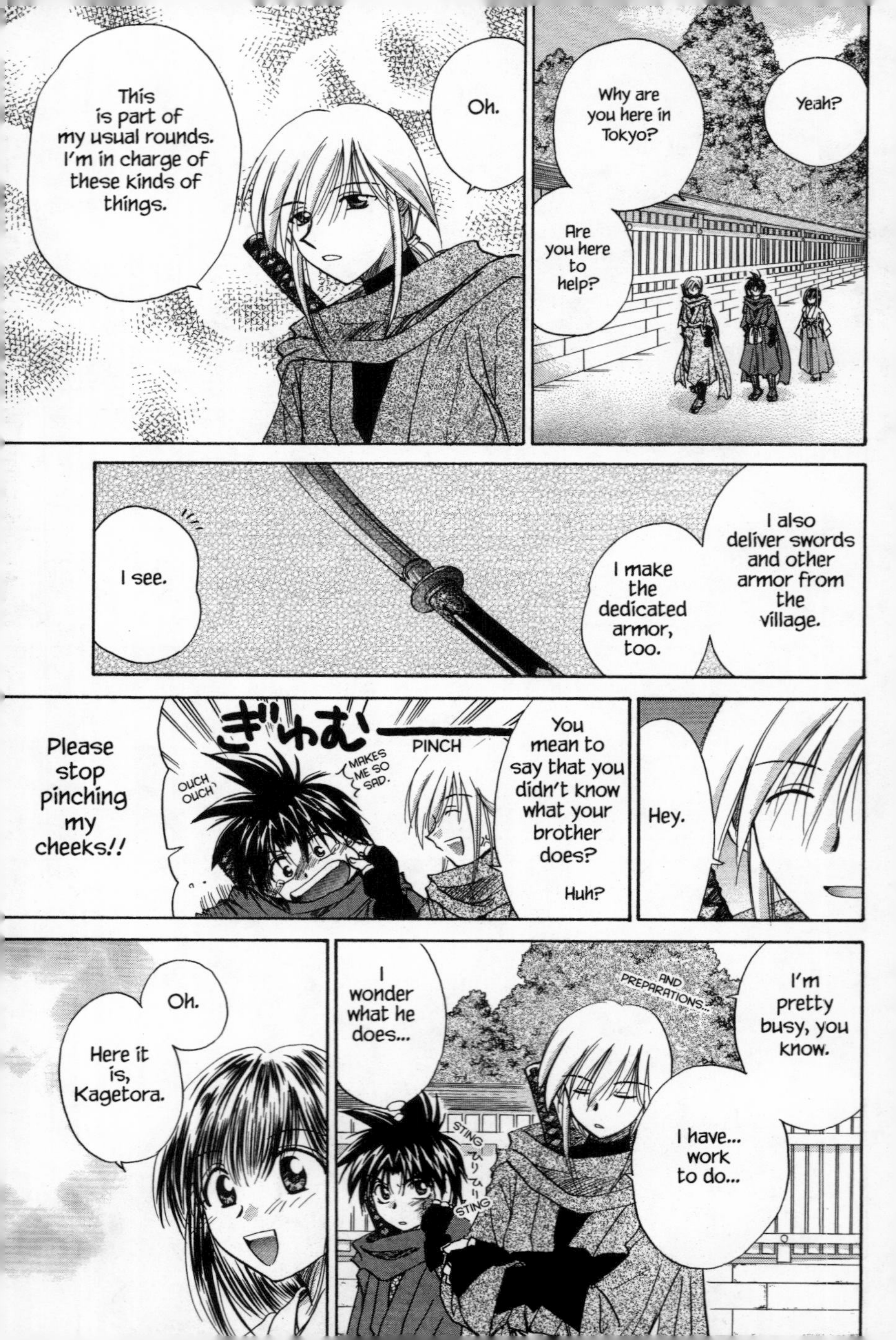
Yeah?
Why are you here in Tokyo?
Are you here to help?
Oh.
This is part of my usual rounds. I'm in charge of these kinds of things.
I also deliver swords and other armor from the village.
I make the dedicated armor, too.
I see.
Hey.
You mean to say that you didn't know what your brother does?
Huh?
PINCH
ぎゅむ
MAKES ME SO SAD.
OUCH OUCH
Please stop pinching my cheeks!!
AND PREPARATIONS...
I'm pretty busy, you know.
I have... work to do...
I wonder what he does...
STING
ひりひり
STING
Oh.
Here it is, Kagetora.

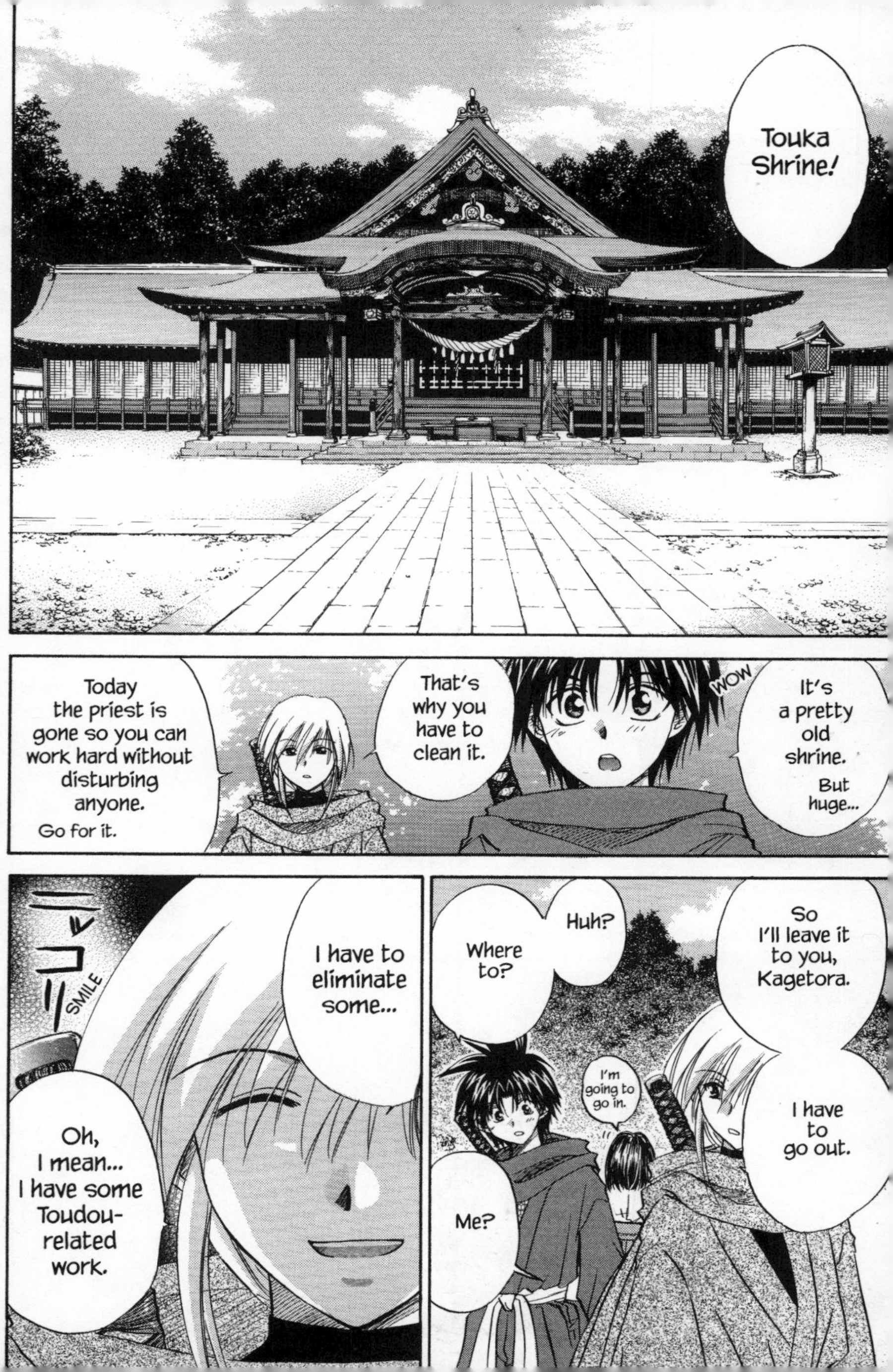
Touka Shrine!
WOW
It's a pretty old shrine.
But huge...
That's why you have to clean it.
Today the priest is gone so you can work hard without disturbing anyone.
Go for it.
So I'll leave it to you, Kagetora.
Huh?
Where to?
I have to go out.
I'm going to go in.
Me?
I have to eliminate some...
SMILE
Oh, I mean... I have some Toudou-related work.

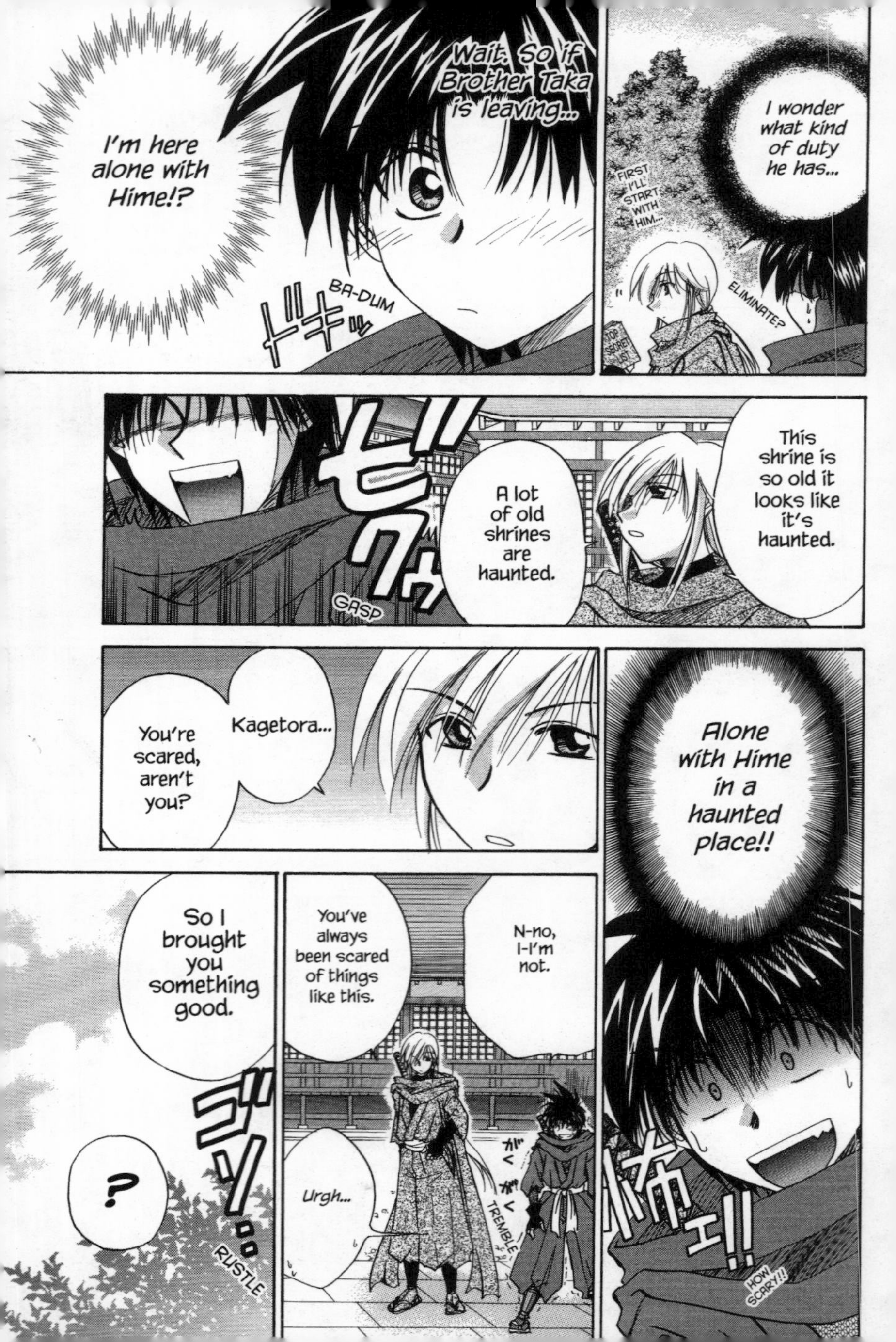
I wonder what kind of duty he has...
FIRST I'LL START WITH HIM...
TOP SECRET LIST
ELIMINATE?
Wait. So if Brother Taka is leaving...
I'm here alone with Hime!?
BA-DUM
This shrine is so old it looks like it's haunted.
A lot of old shrines are haunted.
GASP
Alone with Hime in a haunted place!!
HOW SCARY!!
Kagetora...
You're scared, aren't you?
N-no, I-I'm not.
You've always been scared of things like this.
Urgh...
TREMBLE
So I brought you something good.
?
RUSTLE

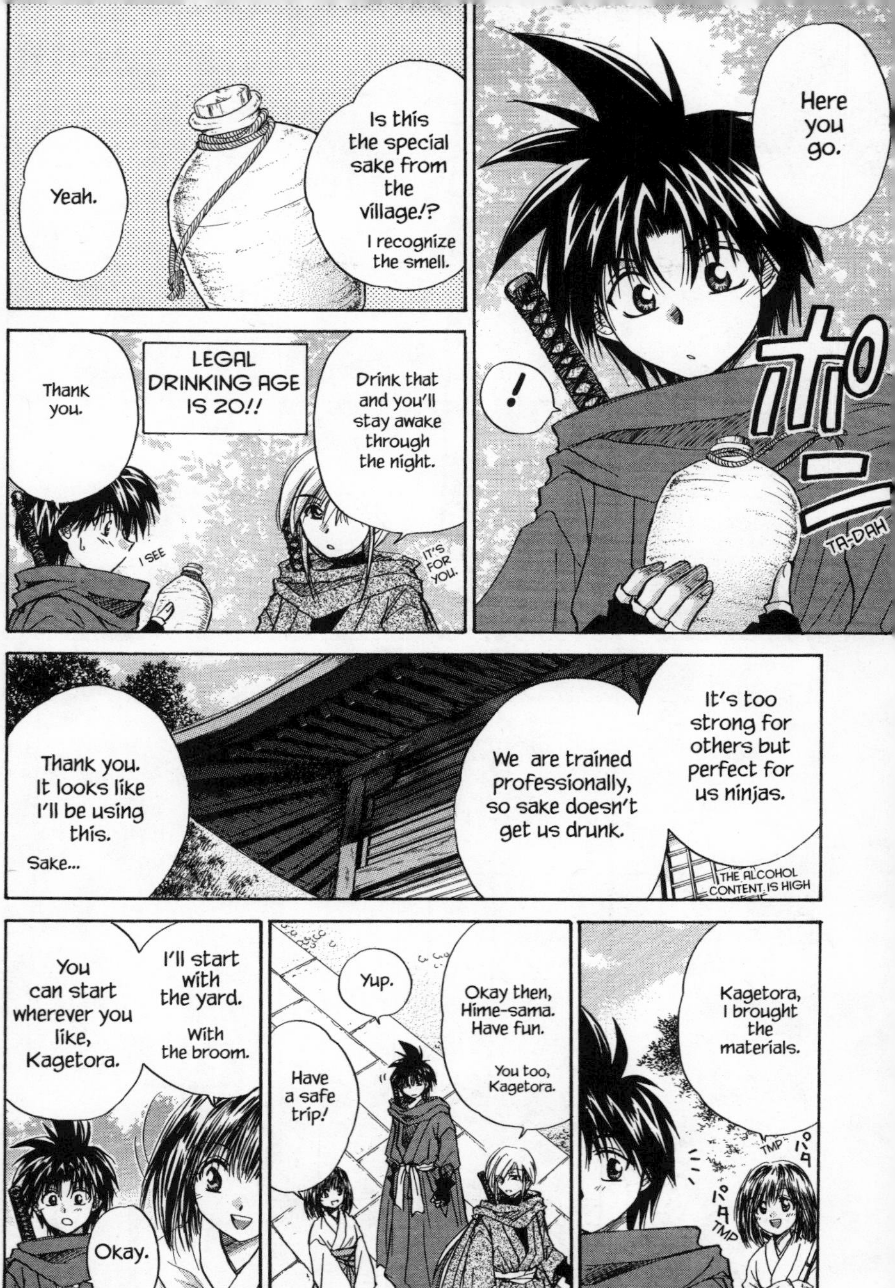
Here you go.
!
TA-DAH
Is this the special sake from the village!?
I recognize the smell.
Yeah.
Drink that and you'll stay awake through the night.
IT'S FOR YOU.
LEGAL DRINKING AGE IS 20!!
Thank you.
I SEE
It's too strong for others but perfect for us ninjas.
We are trained professionally, so sake doesn't get us drunk.
THE ALCOHOL CONTENT IS HIGH
Thank you. It looks like I'll be using this.
Sake...
Kagetora, I brought the materials.
TMP
TMP
Okay then, Hime-sama. Have fun.
You too, Kagetora.
Yup.
Have a safe trip!
I'll start with the yard.
With the broom.
You can start wherever you like, Kagetora.
Okay.

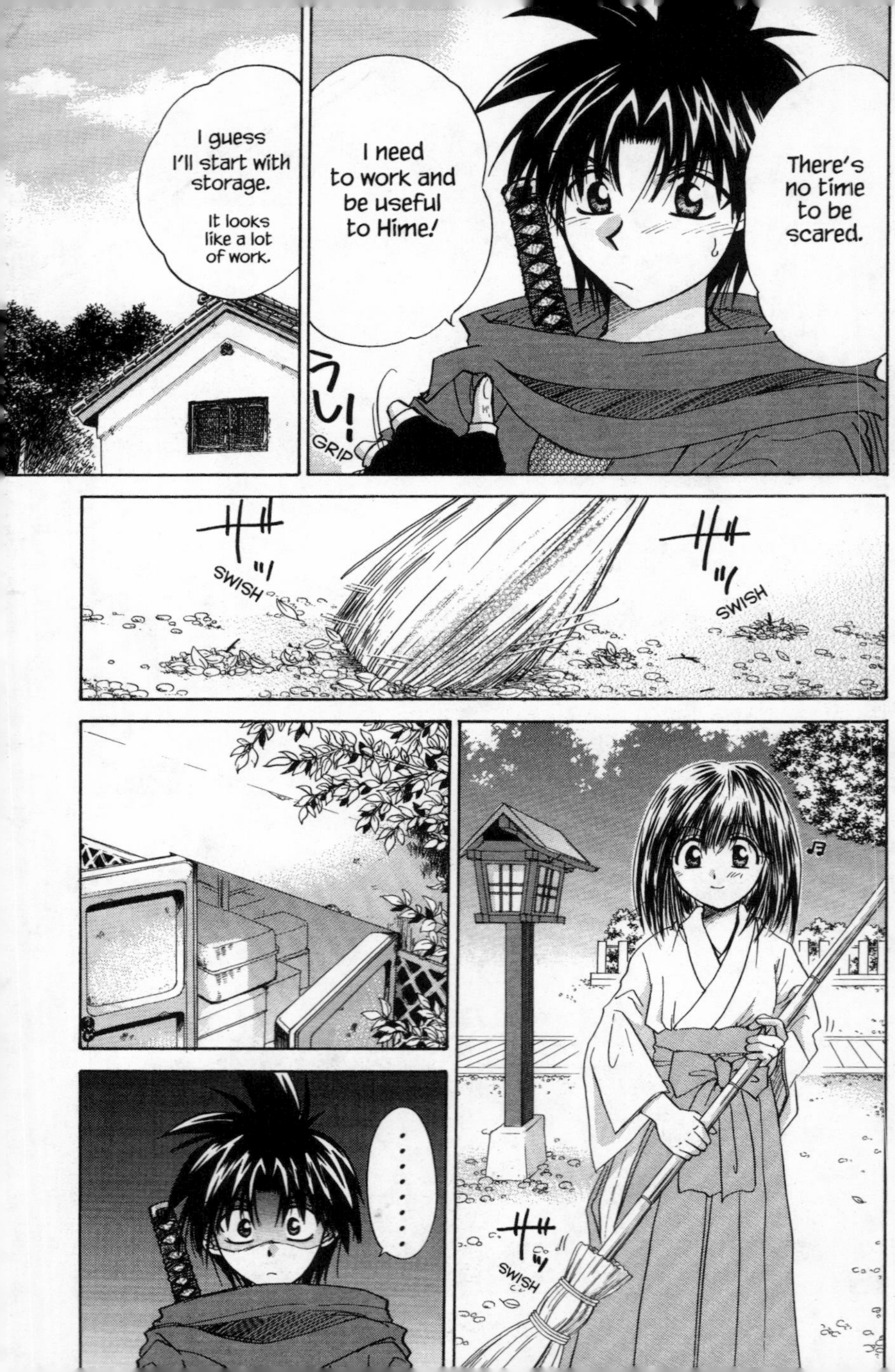
There's no time to be scared.
I need to work and be useful to Hime!
GRIP
I guess I'll start with storage.
It looks like a lot of work.
SWISH
SWISH
SWISH
......

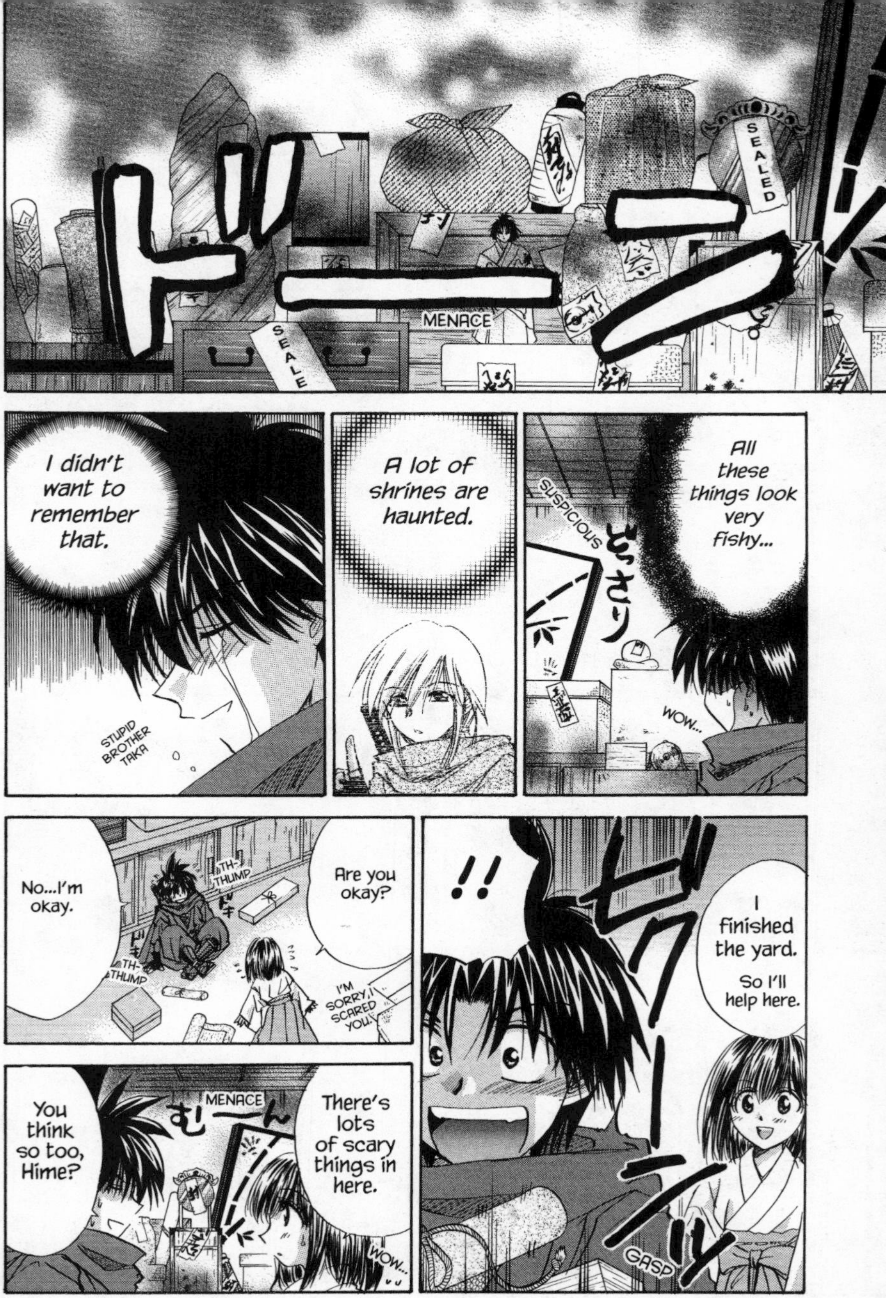
ドーン
SEALED
MENACE
SEALE
All these things look very fishy...
SUSPICIOUS
どっさり
WOW...
A lot of shrines are haunted.
I didn't want to remember that.
STUPID BROTHER TAKA
!!
I finished the yard.
So I'll help here.
GASP
Are you okay?
No...I'm okay.
TH-THUMP
TH-THUMP
I'M SORRY, I SCARED YOU.
There's lots of scary things in here.
You think so too, Hime?
MENACE
むーん
WOW...

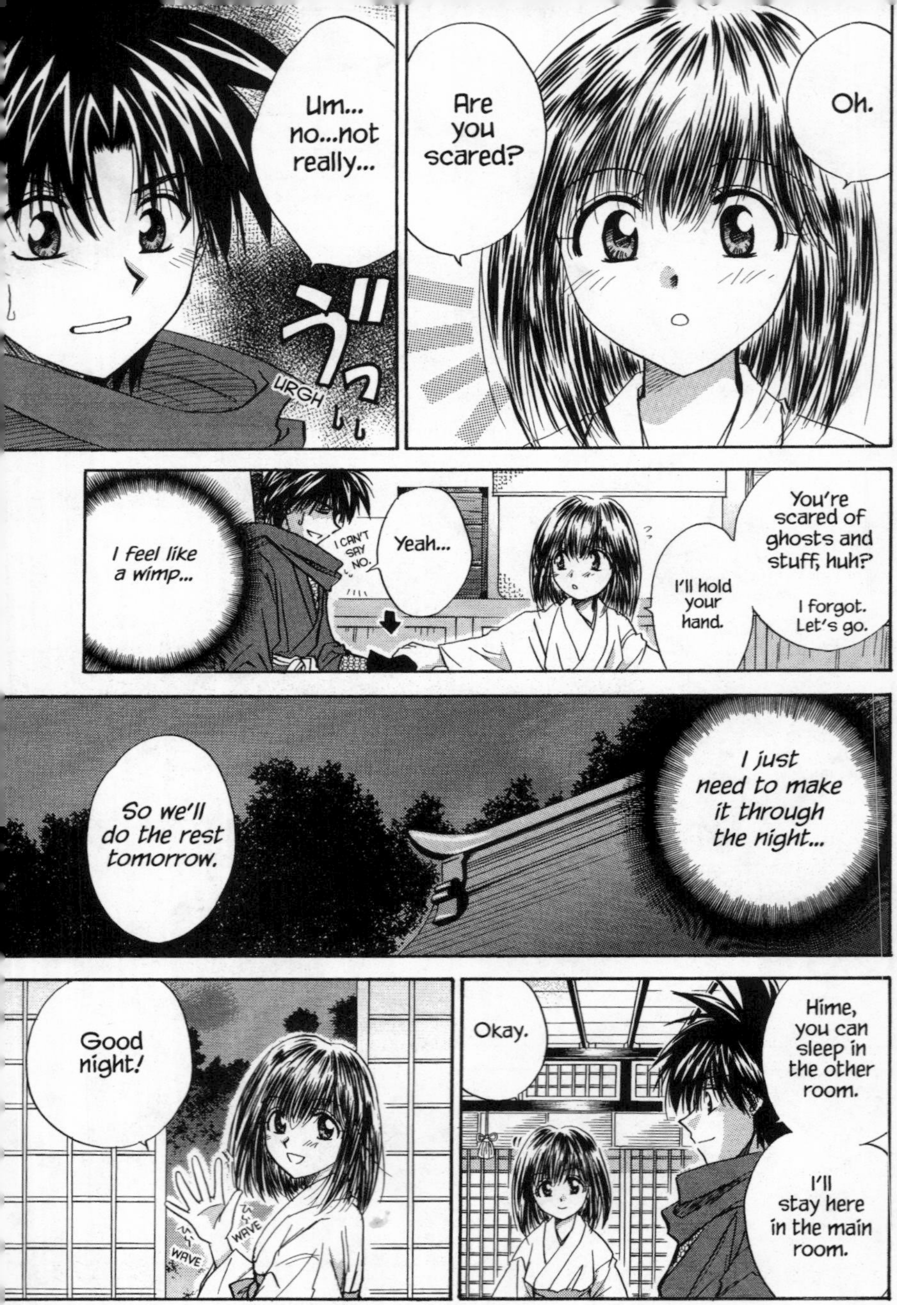
Oh.
Are you scared?
Um... no...not really...
URGH
You're scared of ghosts and stuff, huh?
I forgot. Let's go.
I'll hold your hand.
Yeah...
I CAN'T SAY NO.
I feel like a wimp...
I just need to make it through the night...
So we'll do the rest tomorrow.
Hime, you can sleep in the other room.
I'll stay here in the main room.
Okay.
Good night!
WAVE
WAVE

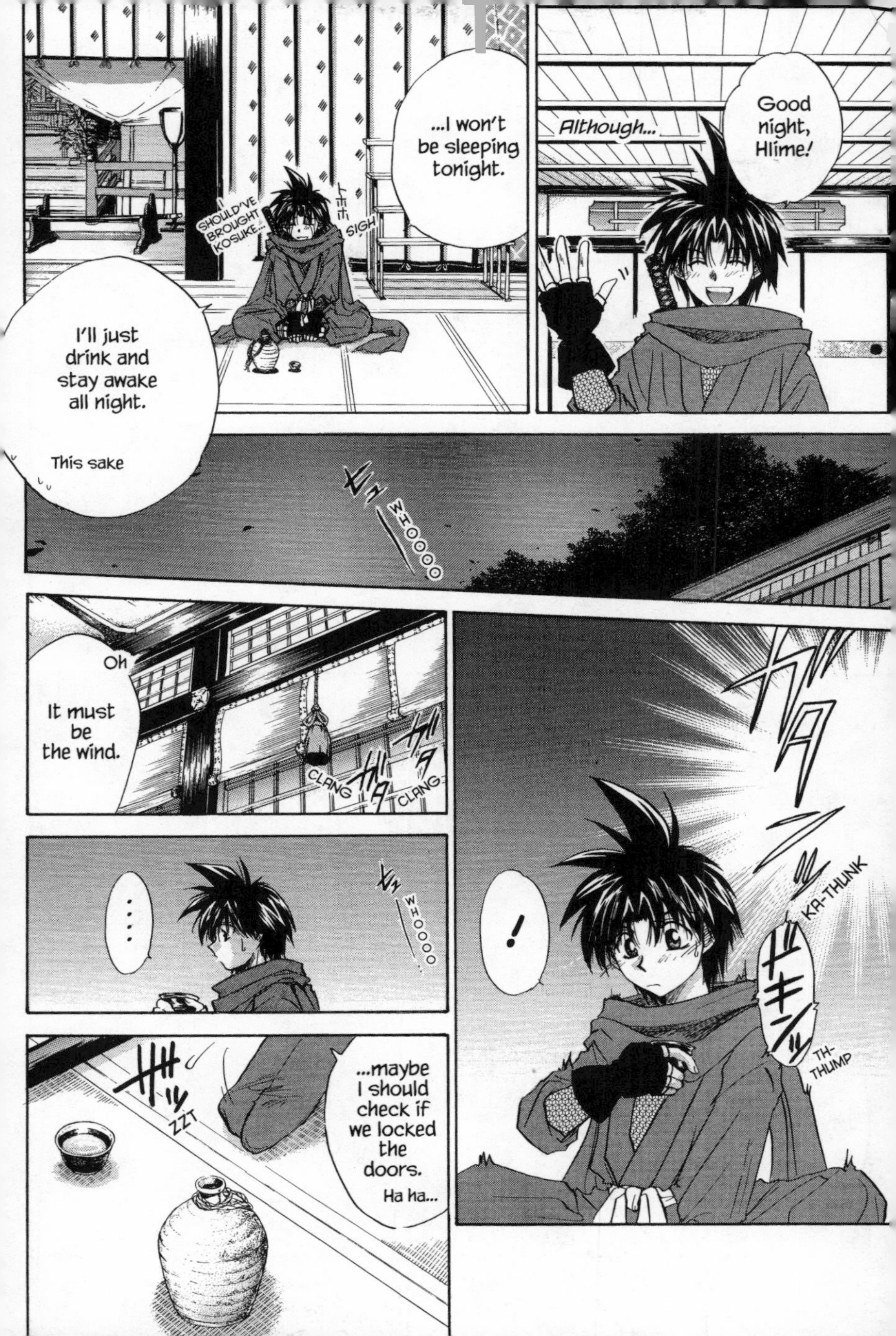
Good night, Hlime!
Although...
...I won't be sleeping tonight.
SIGH
SHOULD'VE BROUGHT KOSUKE...
I'll just drink and stay awake all night.
This sake
WHOOOOO
KA-THUNK
!
TH-THUMP
Oh
It must be the wind.
CLANG
CLANG
....
WHOOOOO...
...maybe I should check if we locked the doors.
Ha ha...
ZZT

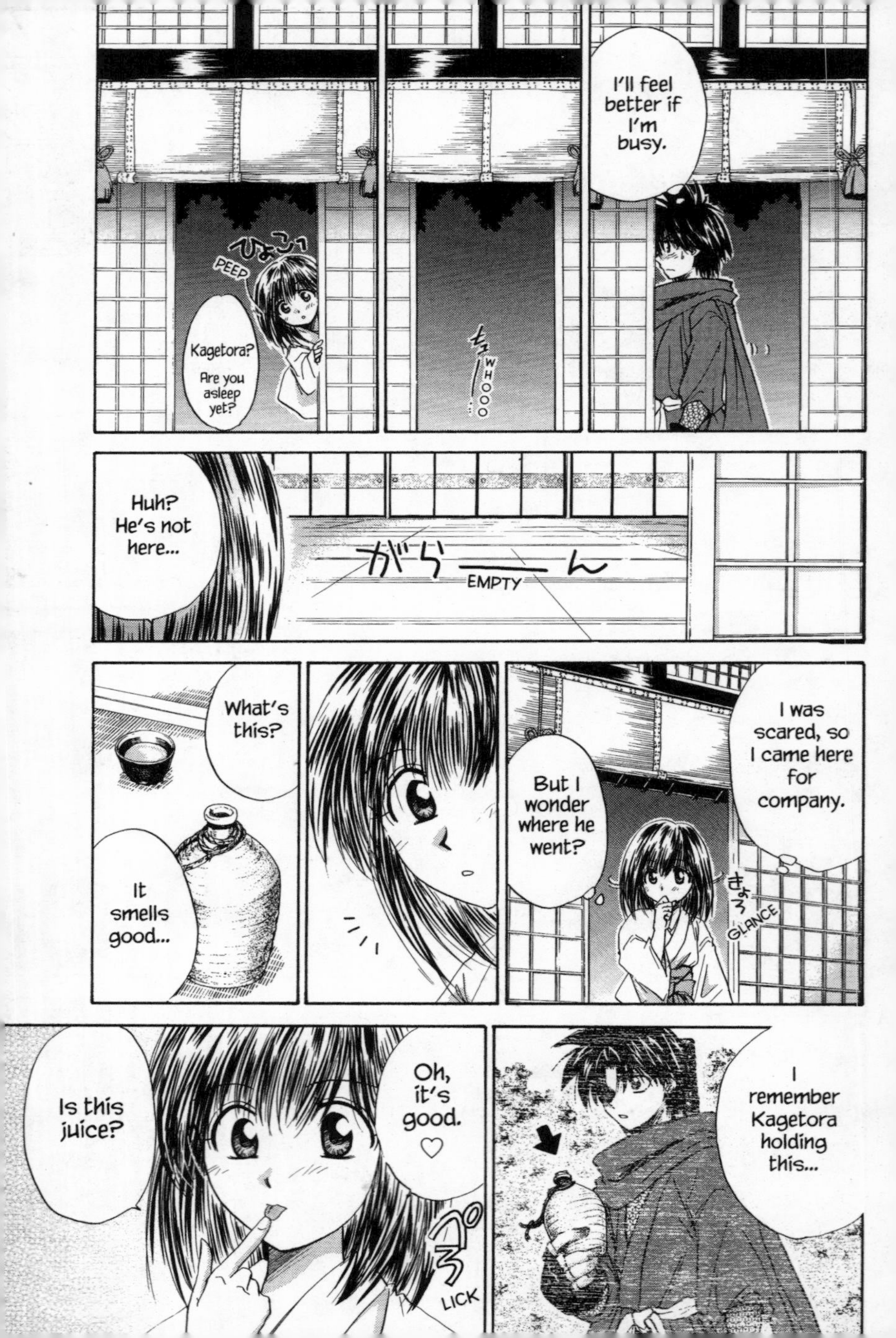
I'll feel better if I'm busy.
WHOOO
ひょこっ
PEEP
Kagetora? Are you asleep yet?
Huh? He's not here...
がら——ん
EMPTY
I was scared, so I came here for company.
But I wonder where he went?
きょろ
GLANCE
What's this?
It smells good...
I remember Kagetora holding this...
Oh, it's good. ♡
Is this juice?
ぺろ
LICK

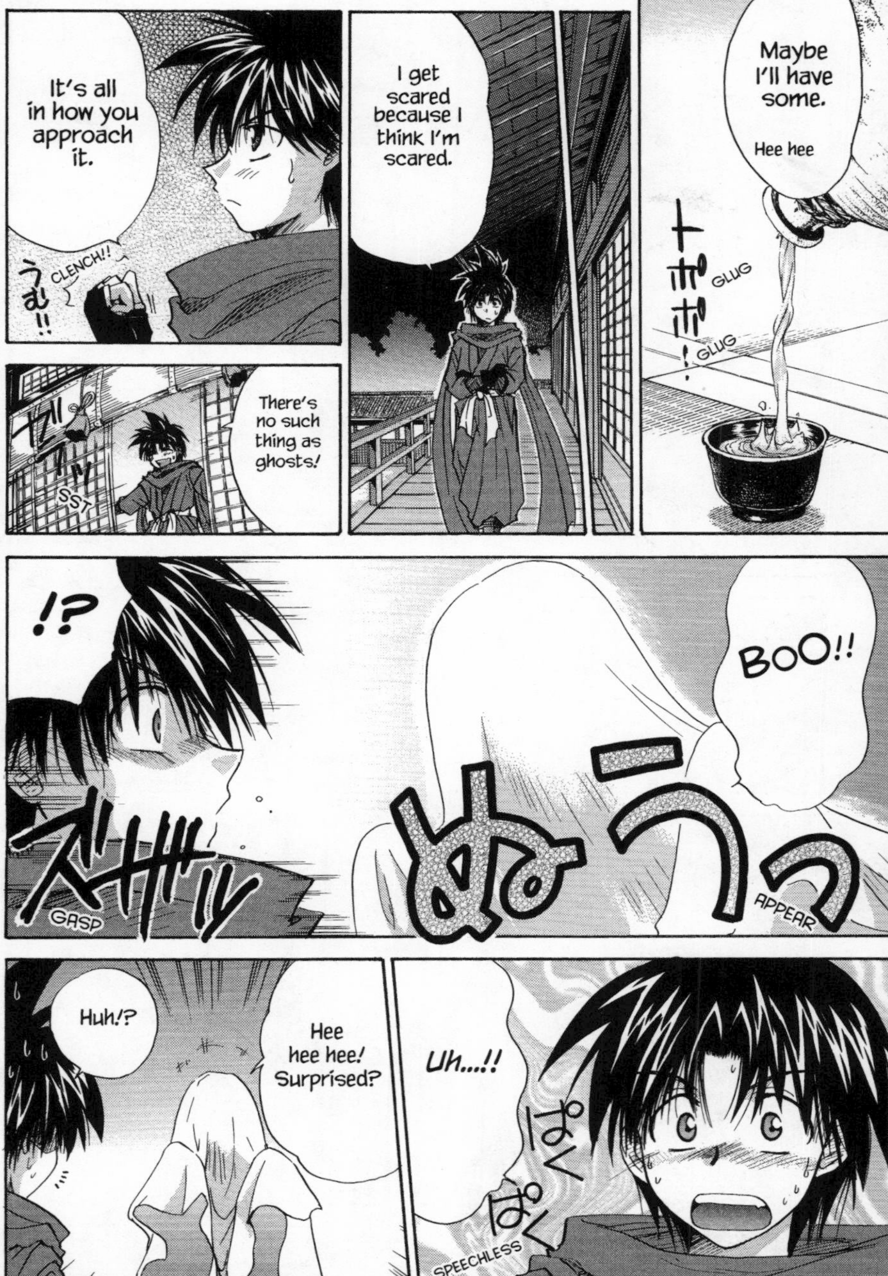
Maybe I'll have some.
Hee hee
トポポ!
GLUG
GLUG
I get scared because I think I'm scared.
It's all in how you approach it.
うむ!!
CLENCH!!
There's no such thing as ghosts!
SST
BOO!!
ぬうっ
APPEAR
!?
GASP
Uh...!!
ぱくぱく
SPEECHLESS
Hee hee hee! Surprised?
Huh!?

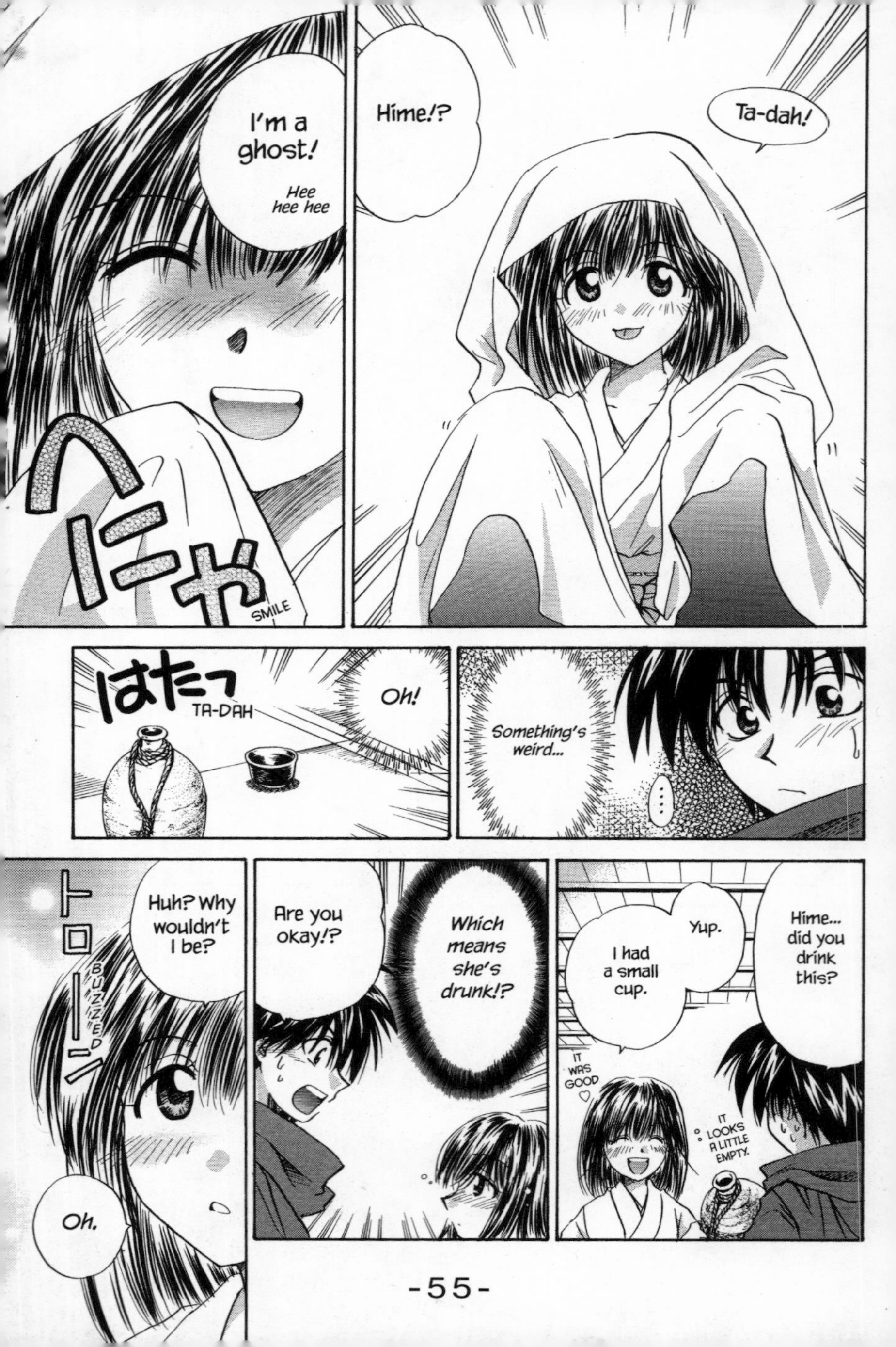
Ta-dah!
Hime!?
I'm a ghost!
Hee hee hee
へにゃ
SMILE
Something's weird...
...
はたっ
TA-DAH
Oh!
Hime... did you drink this?
Yup.
I had a small cup.
IT WAS GOOD ♡
IT LOOKS A LITTLE EMPTY.
Which means she's drunk!?
Are you okay!?
Huh? Why wouldn't I be?
トロ〜ン
BUZZED
Oh.

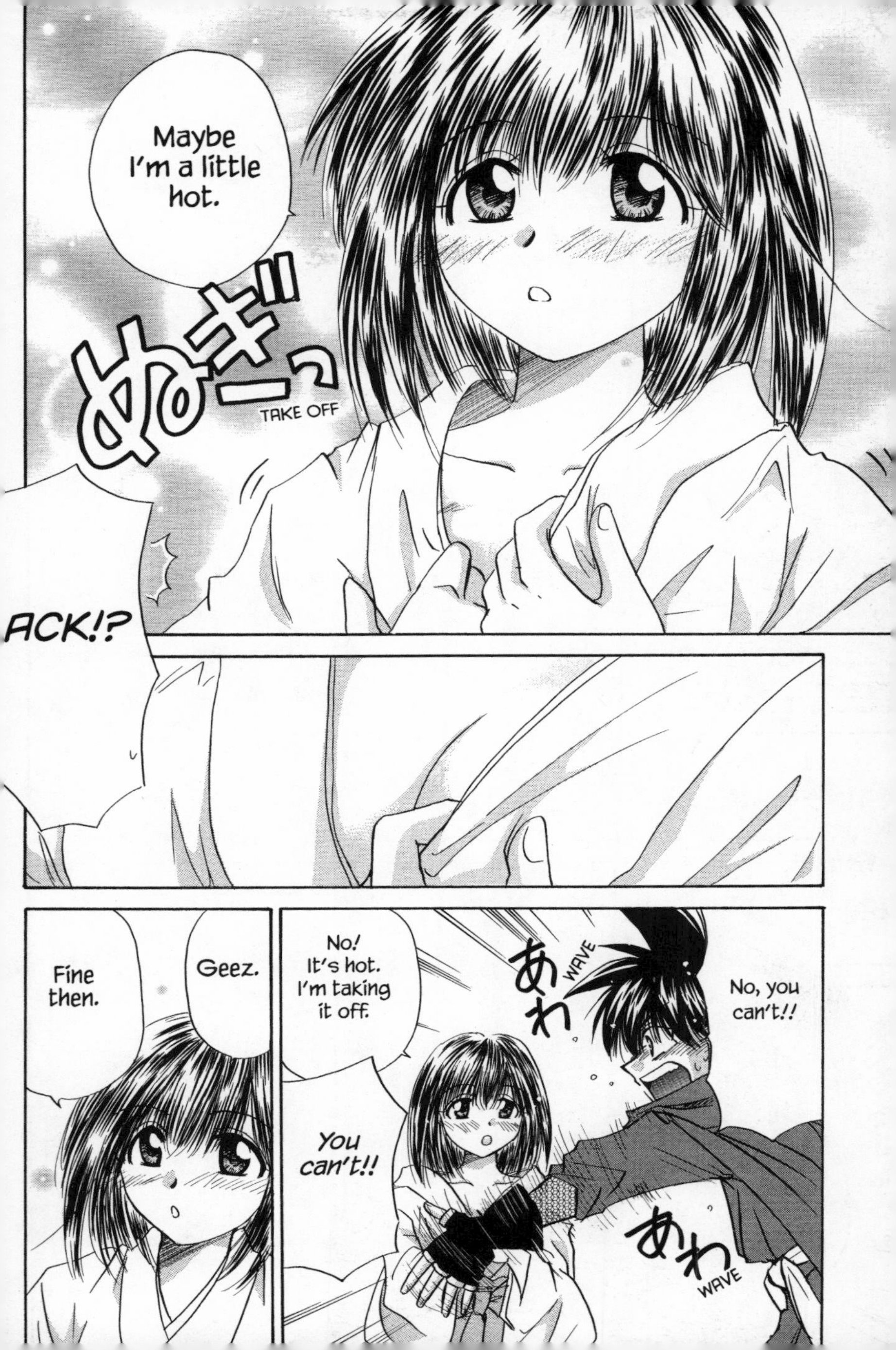
Maybe I'm a little hot.
ぬぎーっ
TAKE OFF
ACK!?
あわ
WAVE
No, you can't!!
No! It's hot. I'm taking it off.
You can't!!
あわ
WAVE
Geez.
Fine then.

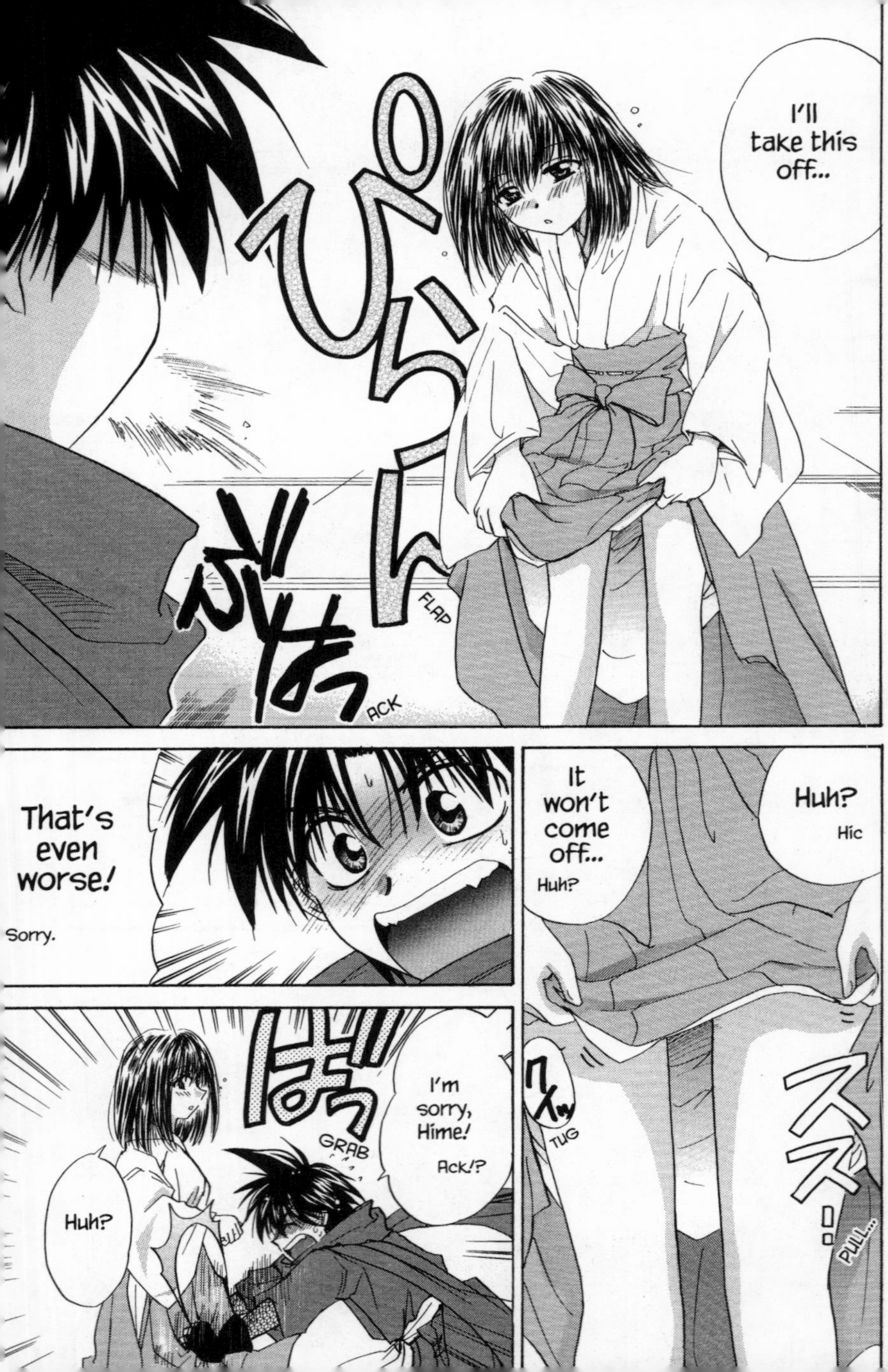

I'll take this off...
ぴらん
FLAP
ぶはっ
ACK
Huh?
Hic
It won't come off...
Huh?
クイッ
TUG
PULL...
That's even worse!
Sorry.
ぼっ
GRAB
I'm sorry, Hime!
Ack!?
Huh?

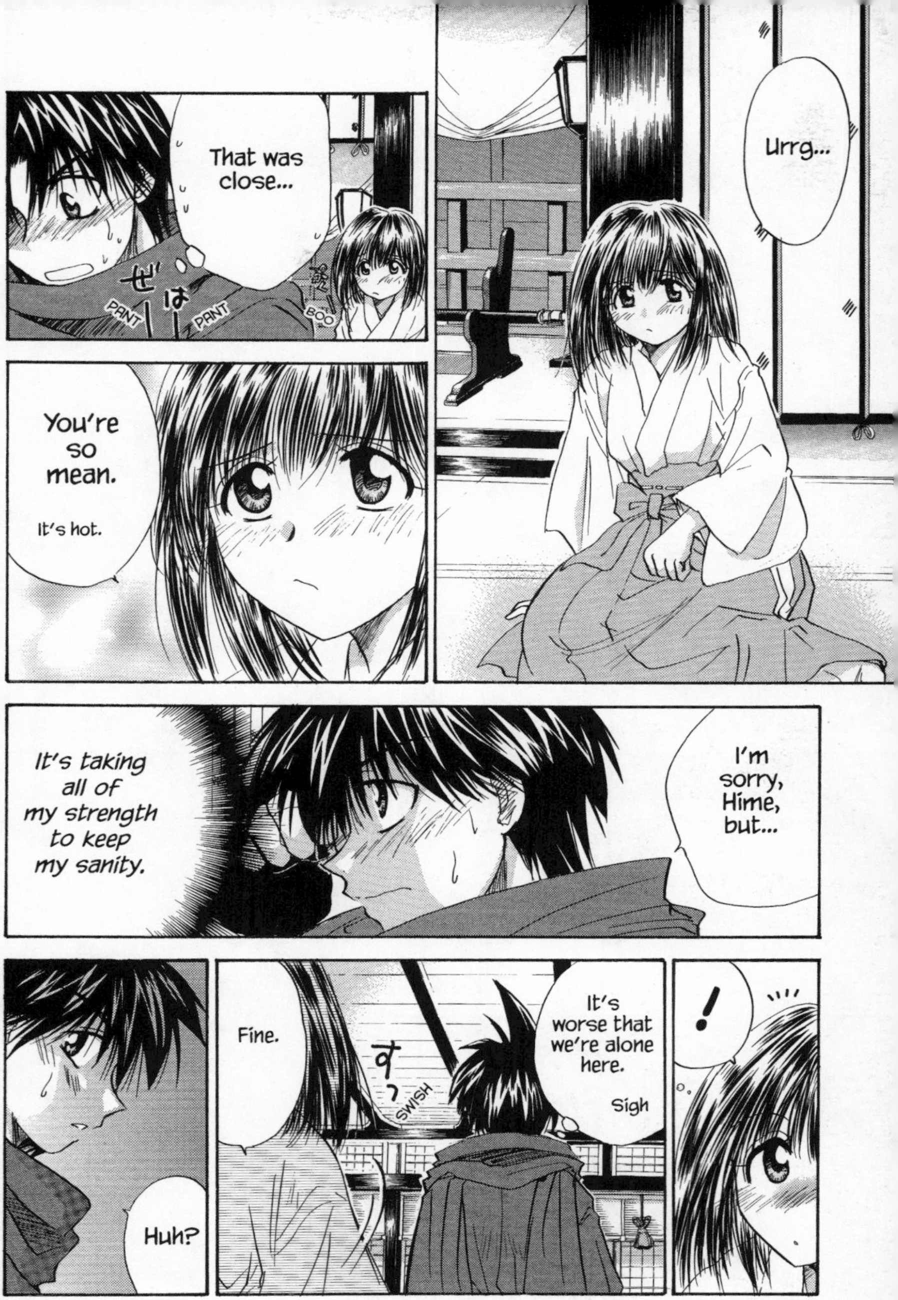
Urrg...
That was close...
ぜ は
PANT PANT
BOO
You're so mean.
It's hot.
I'm sorry, Hime, but...
It's taking all of my strength to keep my sanity.
!
It's worse that we're alone here.
Sigh
Fine.
す
SWISH
Huh?

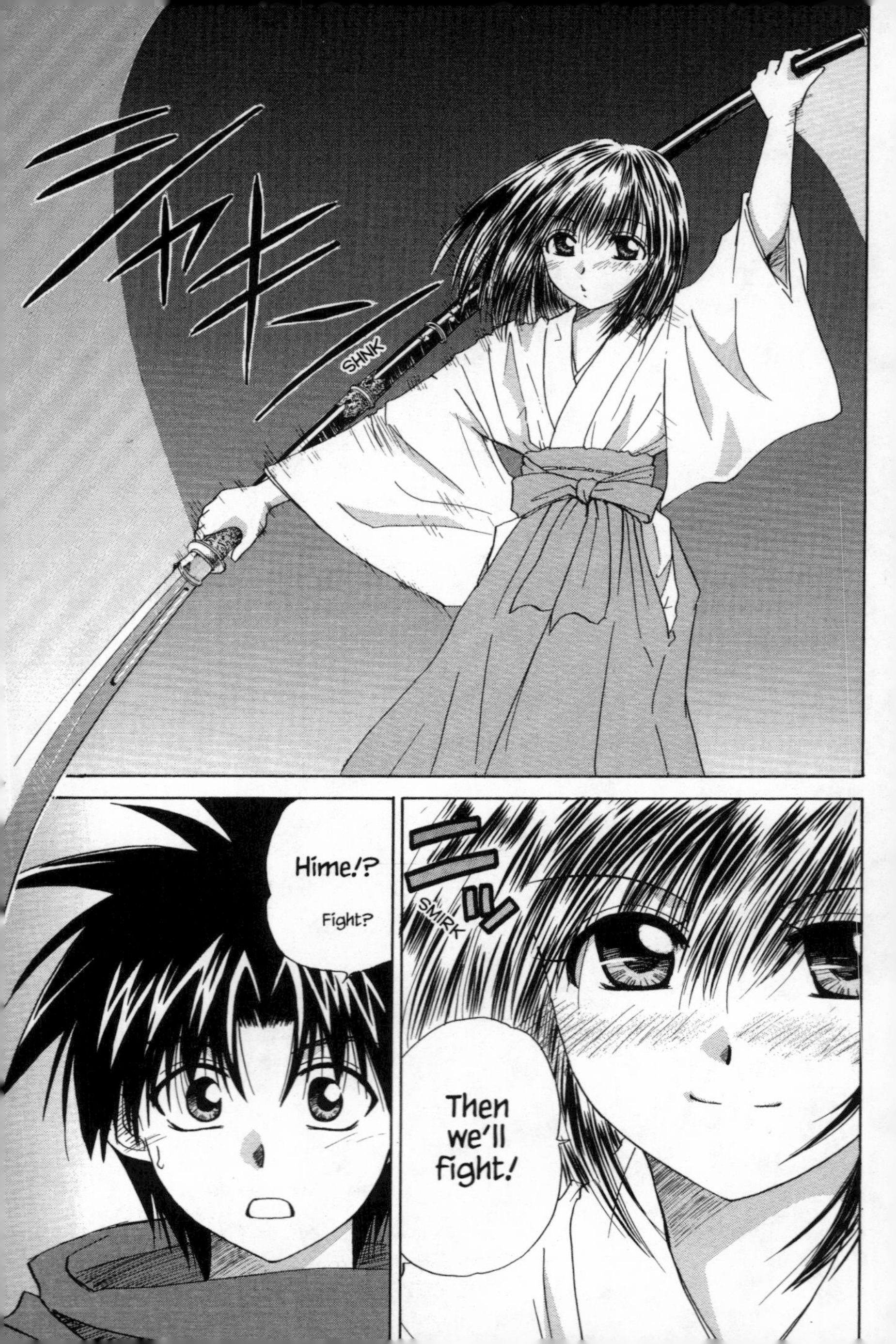
シャキーン
SHNK
SMIRK
Then we'll fight!
Hime!?
Fight?

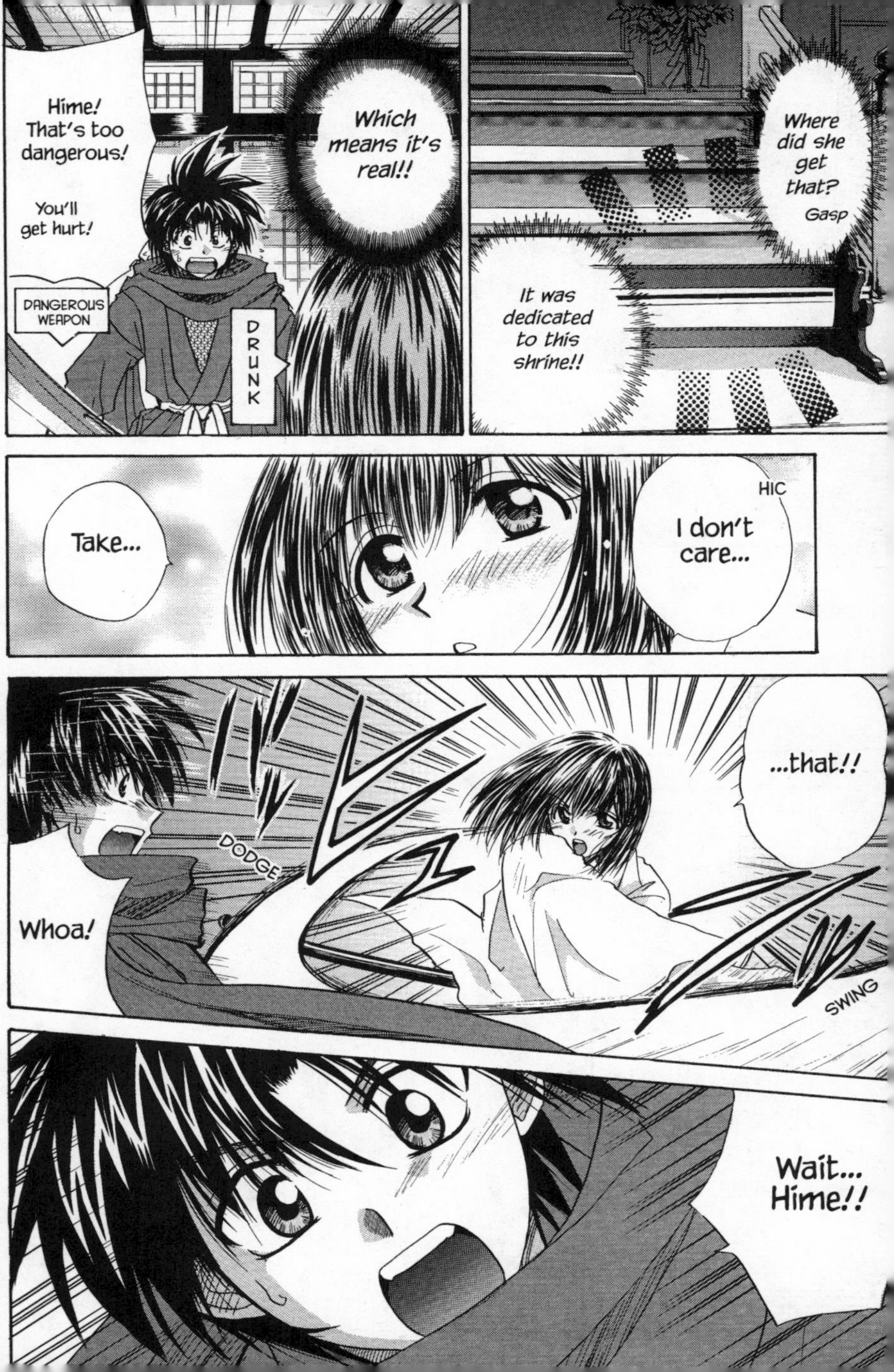

Where did she get that?
Gasp
It was dedicated to this shrine!!
Which means it's real!!
Hime! That's too dangerous!
You'll get hurt!
DANGEROUS WEAPON
DRUNK
HIC
I don't care...
Take...
...that!!
SWING
DODGE
Whoa!
Wait... Hime!!

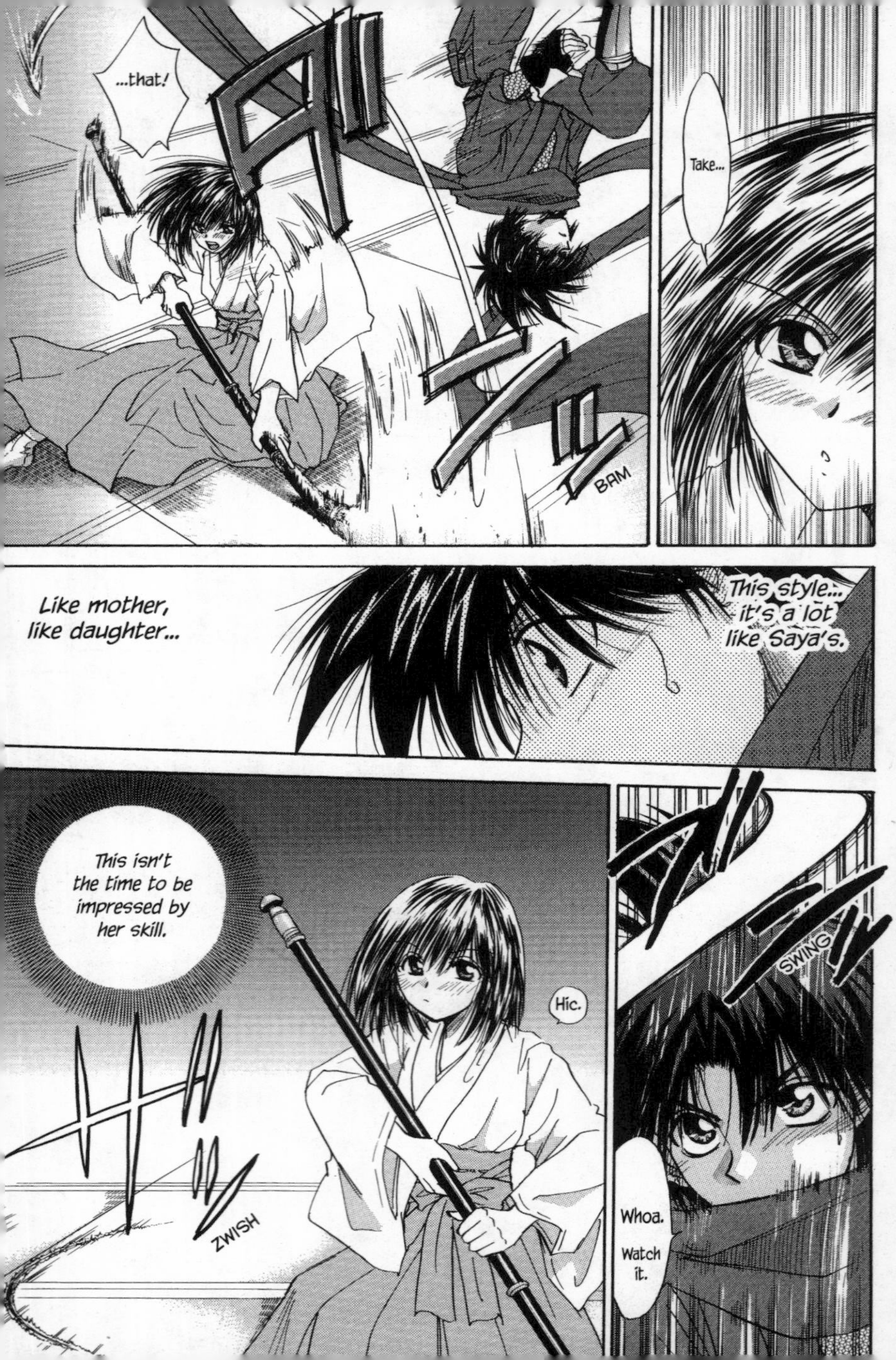
Take...
...that!
BAM
This style... it's a lot like Saya's.
Like mother, like daughter...
SWING
Whoa.
Watch it.
This isn't the time to be impressed by her skill.
Hic.
ZWISH

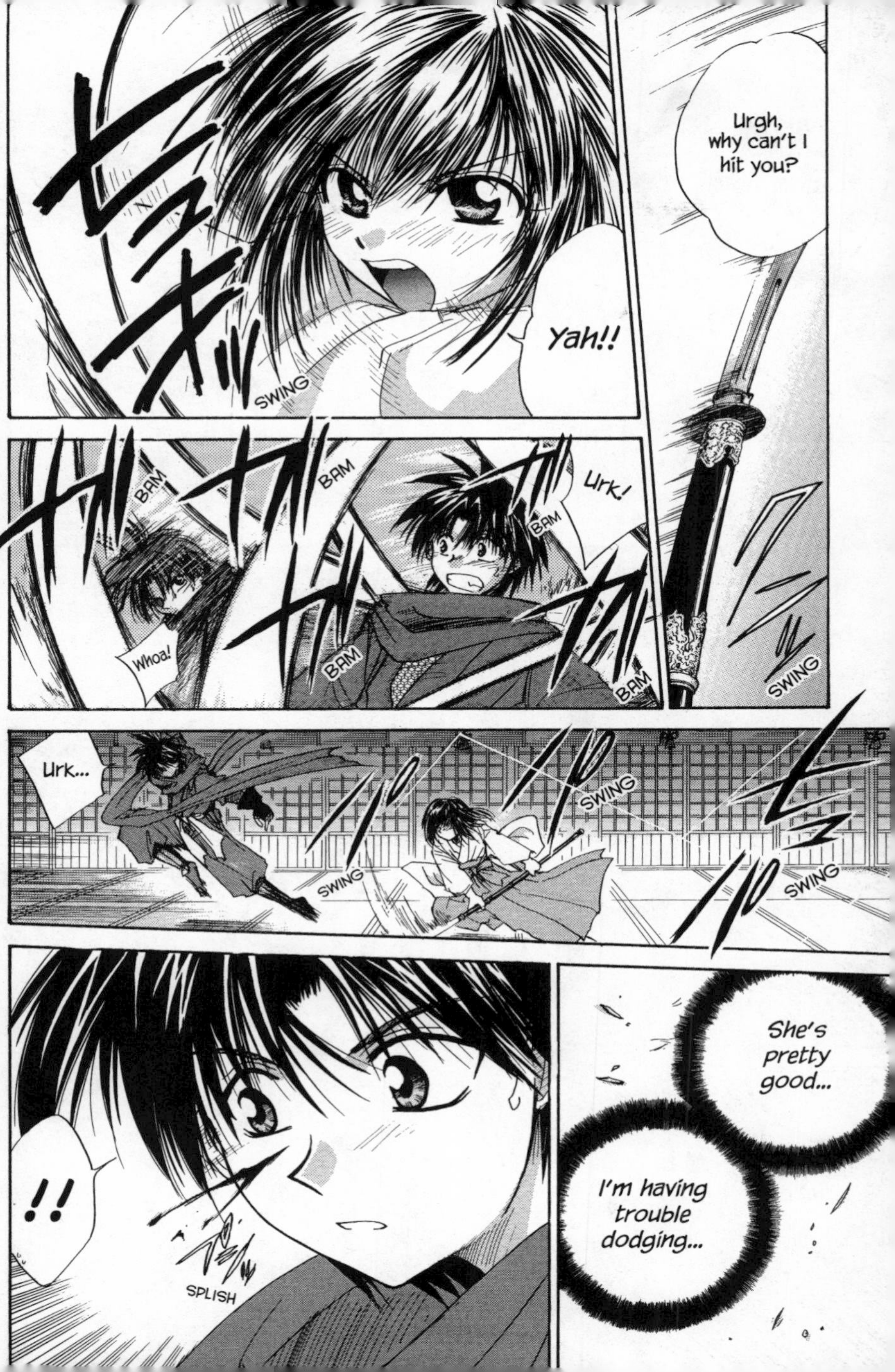
Urgh, why can't I hit you?
Yah!!
SWING
Urk!
BAM
BAM
BAM
BAM
BAM
Whoa!
SWING
SWING
SWING
Urk...
SWING
She's pretty good...
I'm having trouble dodging...
!!
SPLISH

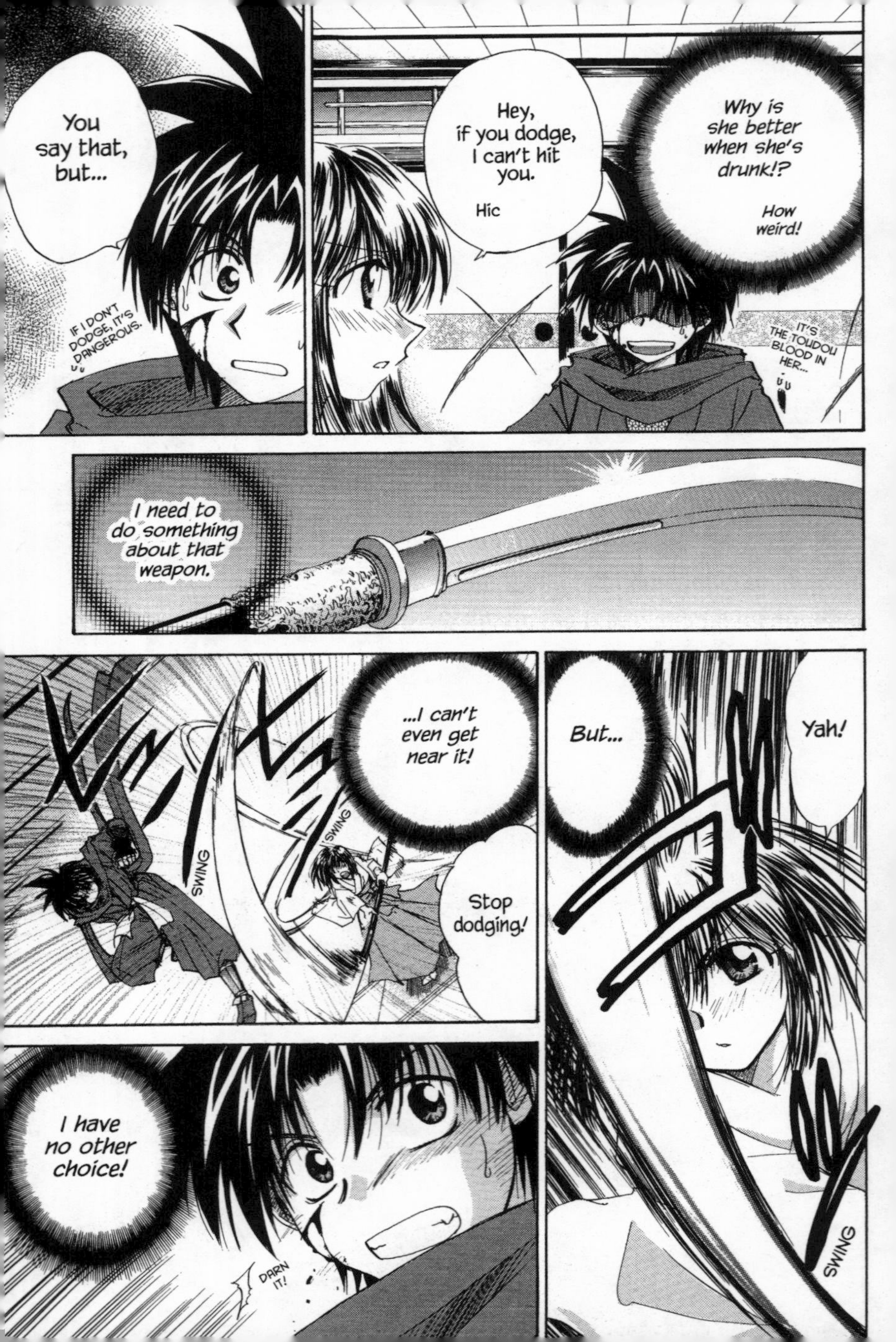
Why is she better when she's drunk!?
How weird!
IT'S THE TOUDOU BLOOD IN HER...
Hey, if you dodge, I can't hit you.
Hic
You say that, but...
IF I DON'T DODGE, IT'S DANGEROUS.
I need to do something about that weapon.
Yah!
But...
SWING
...I can't even get near it!
SWING
Stop dodging!
SWING
I have no other choice!
DARN IT!

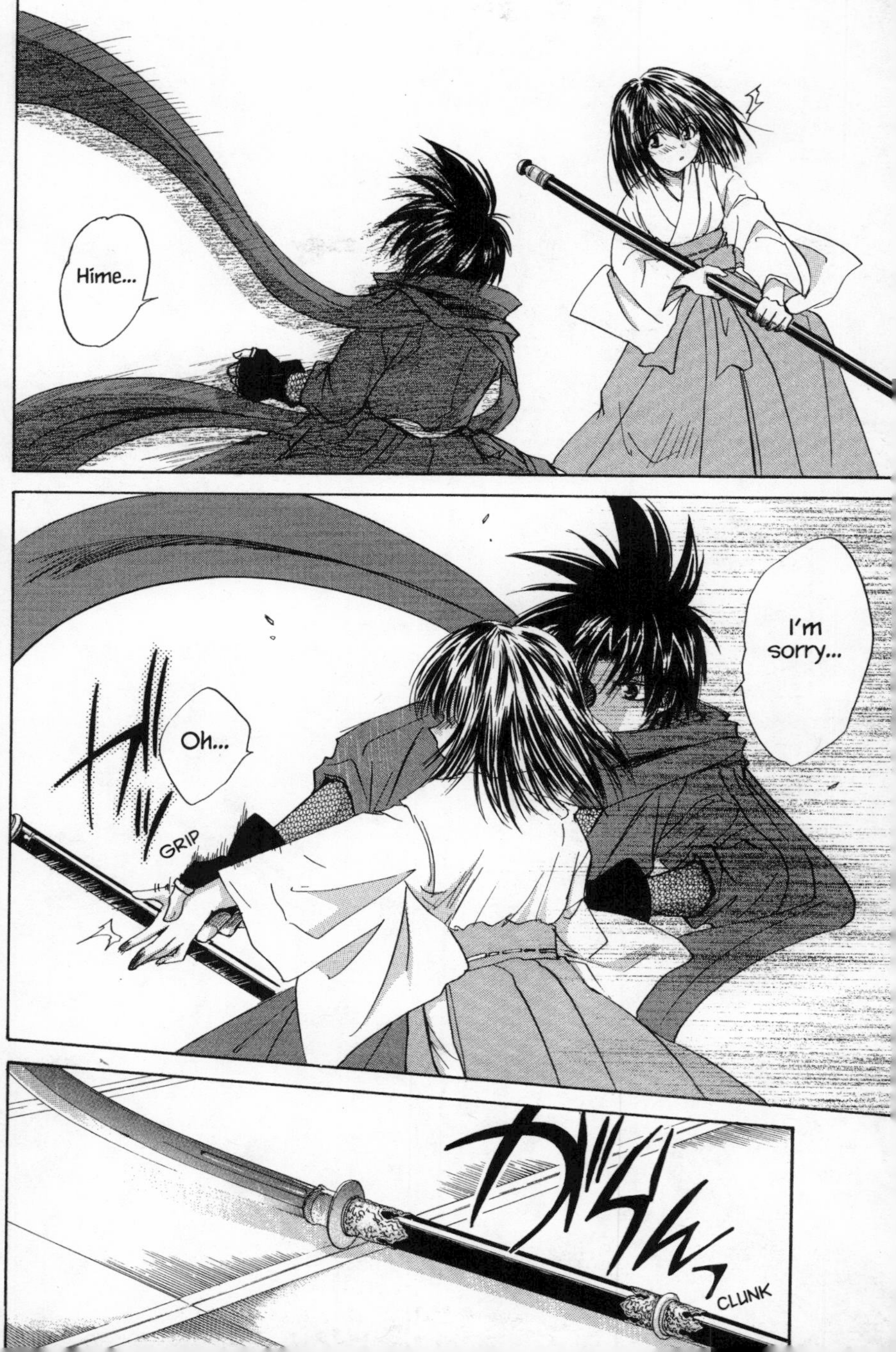
Hime...
I'm sorry...
Oh...
GRIP
CLUNK

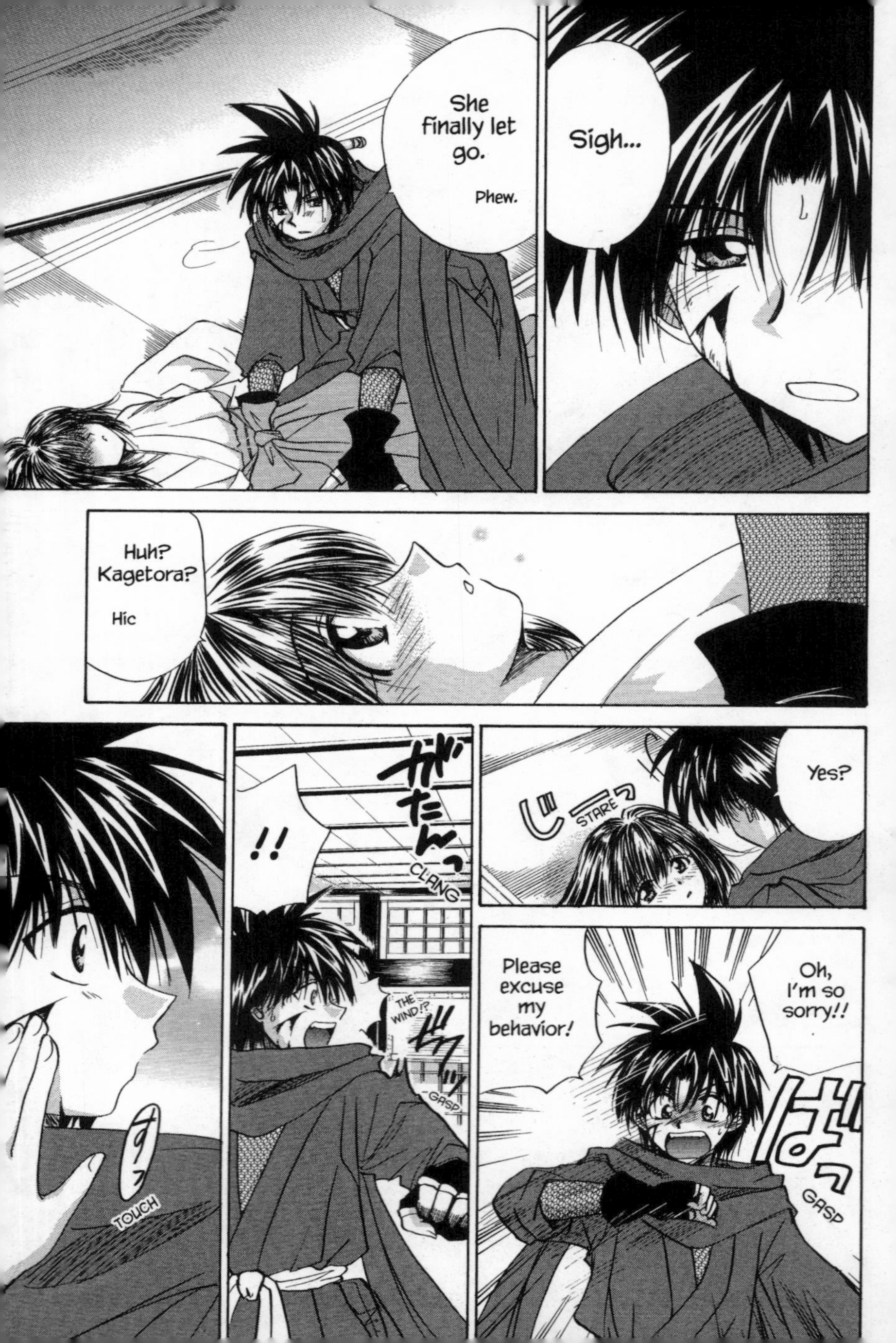
Sigh...
She finally let go.
Phew.
Huh? Kagetora?
Hic
Yes?
じーっ
STARE
Oh, I'm so sorry!!
Please excuse my behavior!
はっ
GASP
がたんっ
CLANG
!!
THE WIND!?
-GASP
すっ
TOUCH

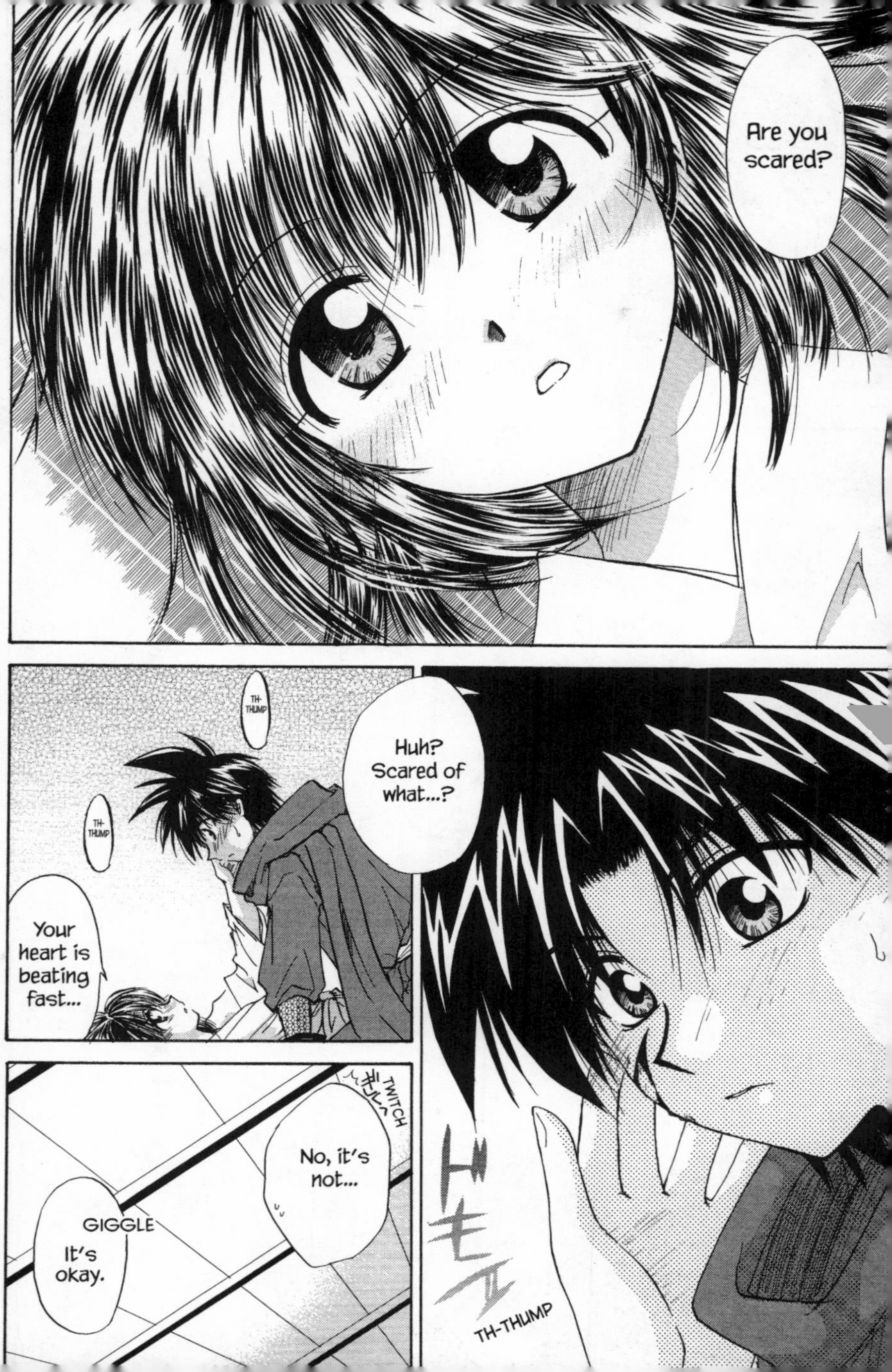
Are you scared?
Huh? Scared of what...?
TH-THUMP
TH-THUMP
TH-THUMP
Your heart is beating fast...
TWITCH
No, it's not...
GIGGLE
It's okay.

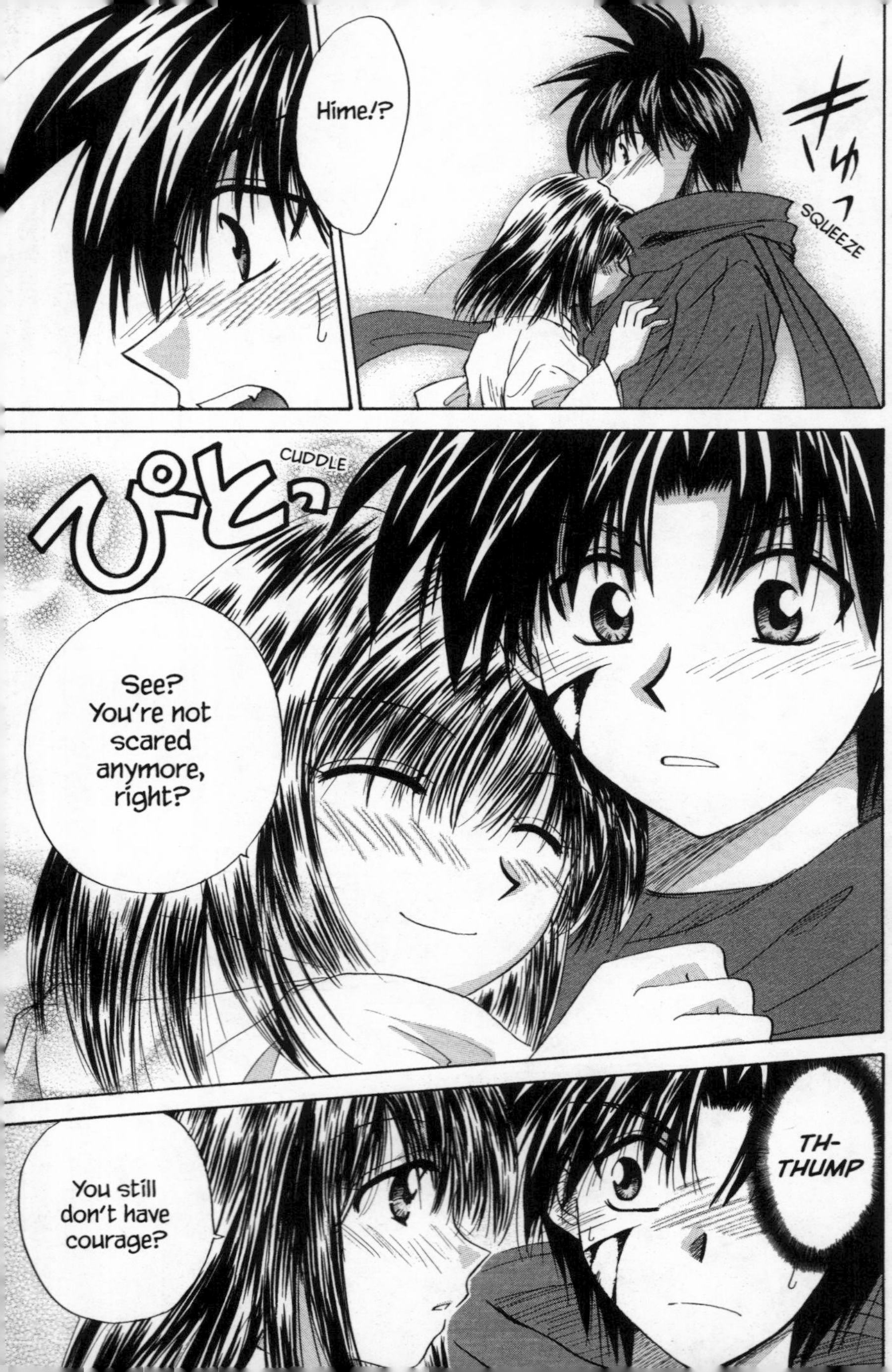
きゅっ
SQUEEZE
Hime!?
ぴとっ
CUDDLE
See? You're not scared anymore, right?
TH-THUMP
You still don't have courage?

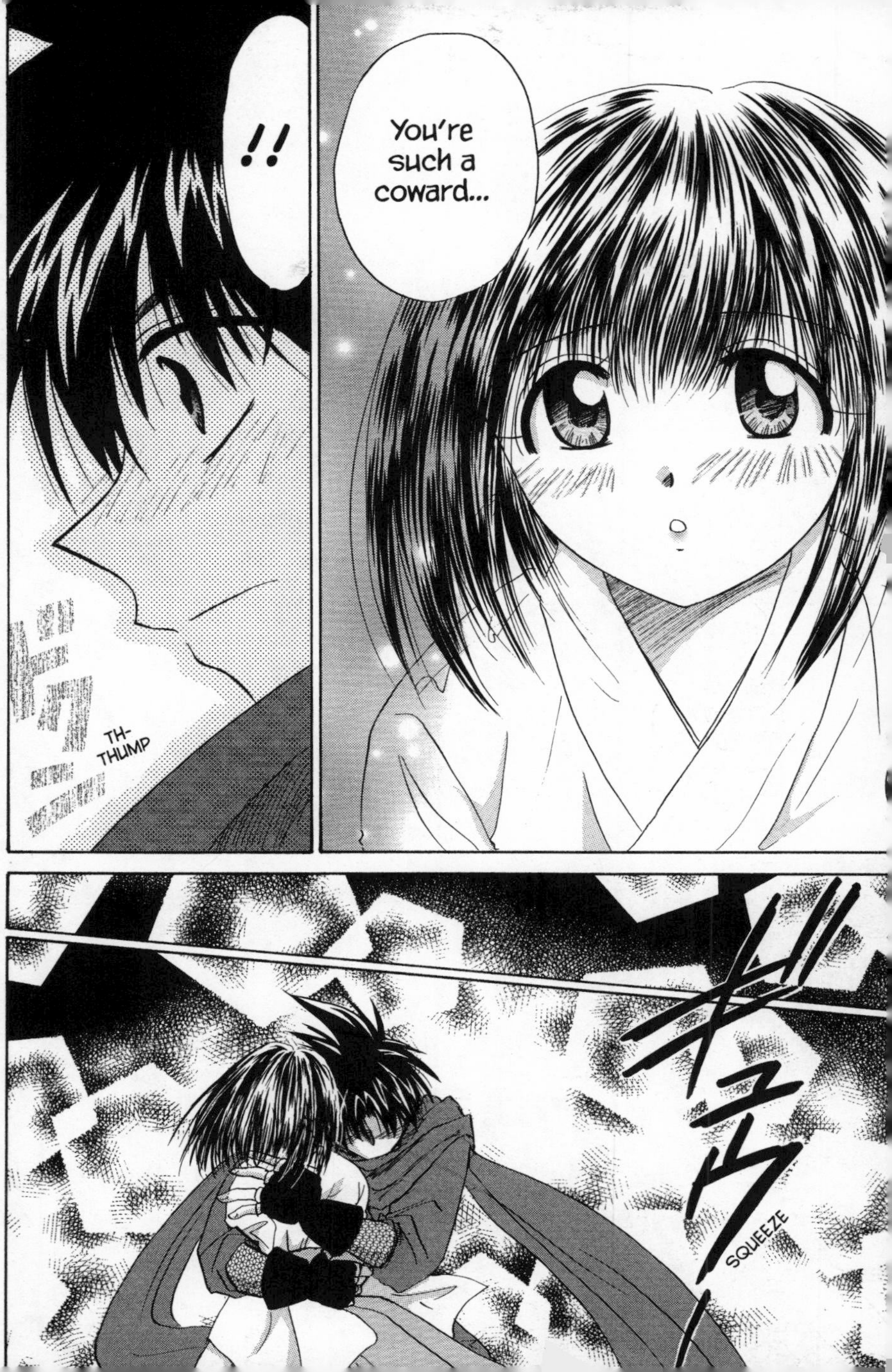
You're such a coward...
!!
TH-THUMP
SQUEEZE

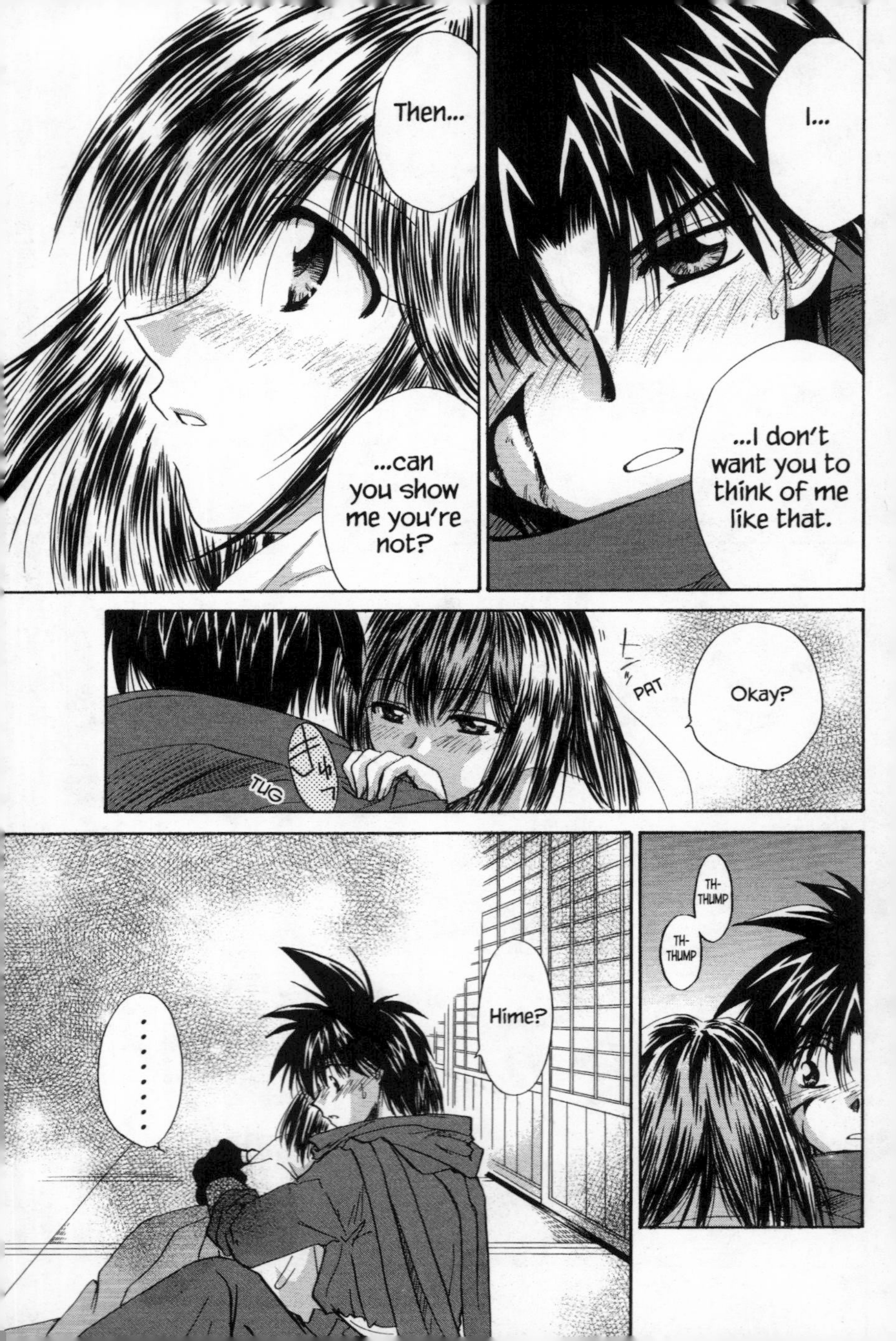
I...
...I don't want you to think of me like that.
Then...
...can you show me you're not?
Okay?
PAT
TUG
TH-THUMP
TH-THUMP
Hime?
....

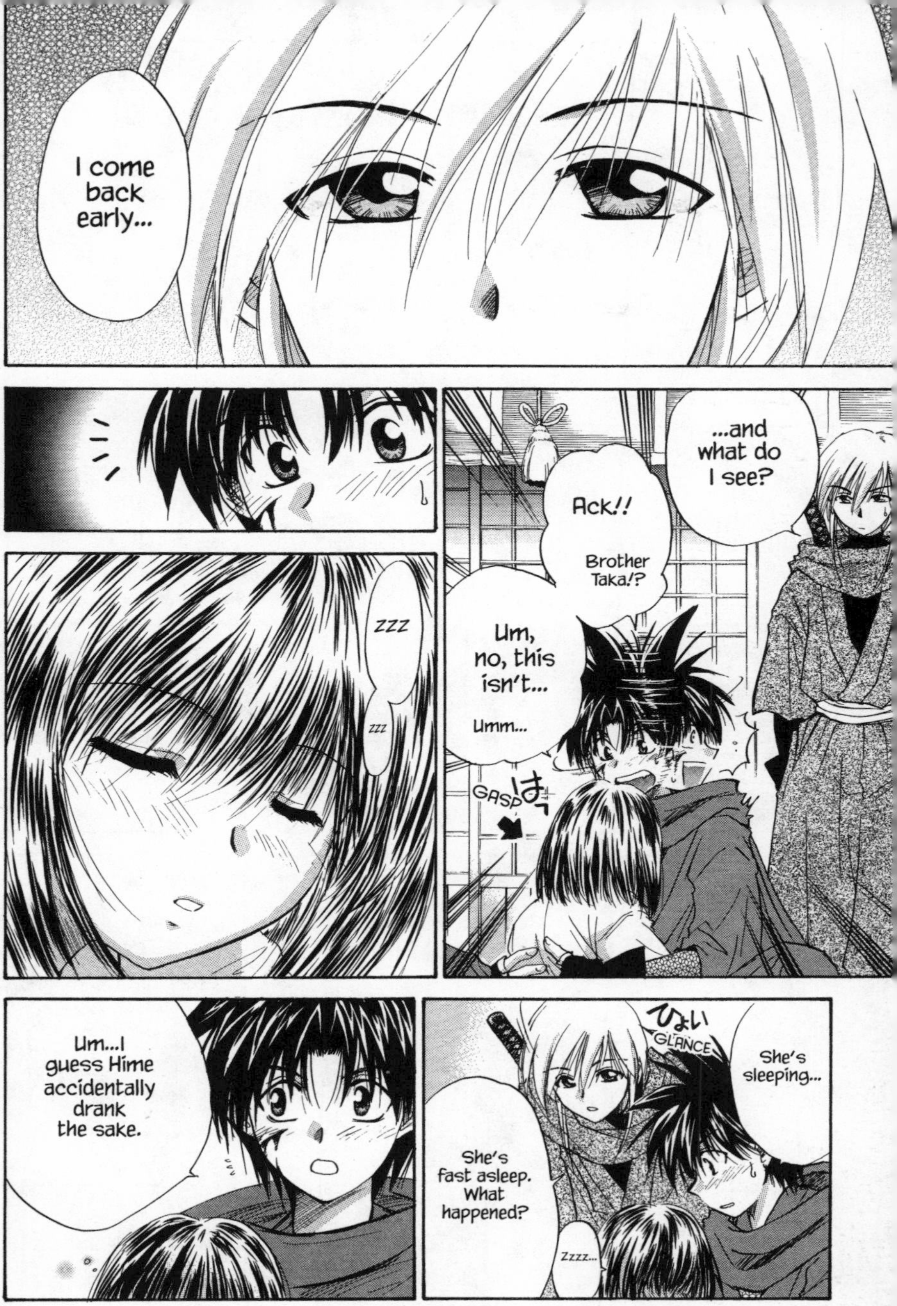
I come back early...
...and what do I see?
Ack!!
Brother Taka!?
Um, no, this isn't...
Umm...
GASP
は
zzz
zzz
ひょい
GLANCE
She's sleeping...
She's fast asleep. What happened?
Zzzz...
Um...I guess Hime accidentally drank the sake.

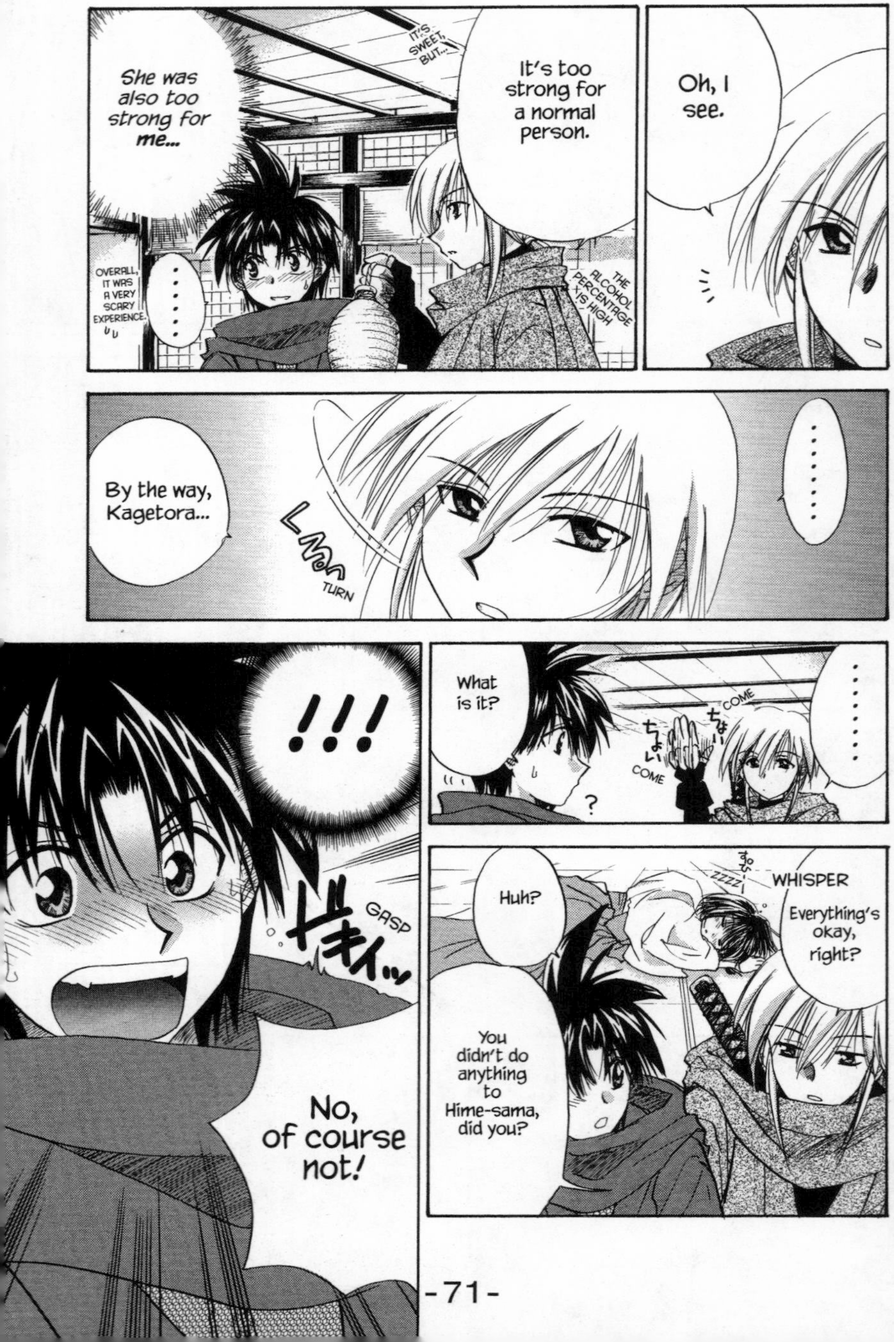
Oh, I see.
It's too strong for a normal person.
IT'S SWEET, BUT...
She was also too strong for me...
THE ALCOHOL PERCENTAGE IS HIGH
......
OVERALL, IT WAS A VERY SCARY EXPERIENCE.
......
By the way, Kagetora...
TURN
......
COME
COME
What is it?
?
WHISPER
Everything's okay, right?
ZZZZ
Huh?
You didn't do anything to Hime-sama, did you?
!!!
GASP
No, of course not!

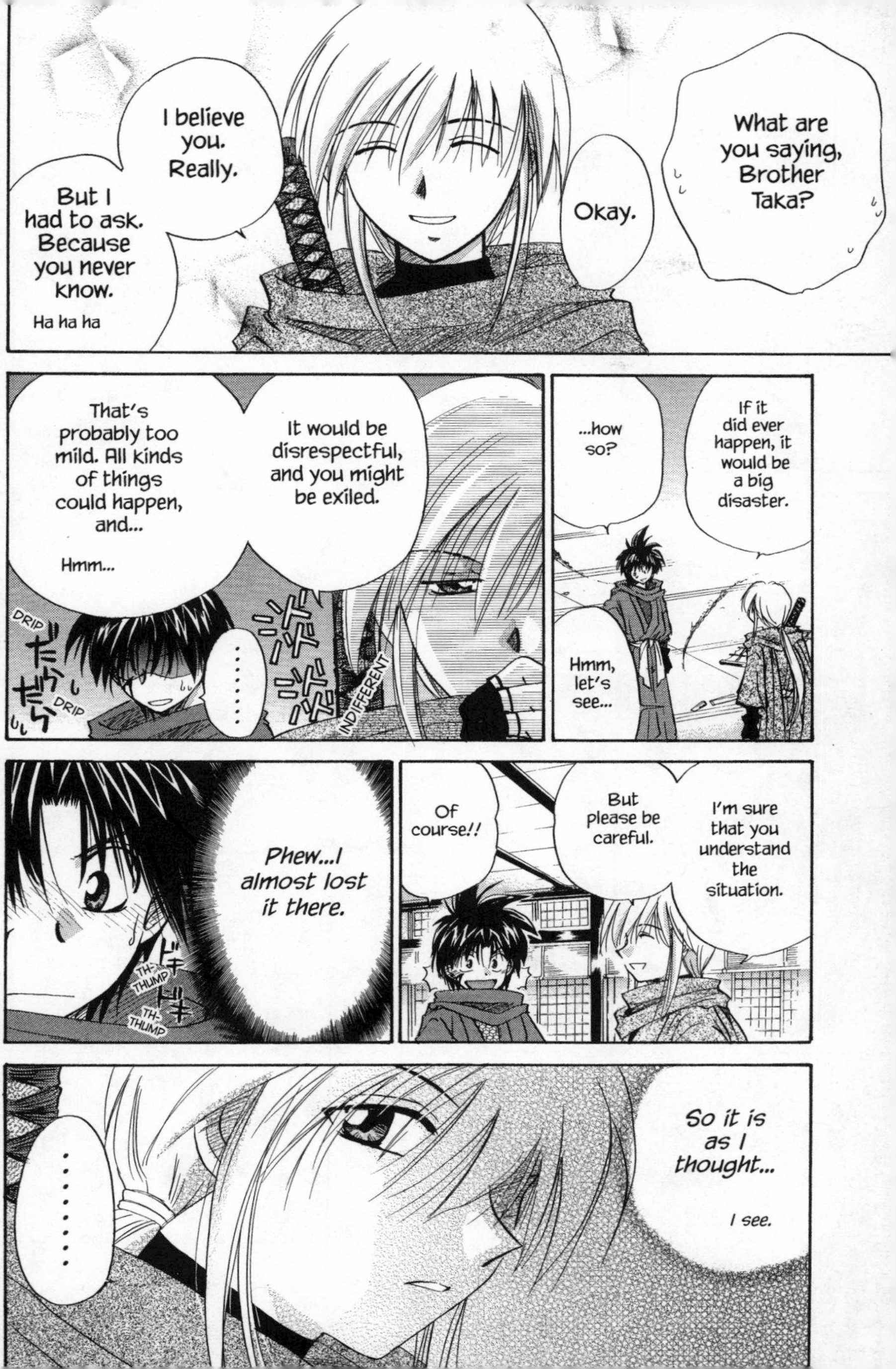
What are you saying, Brother Taka?
Okay.
I believe you. Really.
But I had to ask. Because you never know.
Ha ha ha
If it did ever happen, it would be a big disaster.
...how so?
Hmm, let's see...
It would be disrespectful, and you might be exiled.
That's probably too mild. All kinds of things could happen, and...
Hmm...
INDIFFERENT
......
DRIP
DRIP
I'm sure that you understand the situation.
But please be careful.
Of course!!
Phew...I almost lost it there.
TH-THUMP
TH-THUMP
So it is as I thought...
I see.
....

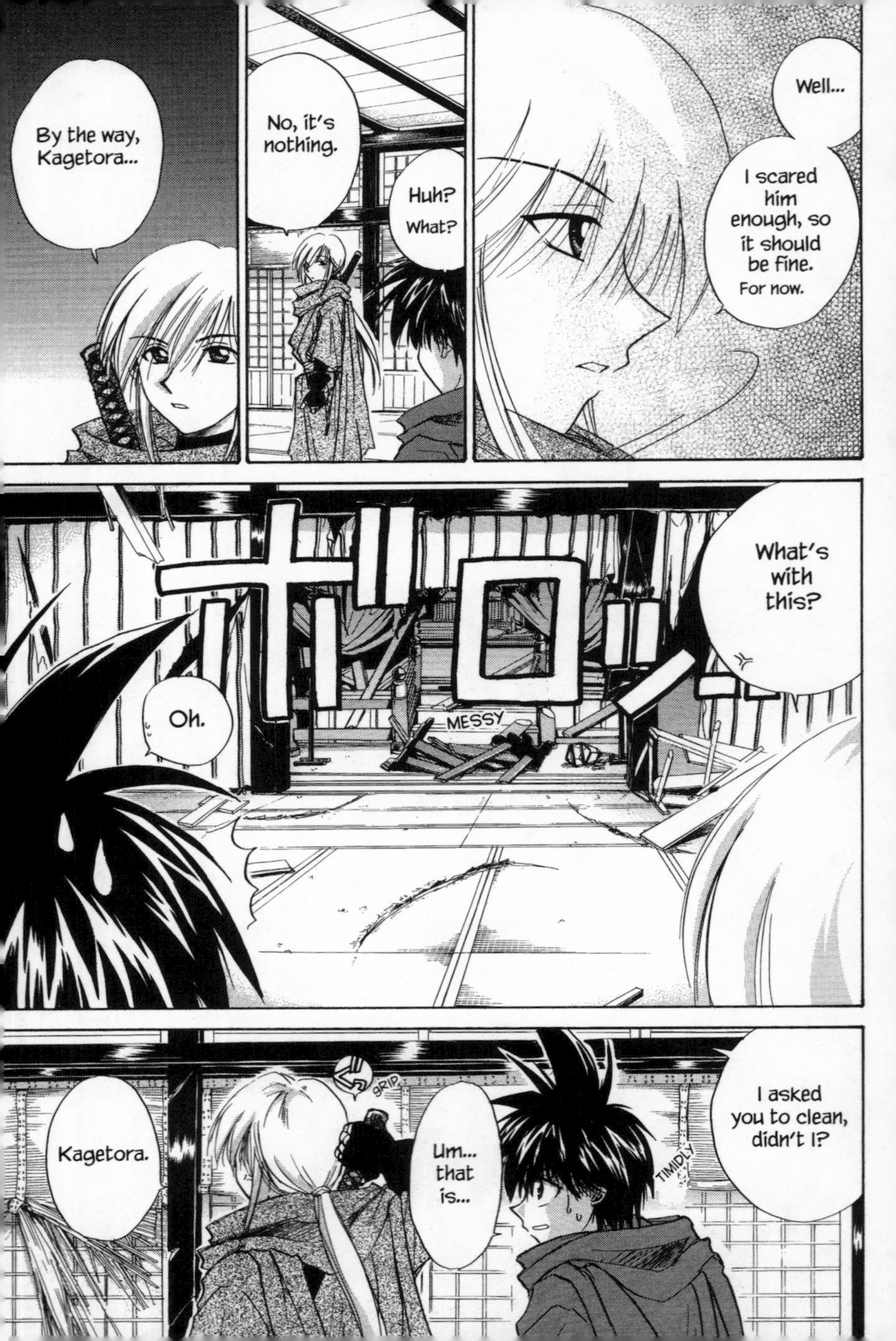
Well...
I scared him enough, so it should be fine. For now.
Huh? What?
No, it's nothing.
By the way, Kagetora...
What's with this?
MESSY
Oh.
I asked you to clean, didn't I?
TIMIDLY
Um... that is...
GRIP
Kagetora.

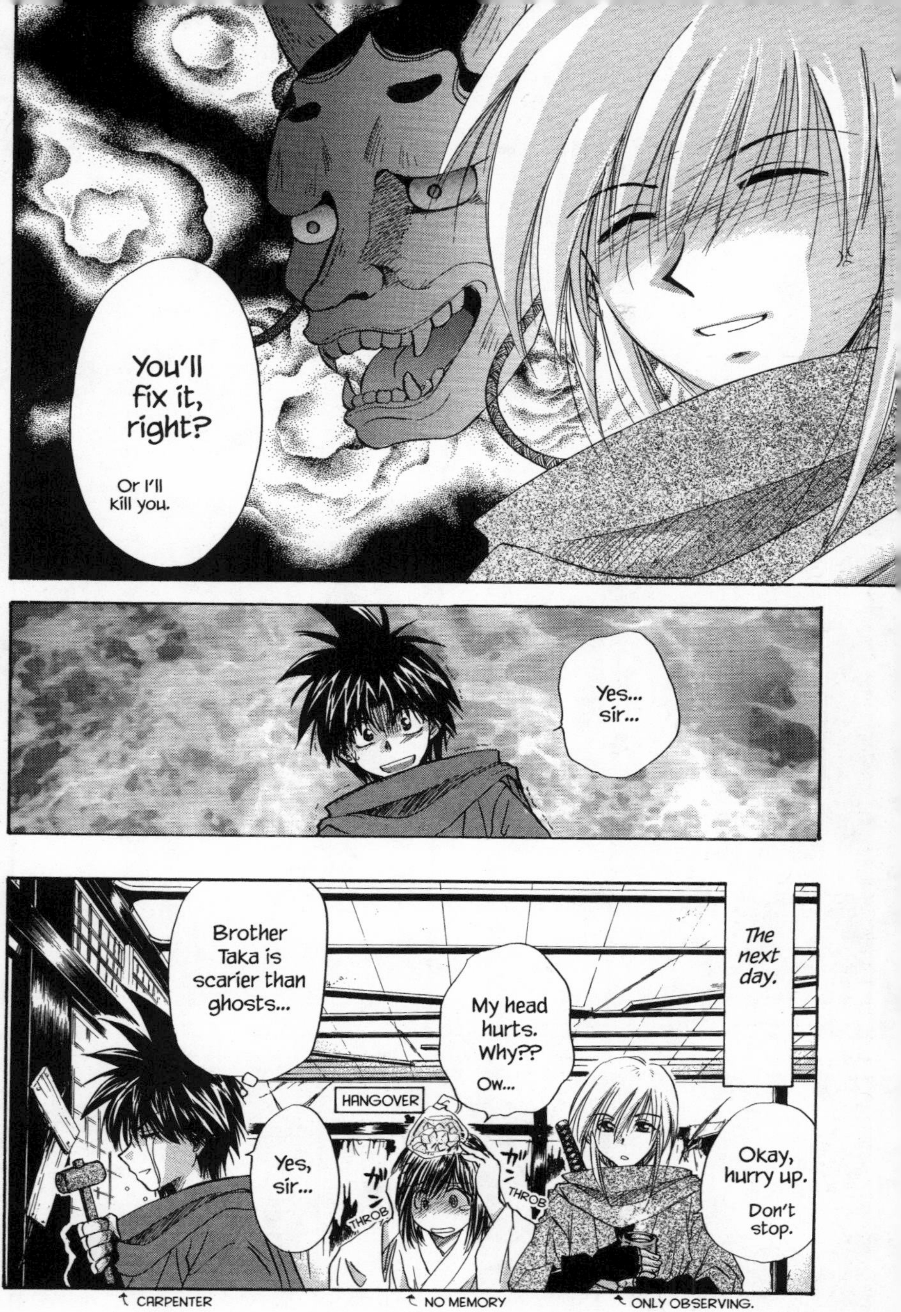
You'll fix it, right?
Or I'll kill you.
Yes... sir...
The next day.
Okay, hurry up.
Don't stop.
My head hurts. Why??
Ow...
HANGOVER
THROB
THROB
Brother Taka is scarier than ghosts...
Yes, sir...
ONLY OBSERVING.
NO MEMORY
CARPENTER

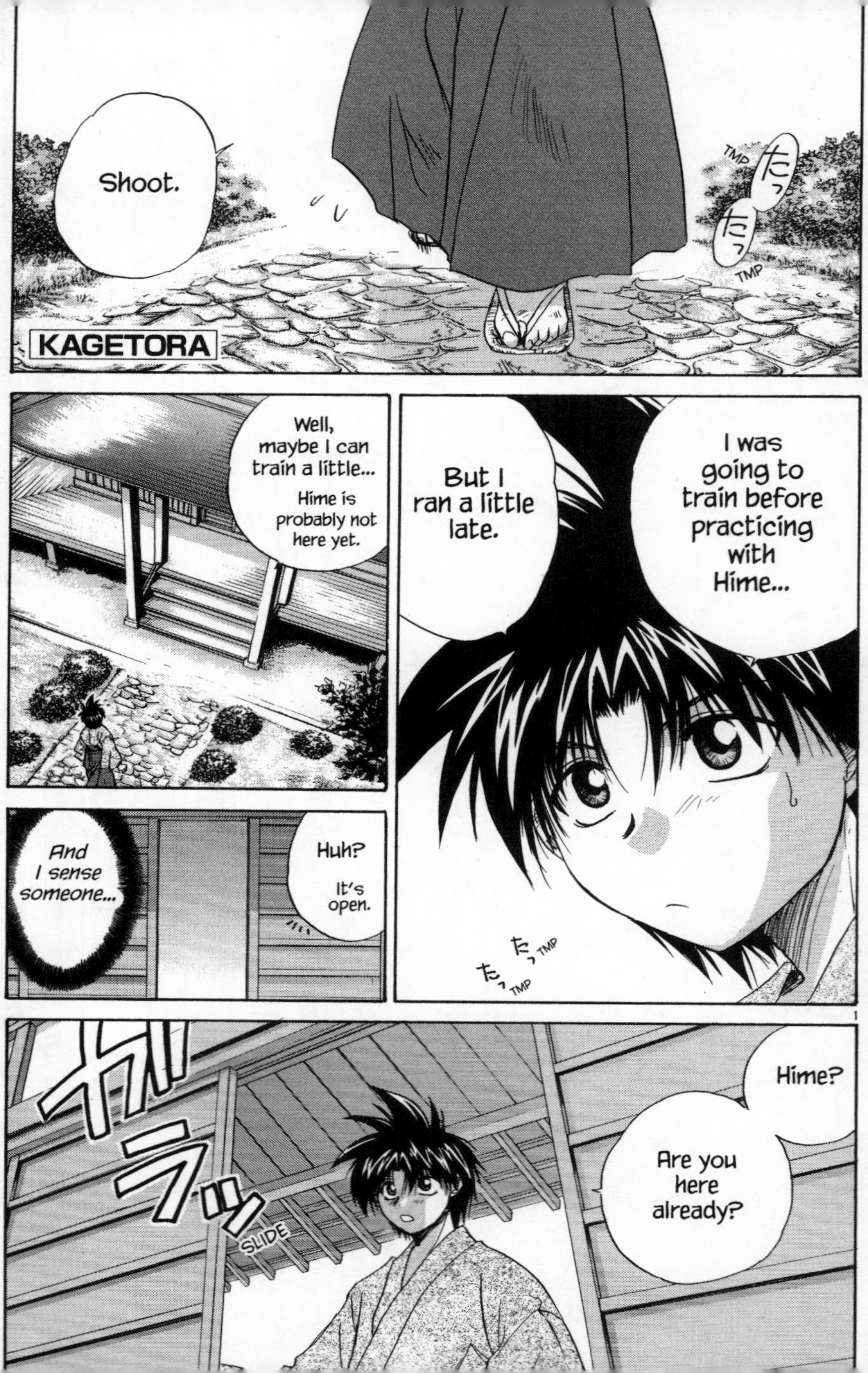
Shoot.
たっ TMP
たっ TMP
KAGETORA
I was going to train before practicing with Hime...
But I ran a little late.
たっ TMP
たっ TMP
Well, maybe I can train a little...
Hime is probably not here yet.
Huh?
It's open.
And I sense someone...
Hime?
Are you here already?
SLIDE

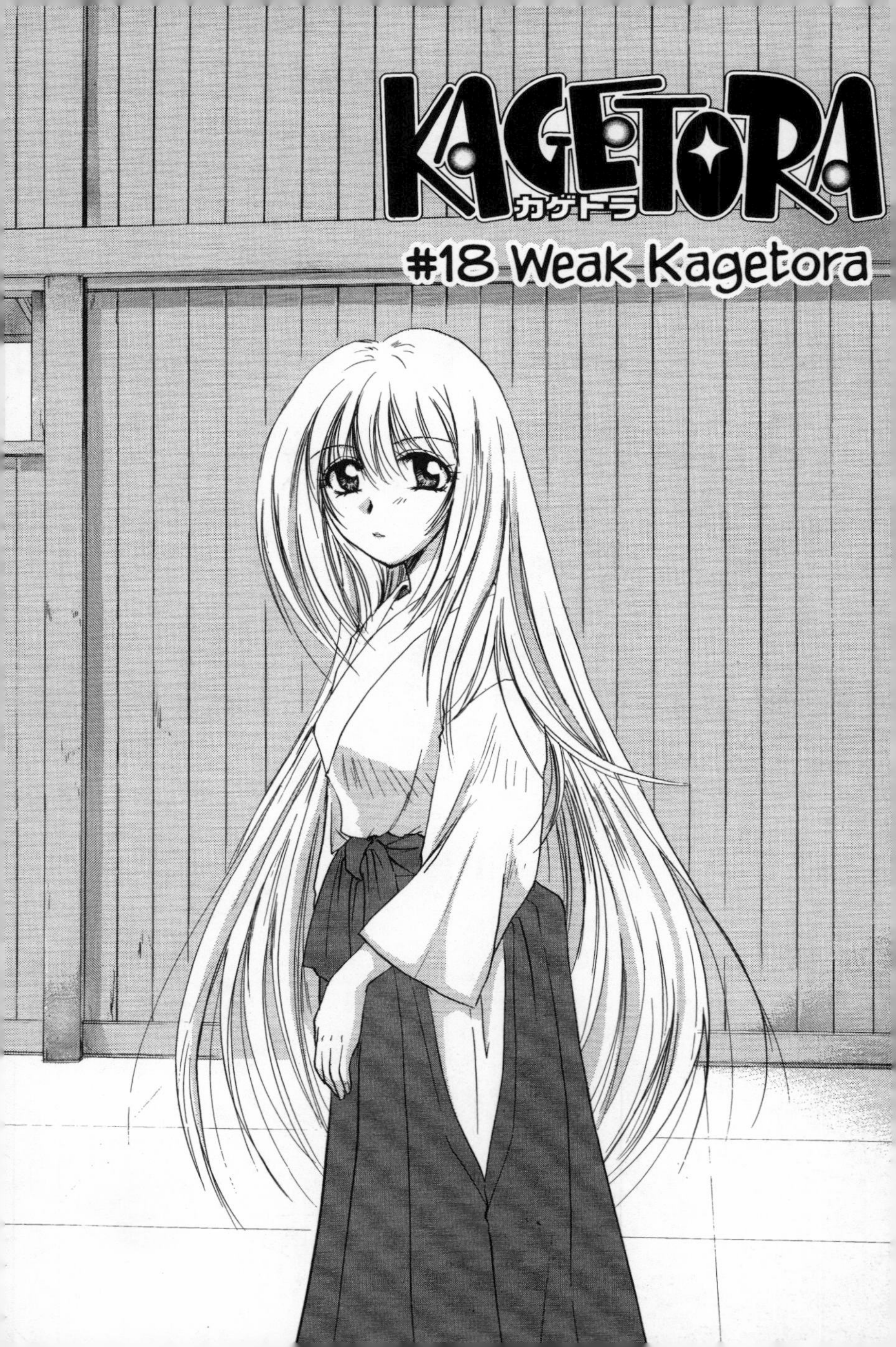
KAGETORA
カゲトラ
#18 Weak Kagetora

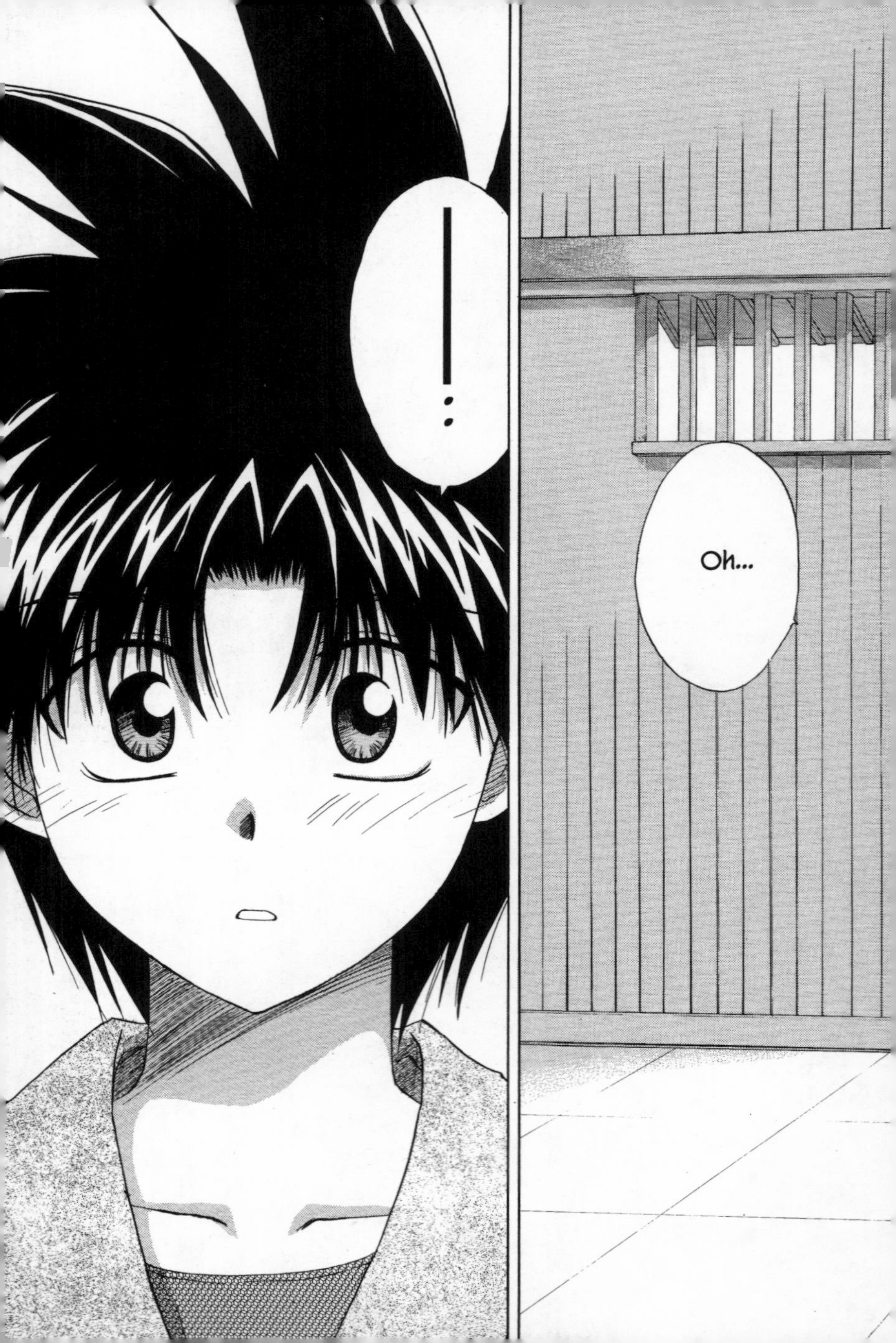
Oh...
—!

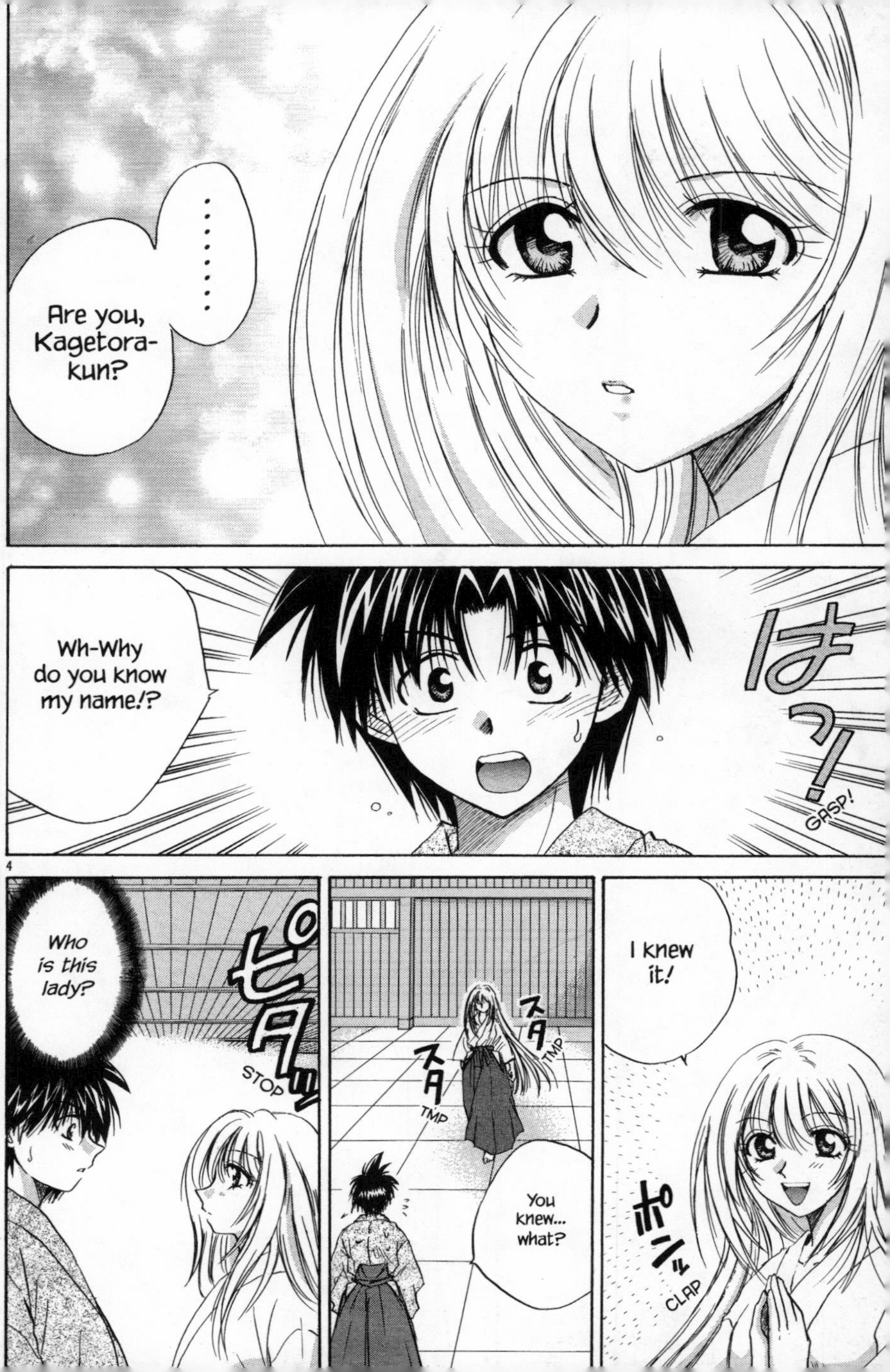
......
Are you, Kagetora-kun?
はっ!
GASP!
Wh-Why do you know my name!?
I knew it!
ポン
CLAP
スタ
TMP
スタ
TMP
You knew... what?
Who is this lady?
ピタッ
STOP

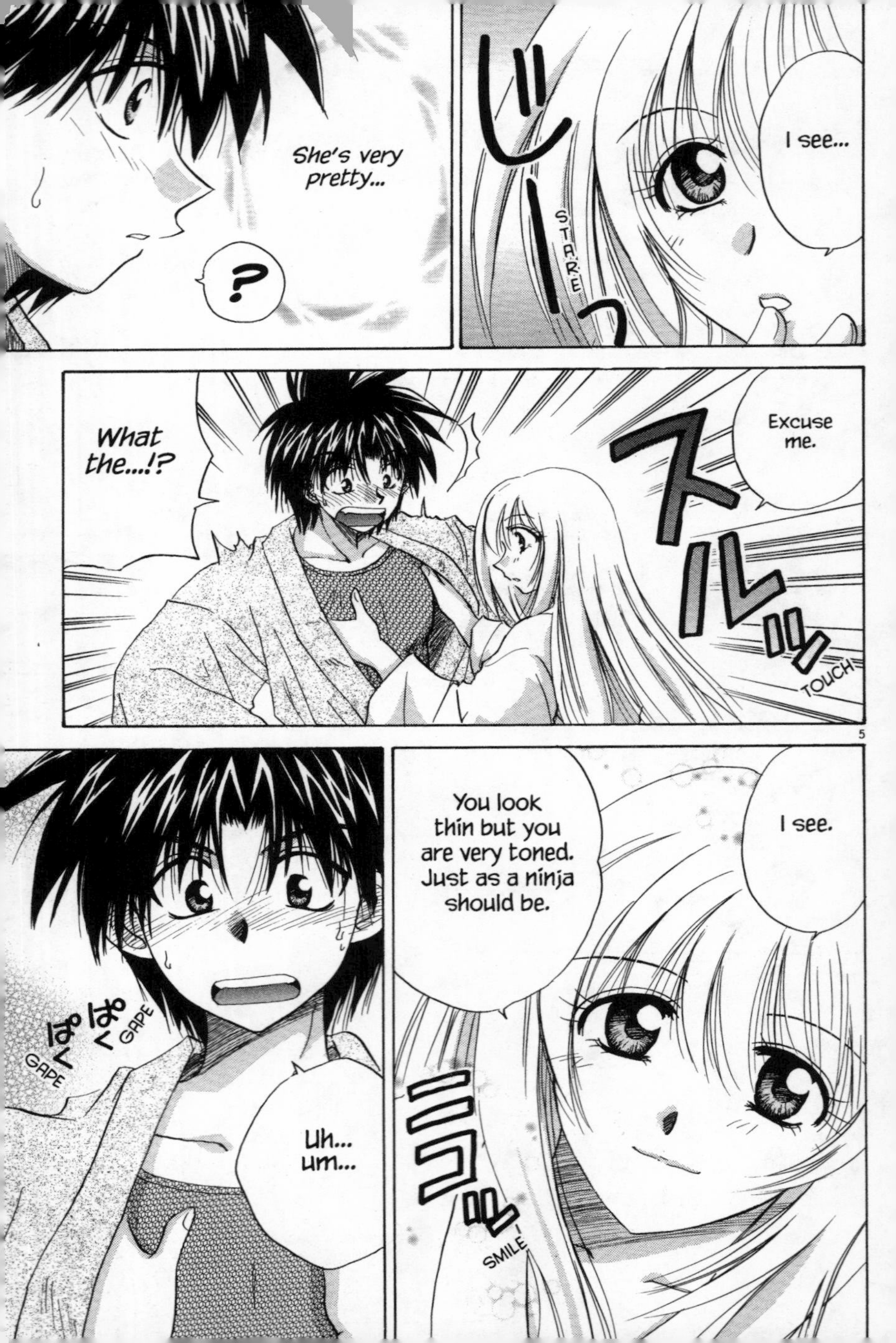
I see...
じーっ
STARE
She's very pretty...
?
Excuse me.
スルッ
TOUCH
What the...!?
I see.
You look thin but you are very toned. Just as a ninja should be.
ニコッ
SMILE
ぱくぱく
GAPE
GAPE
Uh... um...

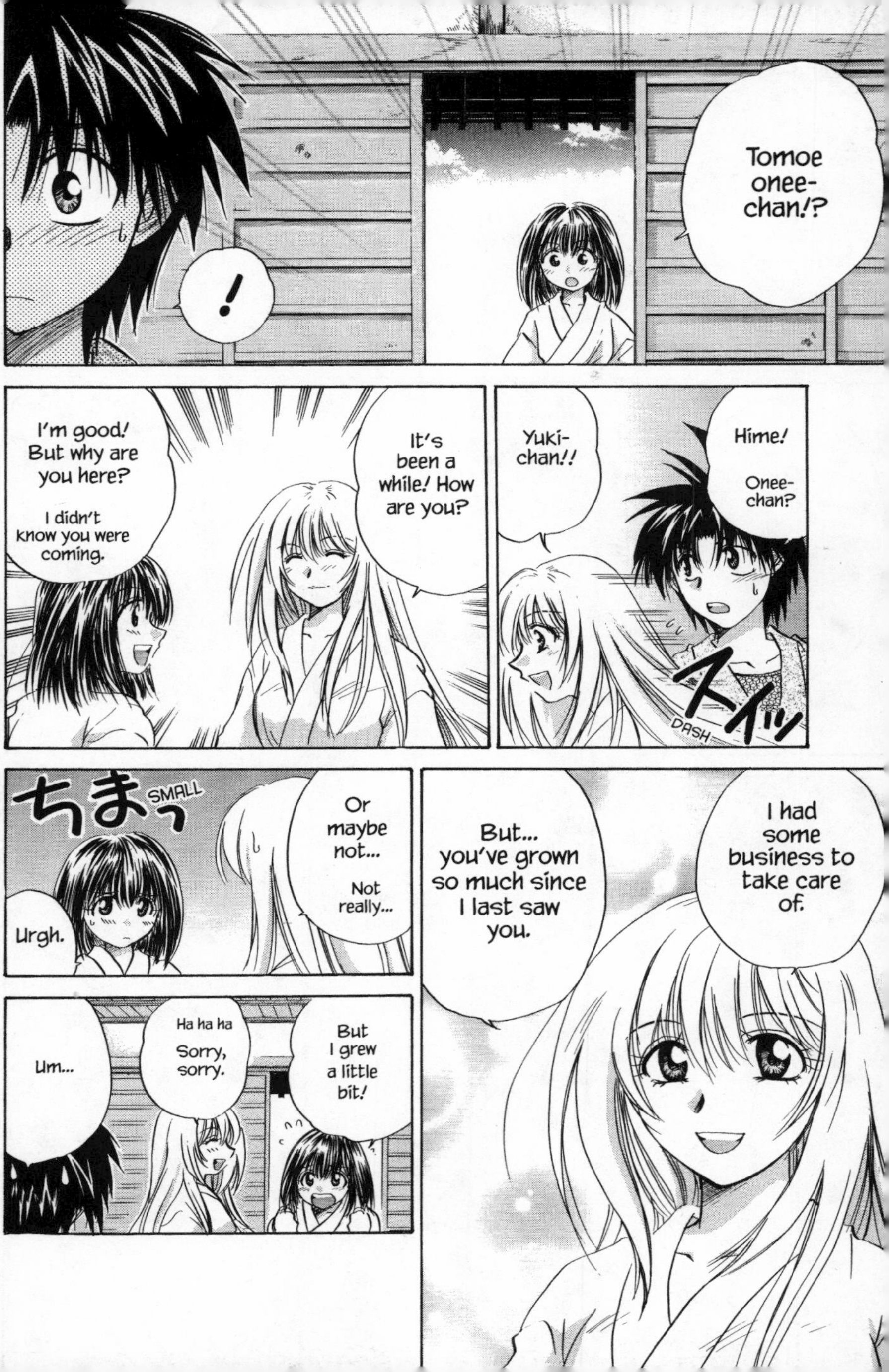

Tomoe onee-chan!?
!
Hime!
Onee-chan?
Yuki-chan!!
スイッ
DASH
It's been a while! How are you?
I'm good! But why are you here?
I didn't know you were coming.
I had some business to take care of.
But... you've grown so much since I last saw you.
Or maybe not...
Not really...
ちまっ
SMALL
Urgh.
But I grew a little bit!
Ha ha ha
Sorry, sorry.
Um...

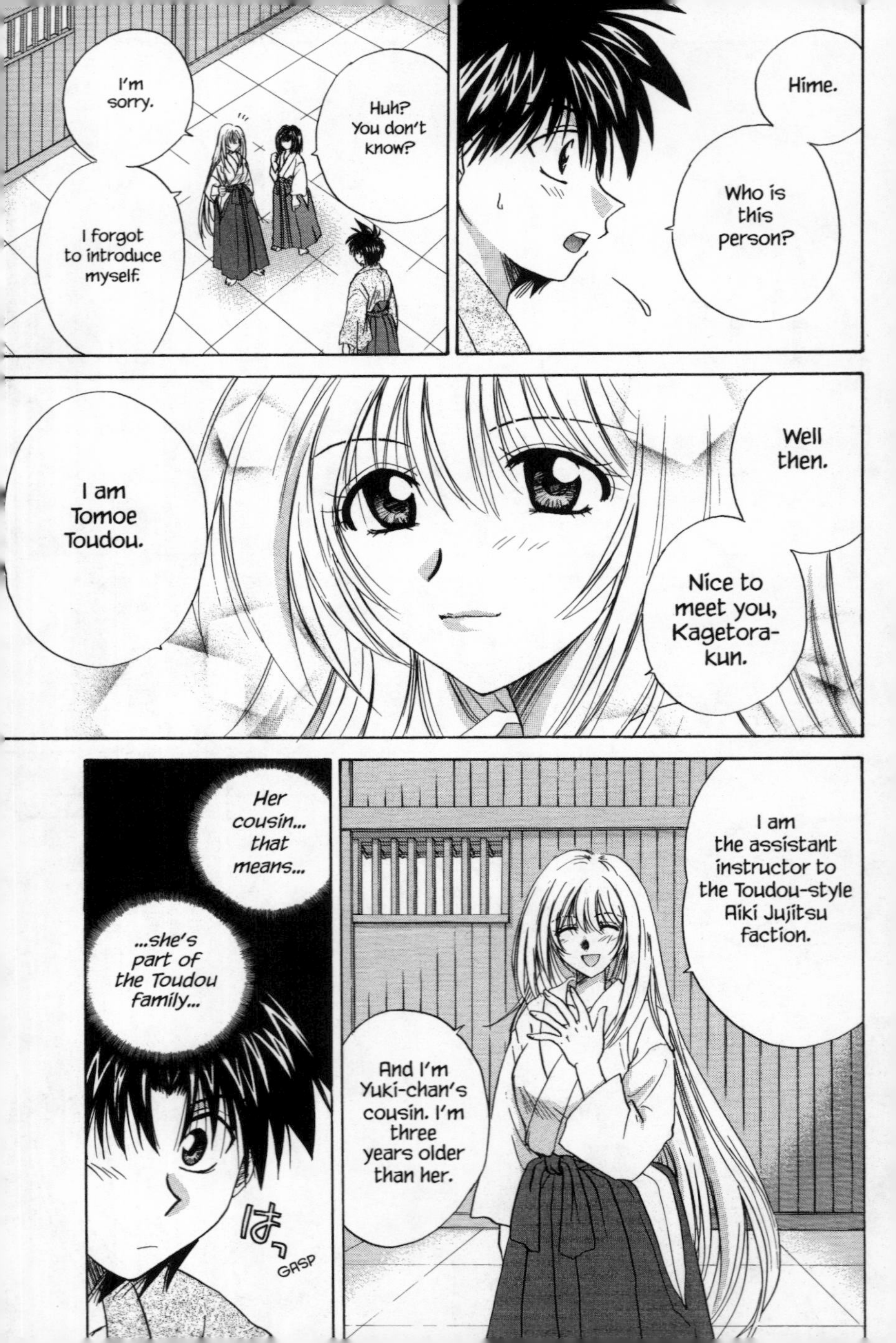
Hime.
Who is this person?
Huh? You don't know?
I'm sorry.
I forgot to introduce myself.
Well then.
Nice to meet you, Kagetora-kun.
I am Tomoe Toudou.
I am the assistant instructor to the Toudou-style Aiki Jujitsu faction.
And I'm Yuki-chan's cousin. I'm three years older than her.
Her cousin... that means...
...she's part of the Toudou family...
はっ
GASP

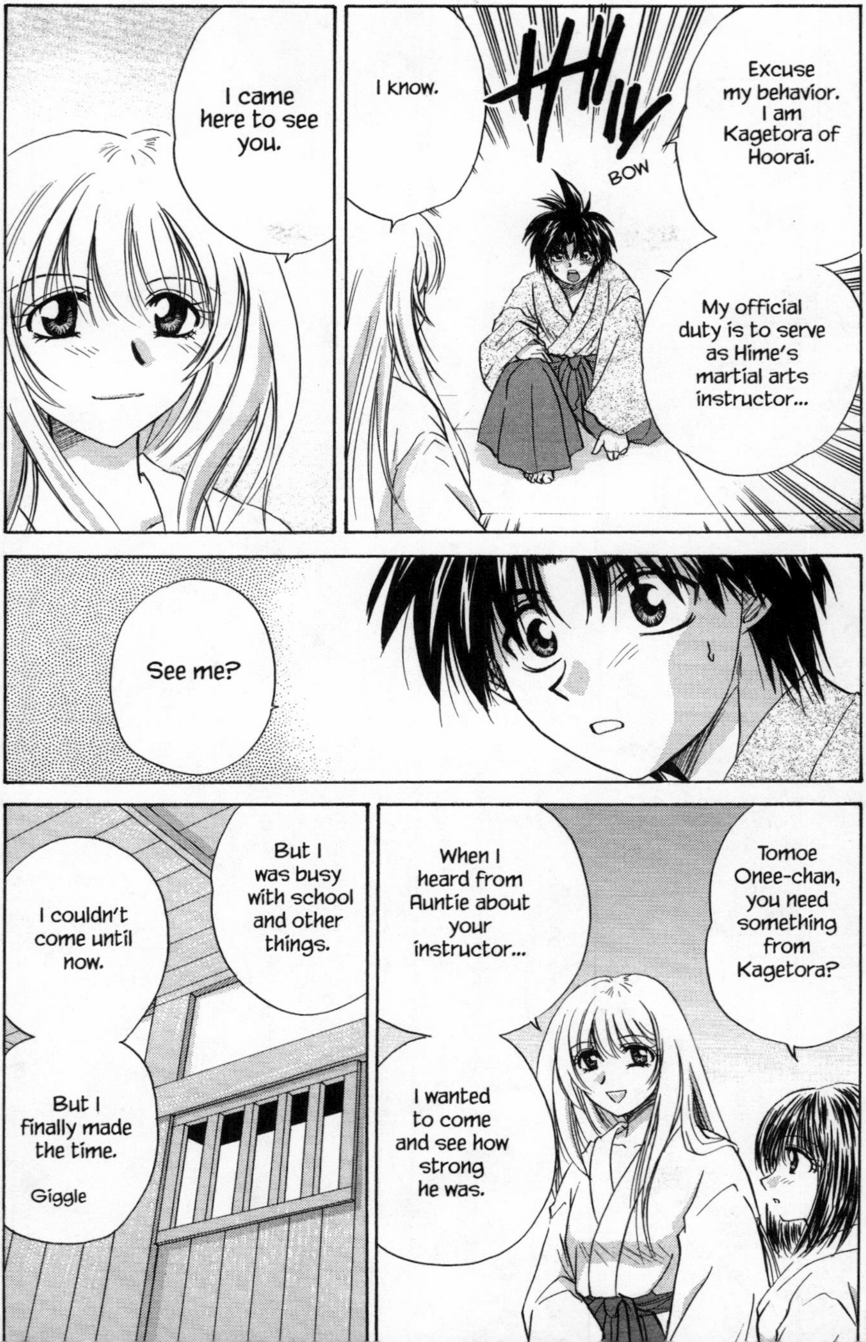
Excuse my behavior. I am Kagetora of Hoorai.
BOW
My official duty is to serve as Hime's martial arts instructor...
I know.
I came here to see you.
See me?
Tomoe Onee-chan, you need something from Kagetora?
When I heard from Auntie about your instructor...
I wanted to come and see how strong he was.
But I was busy with school and other things.
I couldn't come until now.
But I finally made the time.
Giggle

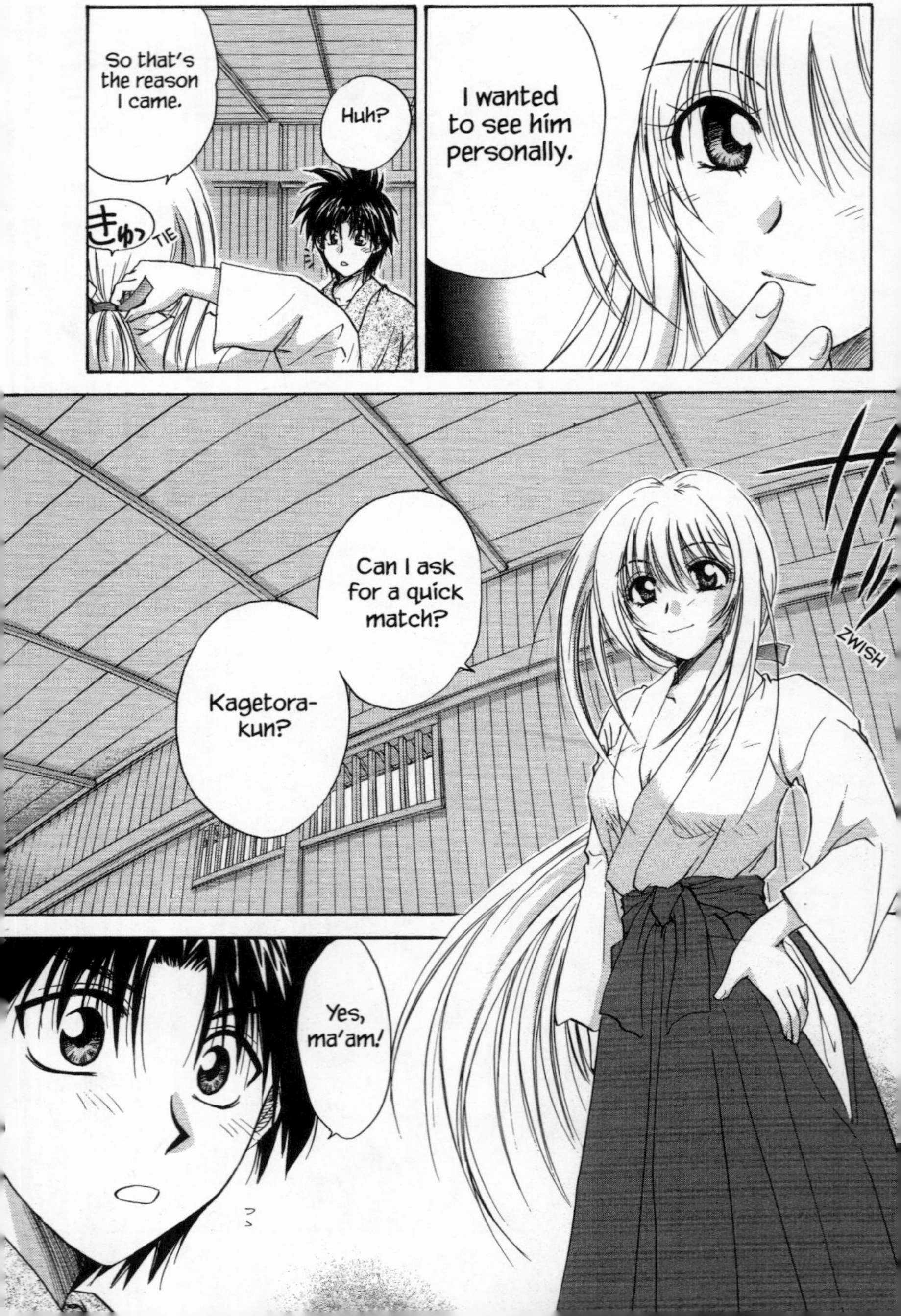
I wanted to see him personally.
So that's the reason I came.
Huh?
きゅっ
TIE
ZWISH
Can I ask for a quick match?
Kagetora-kun?
Yes, ma'am!

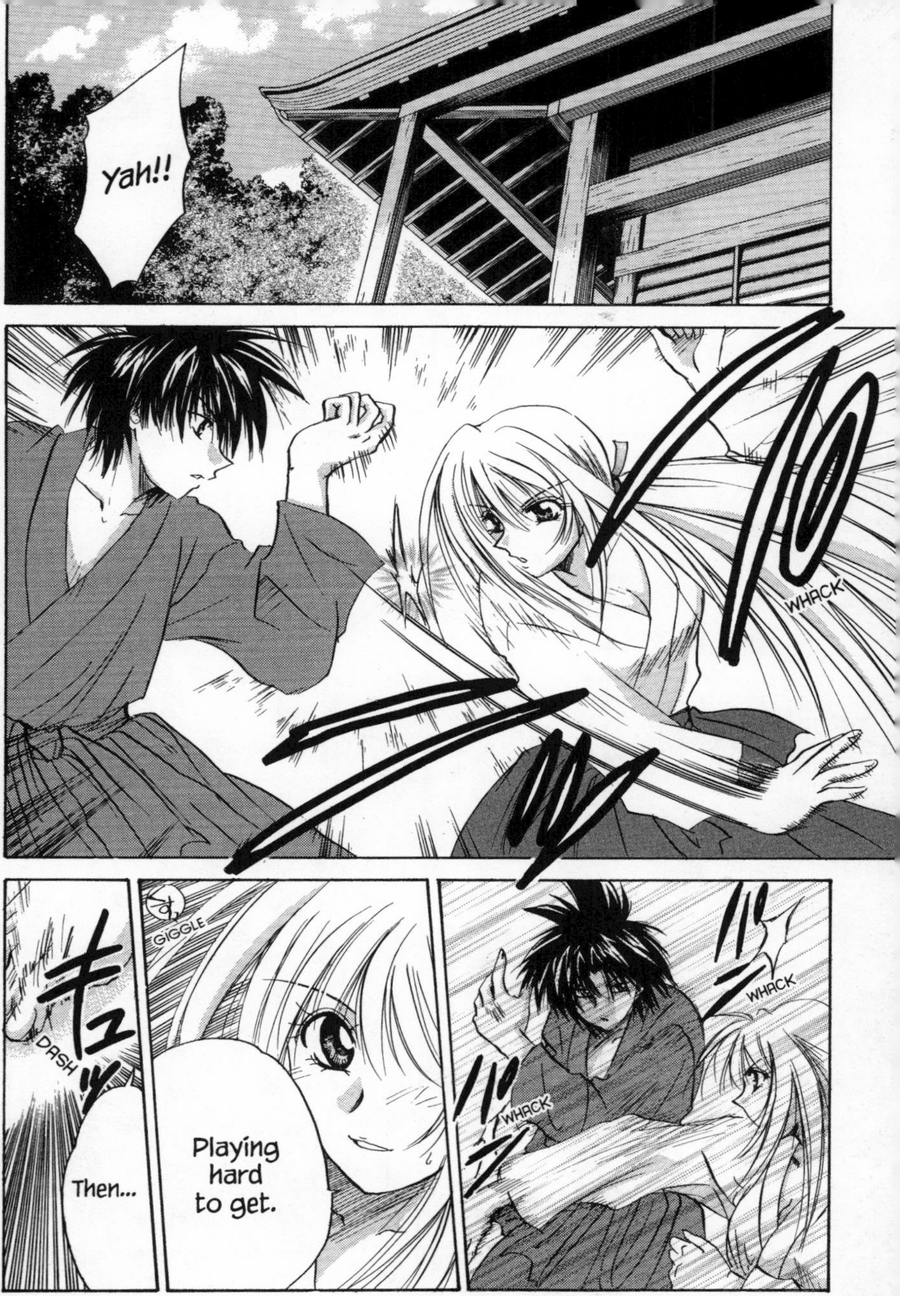
Yah!!
WHACK
WHACK
WHACK
GIGGLE
Playing hard to get.
DASH
Then...

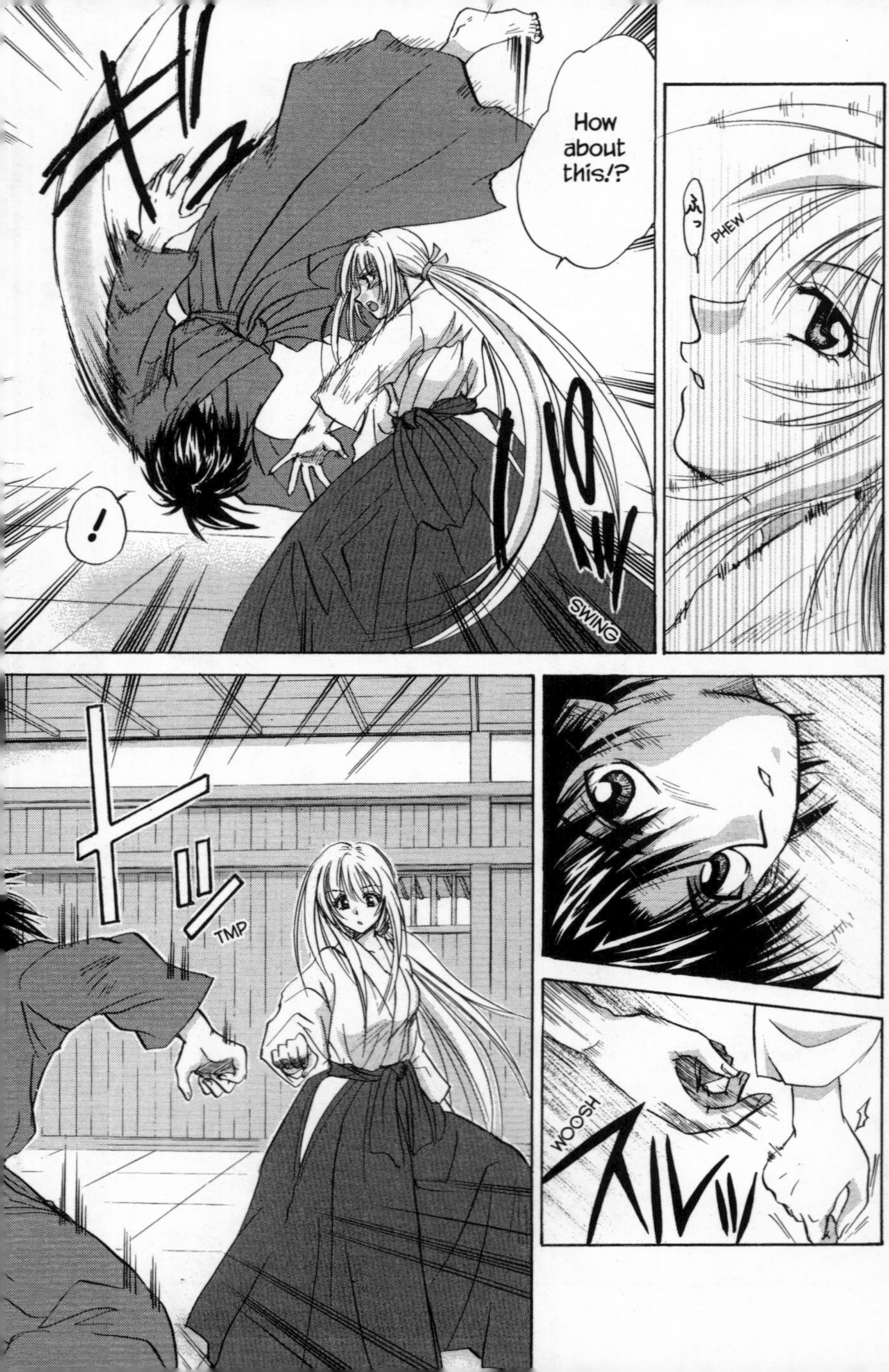
ふっ
PHEW
How about this!?
!
SWING
WOOSH
TMP

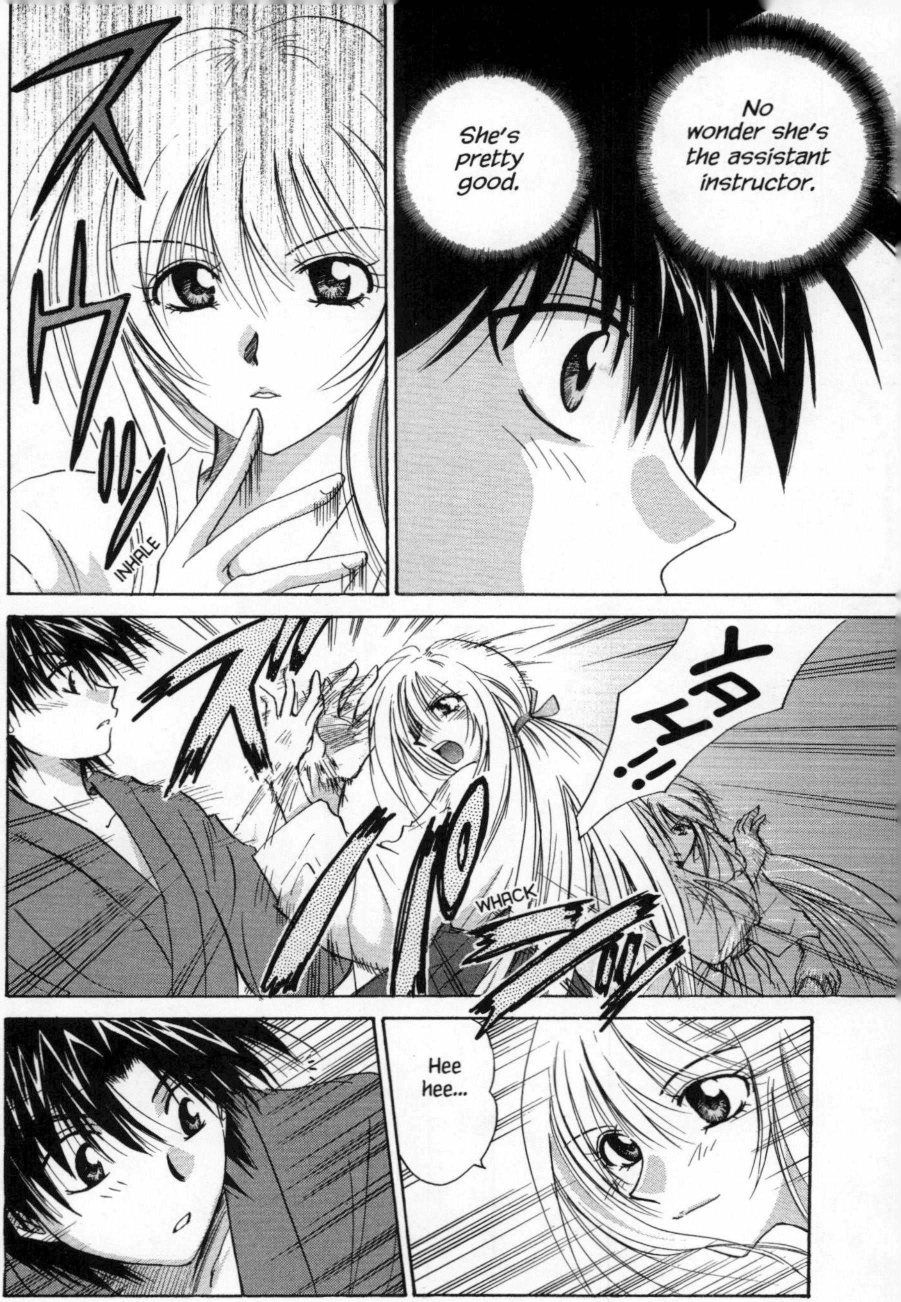

No wonder she's the assistant instructor.
She's pretty good.
INHALE
HEY!!
WHACK
Hee hee...

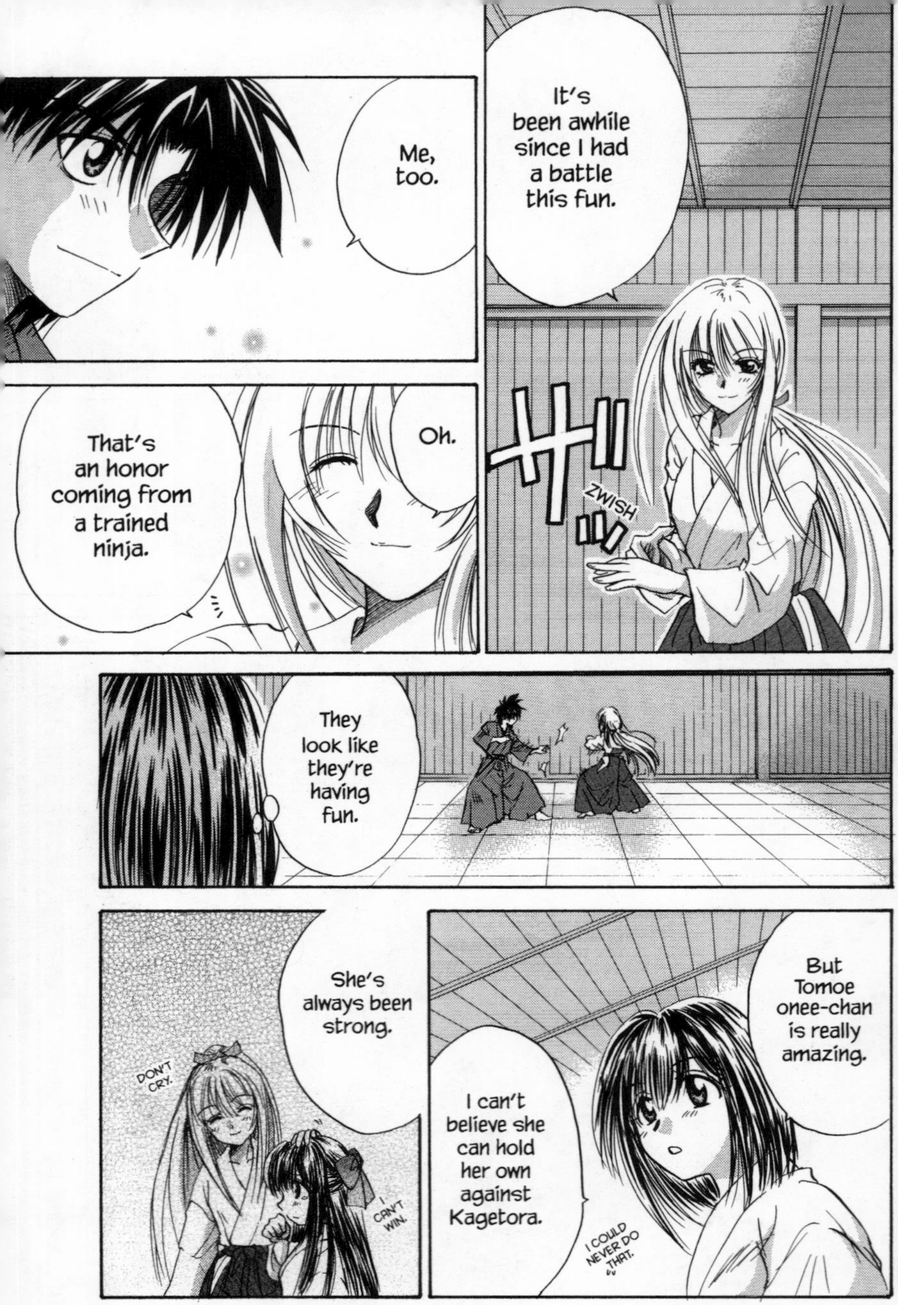
It's been awhile since I had a battle this fun.
ZWISH
Me, too.
Oh.
That's an honor coming from a trained ninja.
They look like they're having fun.
But Tomoe onee-chan is really amazing.
I can't believe she can hold her own against Kagetora.
I could never do that.
She's always been strong.
Don't cry.
I can't win.

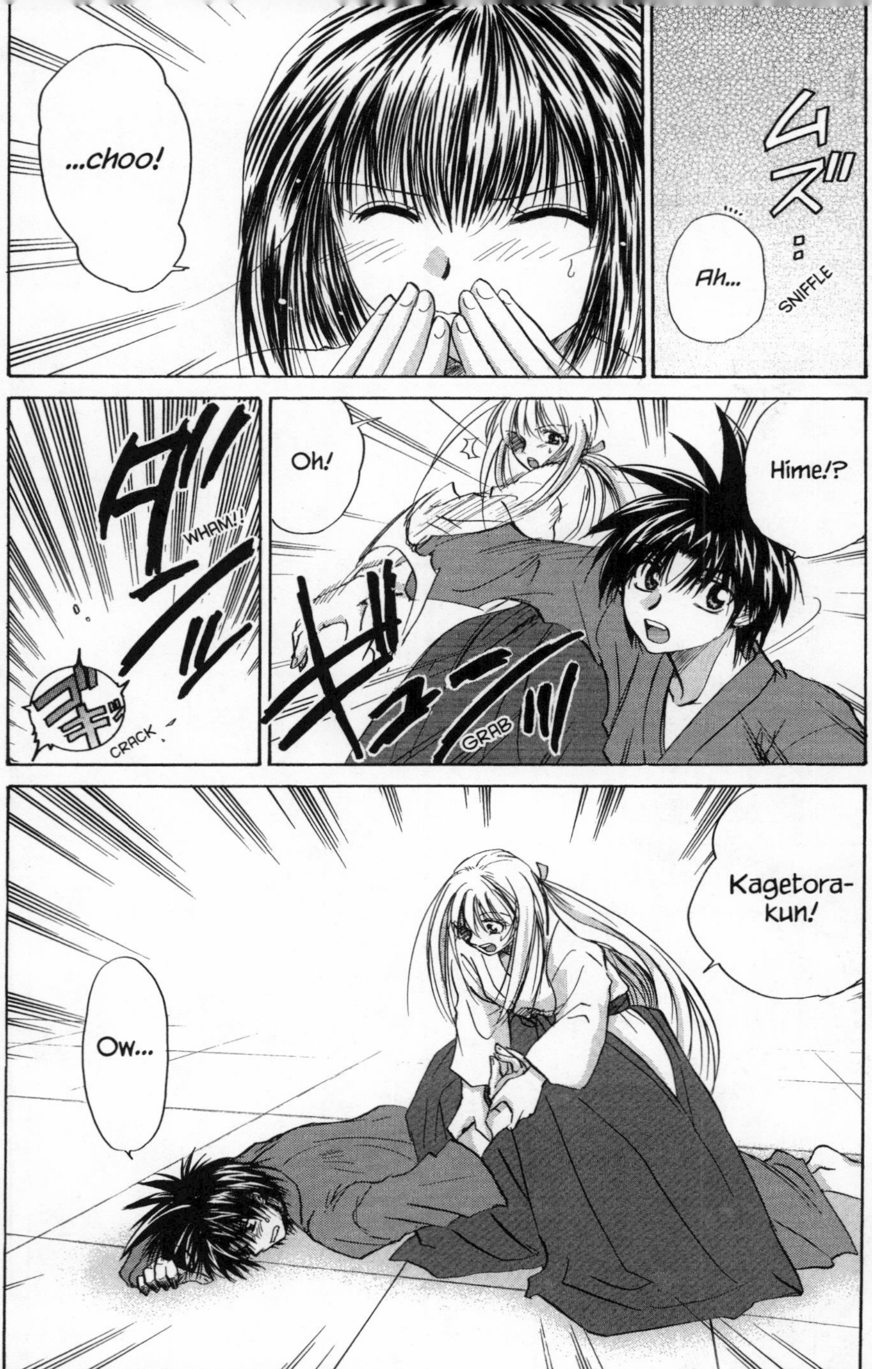
Ah...
SNIFFLE
...choo!
Hime!?
Oh!
GRAB
WHAM!!
CRACK
Kagetora-kun!
Ow...

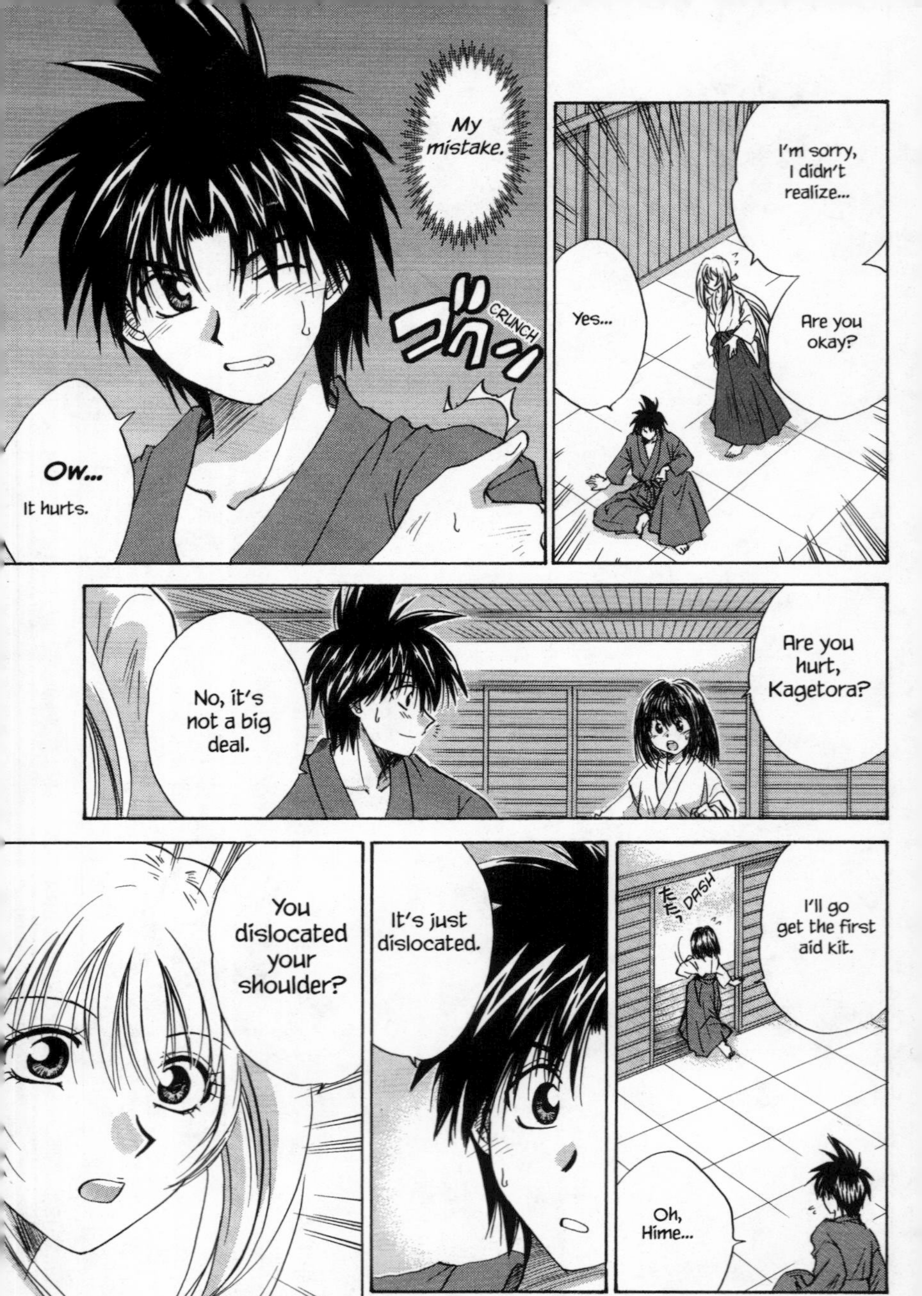
I'm sorry, I didn't realize...
Are you okay?
Yes...
My mistake.
CRUNCH
Ow...
It hurts.
Are you hurt, Kagetora?
No, it's not a big deal.
DASH
I'll go get the first aid kit.
Oh, Hime...
It's just dislocated.
You dislocated your shoulder?

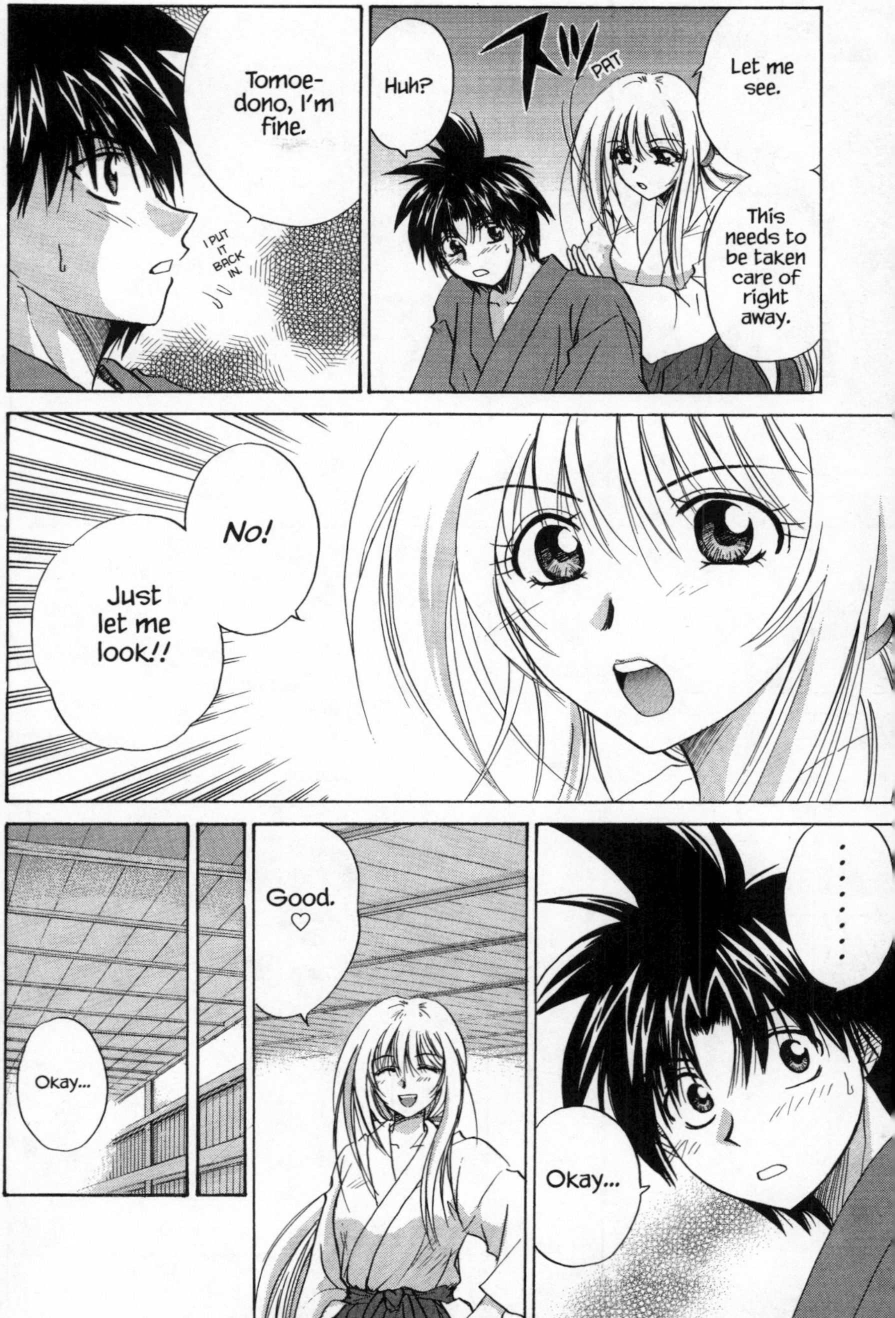
Let me see.
This needs to be taken care of right away.
PAT
Huh?
Tomoe-dono, I'm fine.
I PUT IT BACK IN.
No!
Just let me look!!
......
Okay...
Good. ♡
Okay...

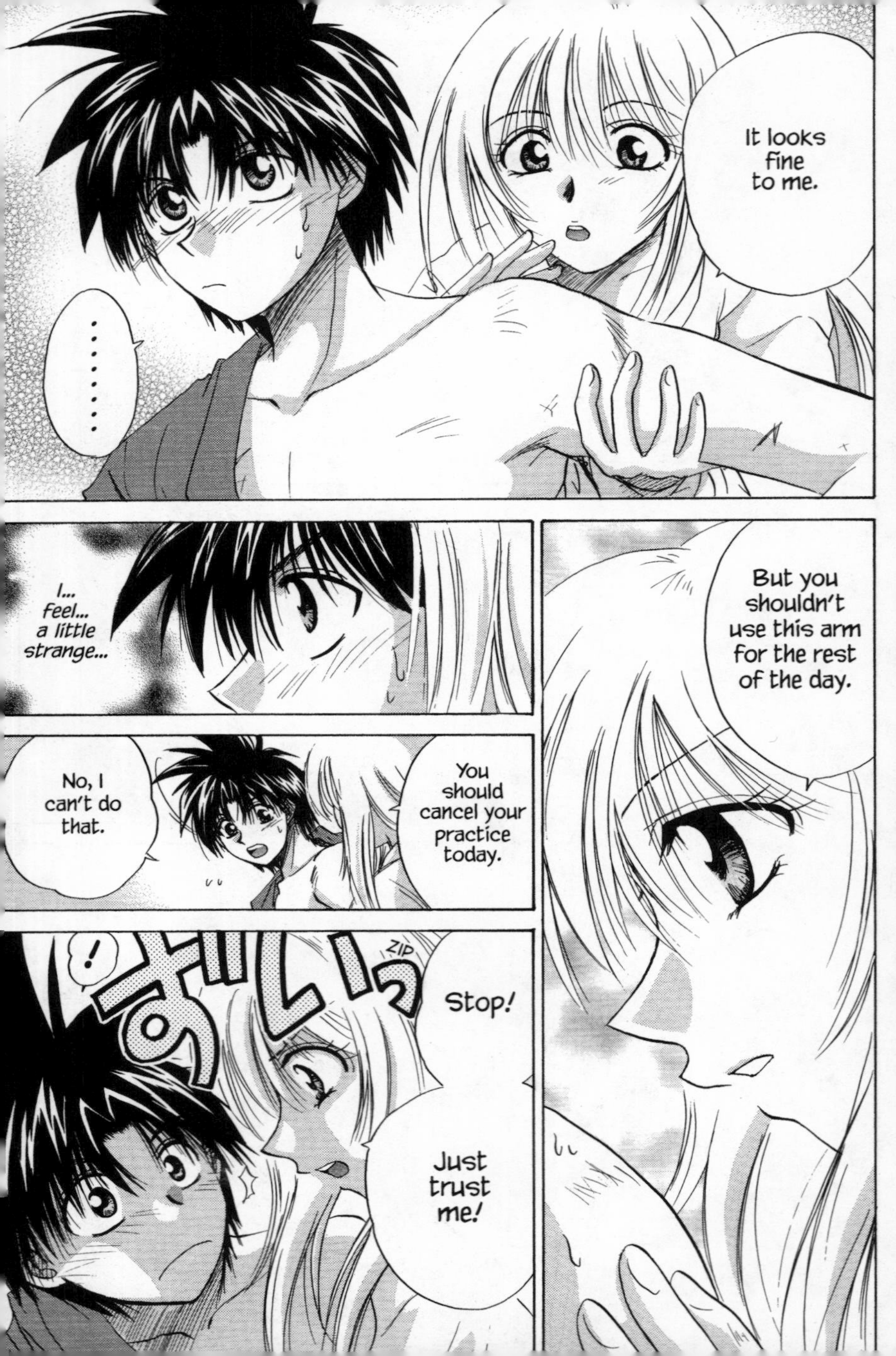
It looks fine to me.
......
But you shouldn't use this arm for the rest of the day.
I... feel... a little strange...
You should cancel your practice today.
No, I can't do that.
Stop!
ZIP
!
Just trust me!

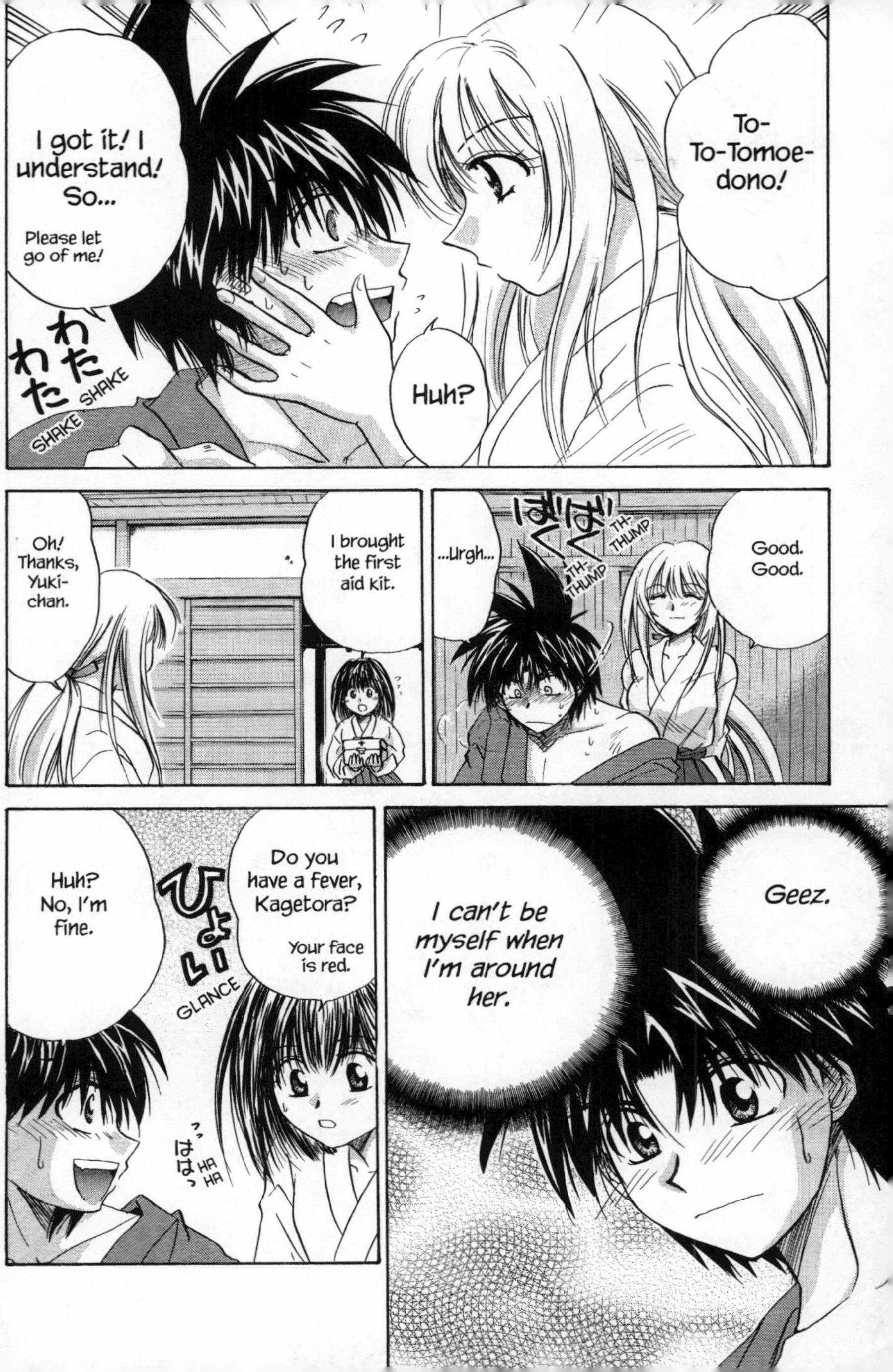
To-
To-Tomoe-dono!
I got it! I understand! So...
Please let go of me!
わたわた
SHAKE SHAKE
Huh?
Good. Good.
...Urgh...
ばくばく
TH-THUMP TH-THUMP
I brought the first aid kit.
Oh! Thanks, Yuki-chan.
Geez.
I can't be myself when I'm around her.
Do you have a fever, Kagetora?
Your face is red.
ひょい
GLANCE
Huh? No, I'm fine.
ははっ
HA HA

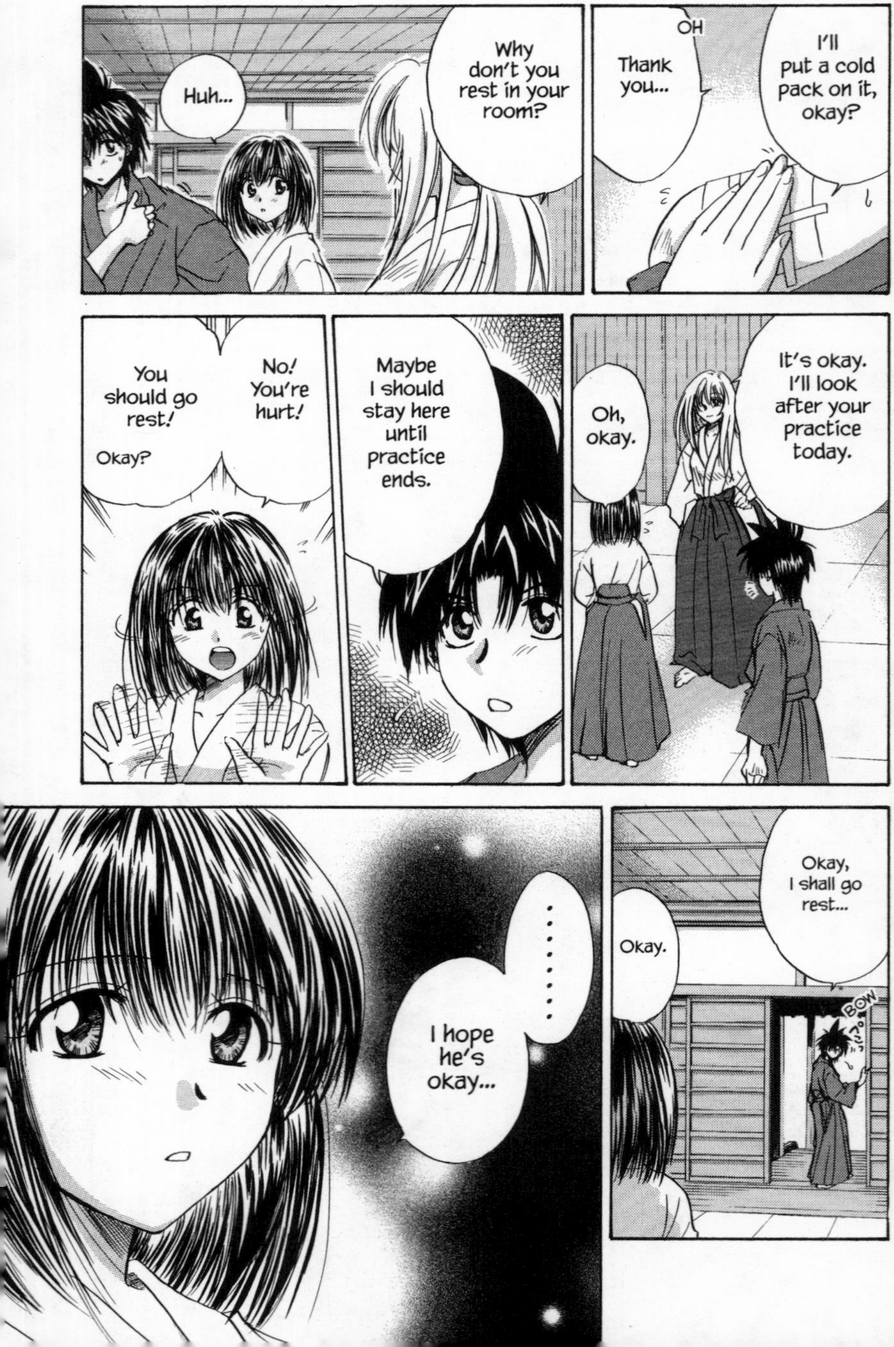
OH
I'll put a cold pack on it, okay?
Thank you...
Why don't you rest in your room?
Huh...
It's okay. I'll look after your practice today.
Oh, okay.
Maybe I should stay here until practice ends.
No! You're hurt!
You should go rest!
Okay?
Okay, I shall go rest...
Okay.
BOW
....
I hope he's okay...

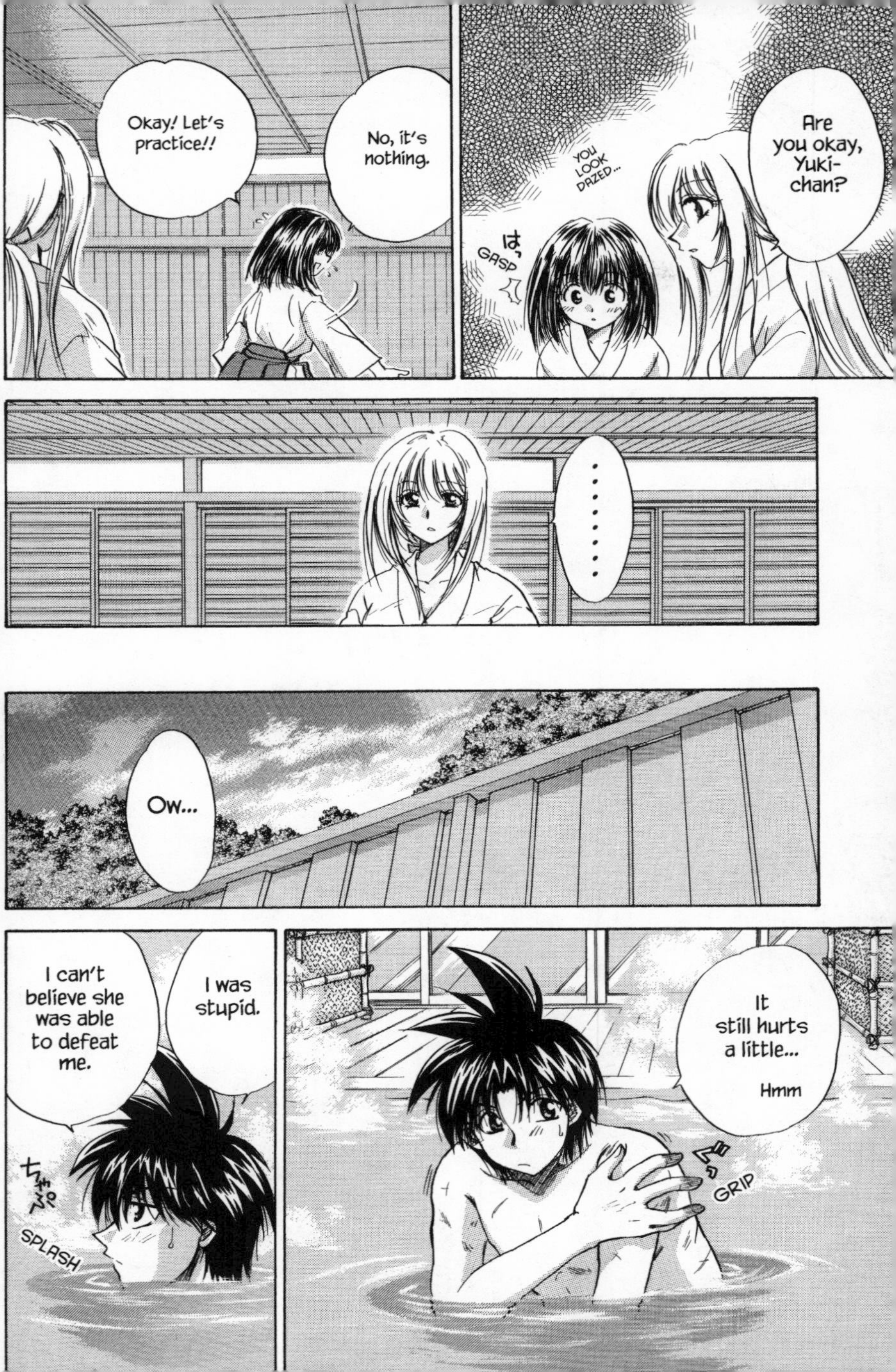
Are you okay, Yuki-chan?
YOU LOOK DAZED...
は、
GASP
No, it's nothing.
Okay! Let's practice!!
....
Ow...
It still hurts a little...
Hmm
GRIP
I was stupid.
I can't believe she was able to defeat me.
SPLASH

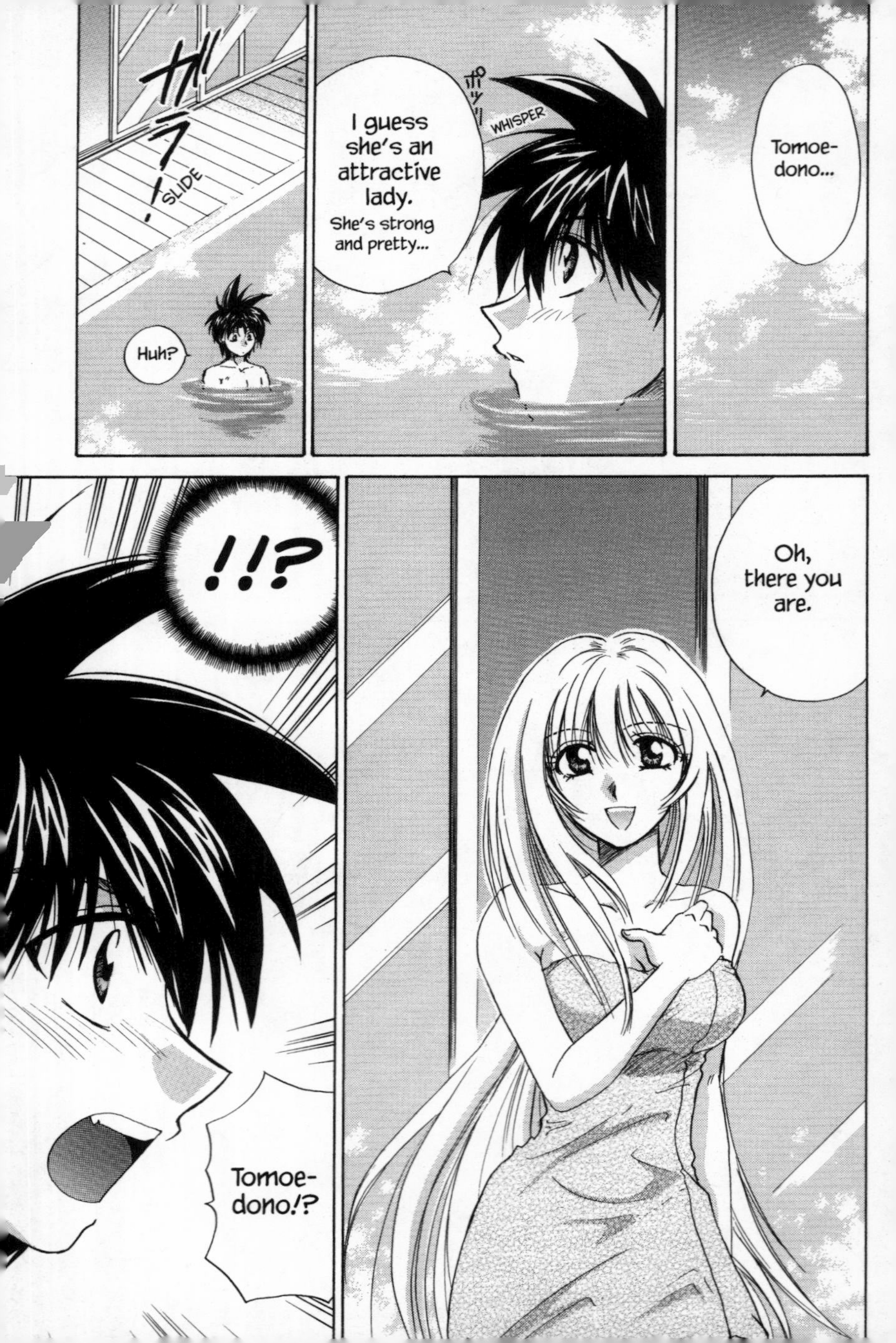
Tomoe-dono...
I guess she's an attractive lady.
She's strong and pretty...
WHISPER
SLIDE
Huh?
Oh, there you are.
!!?
Tomoe-dono!?

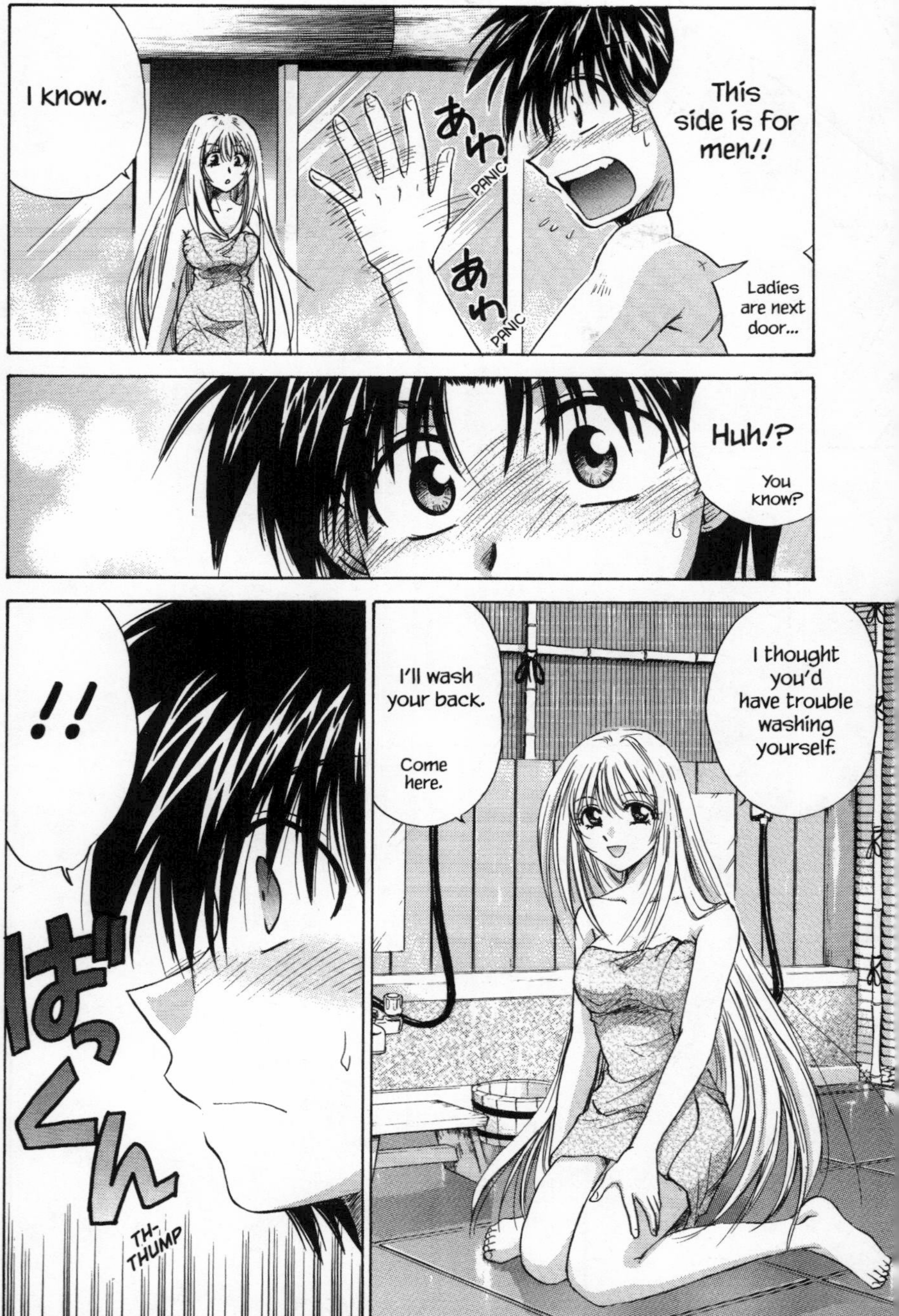
This side is for men!!
Ladies are next door...
あわ
PANIC
あわ
PANIC
I know.
Huh!?
You know?
I thought you'd have trouble washing yourself.
I'll wash your back.
Come here.
!!
ばっくん
TH-THUMP

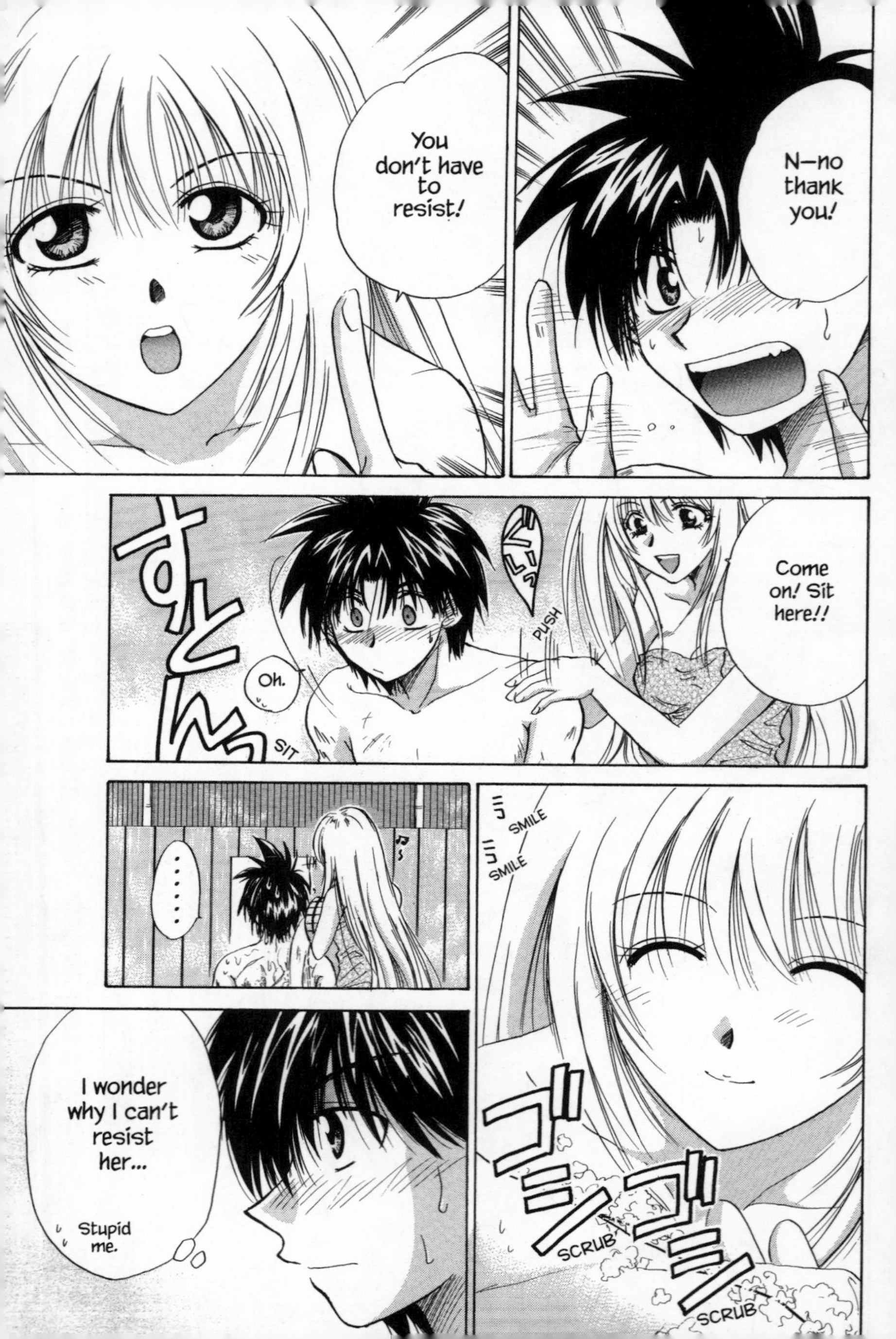
N—no thank you!
You don't have to resist!
Come on! Sit here!!
PUSH
Oh.
すとんっ
SIT
SMILE
SMILE
ゴシゴシ
SCRUB
SCRUB
......
I wonder why I can't resist her...
Stupid me.

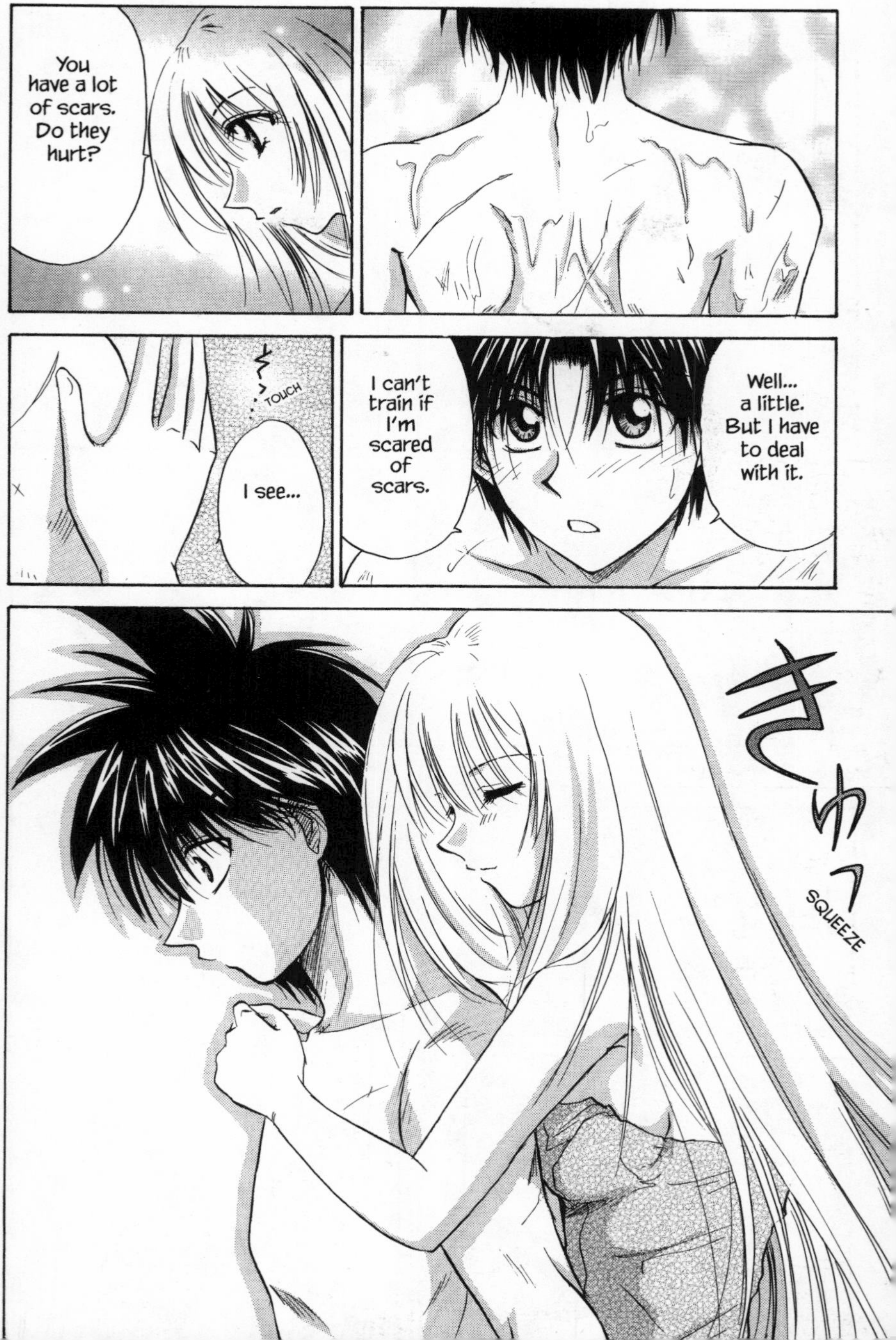
You have a lot of scars. Do they hurt?
Well... a little. But I have to deal with it.
I can't train if I'm scared of scars.
TOUCH
I see...
きゅっ
SQUEEZE

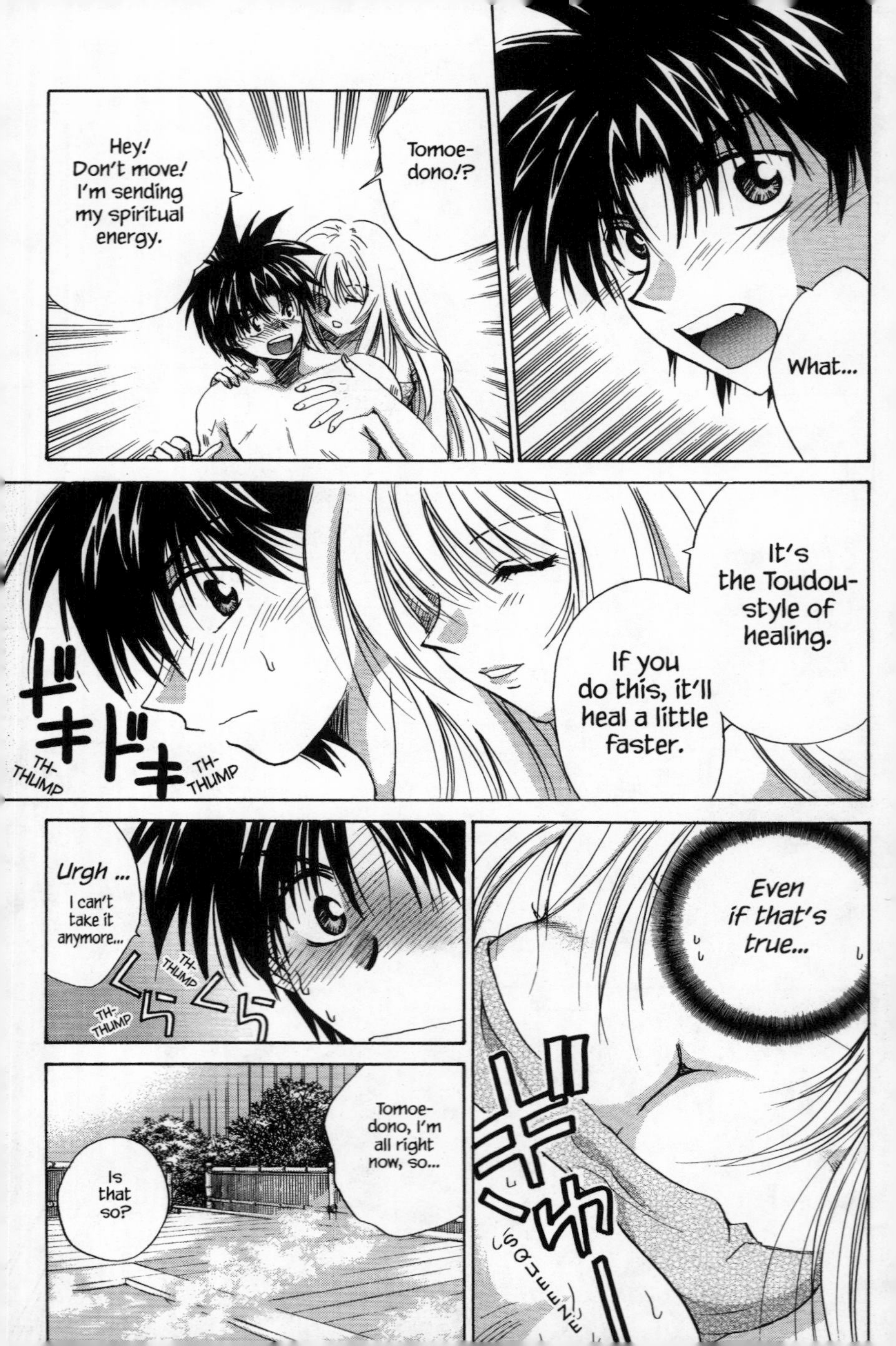
What...
Tomoe-dono!?
Hey! Don't move! I'm sending my spiritual energy.
It's the Toudou-style of healing.
If you do this, it'll heal a little faster.
ドキドキ
TH-THUMP TH-THUMP
Even if that's true...
SQUEEZE
Urgh ... I can't take it anymore...
くらくら
TH-THUMP TH-THUMP
Tomoe-dono, I'm all right now, so...
Is that so?

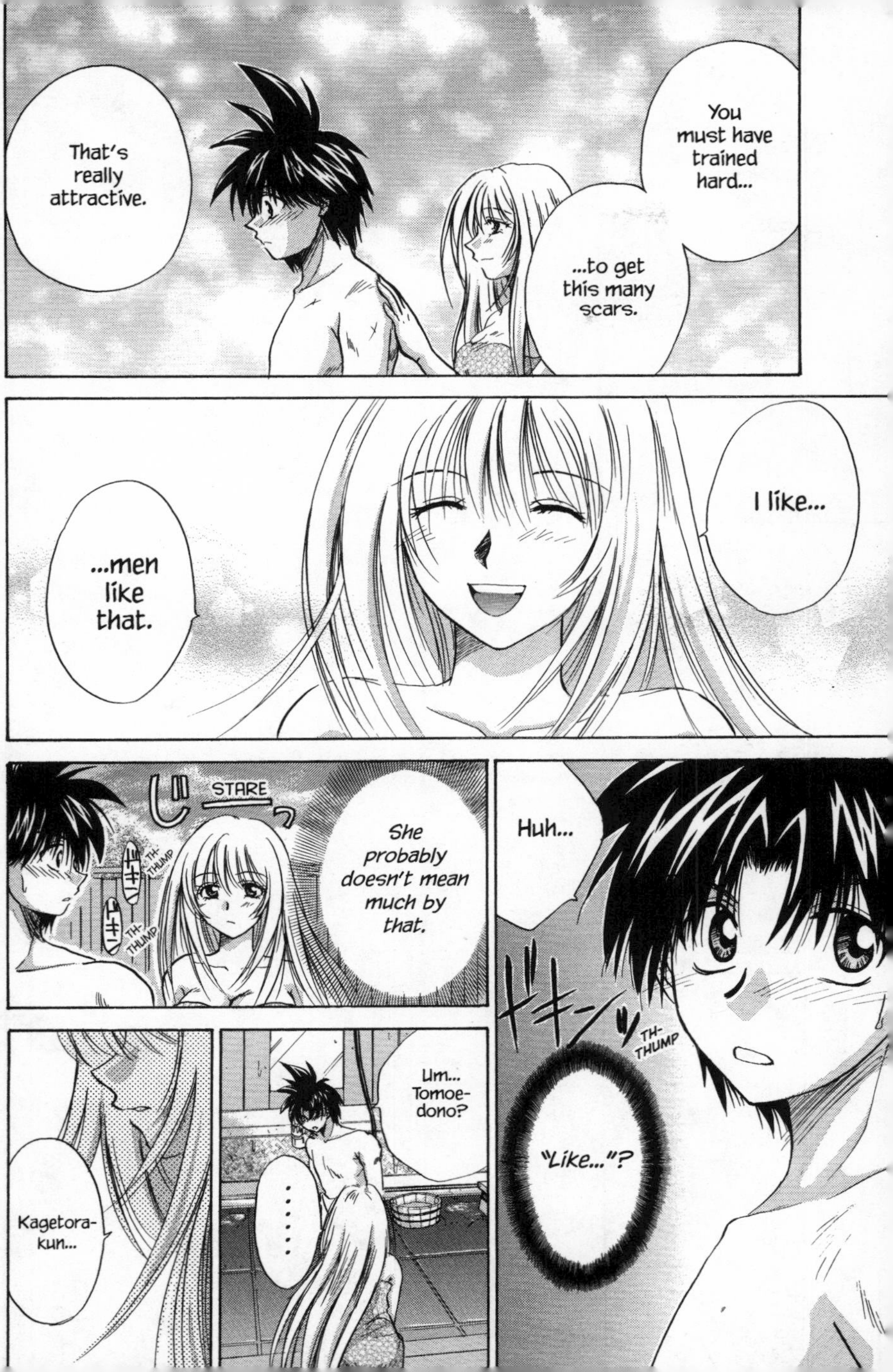

You must have trained hard...
...to get this many scars.
That's really attractive.
I like...
...men like that.
Huh...
TH-THUMP
"Like..."?
STARE
She probably doesn't mean much by that.
TH-THUMP
TH-THUMP
Um... Tomoe-dono?
......
Kagetora-kun...

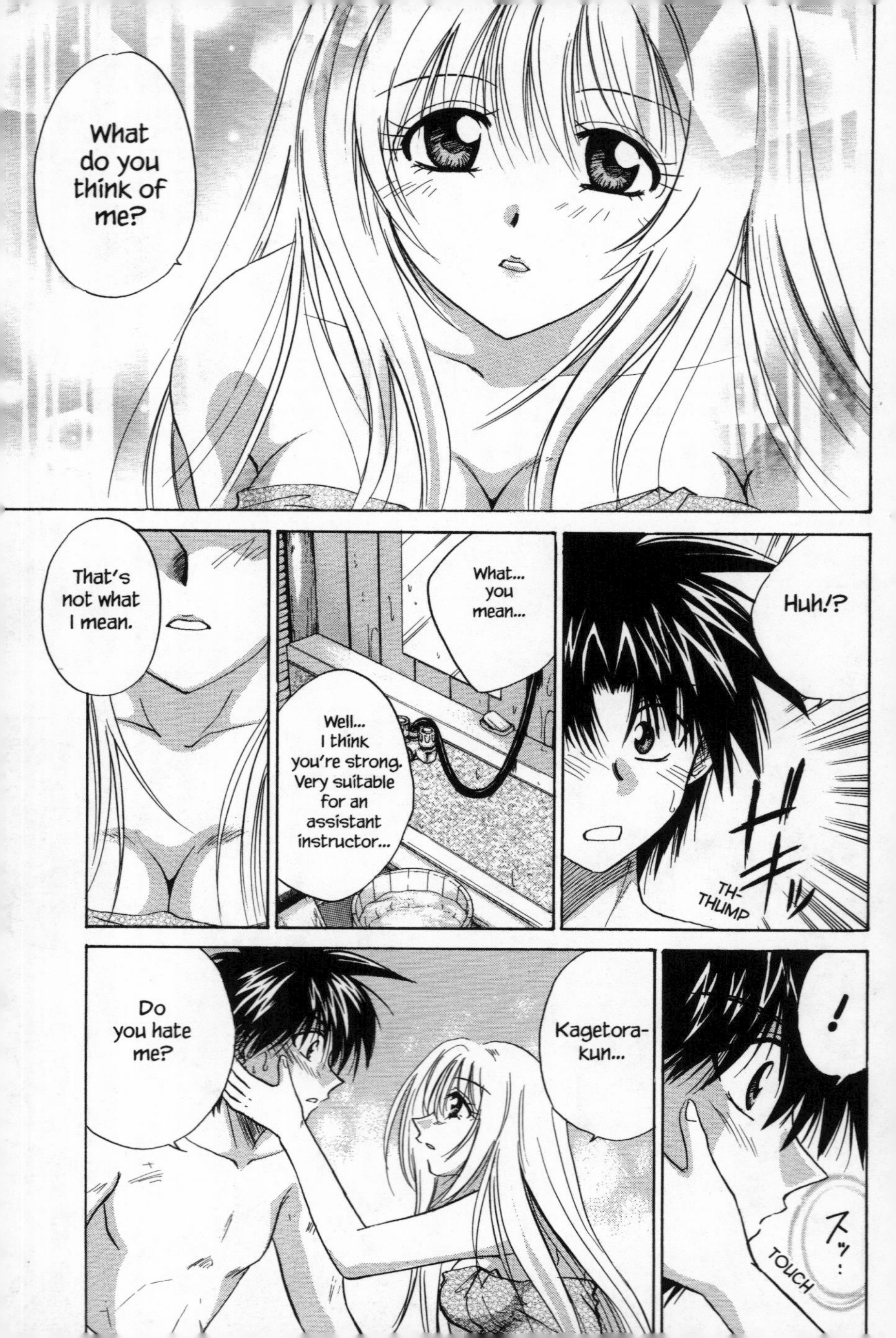
What do you think of me?
Huh!?
TH-THUMP
What... you mean...
Well... I think you're strong. Very suitable for an assistant instructor...
That's not what I mean.
!
TOUCH
Kagetora-kun...
Do you hate me?

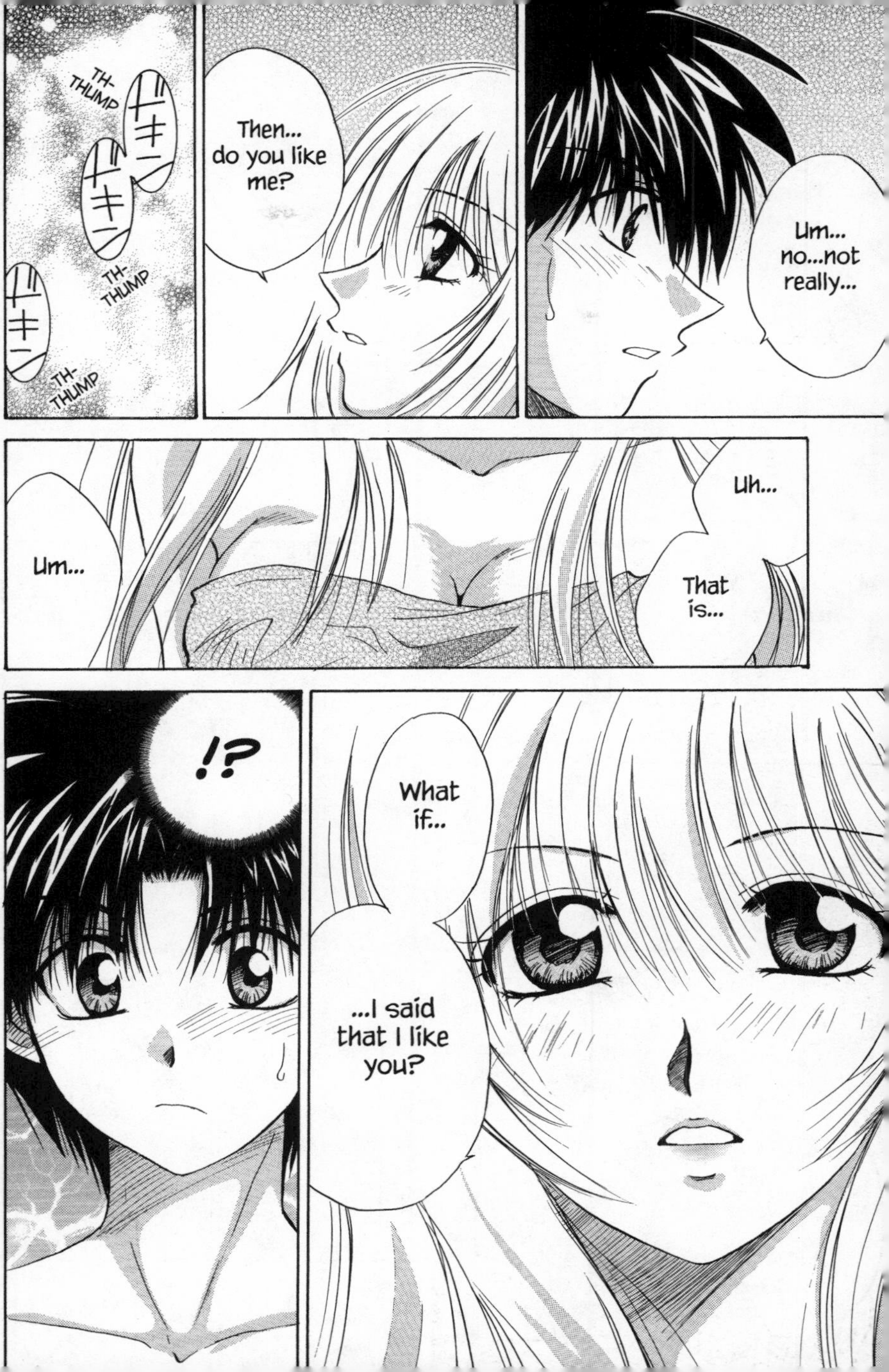
Um...
no...not
really...
Then...
do you like
me?
ドキン
TH-THUMP
ドキン
TH-THUMP
ドキン
TH-THUMP
Uh...
That
is...
Um...
What
if...
...I said
that I like
you?
!?

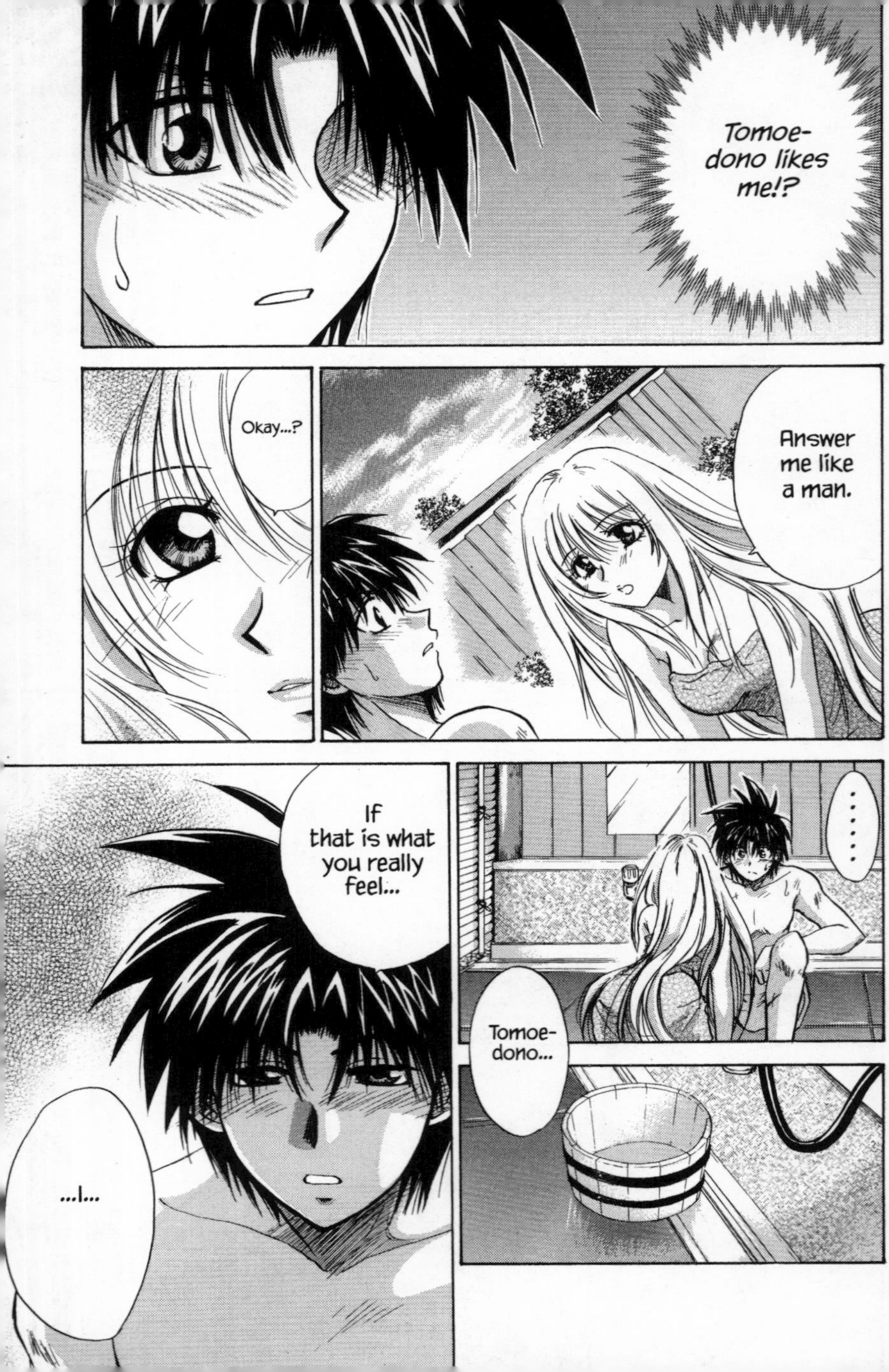
Tomoe-dono likes me!?
Answer me like a man.
Okay...?
......
Tomoe-dono...
If that is what you really feel...
...I...

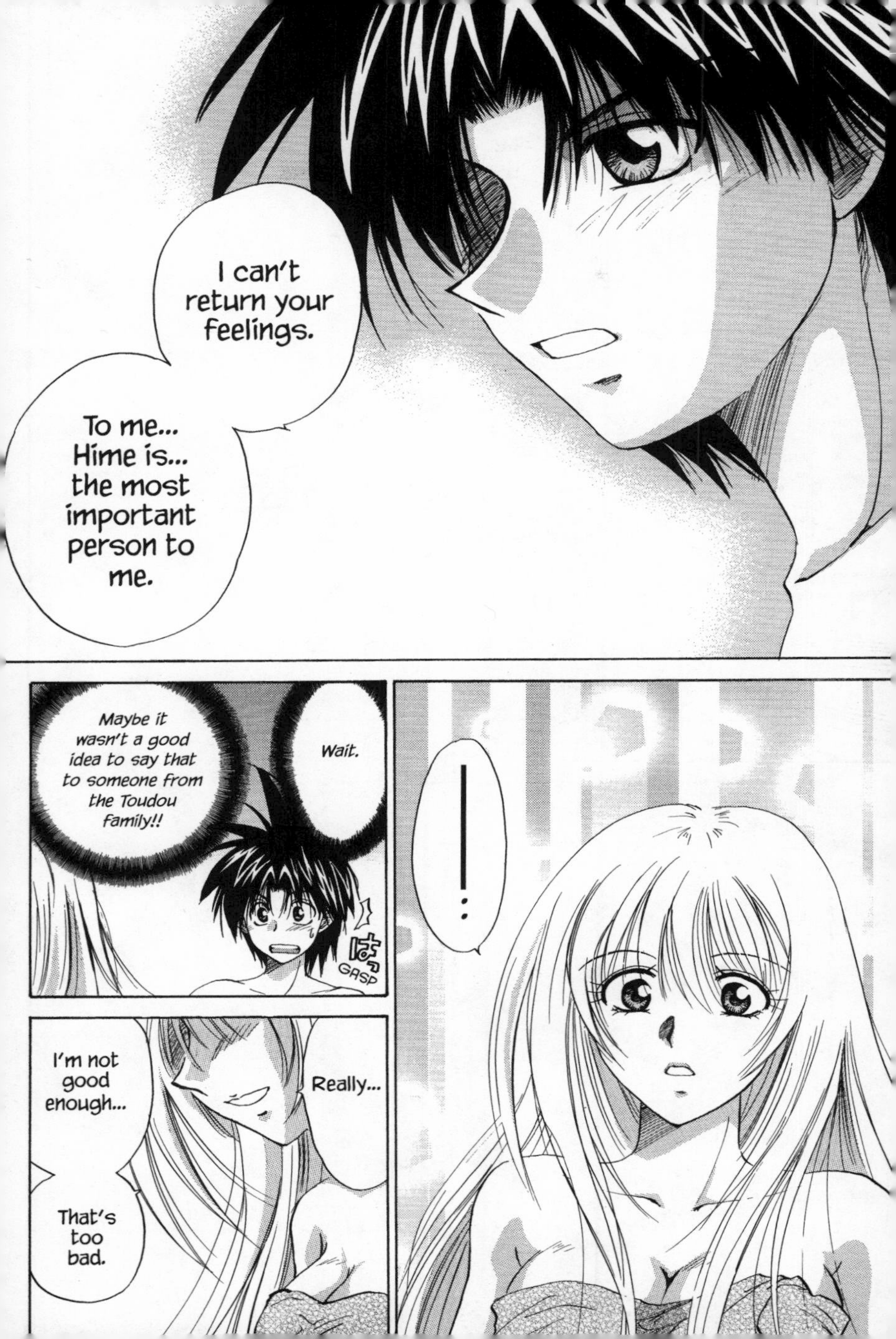
I can't return your feelings.
To me... Hime is... the most important person to me.
—!
Wait.
Maybe it wasn't a good idea to say that to someone from the Toudou family!!
はっ GASP
Really...
I'm not good enough...
That's too bad.

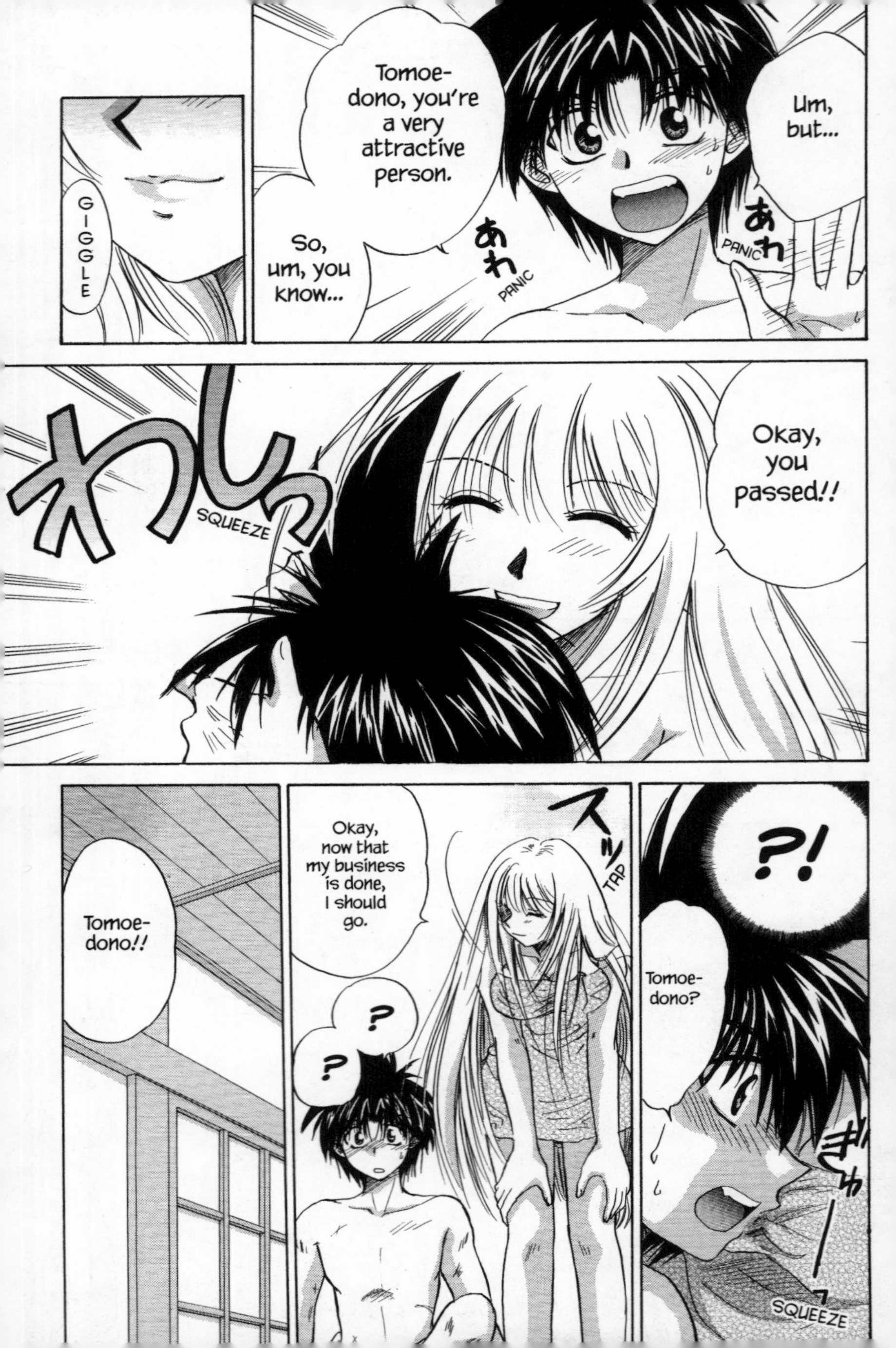

Um, but...
あれ
PANIC
Tomoe-dono, you're a very attractive person.
So, um, you know...
あれ
PANIC
GIGGLE
Okay, you passed!!
わしっ
SQUEEZE
?!
Tomoe-dono?
ぎゅーっ
SQUEEZE
Okay, now that my business is done, I should go.
スッ
TAP
?
?
Tomoe-dono!!

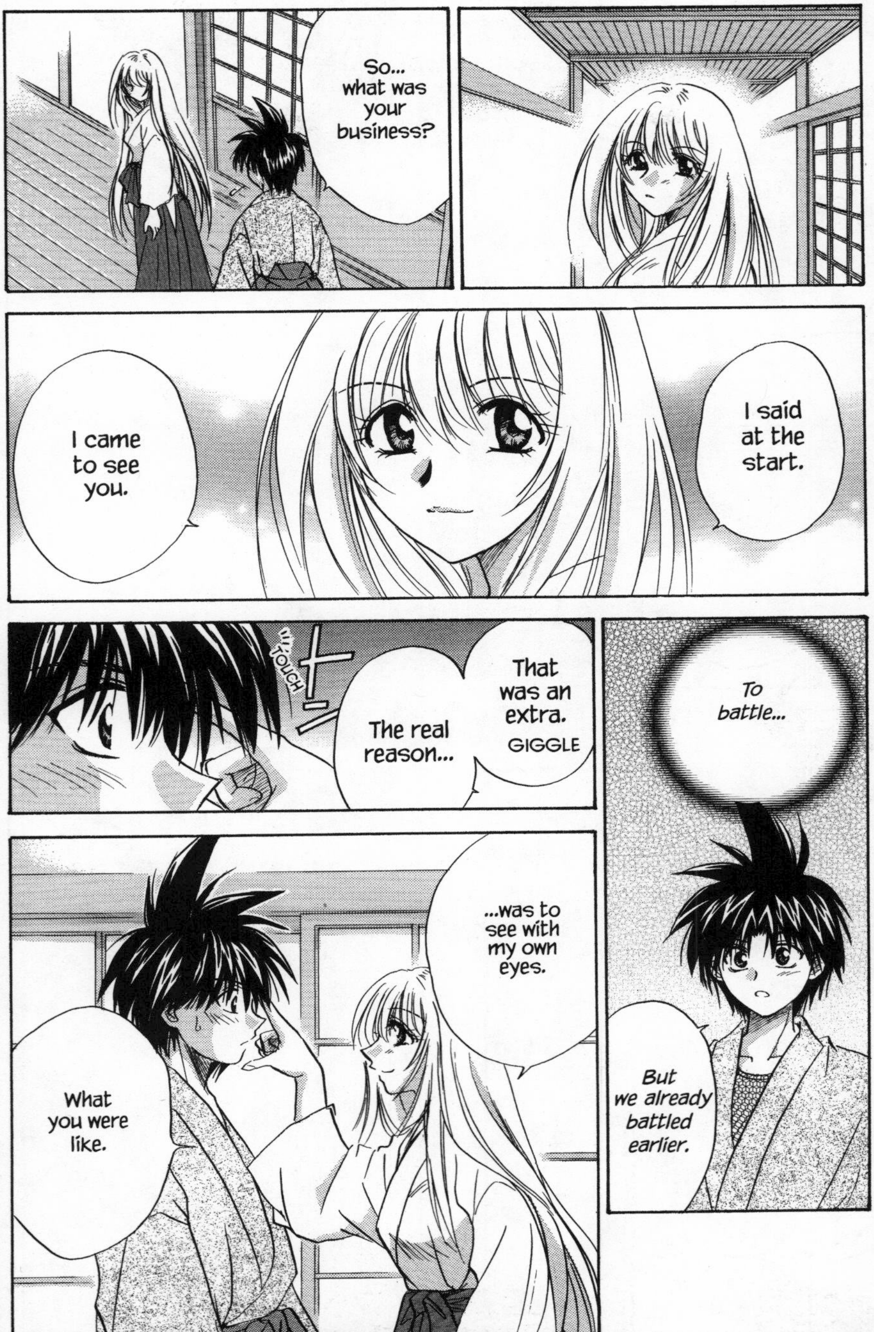
So... what was your business?
I said at the start.
I came to see you.
To battle...
But we already battled earlier.
That was an extra.
GIGGLE
TOUCH
The real reason...
...was to see with my own eyes.
What you were like.

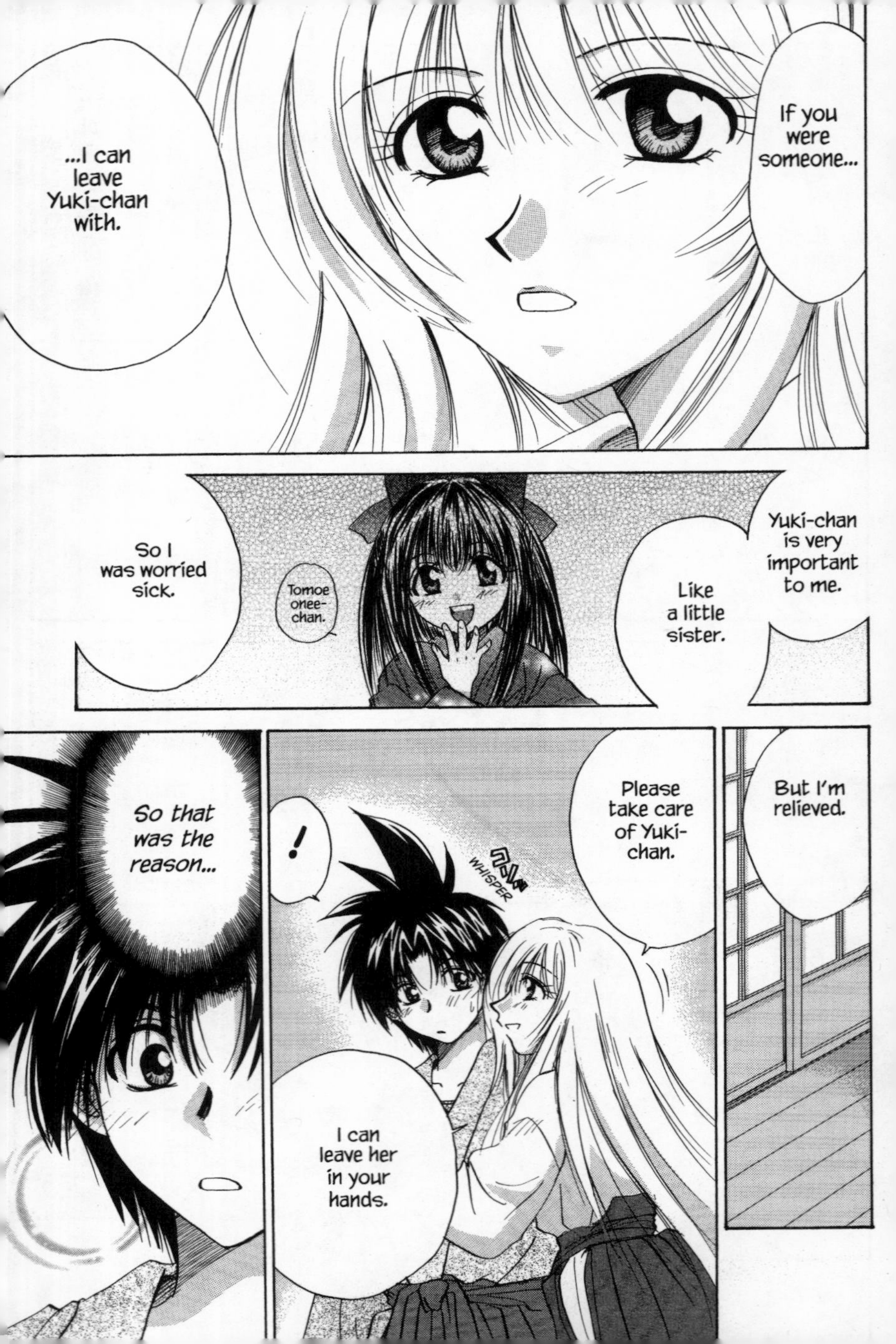

If you were someone...
...I can leave Yuki-chan with.
Yuki-chan is very important to me.
Like a little sister.
Tomoe onee-chan.
So I was worried sick.
But I'm relieved.
Please take care of Yuki-chan.
WHISPER
!
I can leave her in your hands.
So that was the reason...

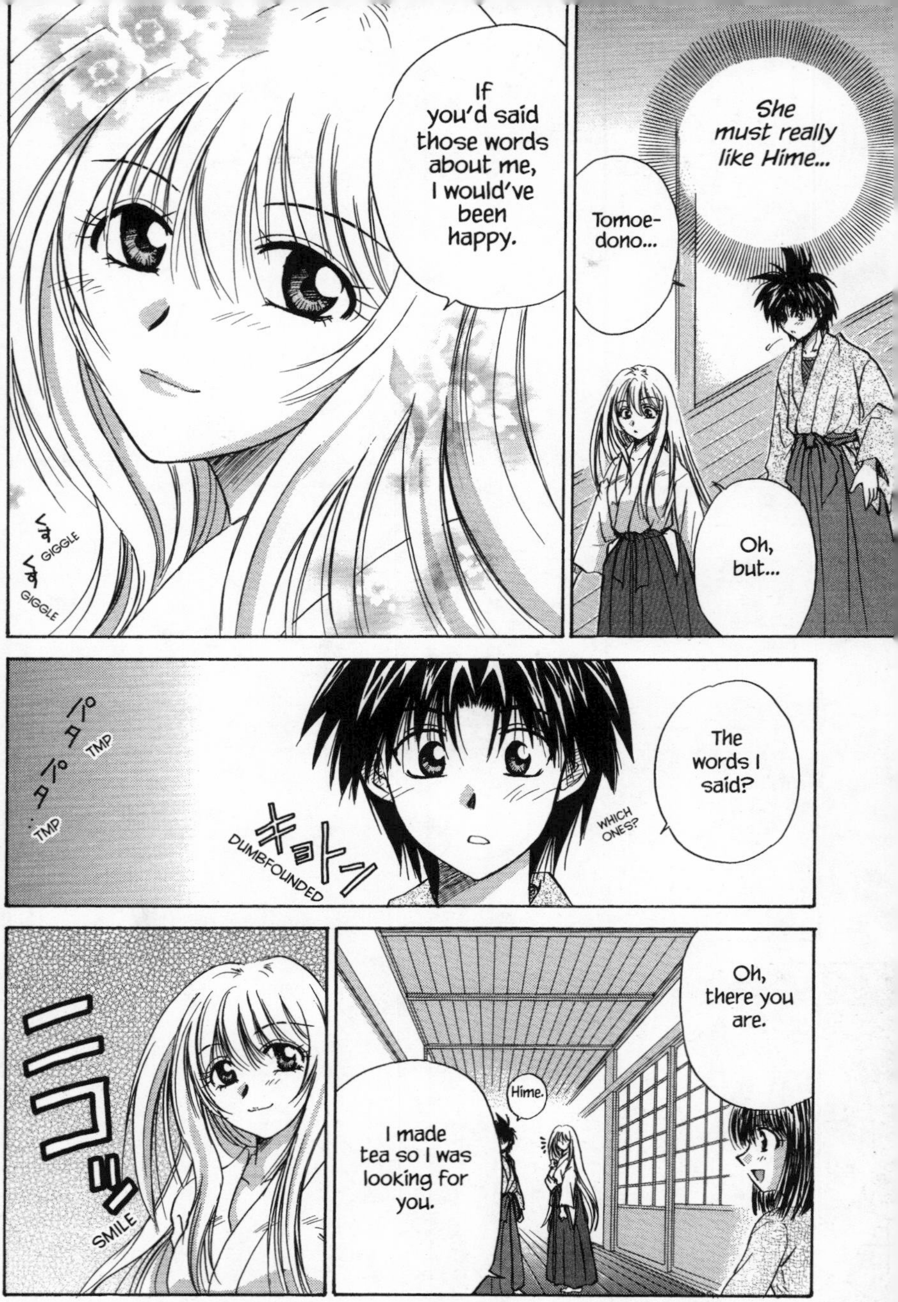

She must really like Hime...
Tomoe-dono...
Oh, but...
If you'd said those words about me, I would've been happy.
GIGGLE
GIGGLE
The words I said?
WHICH ONES?
DUMBFOUNDED
TMP
TMP
Oh, there you are.
Hime.
I made tea so I was looking for you.
SMILE

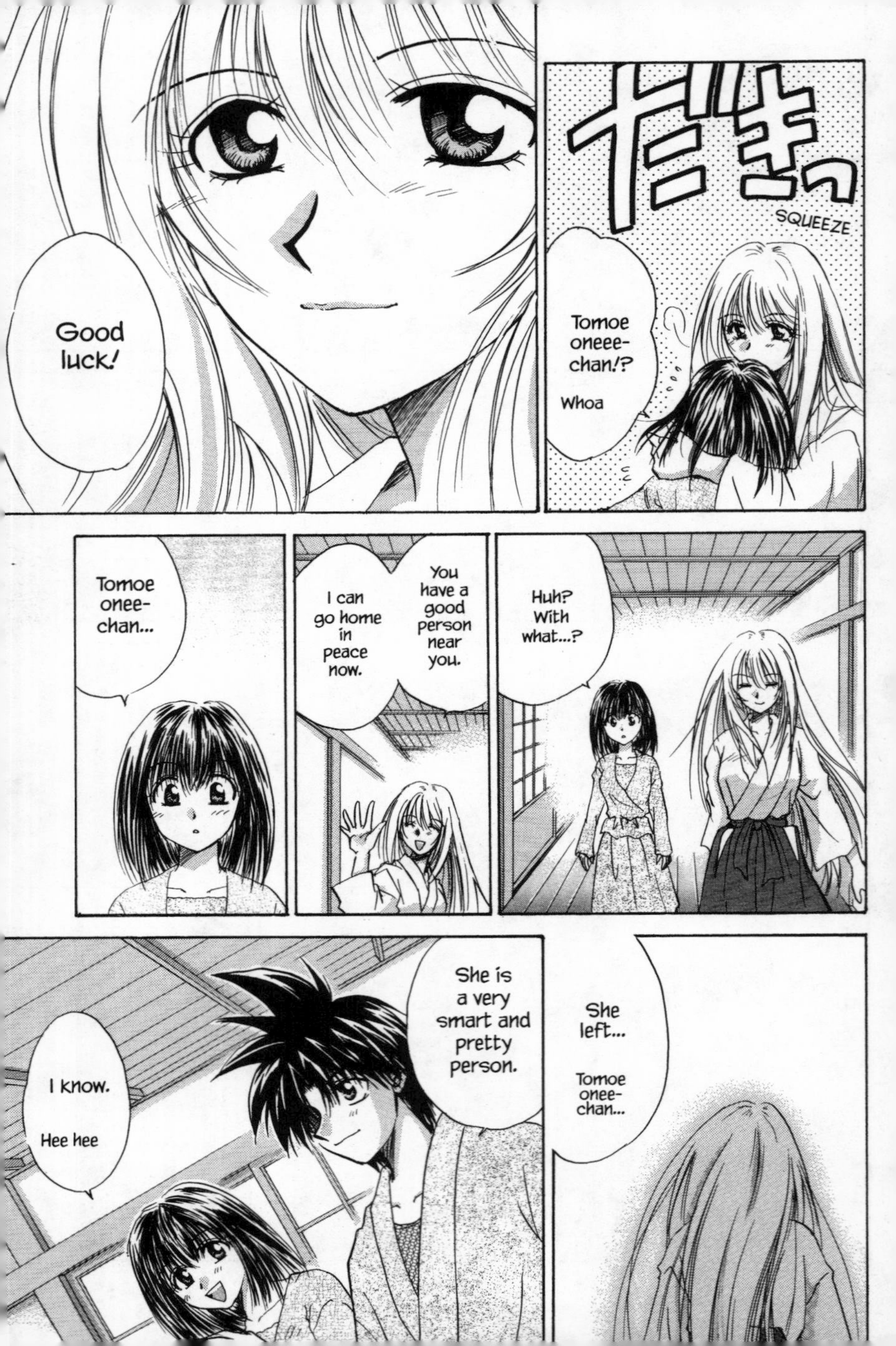
だきっ
SQUEEZE
Tomoe oneee-chan!?
Whoa
Good luck!
Huh? With what...?
You have a good person near you.
I can go home in peace now.
Tomoe onee-chan...
She left...
Tomoe onee-chan...
She is a very smart and pretty person.
I know.
Hee hee

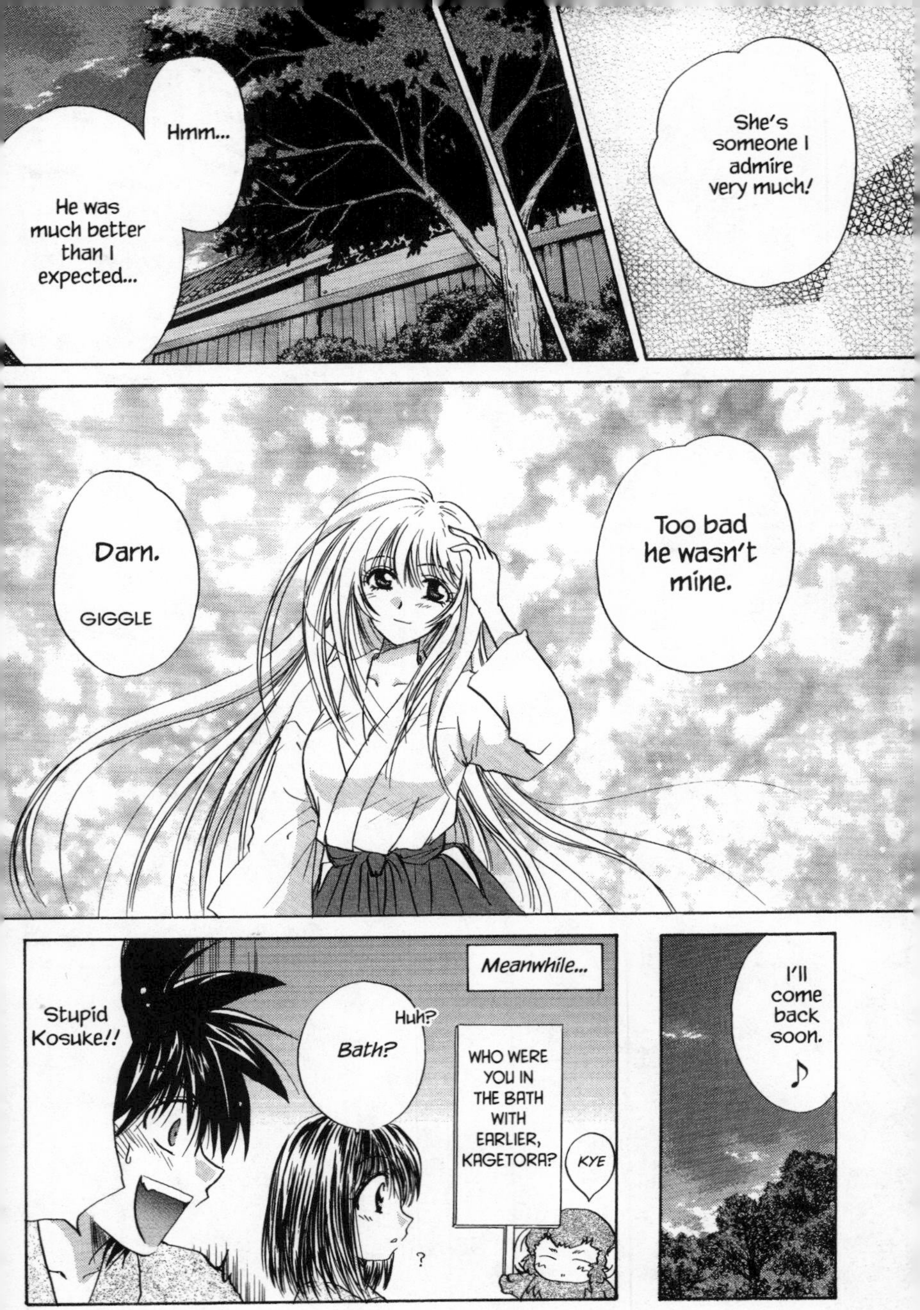
She's someone I admire very much!
Hmm...
He was much better than I expected...
Too bad he wasn't mine.
Darn.
GIGGLE
I'll come back soon. ♪
Meanwhile...
WHO WERE YOU IN THE BATH WITH EARLIER, KAGETORA?
KYE
Huh?
Bath?
Stupid Kosuke!!
?

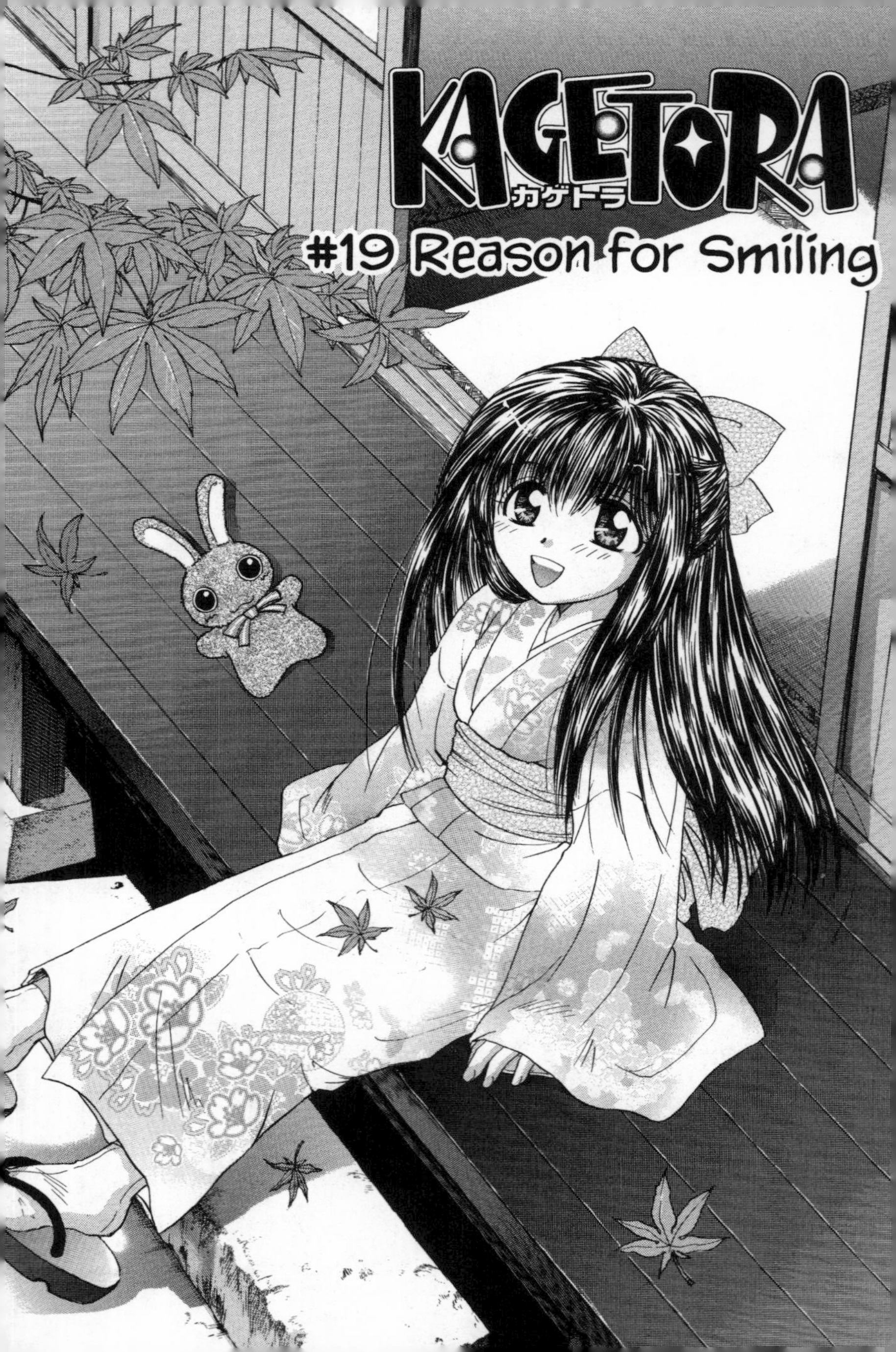
KAGETORA
カゲトラ
#19 Reason for Smiling

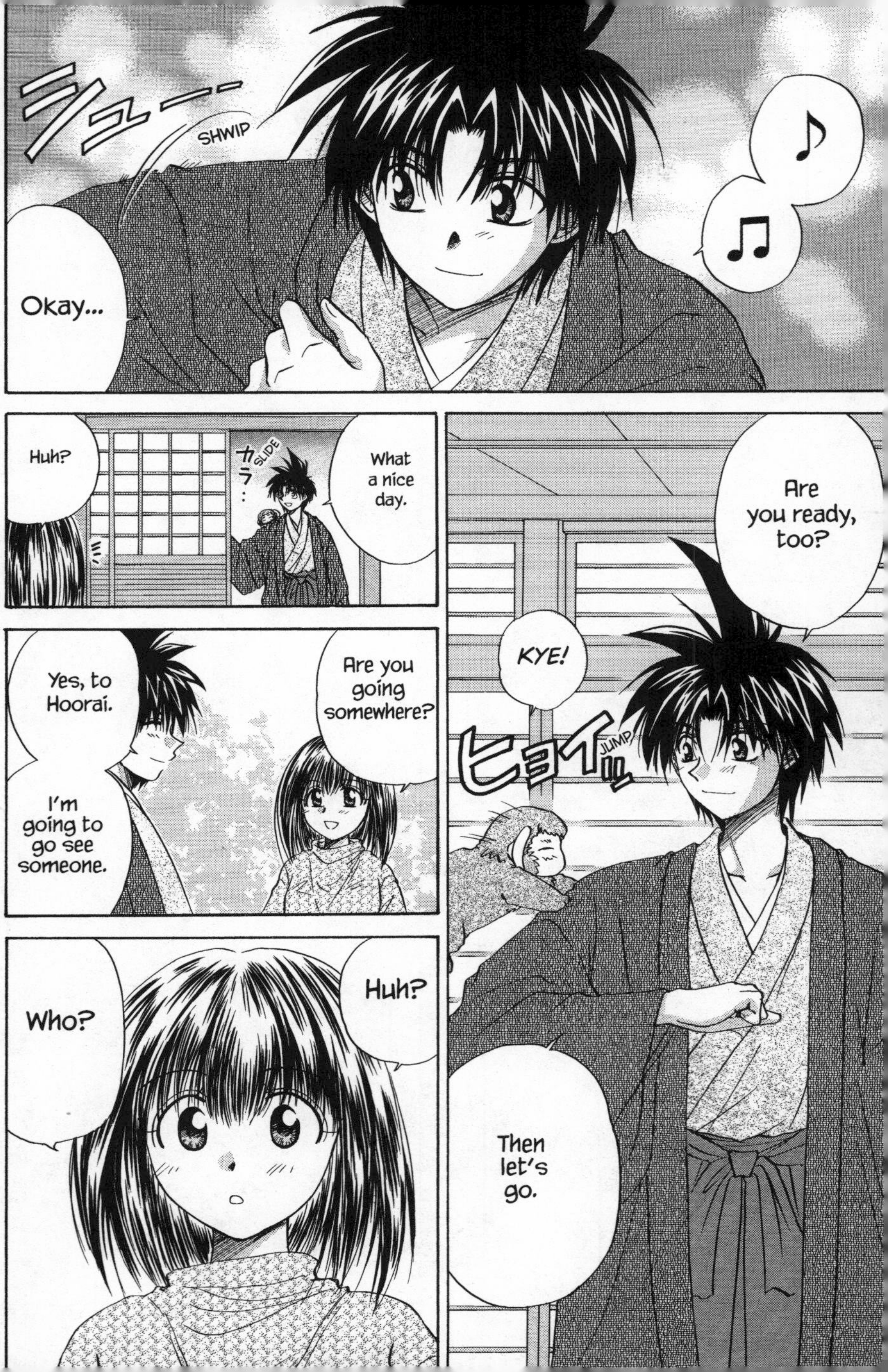
♪ ♫
シューー
SHWIP
Okay...
Are you ready, too?
KYE!
ヒョイ
JUMP
Then let's go.
What a nice day.
カラ…
SLIDE
Huh?
Are you going somewhere?
Yes, to Hoorai.
I'm going to go see someone.
Huh?
Who?

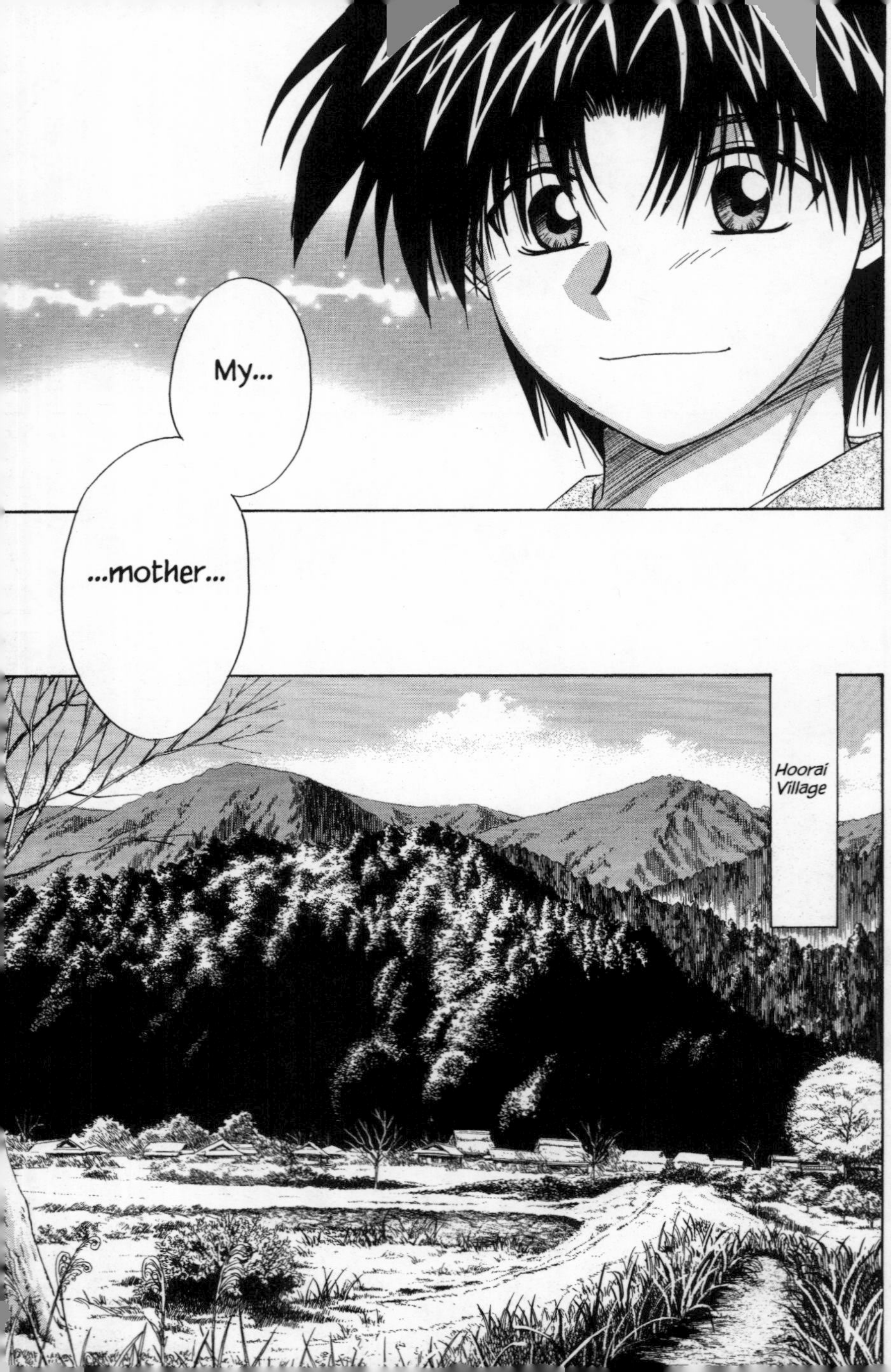
My...
...mother...
Hoorai Village

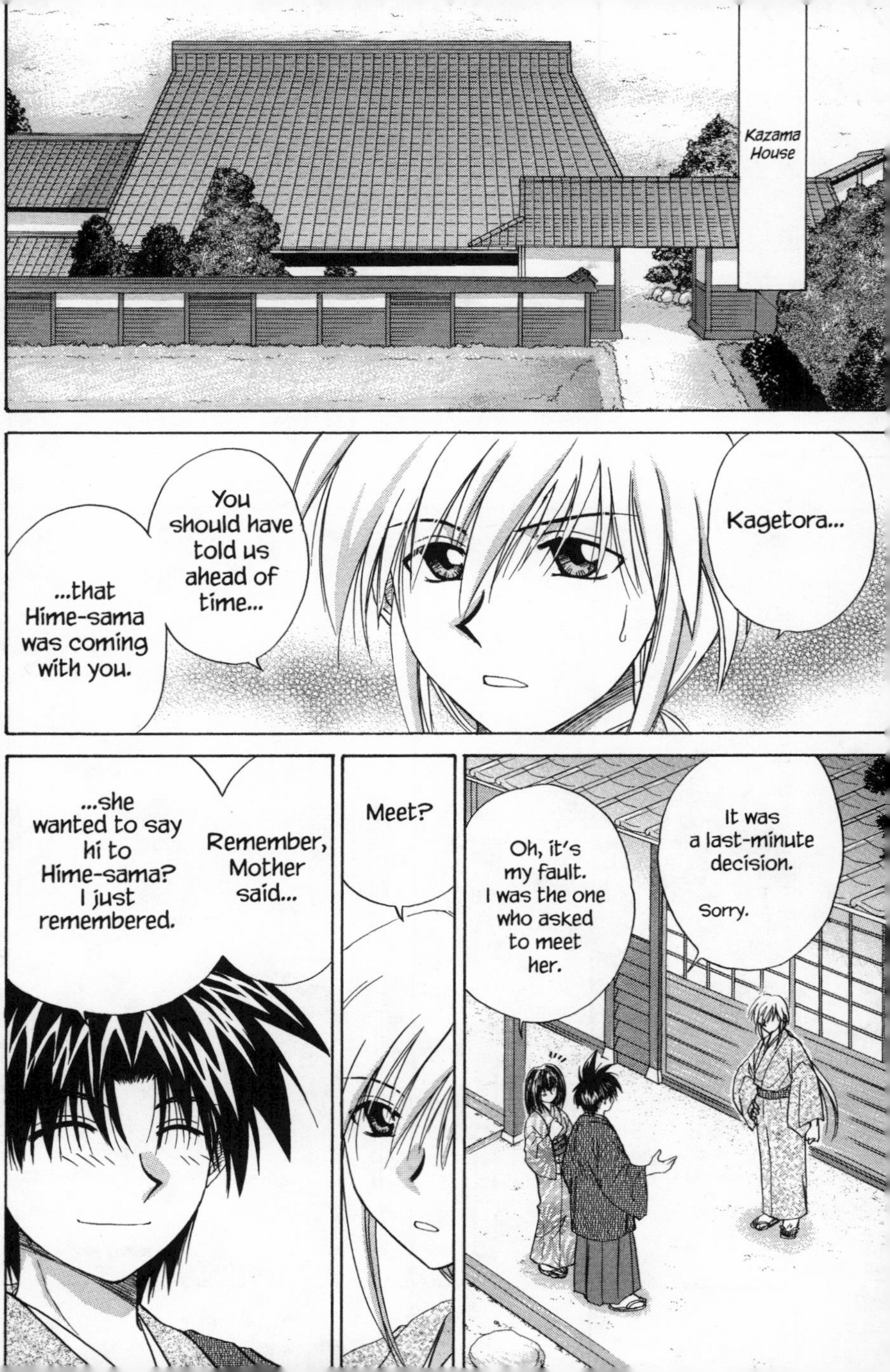
Kazama House
Kagetora...
You should have told us ahead of time...
...that Hime-sama was coming with you.
It was a last-minute decision.
Sorry.
Oh, it's my fault. I was the one who asked to meet her.
Meet?
Remember, Mother said...
...she wanted to say hi to Hime-sama? I just remembered.

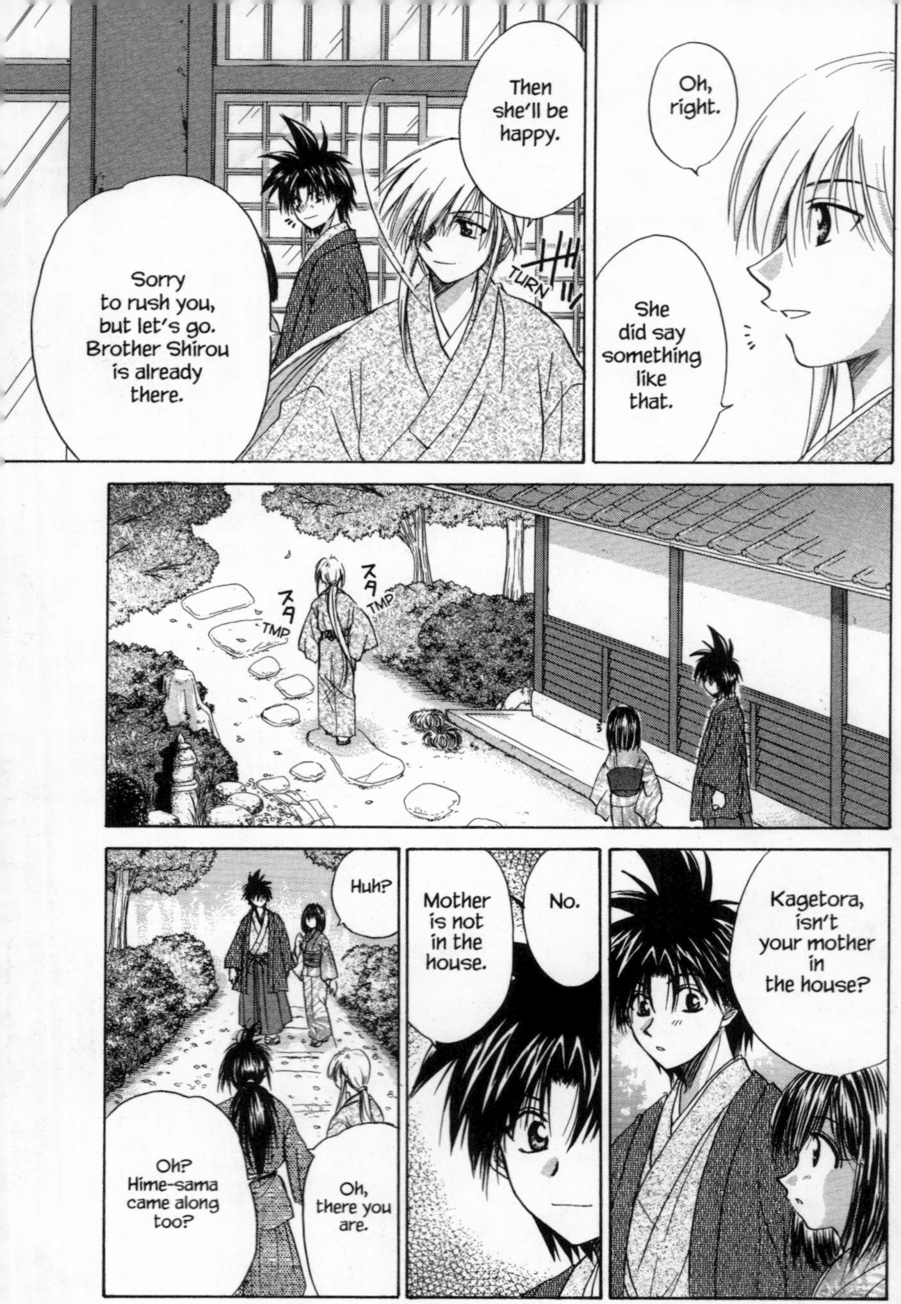
Oh, right.
She did say something like that.
Then she'll be happy.
TURN
Sorry to rush you, but let's go. Brother Shirou is already there.
スタ
TMP
スタ
TMP
Kagetora, isn't your mother in the house?
No.
Mother is not in the house.
Huh?
Oh, there you are.
Oh? Hime-sama came along too?

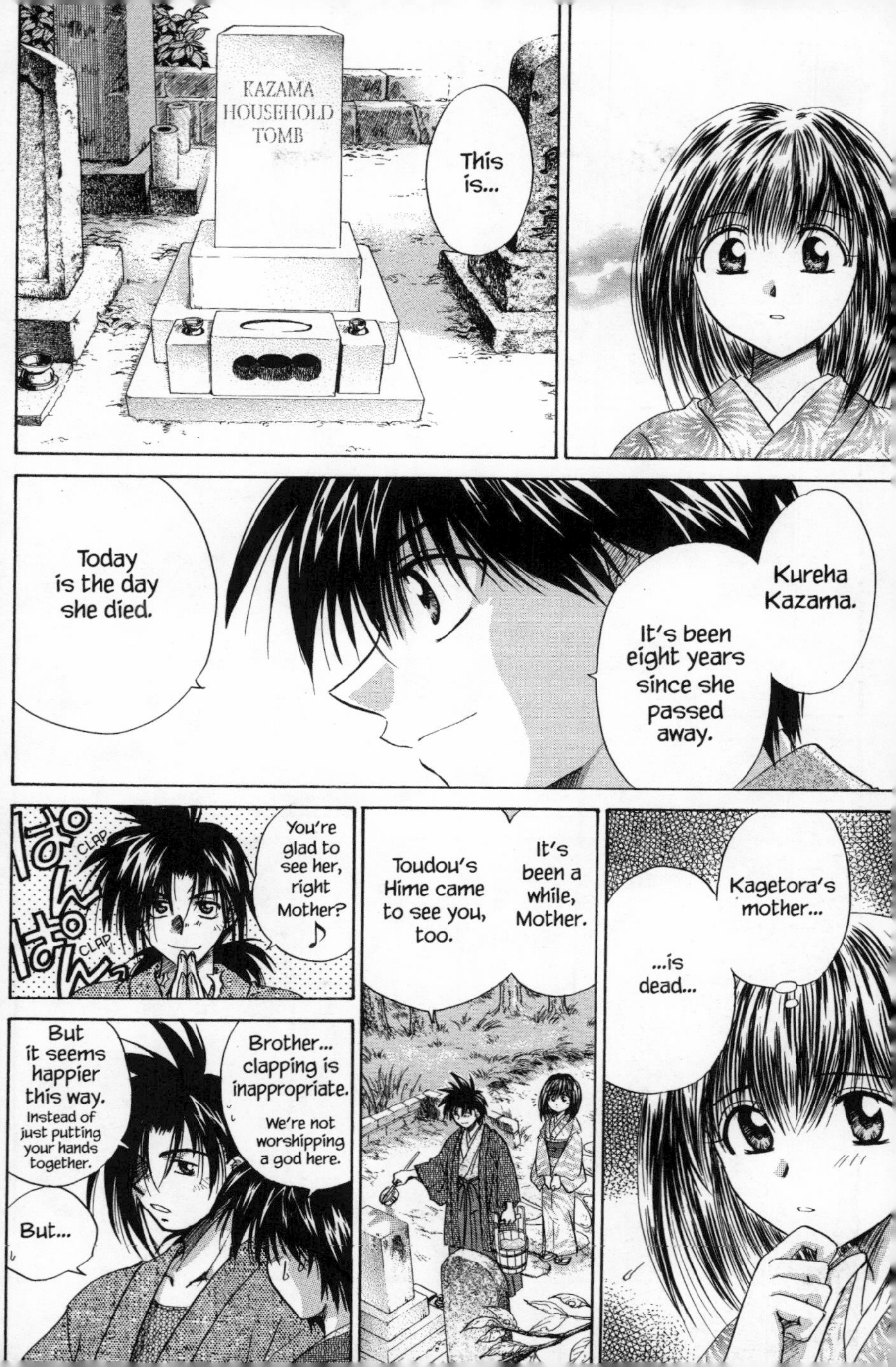
KAZAMA HOUSEHOLD TOMB
This is...
Kureha Kazama.
It's been eight years since she passed away.
Today is the day she died.
Kagetora's mother...
...is dead...
It's been a while, Mother.
Toudou's Hime came to see you, too.
You're glad to see her, right Mother? ♪
CLAP
CLAP
Brother... clapping is inappropriate.
We're not worshipping a god here.
But it seems happier this way.
Instead of just putting your hands together.
But...

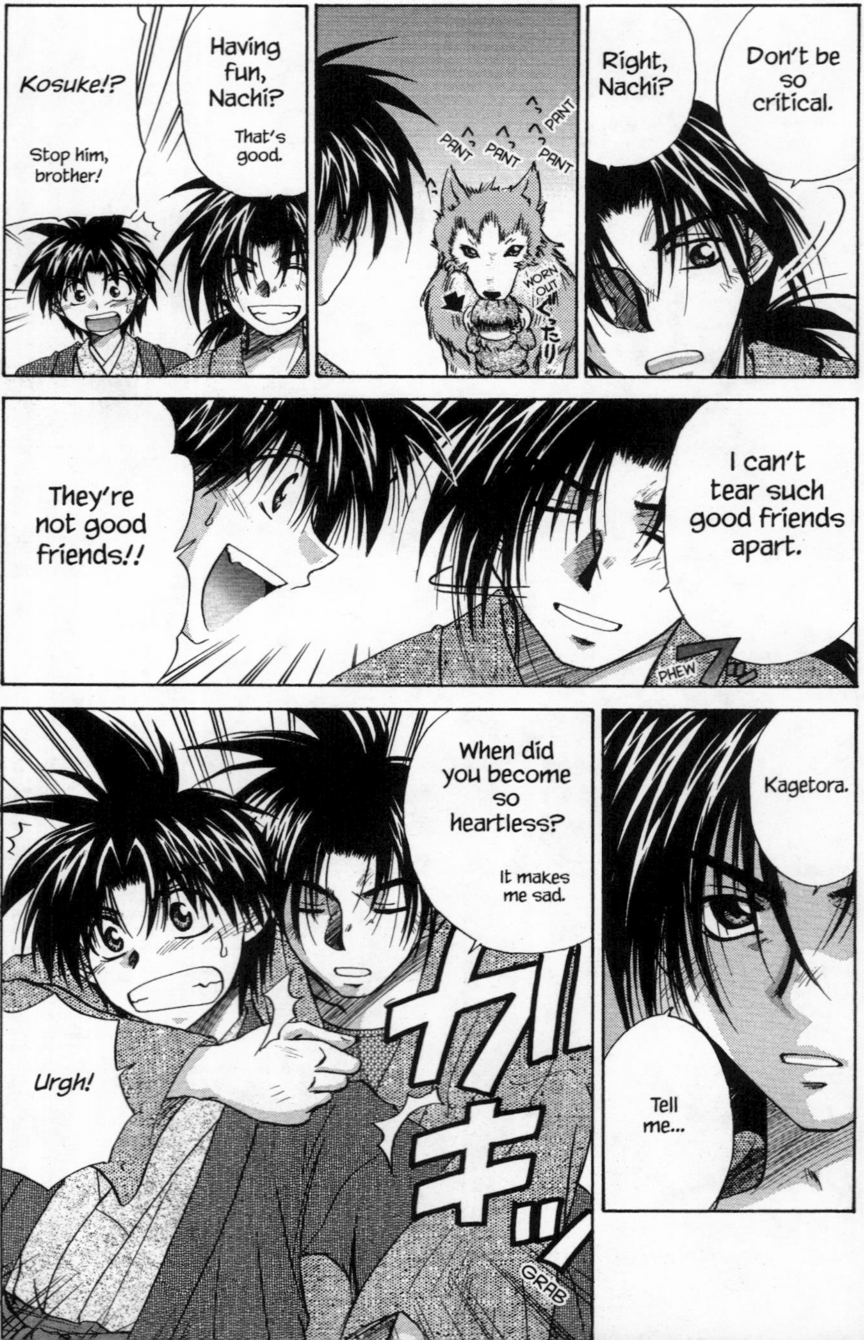
Don't be so critical.
Right, Nachi?
PANT
PANT
PANT
PANT
WORN OUT
ぐったり
Having fun, Nachi?
That's good.
Kosuke!?
Stop him, brother!
I can't tear such good friends apart.
PHEW
They're not good friends!!
Kagetora.
Tell me...
When did you become so heartless?
It makes me sad.
Urgh!
GRAB

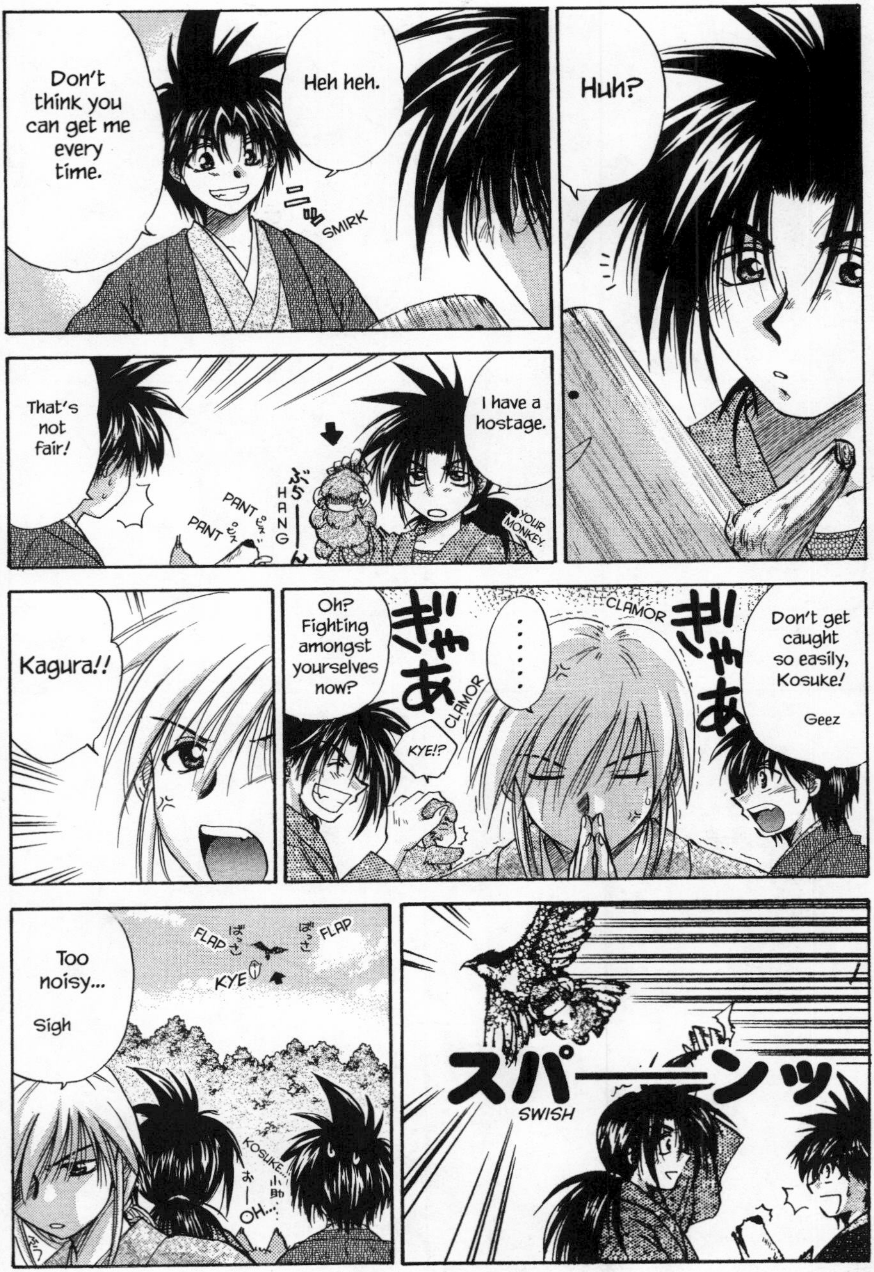
Huh?
Heh heh.
Don't think you can get me every time.
SMIRK
I have a hostage.
YOUR MONKEY.
ぶら——ん
HANG
PANT PANT
That's not fair!
Don't get caught so easily, Kosuke!
Geez
ぎゃあ
CLAMOR
......
ぎゃあ
CLAMOR
Oh? Fighting amongst yourselves now?
KYE!?
Kagura!!
スパーンッ
SWISH
ばっさ
FLAP
ばっさ
FLAP
KYE
Too noisy...
Sigh
小助
KOSUKE...
おー
OH...

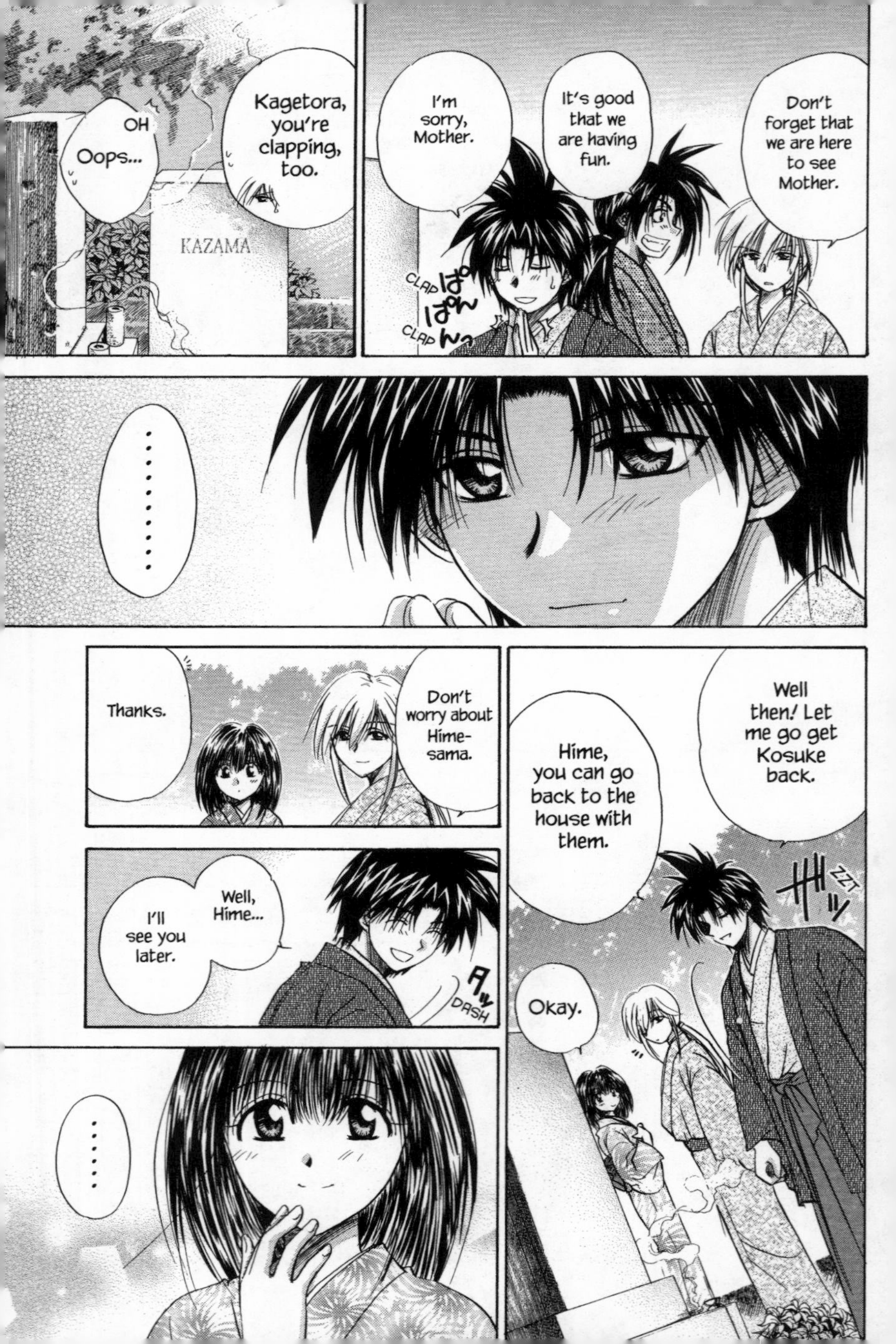
Don't forget that we are here to see Mother.
It's good that we are having fun.
I'm sorry, Mother.
CLAP ぱん
CLAP ぱん
Kagetora, you're clapping, too.
OH
Oops...
KAZAMA
......
Well then! Let me go get Kosuke back.
Hime, you can go back to the house with them.
ZZT
Okay.
Don't worry about Hime-sama.
Thanks.
Well, Hime...
I'll see you later.
DASH
......

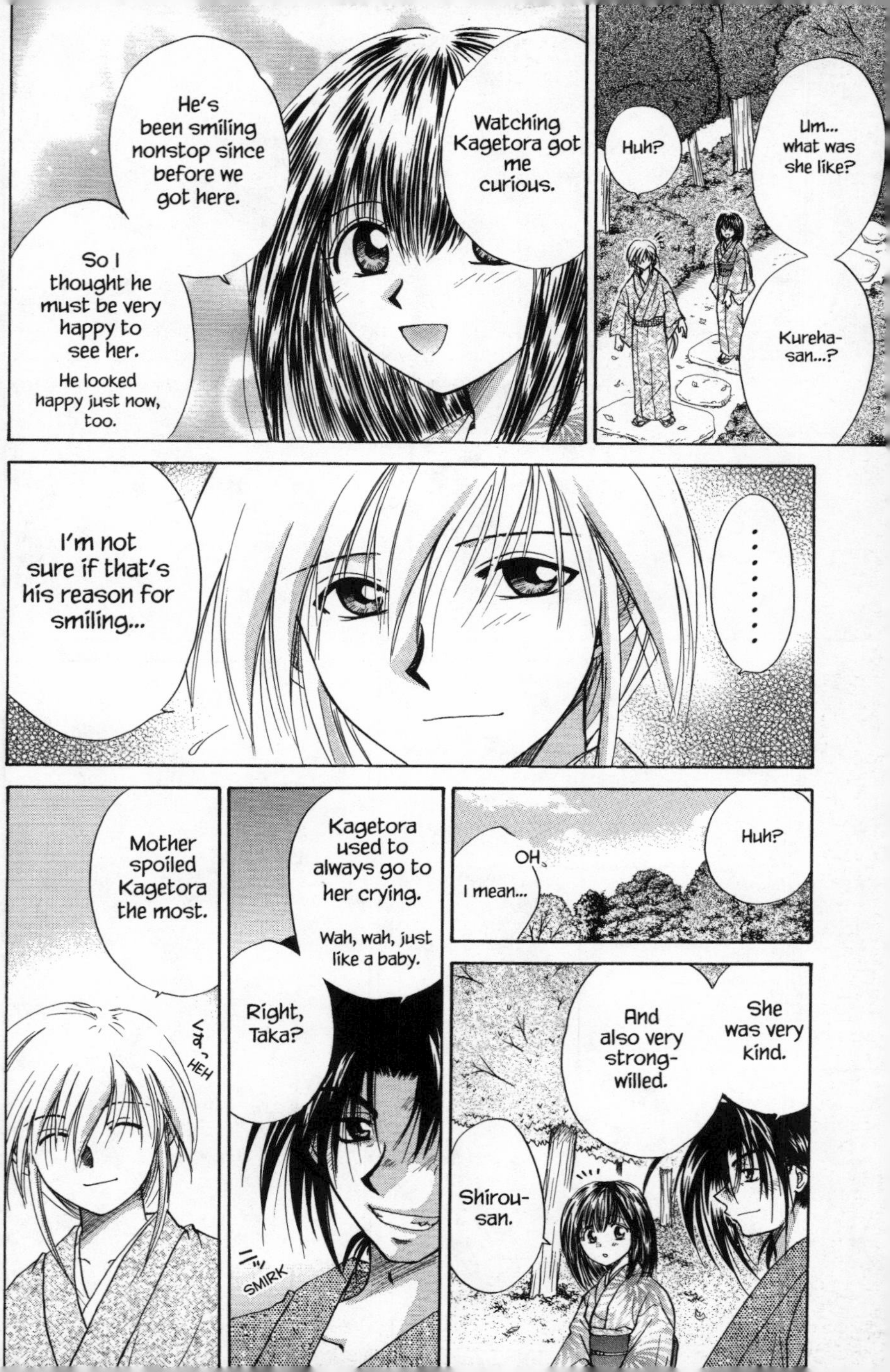
Um... what was she like?
Kureha-san...?
Huh?
Watching Kagetora got me curious.
He's been smiling nonstop since before we got here.
So I thought he must be very happy to see her.
He looked happy just now, too.
......
I'm not sure if that's his reason for smiling...
Huh?
OH,
I mean...
She was very kind.
And also very strong-willed.
Shirou-san.
Kagetora used to always go to her crying.
Wah, wah, just like a baby.
Right, Taka?
SMIRK
Mother spoiled Kagetora the most.
HEH

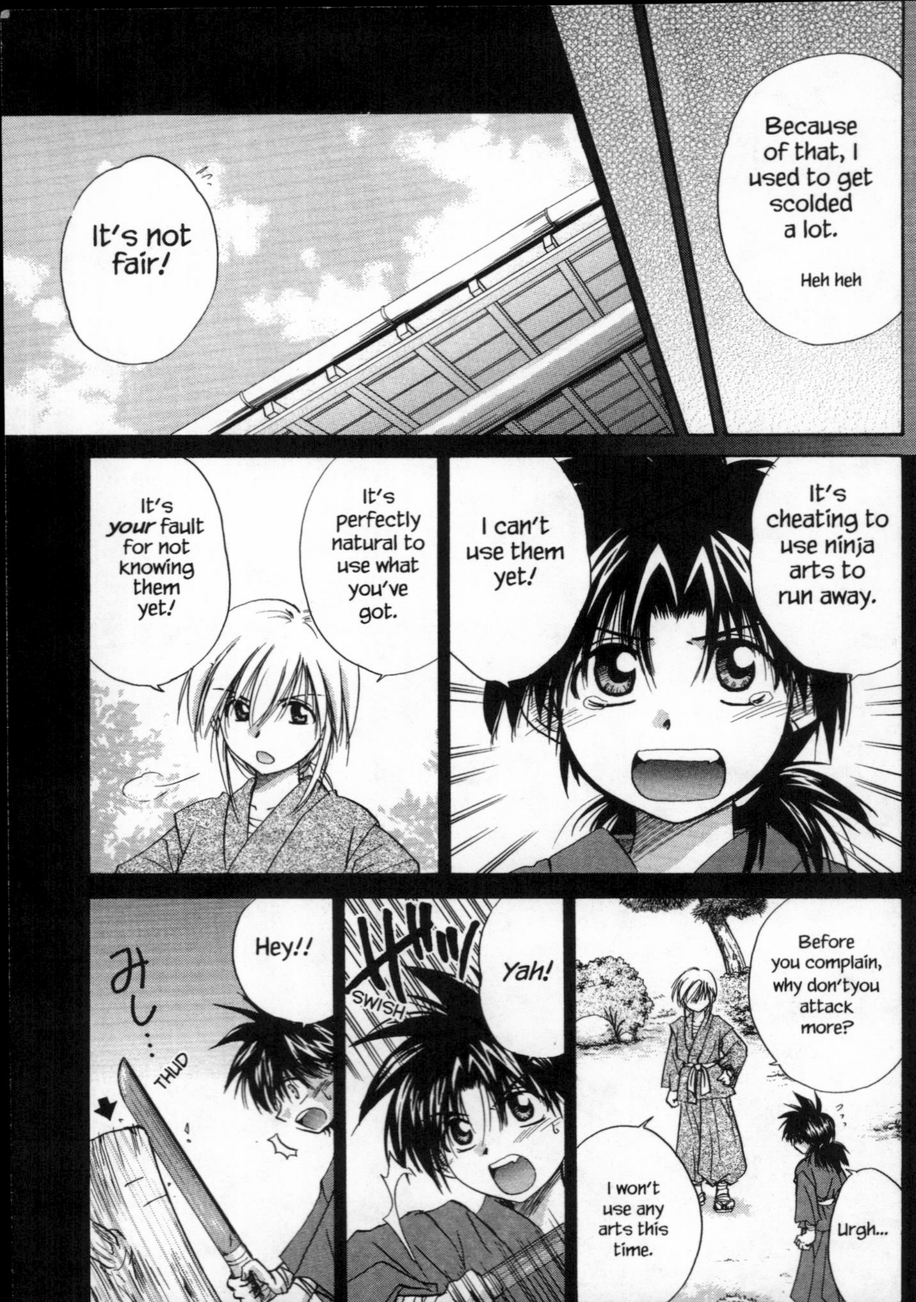
Because of that, I used to get scolded a lot.
Heh heh
It's not fair!
It's cheating to use ninja arts to run away.
I can't use them yet!
It's perfectly natural to use what you've got.
It's *your* fault for not knowing them yet!
Before you complain, why don'tyou attack more?
I won't use any arts this time.
Urgh...
Yah!
SWISH
Hey!!
みし…
THUD

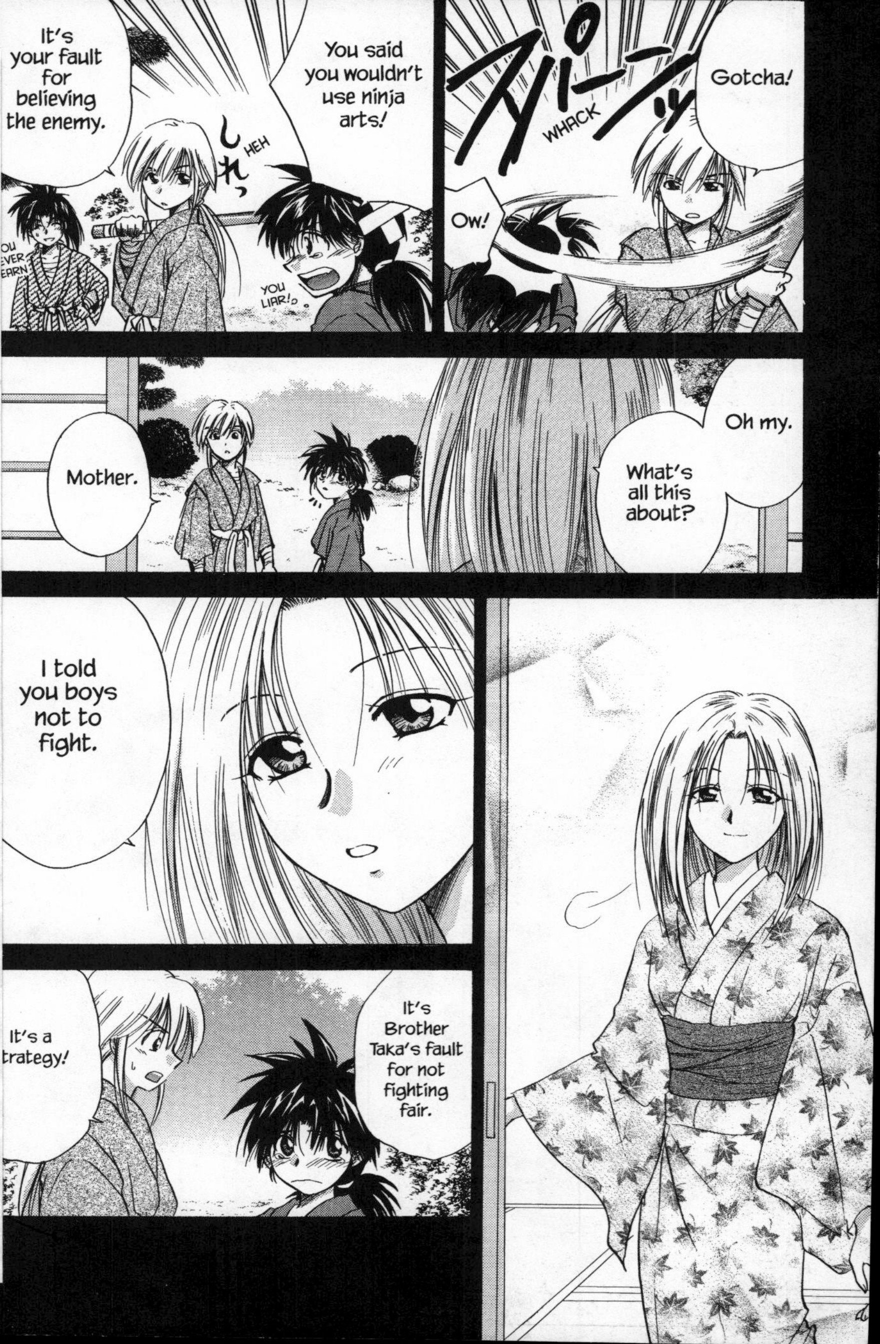

Gotcha!
スパーンッ
WHACK
Ow!
You said you wouldn't use ninja arts!
It's your fault for believing the enemy.
しれっ
HEH
OU EVER EARN
YOU LIAR!
Oh my.
What's all this about?
Mother.
I told you boys not to fight.
It's Brother Taka's fault for not fighting fair.
It's a trategy!

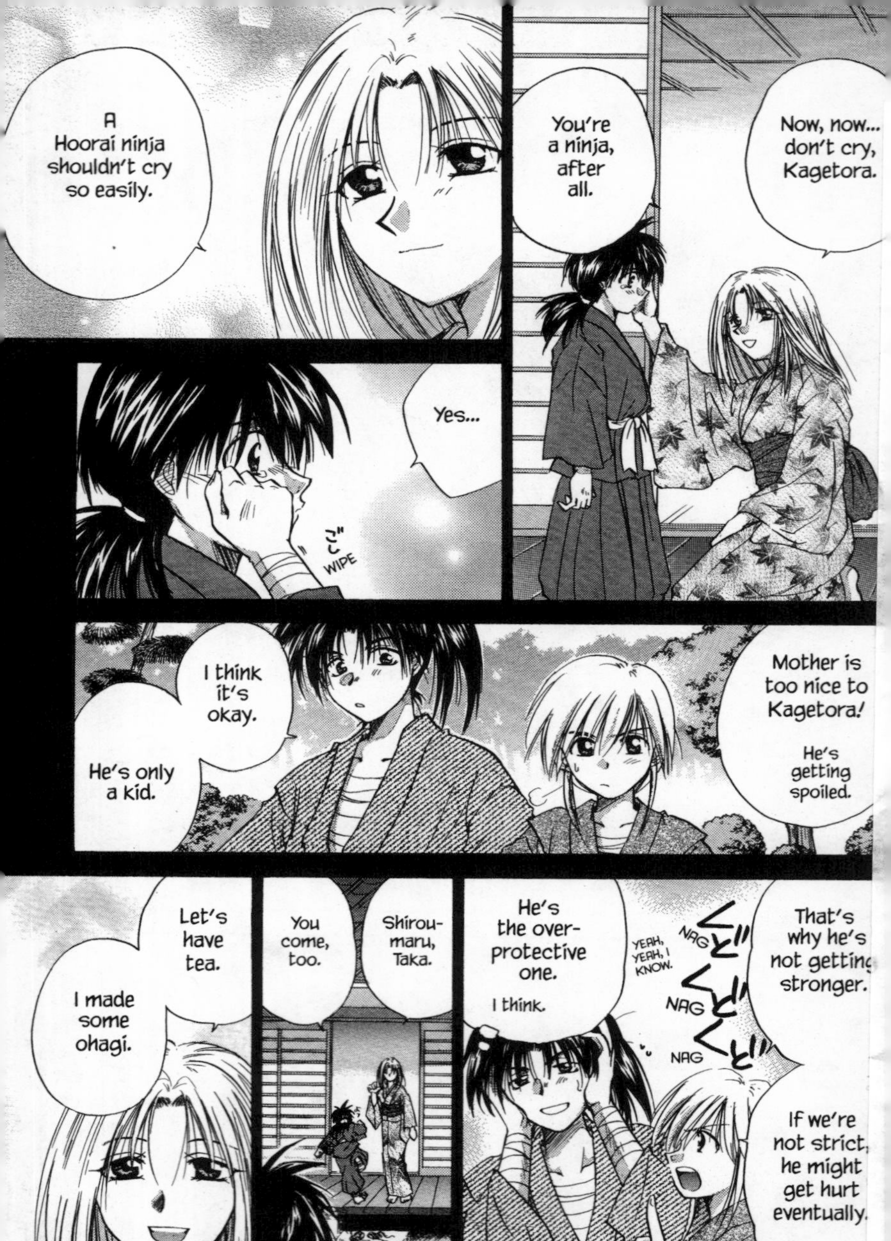
Now, now... don't cry, Kagetora.
You're a ninja, after all.
A Hoorai ninja shouldn't cry so easily.
Yes...
WIPE
Mother is too nice to Kagetora!
He's getting spoiled.
I think it's okay.
He's only a kid.
That's why he's not getting stronger.
NAG
NAG
NAG
YEAH, YEAH, I KNOW.
He's the over-protective one.
I think.
If we're not strict, he might get hurt eventually.
Shirou-maru, Taka.
You come, too.
Let's have tea.
I made some ohagi.

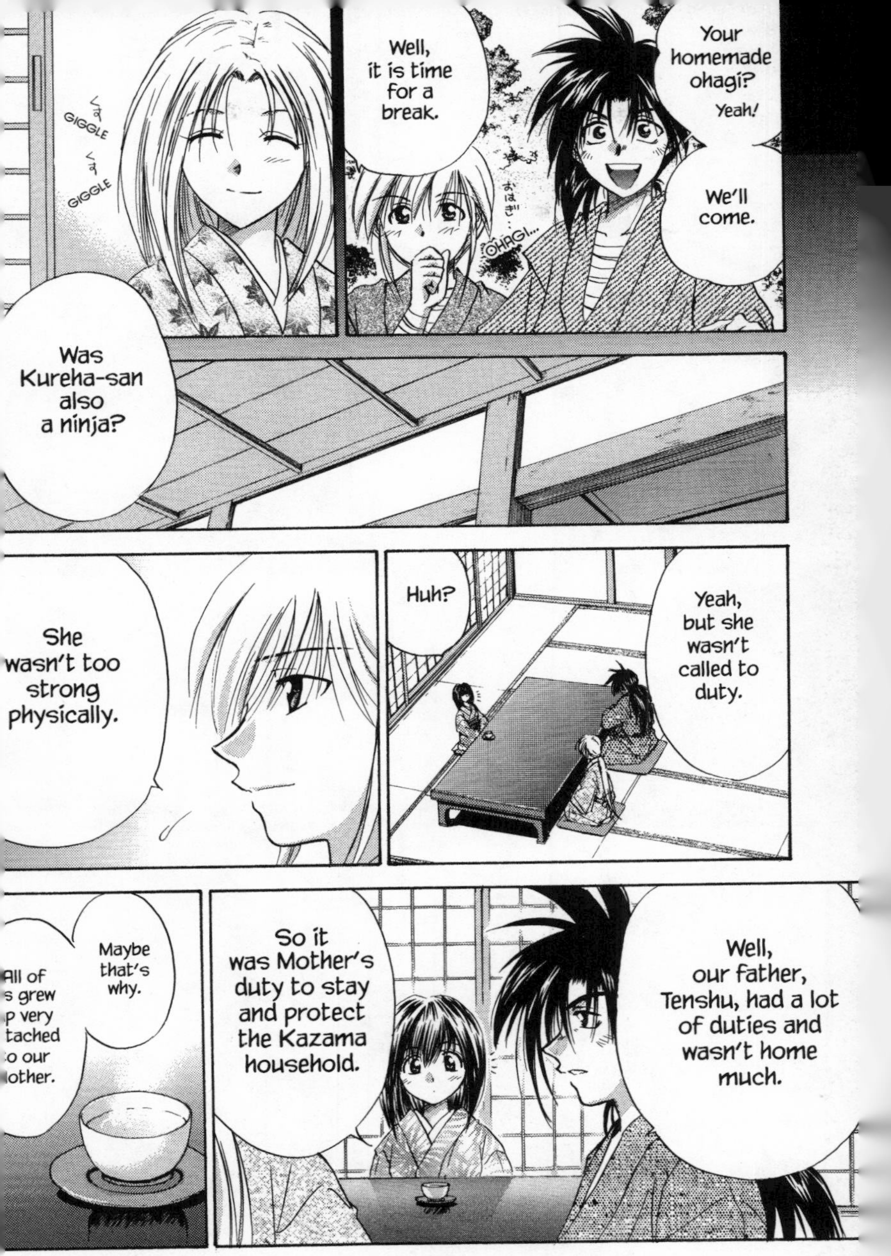

Your homemade ohagi?
Yeah!
We'll come.
Well, it is time for a break.
おはぎ…
OHAGI...
くす
GIGGLE
くす
GIGGLE
Was Kureha-san also a ninja?
Yeah, but she wasn't called to duty.
Huh?
She wasn't too strong physically.
Well, our father, Tenshu, had a lot of duties and wasn't home much.
So it was Mother's duty to stay and protect the Kazama household.
Maybe that's why.
All of s grew p very tached o our other.

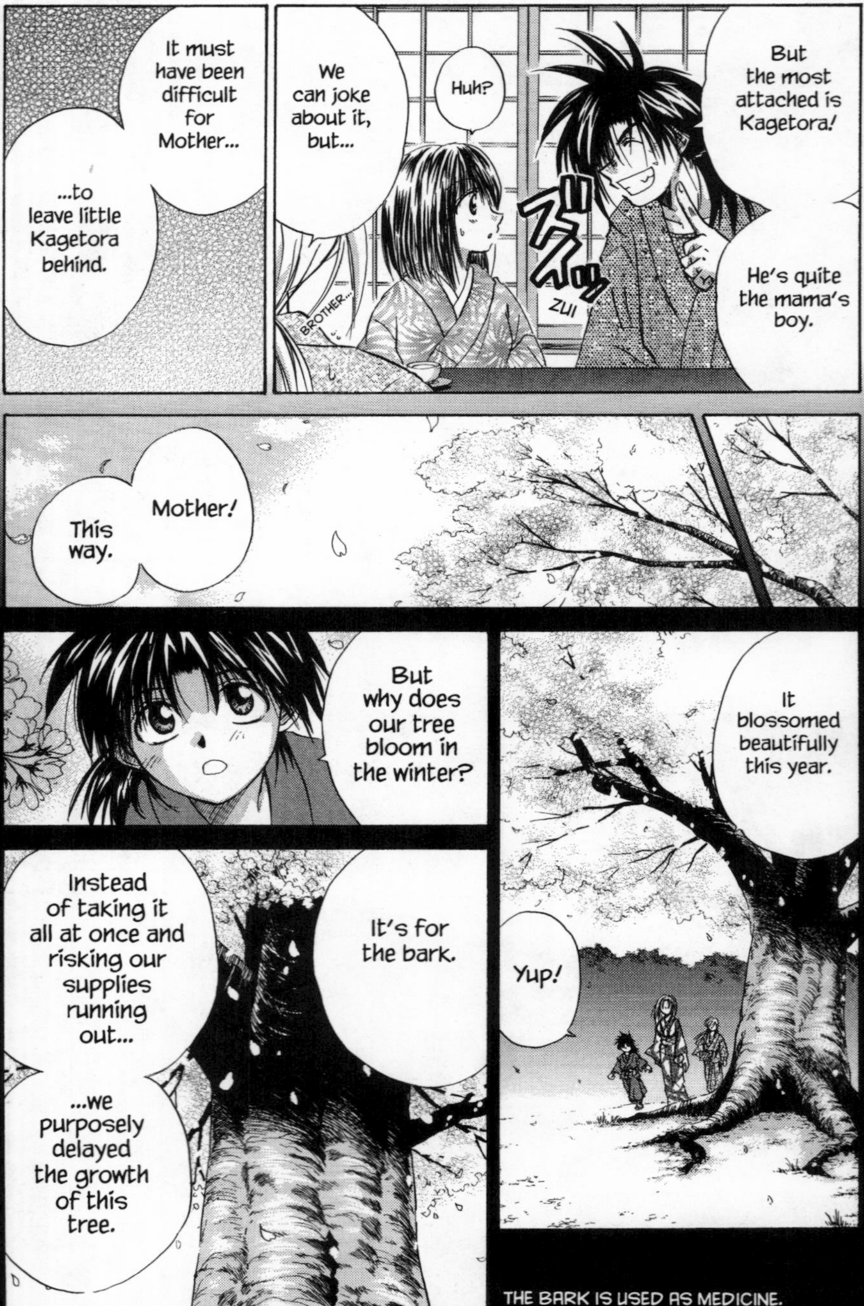
But the most attached is Kagetora!
He's quite the mama's boy.
ZUI
Huh?
We can joke about it, but...
BROTHER...
It must have been difficult for Mother...
...to leave little Kagetora behind.
Mother!
This way.
It blossomed beautifully this year.
Yup!
THE BARK IS USED AS MEDICINE.
But why does our tree bloom in the winter?
It's for the bark.
Instead of taking it all at once and risking our supplies running out...
...we purposely delayed the growth of this tree.

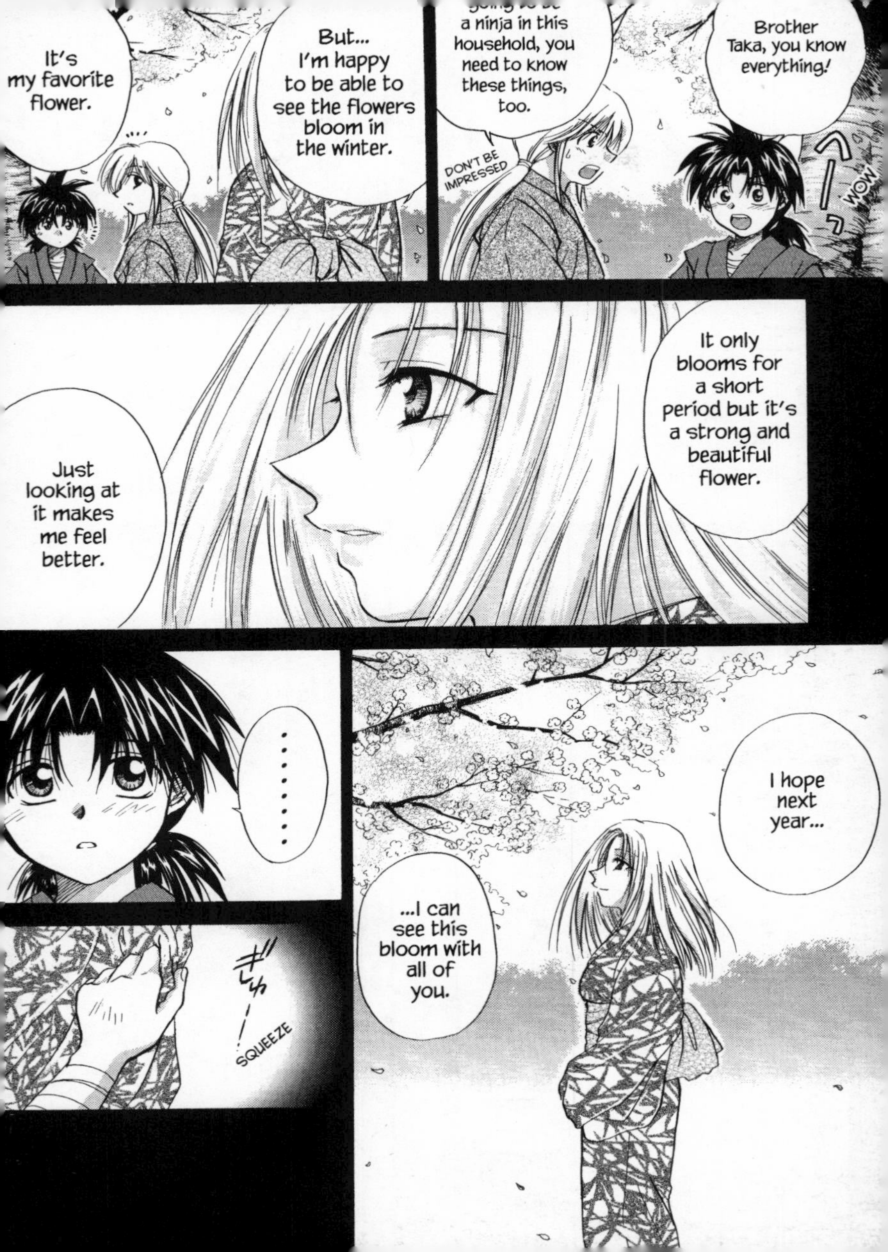
Brother Taka, you know everything!
WOW
a ninja in this household, you need to know these things, too.
DON'T BE IMPRESSED
But... I'm happy to be able to see the flowers bloom in the winter.
It's my favorite flower.
It only blooms for a short period but it's a strong and beautiful flower.
Just looking at it makes me feel better.
I hope next year...
...I can see this bloom with all of you.
....
SQUEEZE

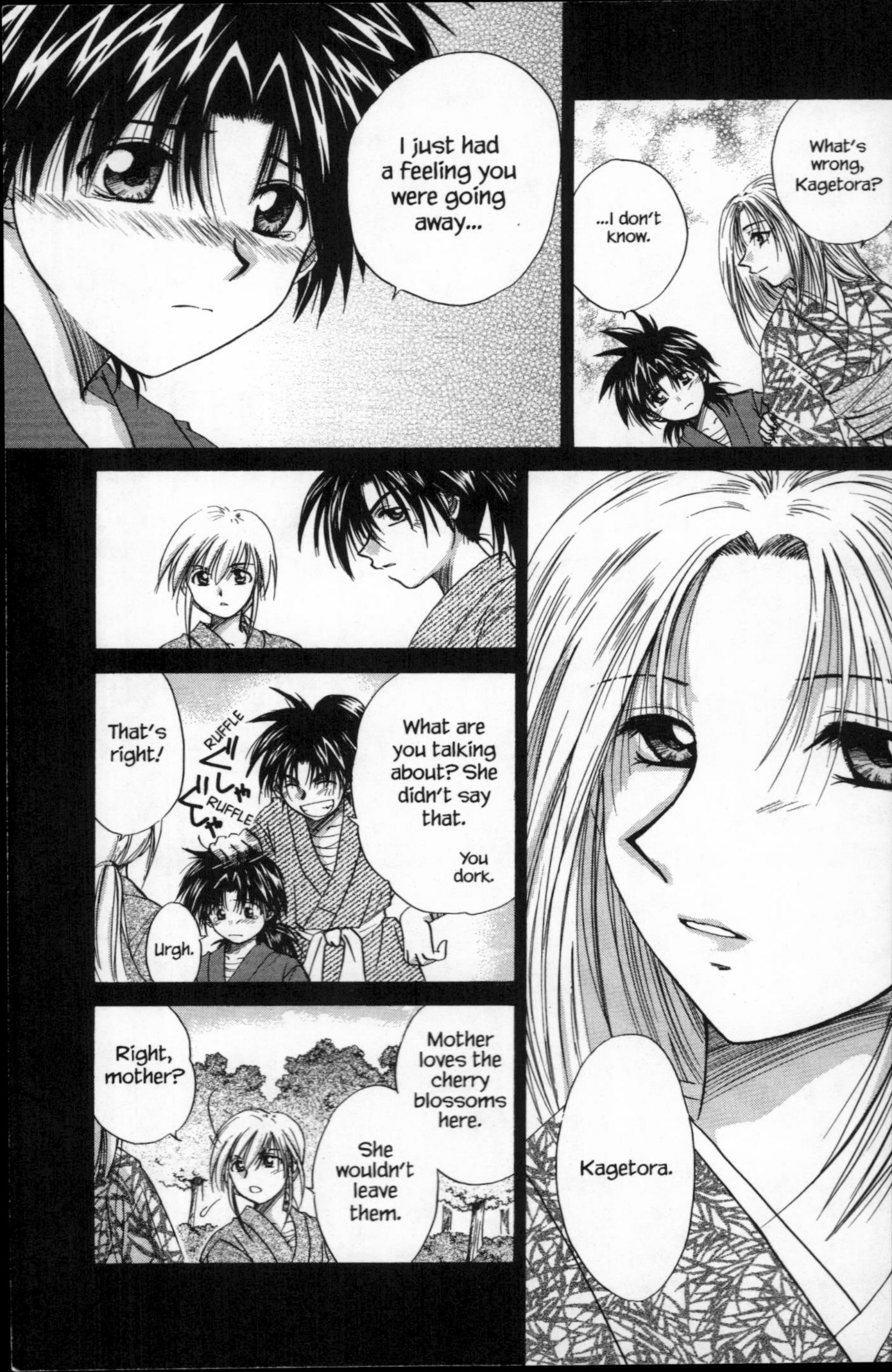
What's wrong, Kagetora?
...I don't know.
I just had a feeling you were going away...
Kagetora.
What are you talking about? She didn't say that.
You dork.
RUFFLE ぐしゃ
RUFFLE ぐしゃ
That's right!
Urgh.
Mother loves the cherry blossoms here.
She wouldn't leave them.
Right, mother?

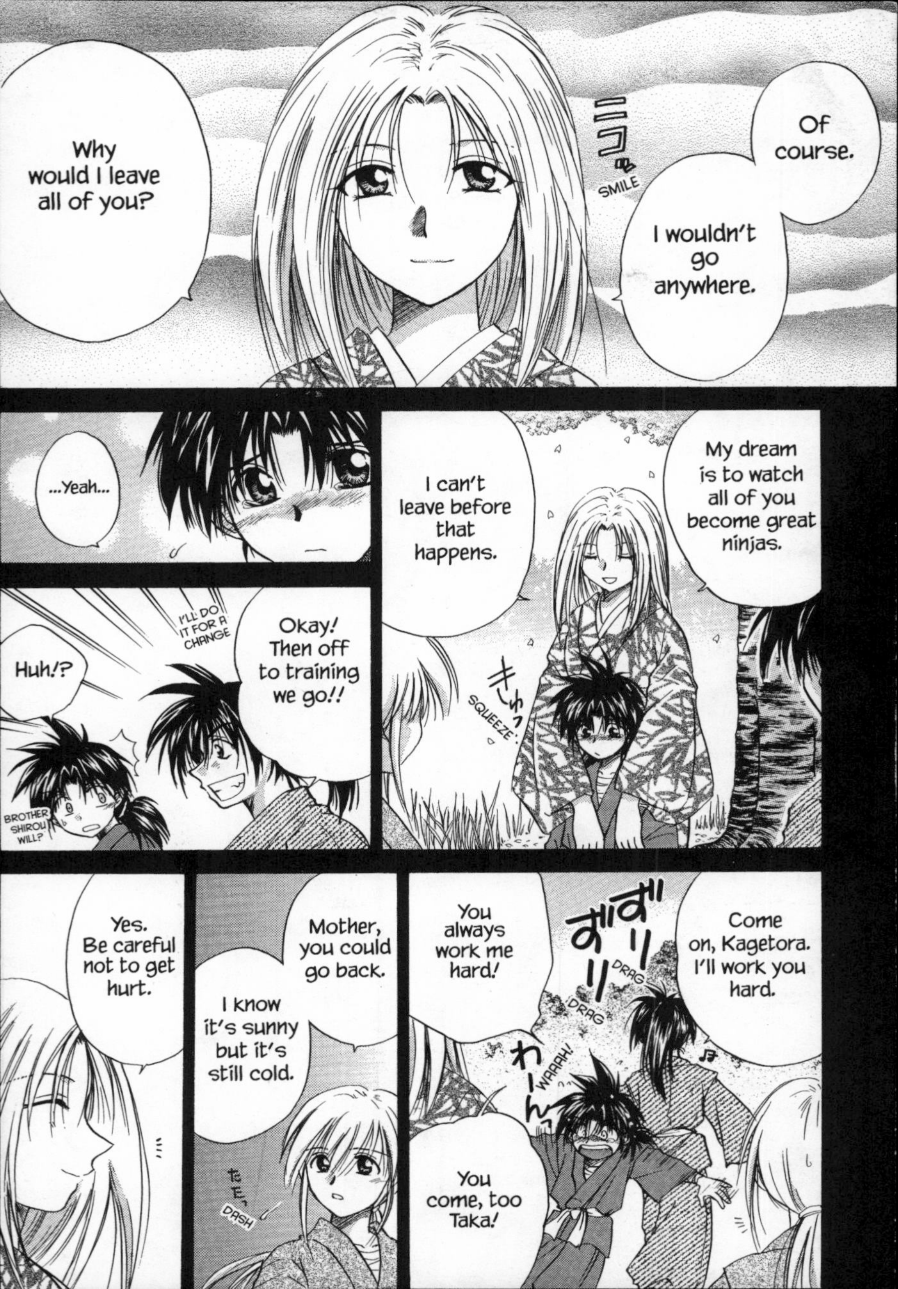
Of course.
I wouldn't go anywhere.
ニコ
SMILE
Why would I leave all of you?
My dream is to watch all of you become great ninjas.
I can't leave before that happens.
きゅっ
SQUEEZE
...Yeah...
Okay! Then off to training we go!!
I'LL DO IT FOR A CHANGE
Huh!?
BROTHER SHIROU WILL?
Come on, Kagetora. I'll work you hard.
ずりずり
DRAG DRAG
You always work me hard!
わーん
WAAAH!
You come, too Taka!
Mother, you could go back.
I know it's sunny but it's still cold.
たた
DASH
Yes. Be careful not to get hurt.

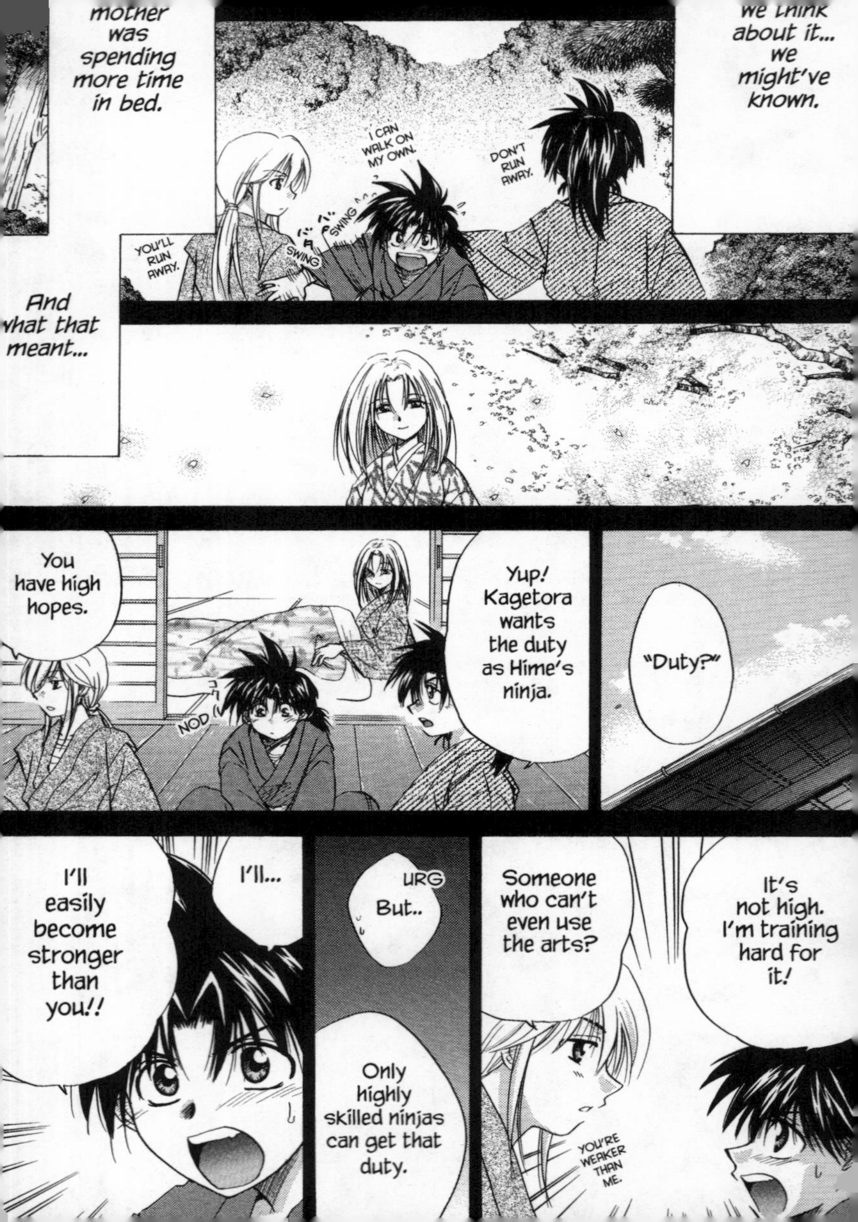
we think about it... we might've known.
DON'T RUN AWAY.
I CAN WALK ON MY OWN.
SWING
SWING
YOU'LL RUN AWAY.
mother was spending more time in bed.
And what that meant...
"Duty?"
Yup! Kagetora wants the duty as Hime's ninja.
NOD
You have high hopes.
It's not high. I'm training hard for it!
Someone who can't even use the arts?
YOU'RE WEAKER THAN ME.
URG
But..
Only highly skilled ninjas can get that duty.
I'll...
I'll easily become stronger than you!!

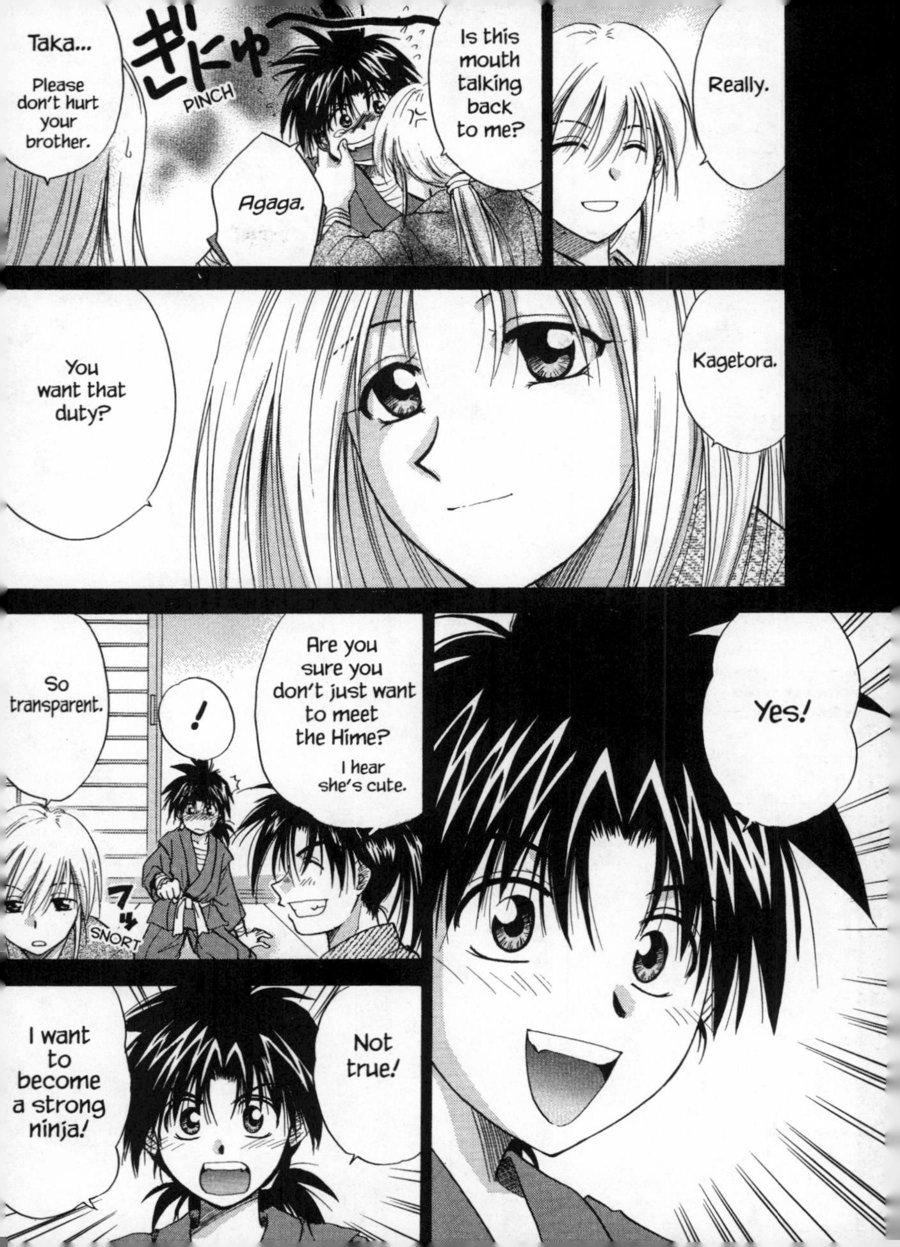
Really.
Is this mouth talking back to me?
ぎにゅ
PINCH
Taka... Please don't hurt your brother.
Agaga.
Kagetora.
You want that duty?
Yes!
Are you sure you don't just want to meet the Hime?
I hear she's cute.
!
So transparent.
SNORT
Not true!
I want to become a strong ninja!

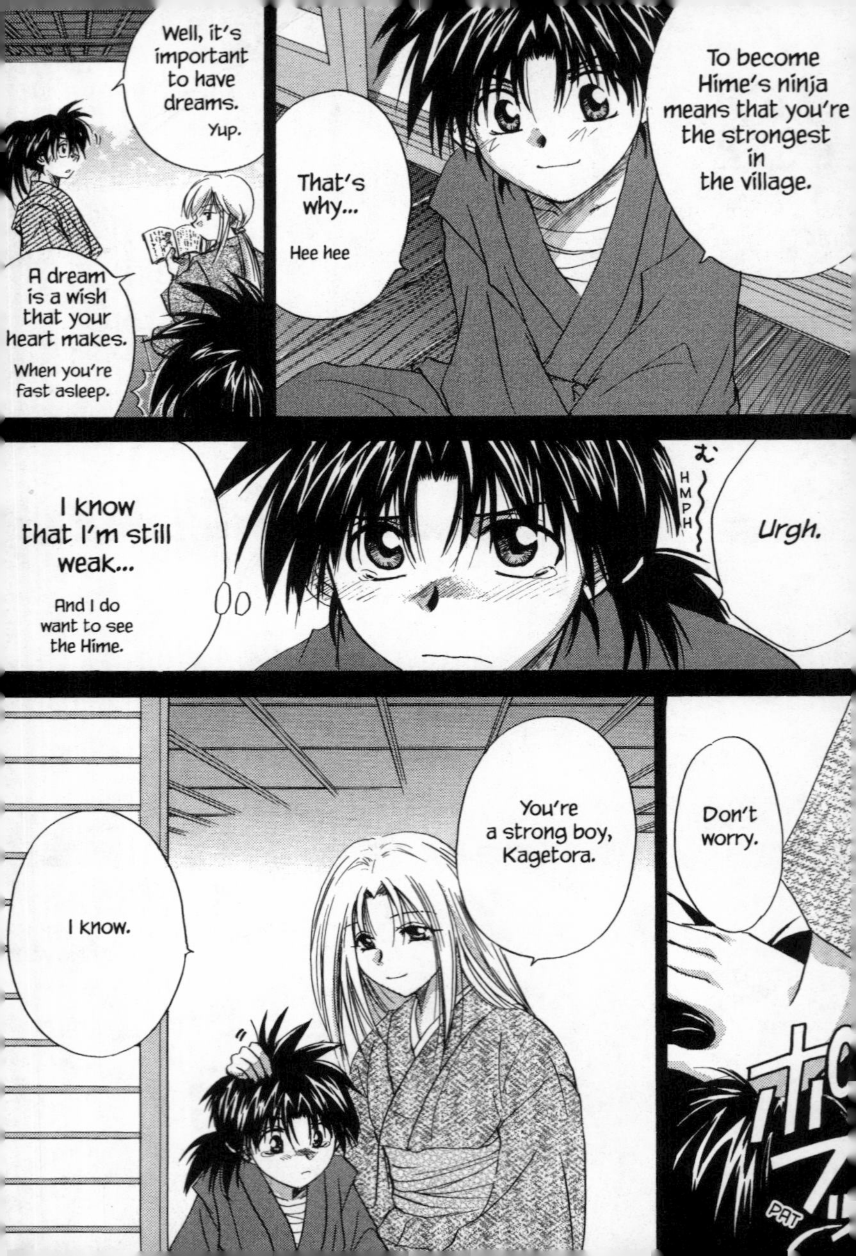
To become Hime's ninja means that you're the strongest in the village.
That's why...
Hee hee
Well, it's important to have dreams.
Yup.
A dream is a wish that your heart makes.
When you're fast asleep.
む
HMPH
Urgh.
I know that I'm still weak...
And I do want to see the Hime.
Don't worry.
PAT
You're a strong boy, Kagetora.
I know.

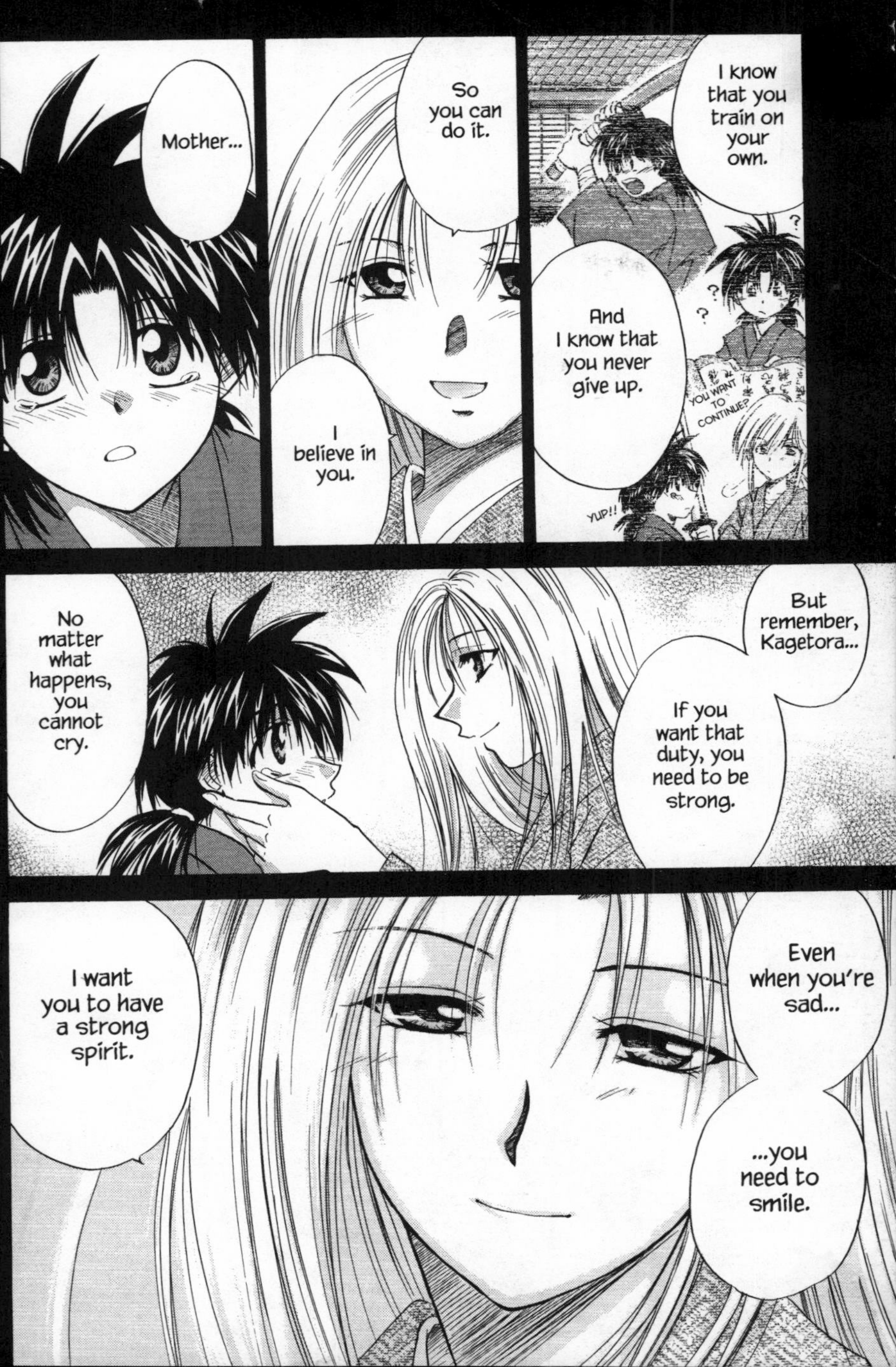
I know that you train on your own.
And I know that you never give up.
YOU WANT TO CONTINUE?
YUP!!
So you can do it.
I believe in you.
Mother...
But remember, Kagetora...
If you want that duty, you need to be strong.
No matter what happens, you cannot cry.
Even when you're sad...
...you need to smile.
I want you to have a strong spirit.

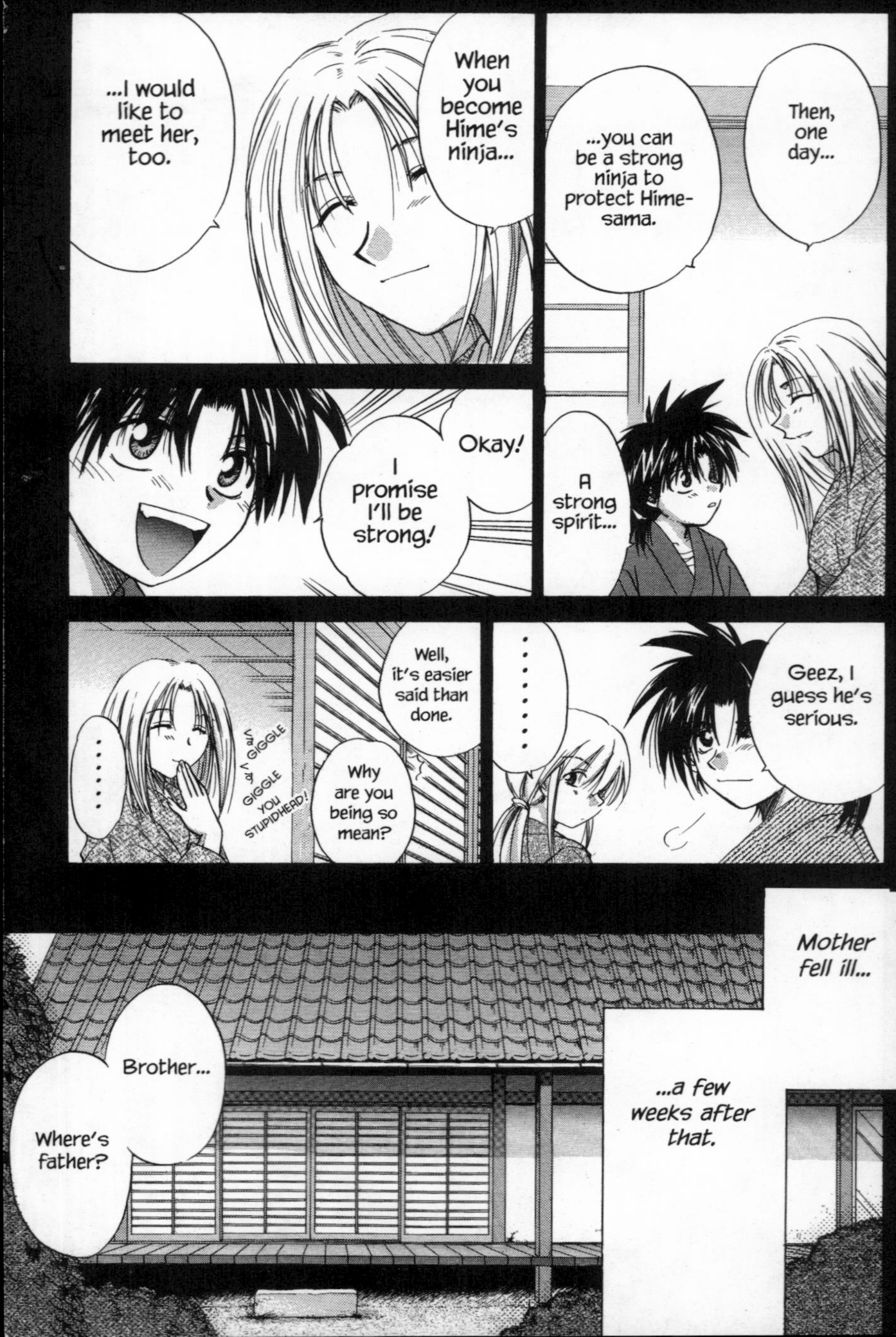
Then, one day...
...you can be a strong ninja to protect Hime-sama.
A strong spirit...
When you become Hime's ninja...
...I would like to meet her, too.
Okay!
I promise I'll be strong!
Geez, I guess he's serious.
......
Well, it's easier said than done.
Why are you being so mean?
GIGGLE GIGGLE
YOU STUPIDHEAD!
......
Mother fell ill...
...a few weeks after that.
Brother...
Where's father?

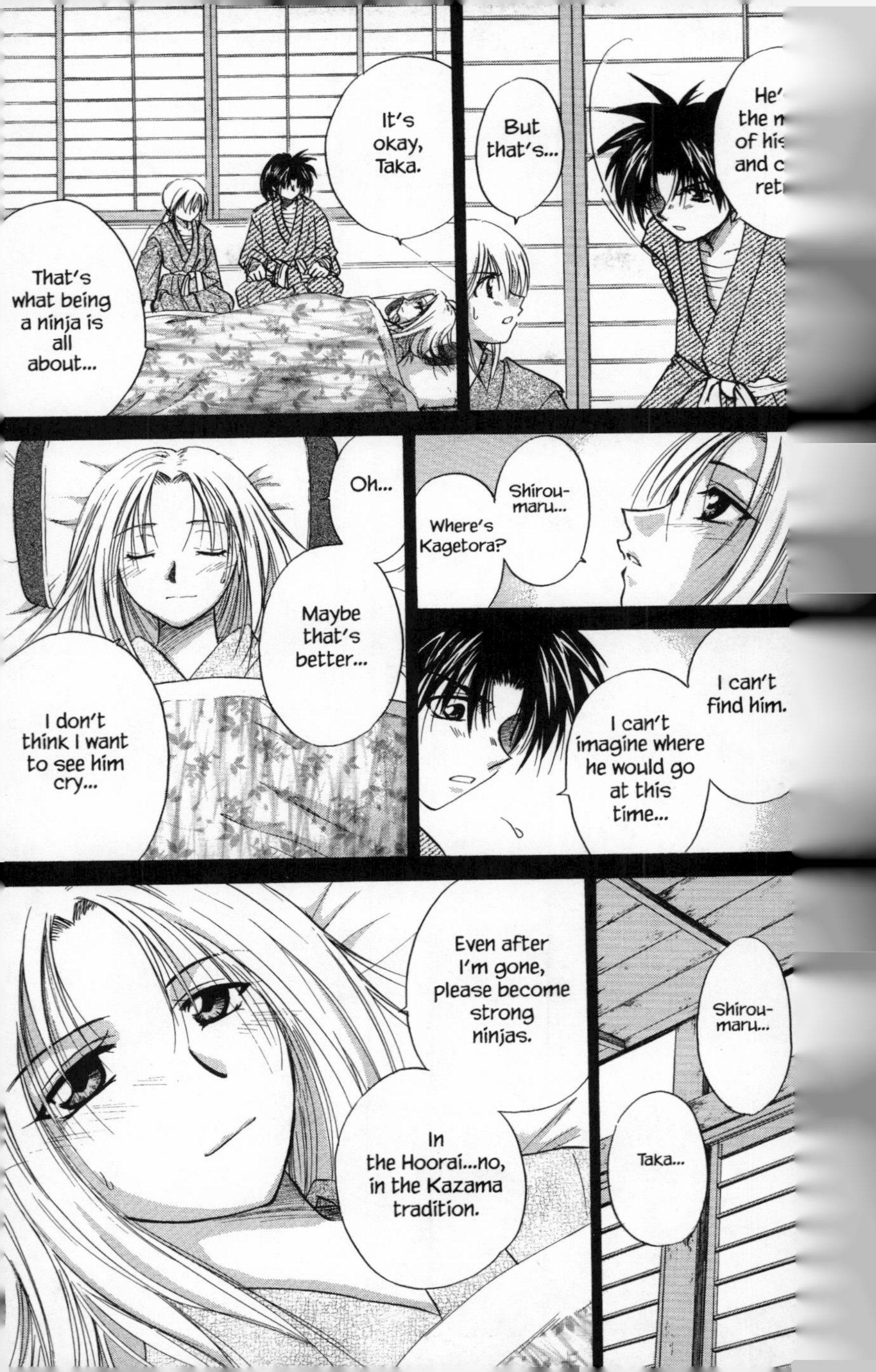
But that's...
It's okay, Taka.
That's what being a ninja is all about...
Shirou-maru...
Where's Kagetora?
I can't find him.
I can't imagine where he would go at this time...
Oh...
Maybe that's better...
I don't think I want to see him cry...
Shirou-maru...
Taka...
Even after I'm gone, please become strong ninjas.
In the Hoorai...no, in the Kazama tradition.

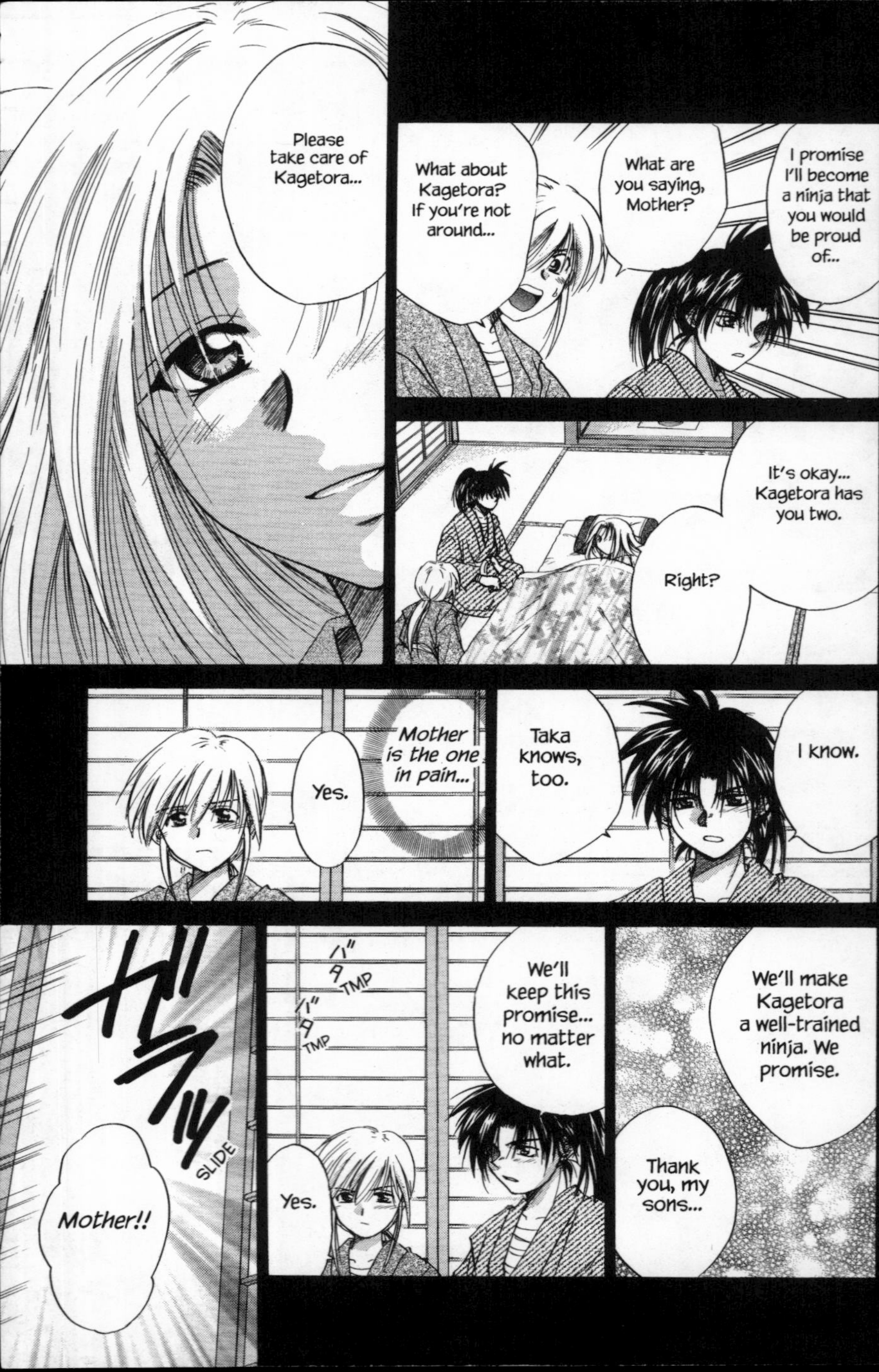
I promise I'll become a ninja that you would be proud of...
What are you saying, Mother?
What about Kagetora? If you're not around...
It's okay... Kagetora has you two.
Right?
Please take care of Kagetora...
I know.
Taka knows, too.
Mother is the one in pain...
Yes.
We'll make Kagetora a well-trained ninja. We promise.
Thank you, my sons...
We'll keep this promise... no matter what.
バタ TMP
バタ TMP
Yes.
ガラッ SLIDE
Mother!!

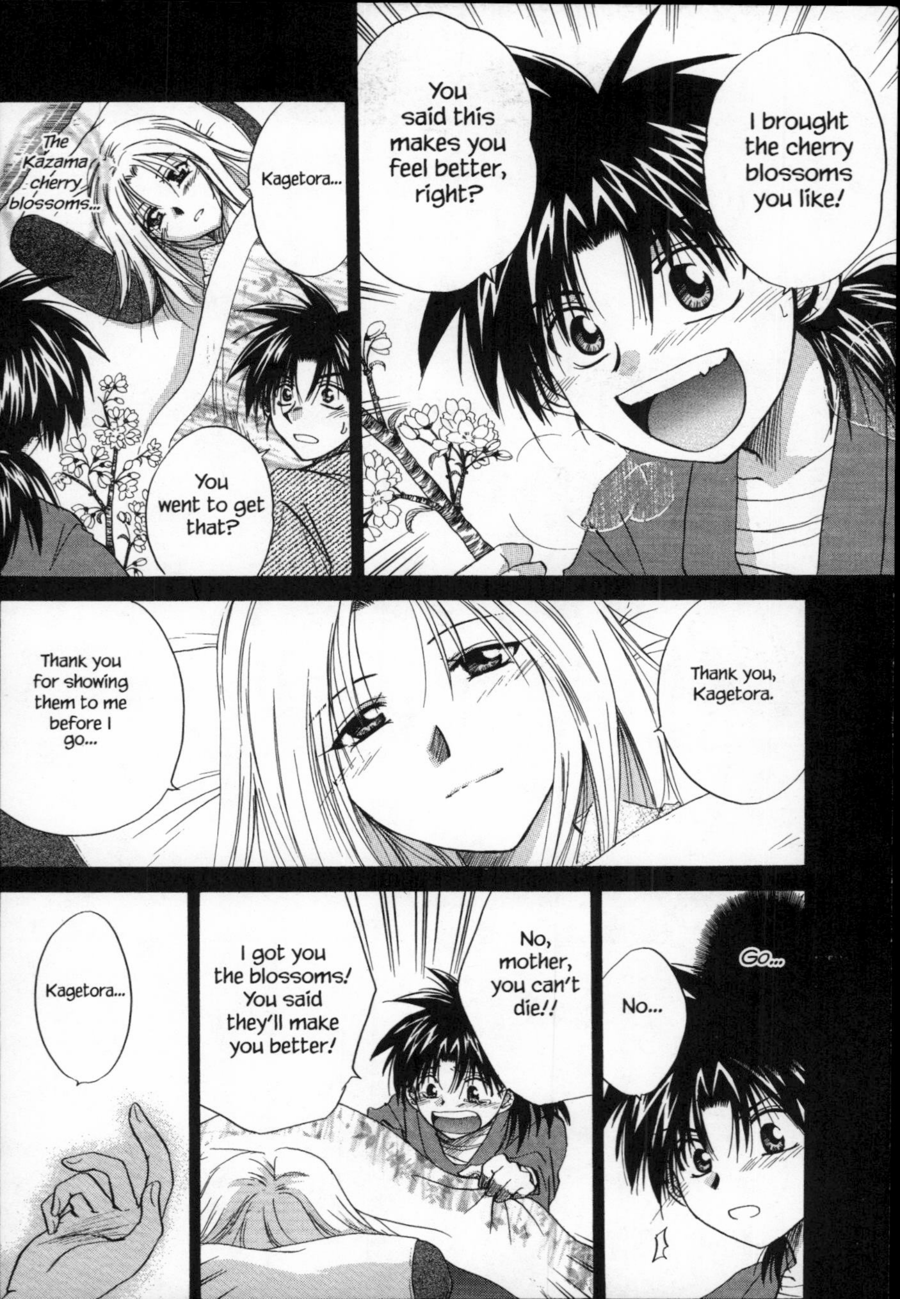

I brought the cherry blossoms you like!
You said this makes you feel better, right?
Kagetora...
The Kazama cherry blossoms...
You went to get that?
Thank you, Kagetora.
Thank you for showing them to me before I go...
Go...
No...
No, mother, you can't die!!
I got you the blossoms! You said they'll make you better!
Kagetora...

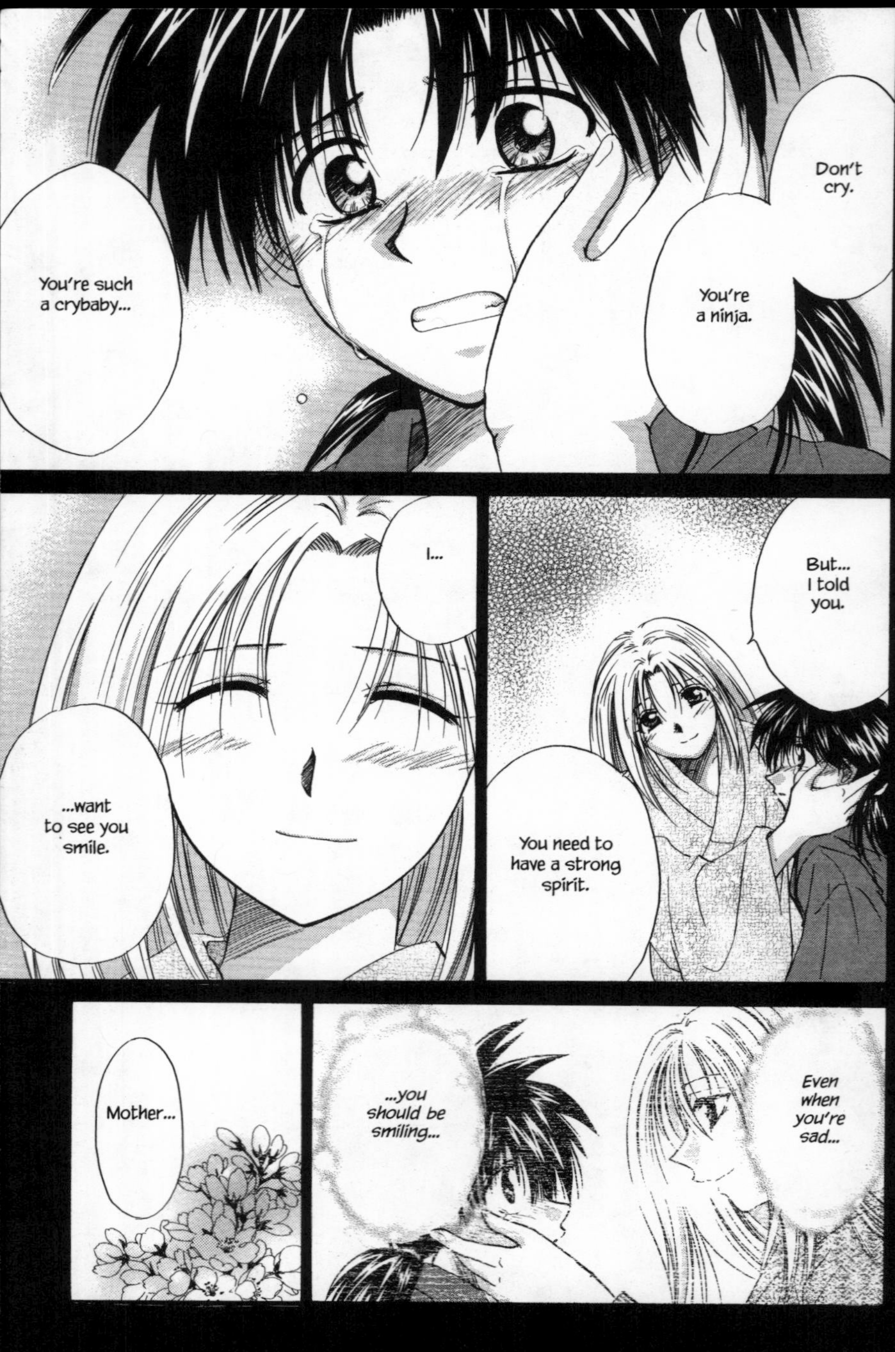
Don't cry.
You're a ninja.
You're such a crybaby...
But... I told you.
You need to have a strong spirit.
I...
...want to see you smile.
Even when you're sad...
...you should be smiling...
Mother...

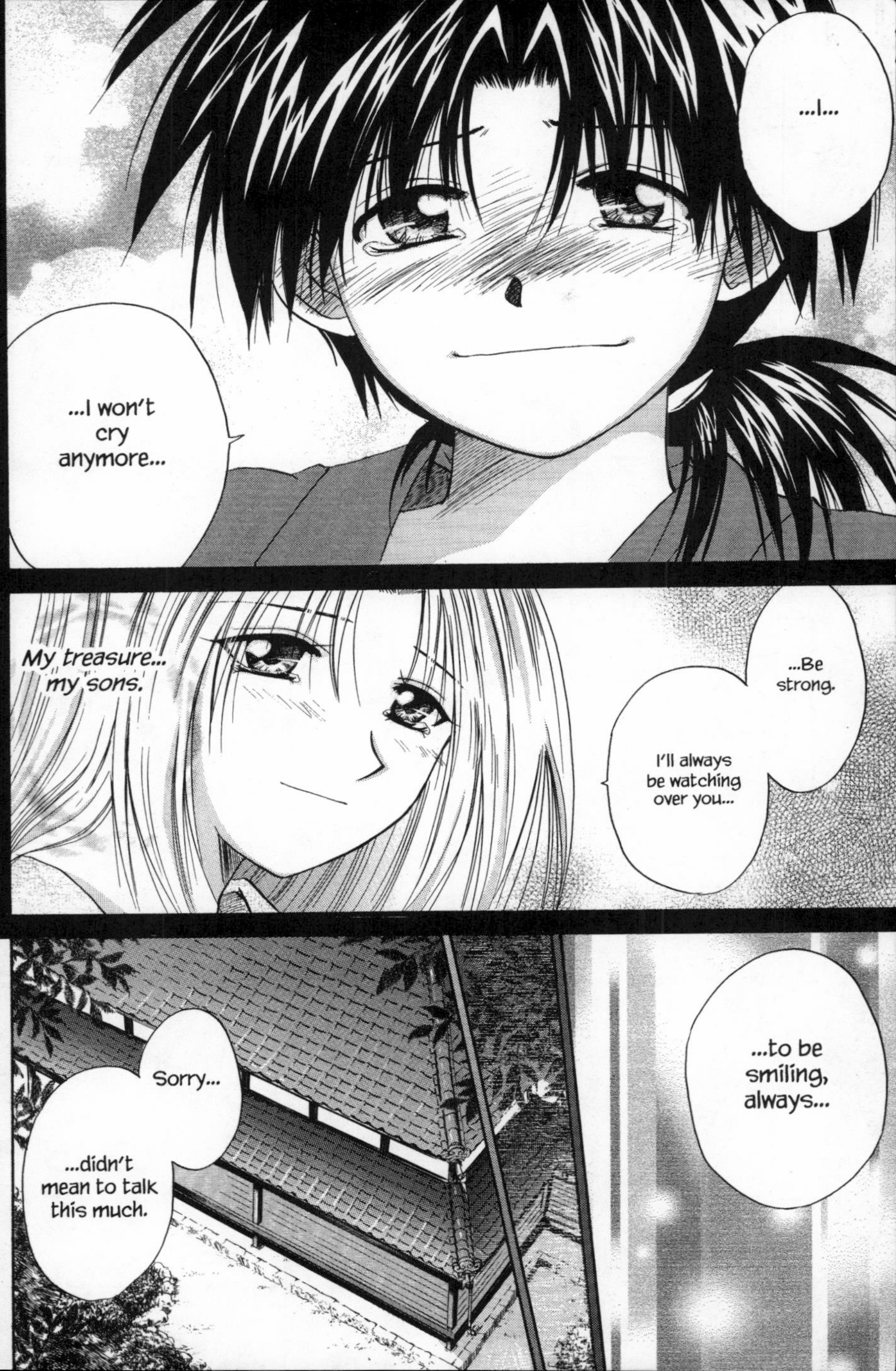
...I...
...I won't cry anymore...
...Be strong.
I'll always be watching over you...
My treasure... my sons.
...to be smiling, always...
Sorry...
...didn't mean to talk this much.

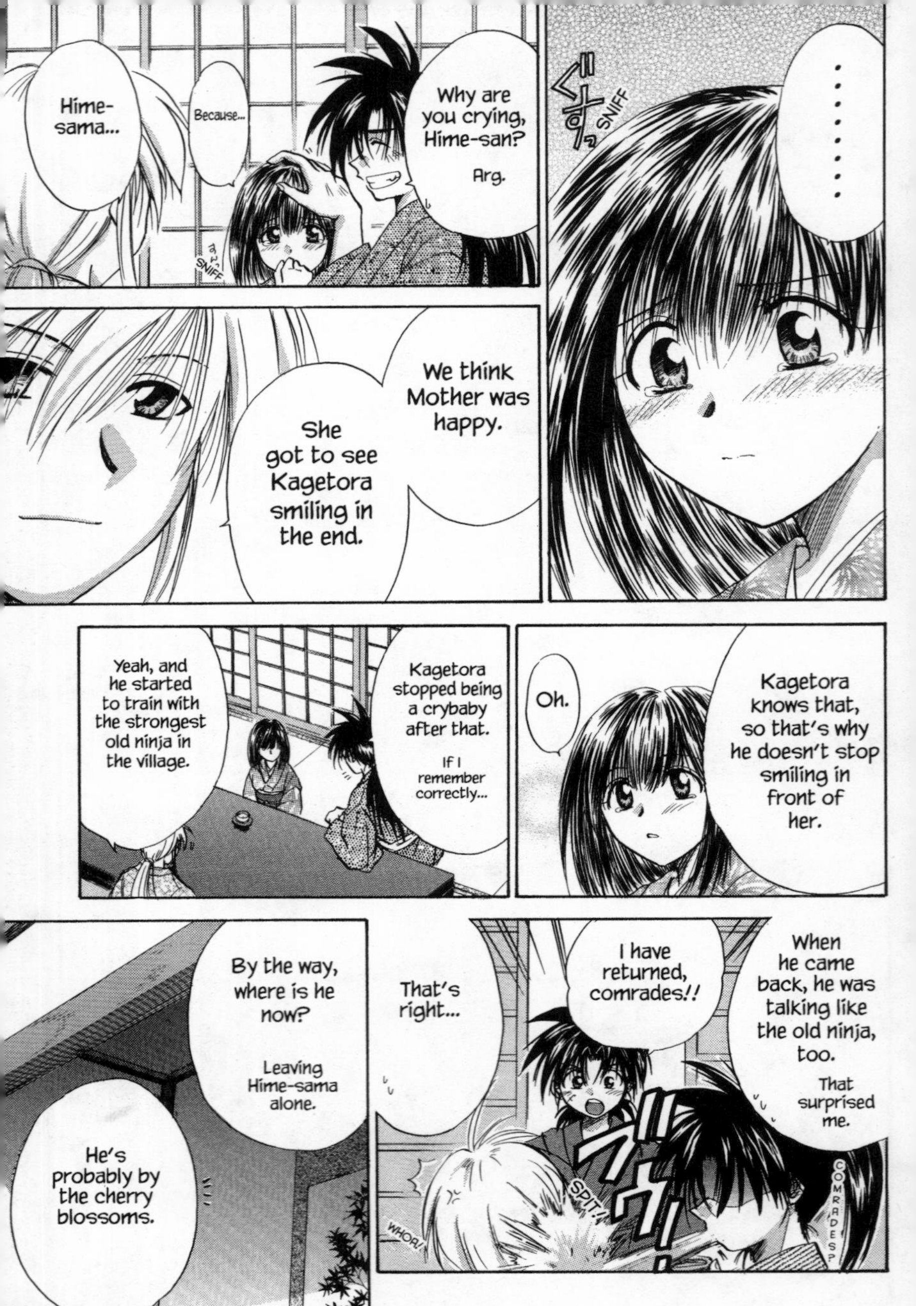
......
SNIFF
Why are you crying, Hime-san?
Arg.
Because...
Hime-sama...
SNIFF
We think Mother was happy.
She got to see Kagetora smiling in the end.
Kagetora knows that, so that's why he doesn't stop smiling in front of her.
Oh.
Kagetora stopped being a crybaby after that.
If I remember correctly...
Yeah, and he started to train with the strongest old ninja in the village.
When he came back, he was talking like the old ninja, too.
That surprised me.
I have returned, comrades!!
COMRADES?
SPIT!
WHOA!
That's right...
By the way, where is he now?
Leaving Hime-sama alone.
He's probably by the cherry blossoms.

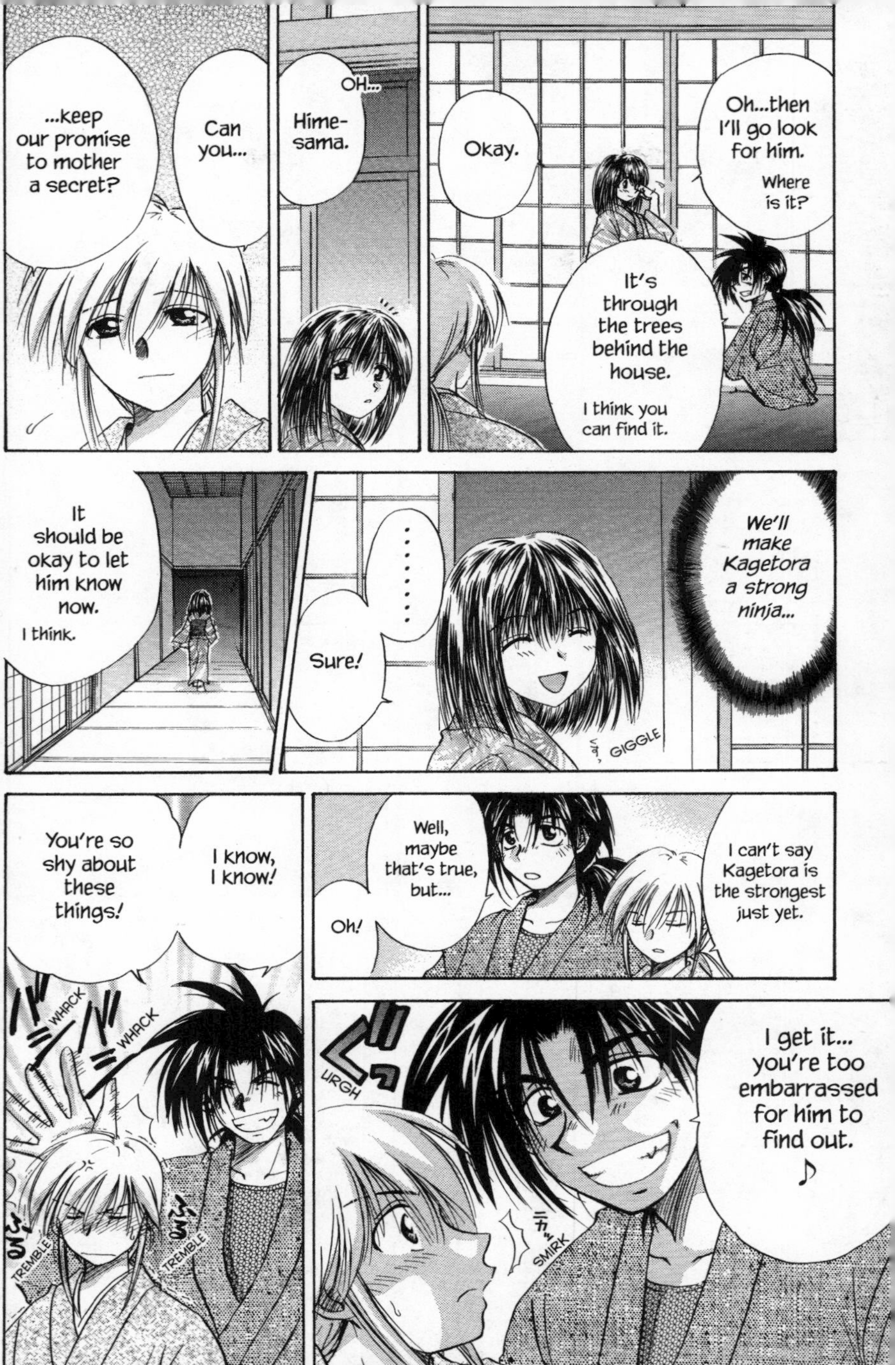
Oh...then I'll go look for him.
Where is it?
It's through the trees behind the house.
I think you can find it.
Okay.
OH...
Hime-sama.
Can you...
...keep our promise to mother a secret?
We'll make Kagetora a strong ninja...
......
Sure!
GIGGLE
It should be okay to let him know now.
I think.
I can't say Kagetora is the strongest just yet.
Well, maybe that's true, but...
Oh!
I get it... you're too embarrassed for him to find out. ♪
URGH
SMIRK
I know, I know!
You're so shy about these things!
WHACK
WHACK
TREMBLE
TREMBLE

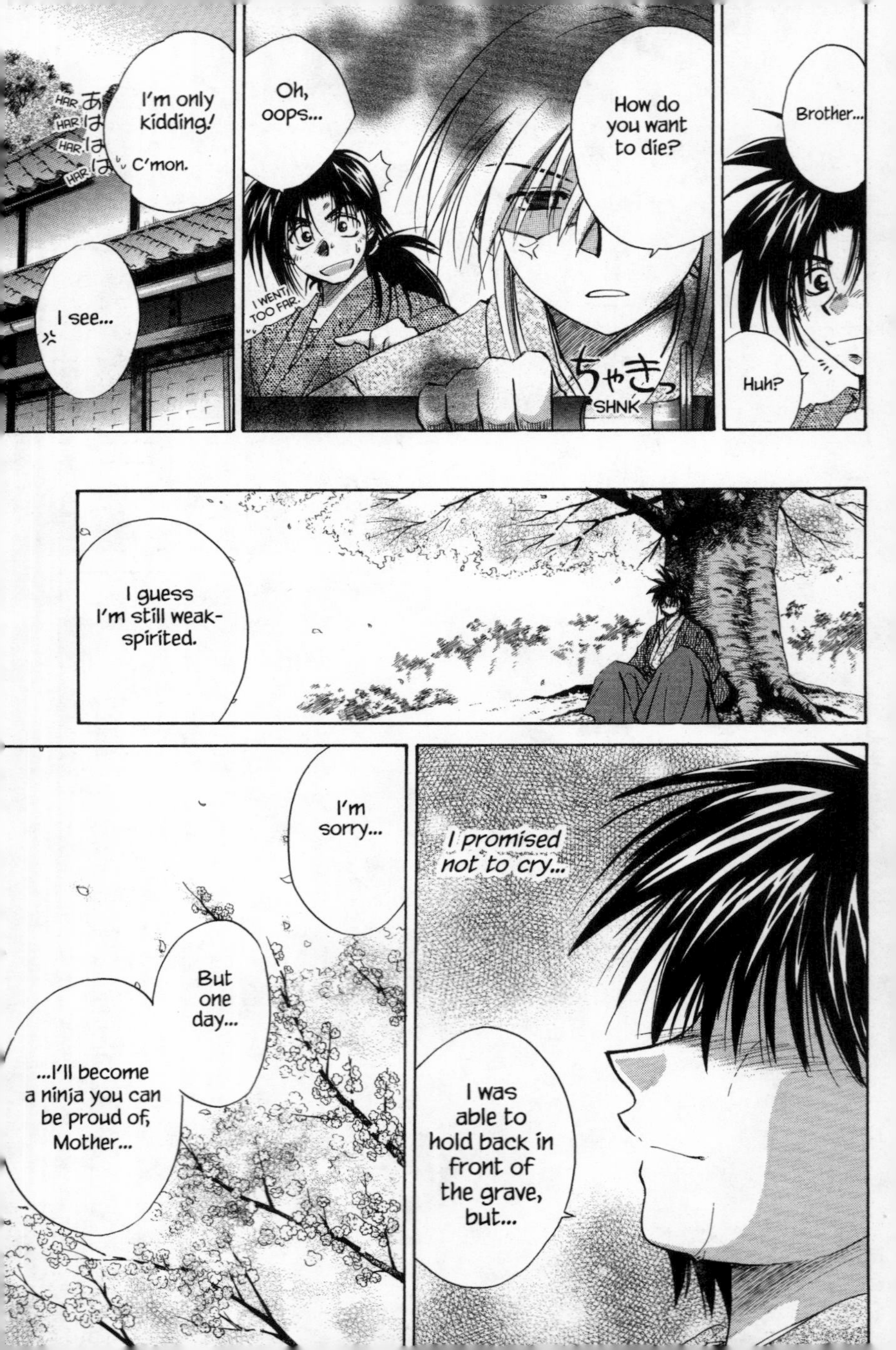
Brother...
Huh?
How do you want to die?
Oh, oops...
I WENT TOO FAR.
ちゃきっ
SHNK
I'm only kidding! C'mon.
HAR HAR HAR HAR
I see...
I guess I'm still weak-spirited.
I promised not to cry...
I was able to hold back in front of the grave, but...
I'm sorry...
But one day...
...I'll become a ninja you can be proud of, Mother...

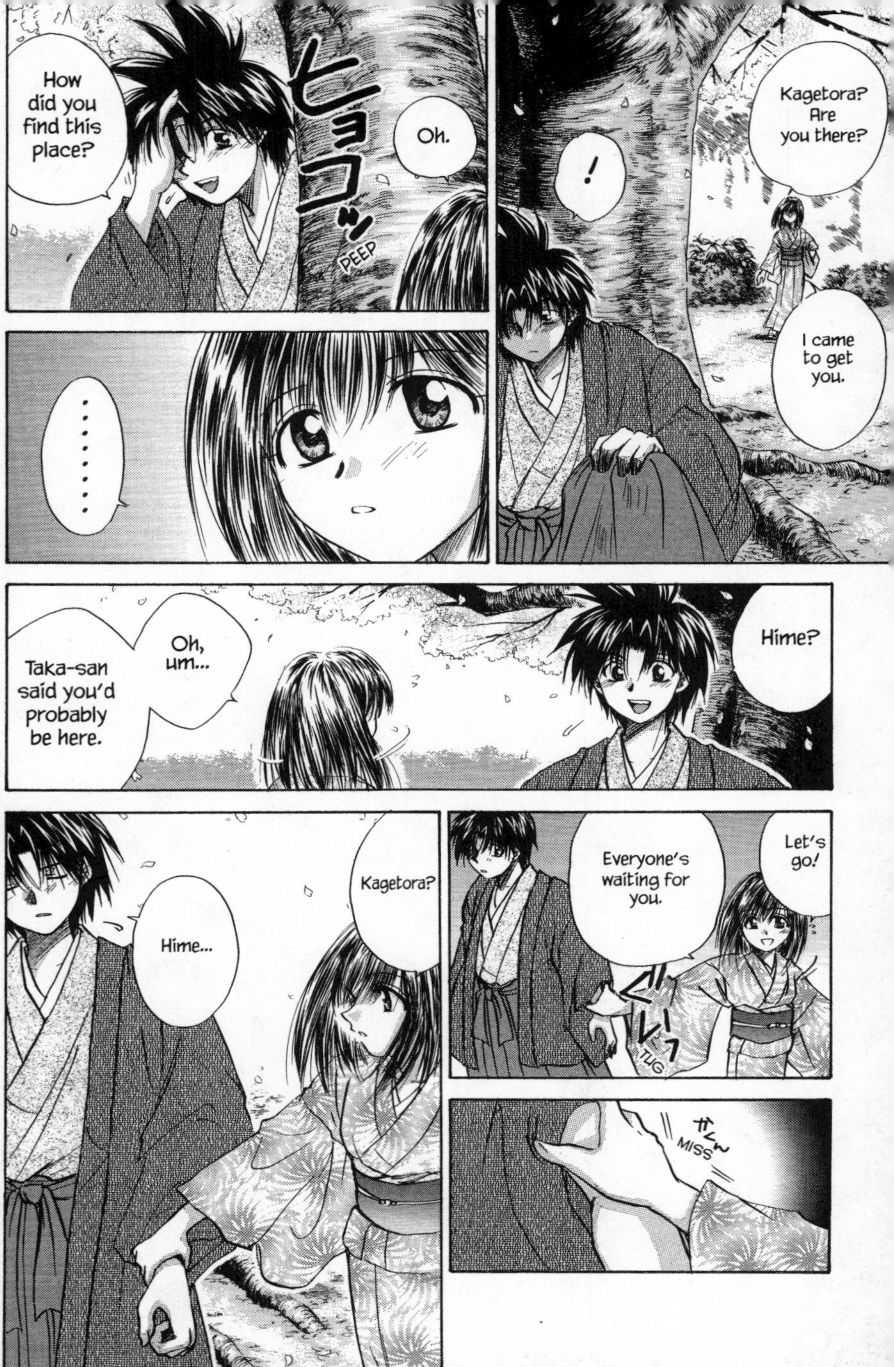

Kagetora? Are you there?
!
I came to get you.
Oh.
How did you find this place?
PEEP
......
Hime?
Oh, um...
Taka-san said you'd probably be here.
Let's go!
Everyone's waiting for you.
TUG
MISS
Kagetora?
Hime...

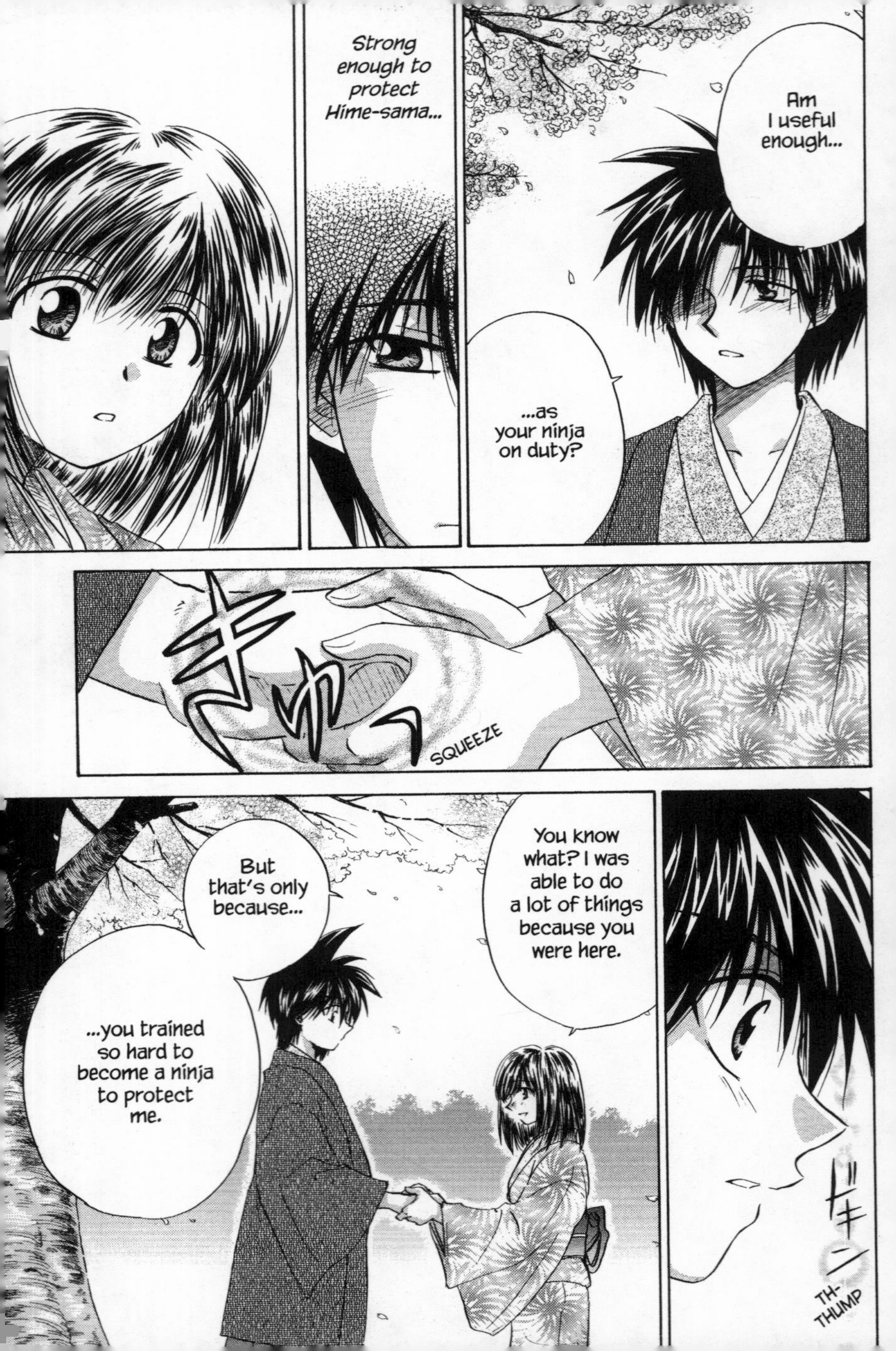
Am I useful enough...
...as your ninja on duty?
Strong enough to protect Hime-sama...
SQUEEZE
TH-THUMP
You know what? I was able to do a lot of things because you were here.
But that's only because...
...you trained so hard to become a ninja to protect me.

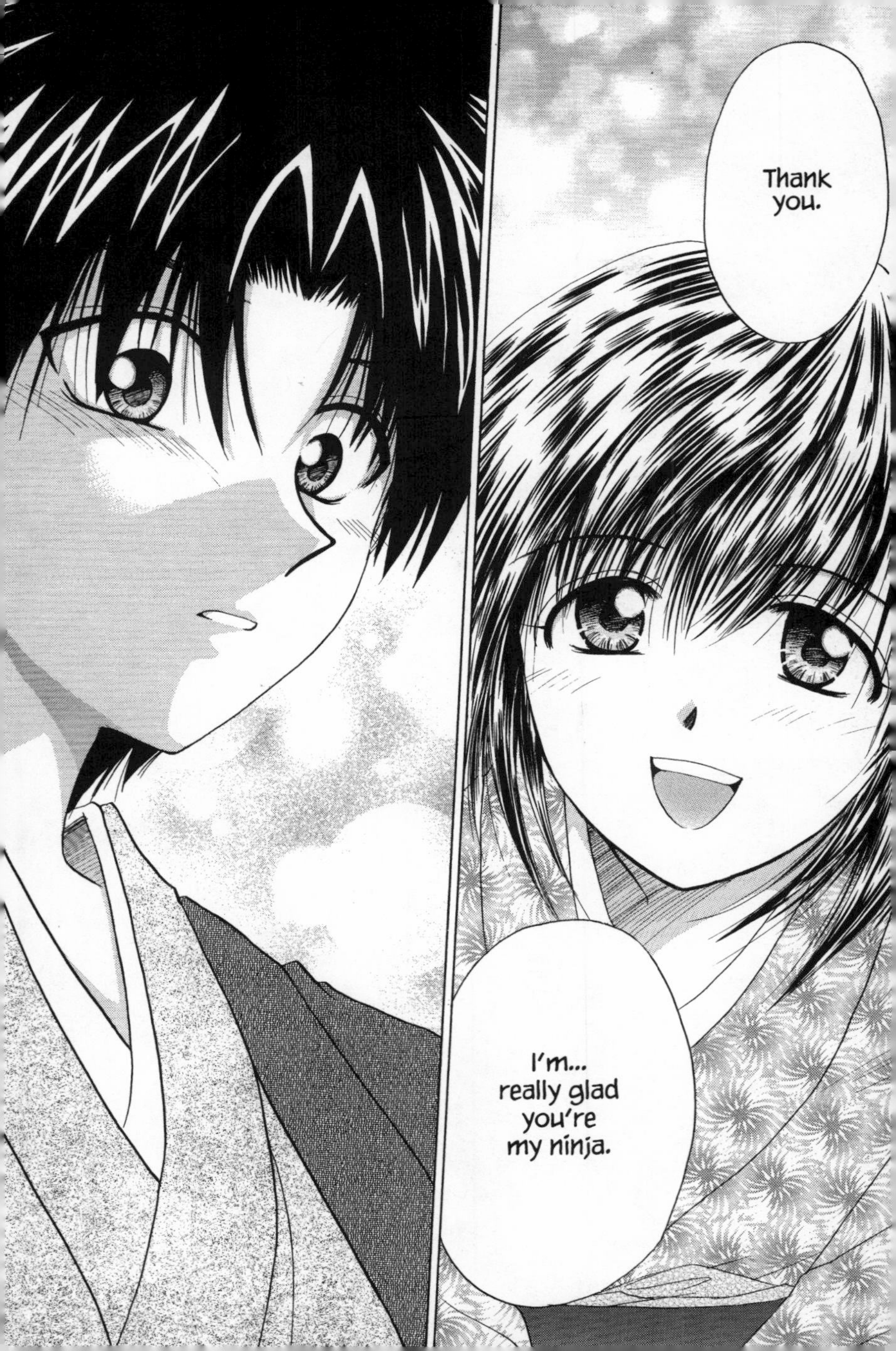
Thank you.
I'm... really glad you're my ninja.

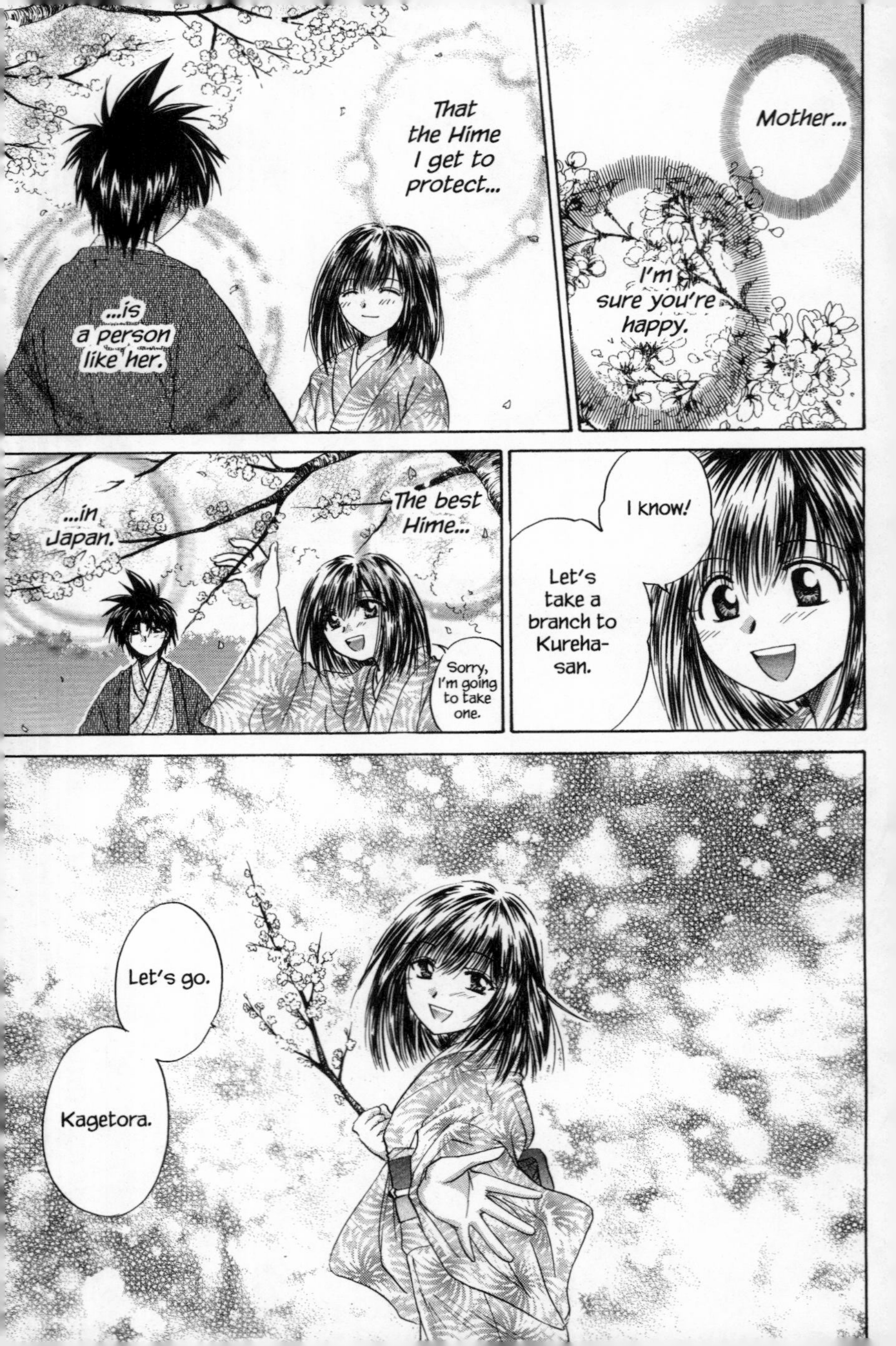
Mother...
I'm sure you're happy.
That the Hime I get to protect...
...is a person like her.
I know!
Let's take a branch to Kureha-san.
The best Hime...
...in Japan.
Sorry, I'm going to take one.
Let's go.
Kagetora.

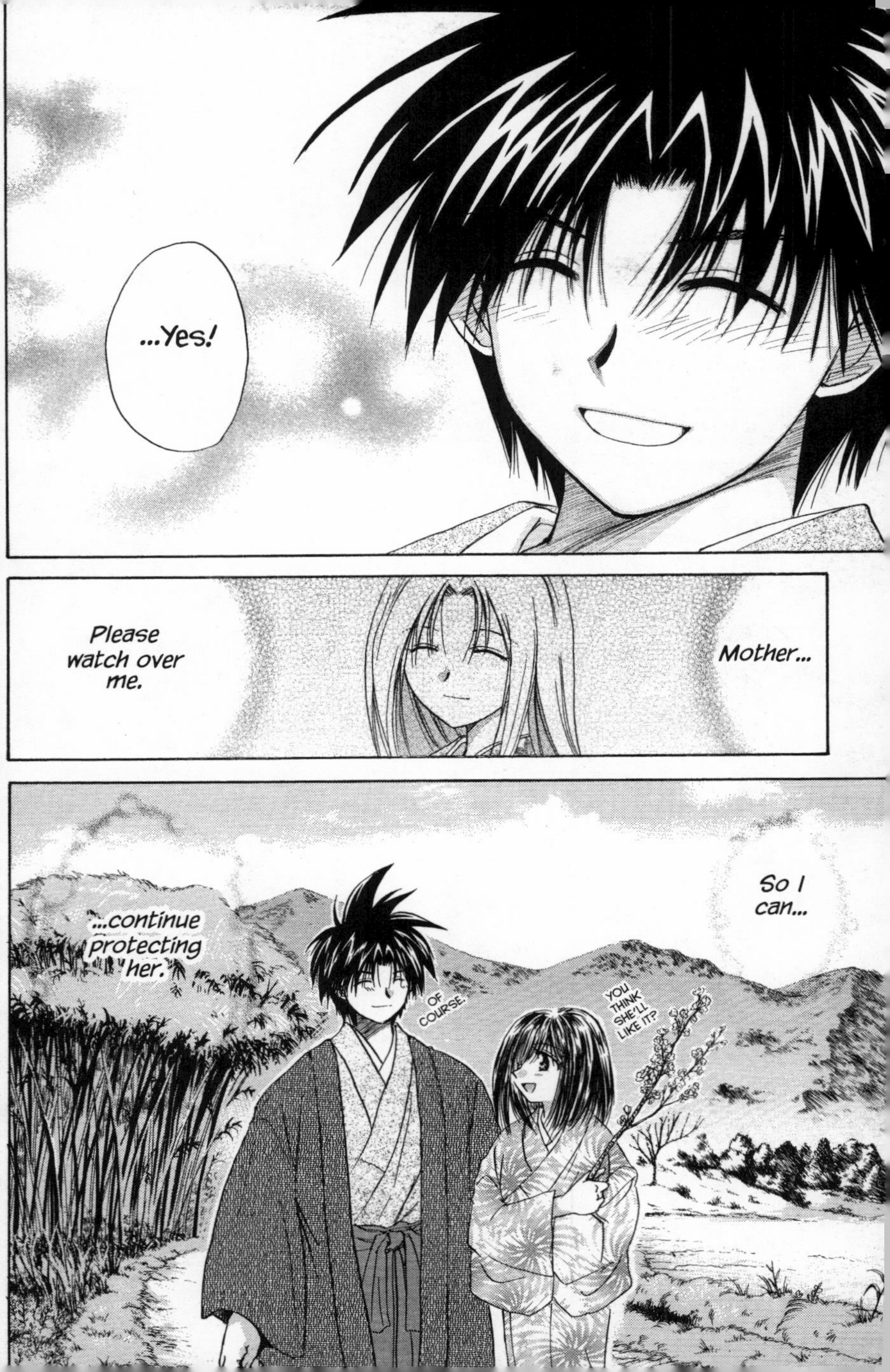

...Yes!
Mother...
Please watch over me.
So I can...
...continue protecting her.
YOU THINK SHE'LL LIKE IT?
OF COURSE.

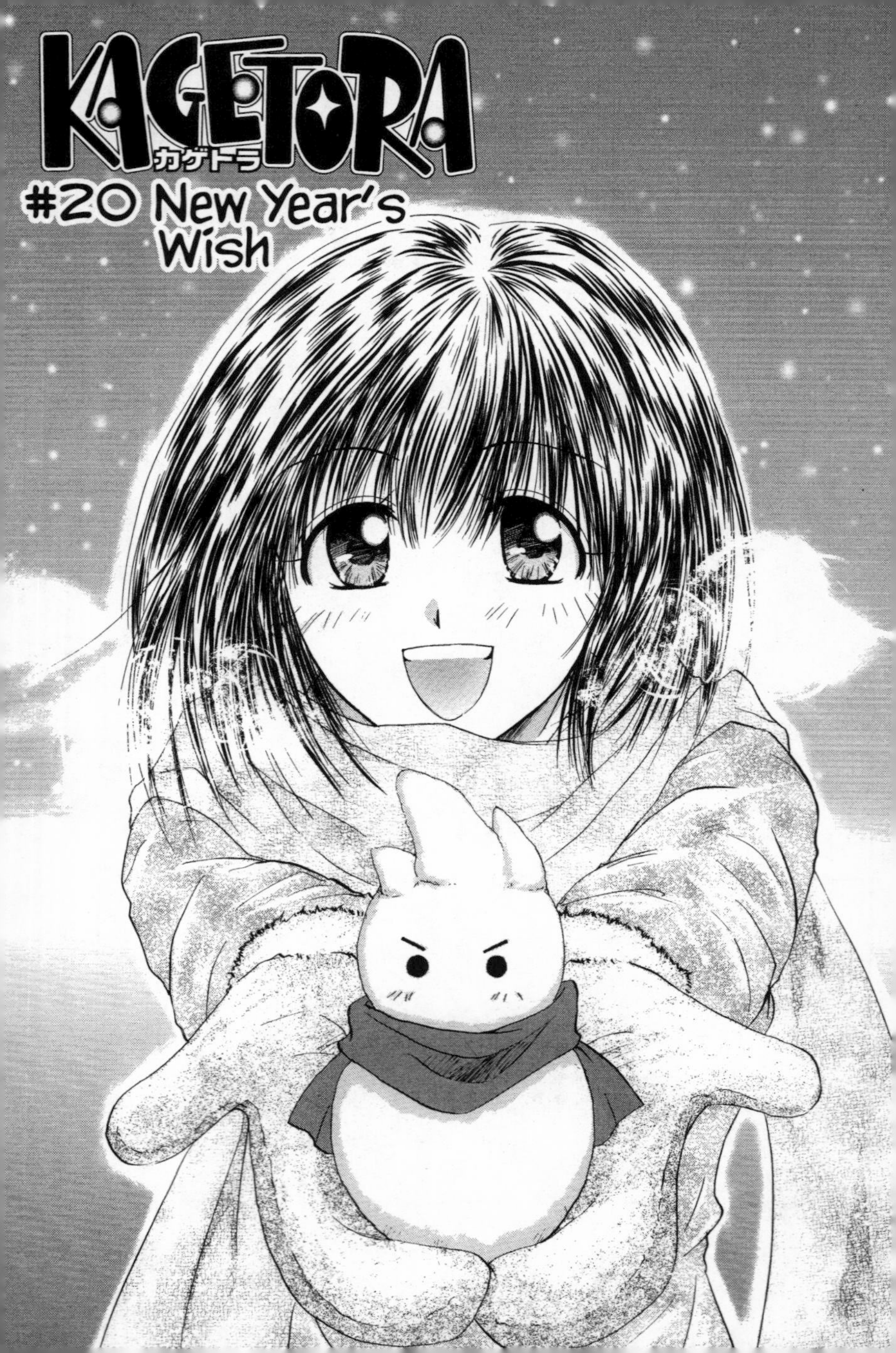
KAGETORA
カゲトラ
#20 New Year's Wish

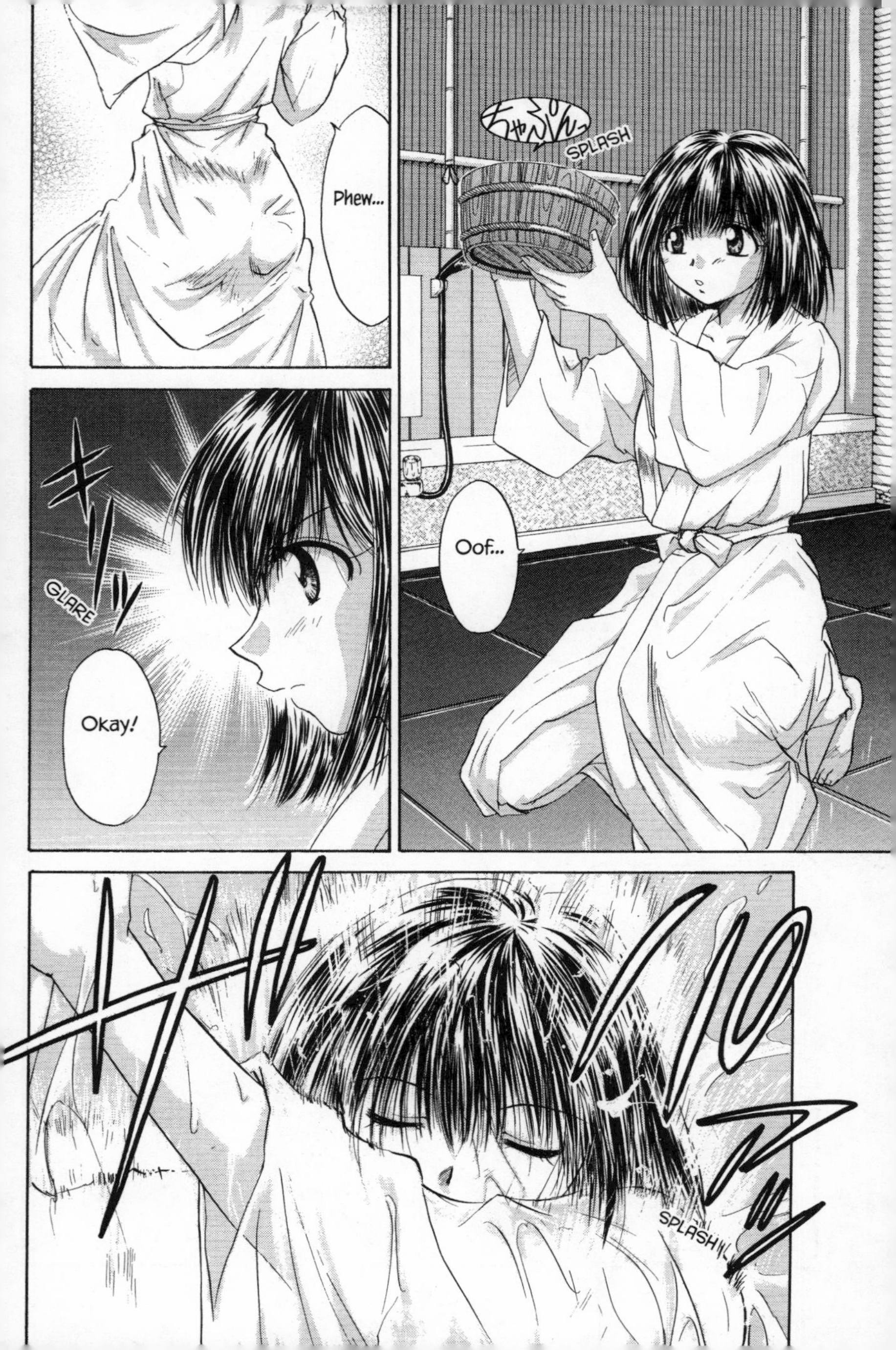

ちゃぷんっ
SPLASH
Oof...
Phew...
GLARE
Okay!
SPLASH!

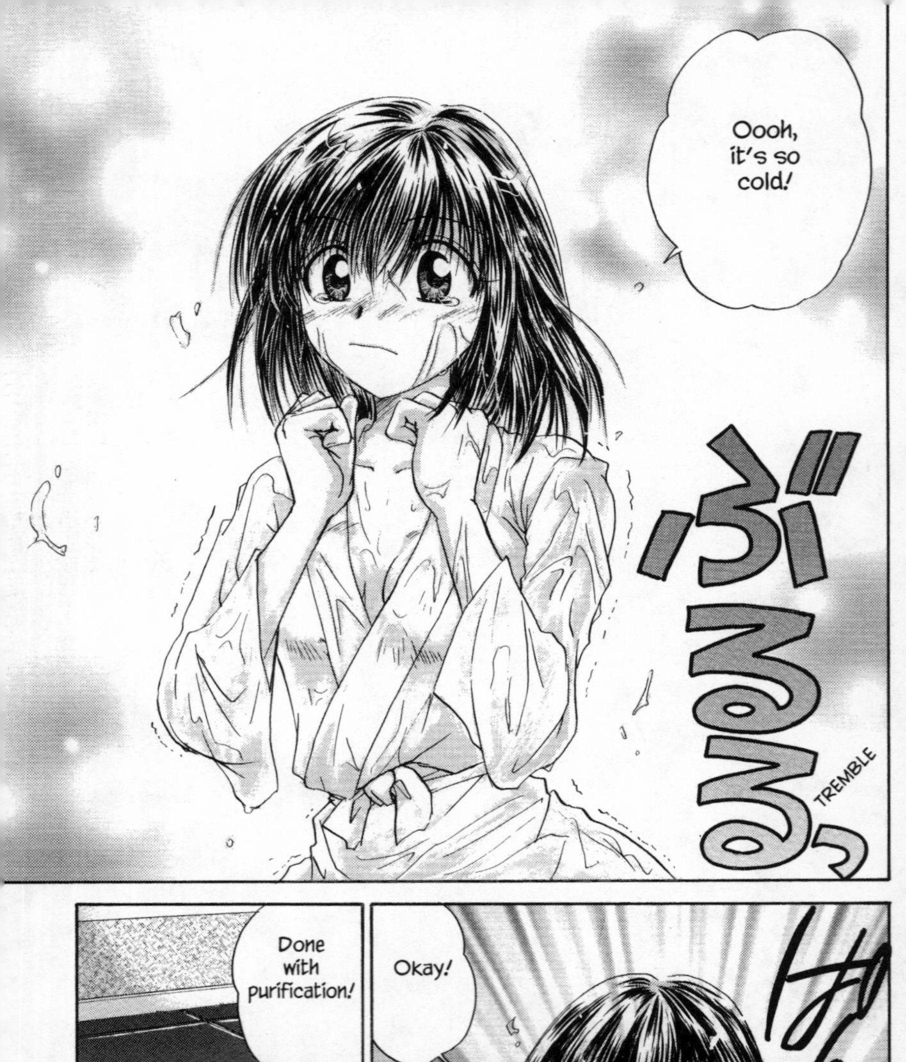
Oooh, it's so cold!
ぶるるっ
TREMBLE

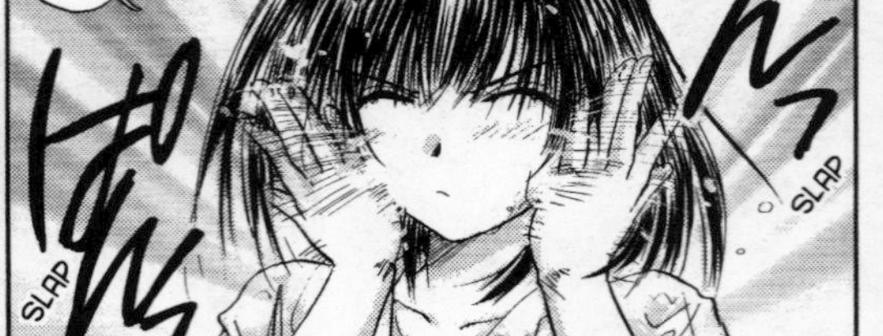
Okay!
ぱんっ
SLAP
ぱんっ
SLAP

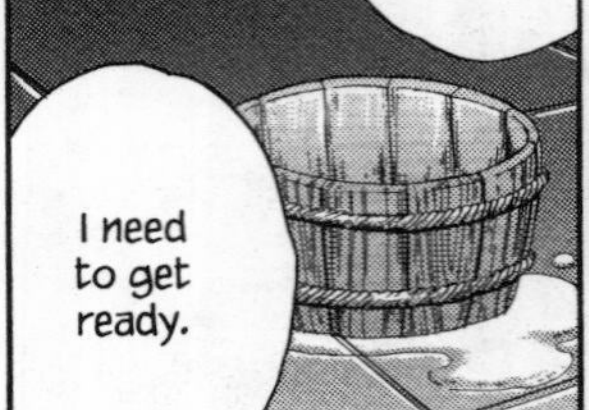
Done with purification!
I need to get ready.

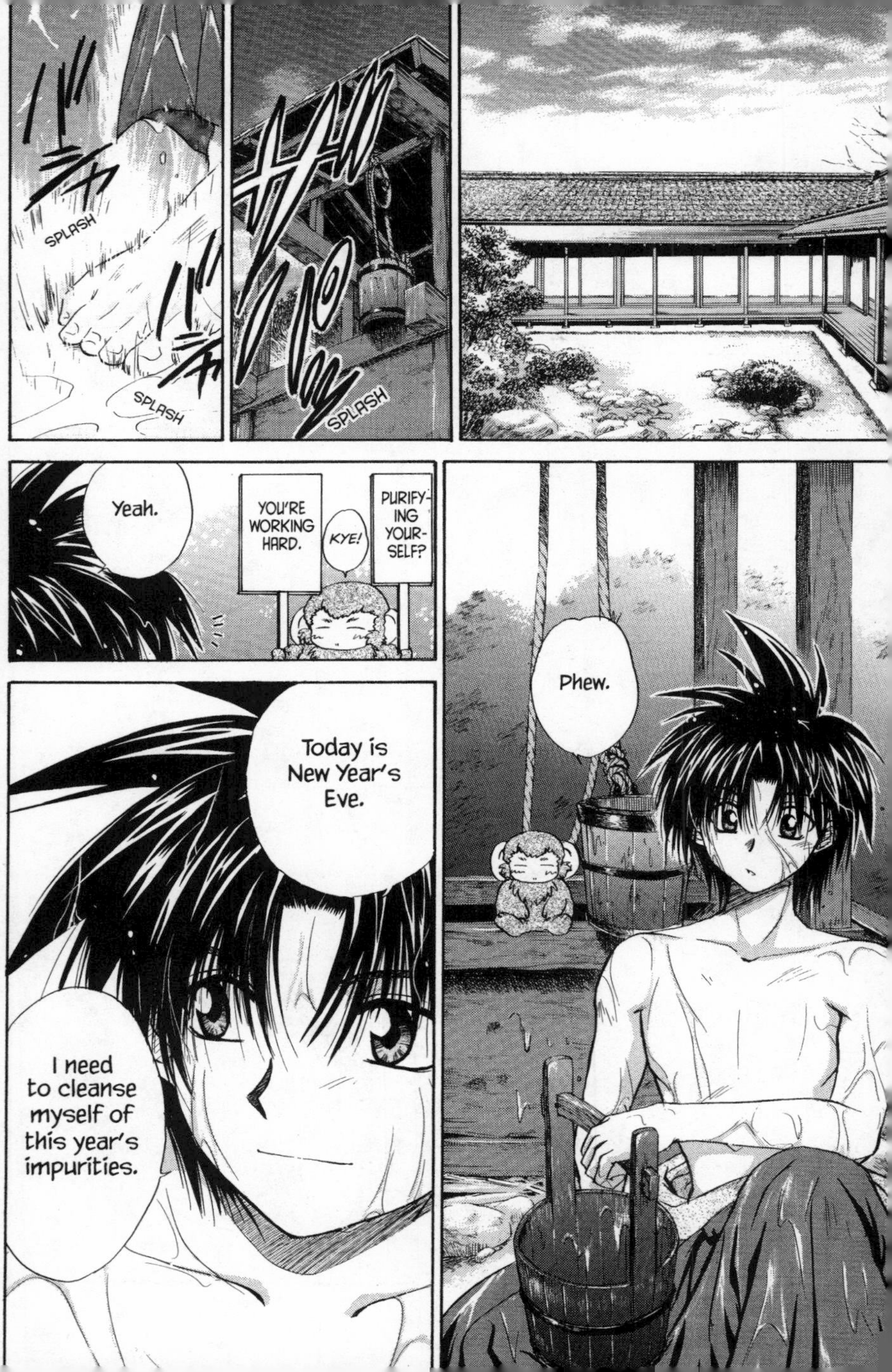
SPLASH
SPLASH
SPLASH
Phew.
PURIFYING YOURSELF?
KYE!
YOU'RE WORKING HARD.
Yeah.
Today is New Year's Eve.
I need to cleanse myself of this year's impurities.

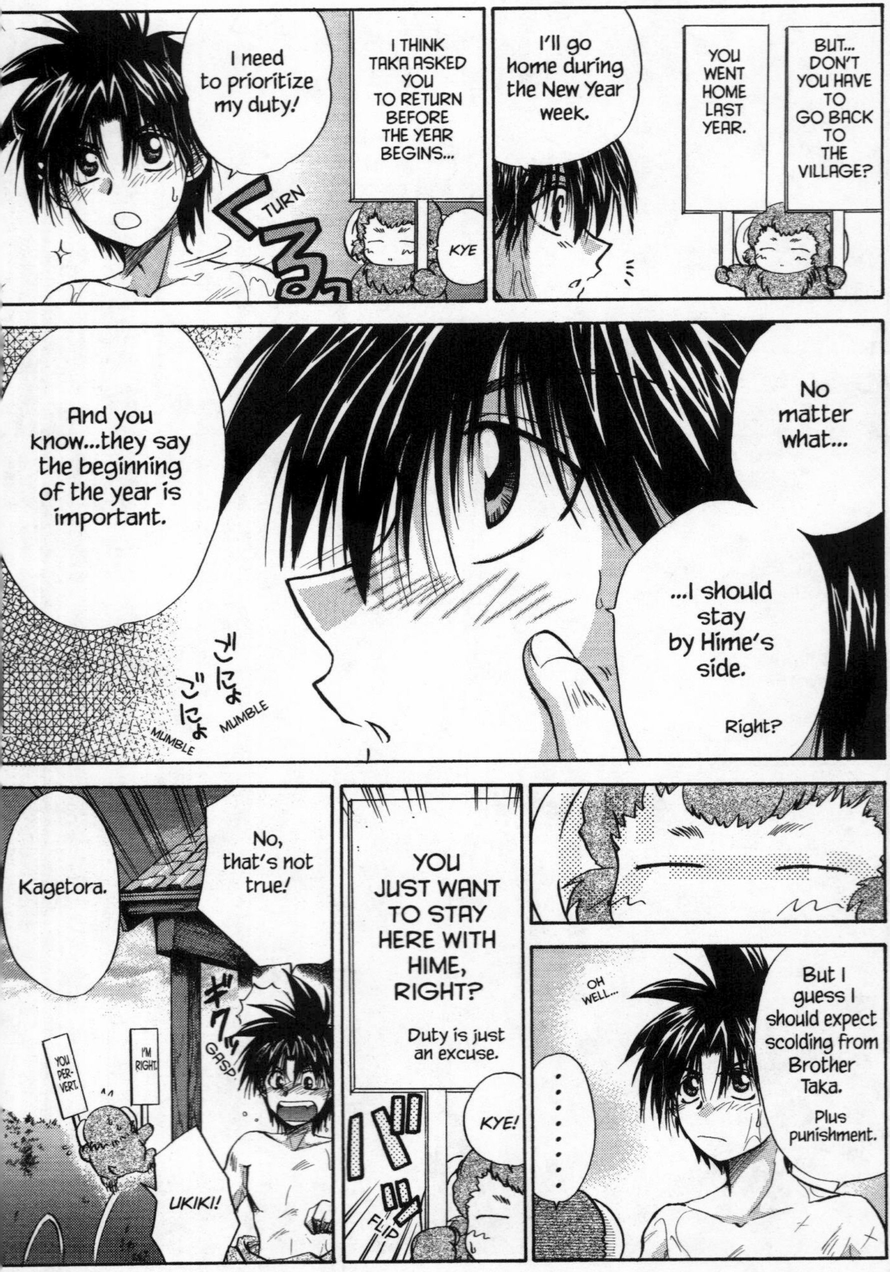
BUT... DON'T YOU HAVE TO GO BACK TO THE VILLAGE?
YOU WENT HOME LAST YEAR.
I'll go home during the New Year week.
I THINK TAKA ASKED YOU TO RETURN BEFORE THE YEAR BEGINS...
I need to prioritize my duty!
KYE
TURN
No matter what...
...I should stay by Hime's side.
Right?
And you know...they say the beginning of the year is important.
ごにょごにょ
MUMBLE MUMBLE
But I guess I should expect scolding from Brother Taka.
Plus punishment.
OH WELL...
......
YOU JUST WANT TO STAY HERE WITH HIME, RIGHT?
Duty is just an excuse.
KYE!
FLIP
No, that's not true!
Kagetora.
GASP
I'M RIGHT.
YOU PERVERT.
UKIKI!

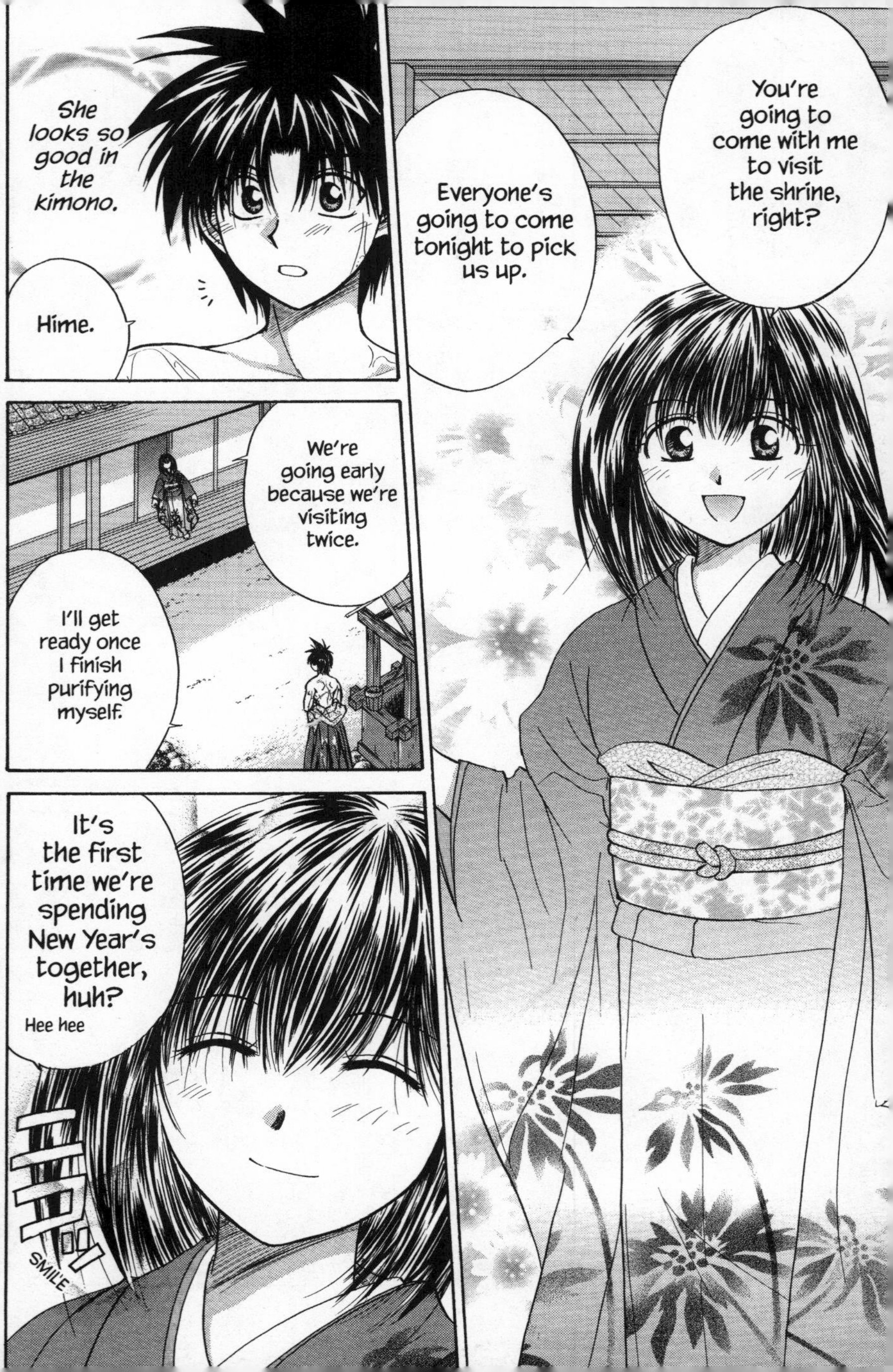
You're going to come with me to visit the shrine, right?
Everyone's going to come tonight to pick us up.
She looks so good in the kimono.
Hime.
We're going early because we're visiting twice.
I'll get ready once I finish purifying myself.
It's the first time we're spending New Year's together, huh?
Hee hee
SMILE

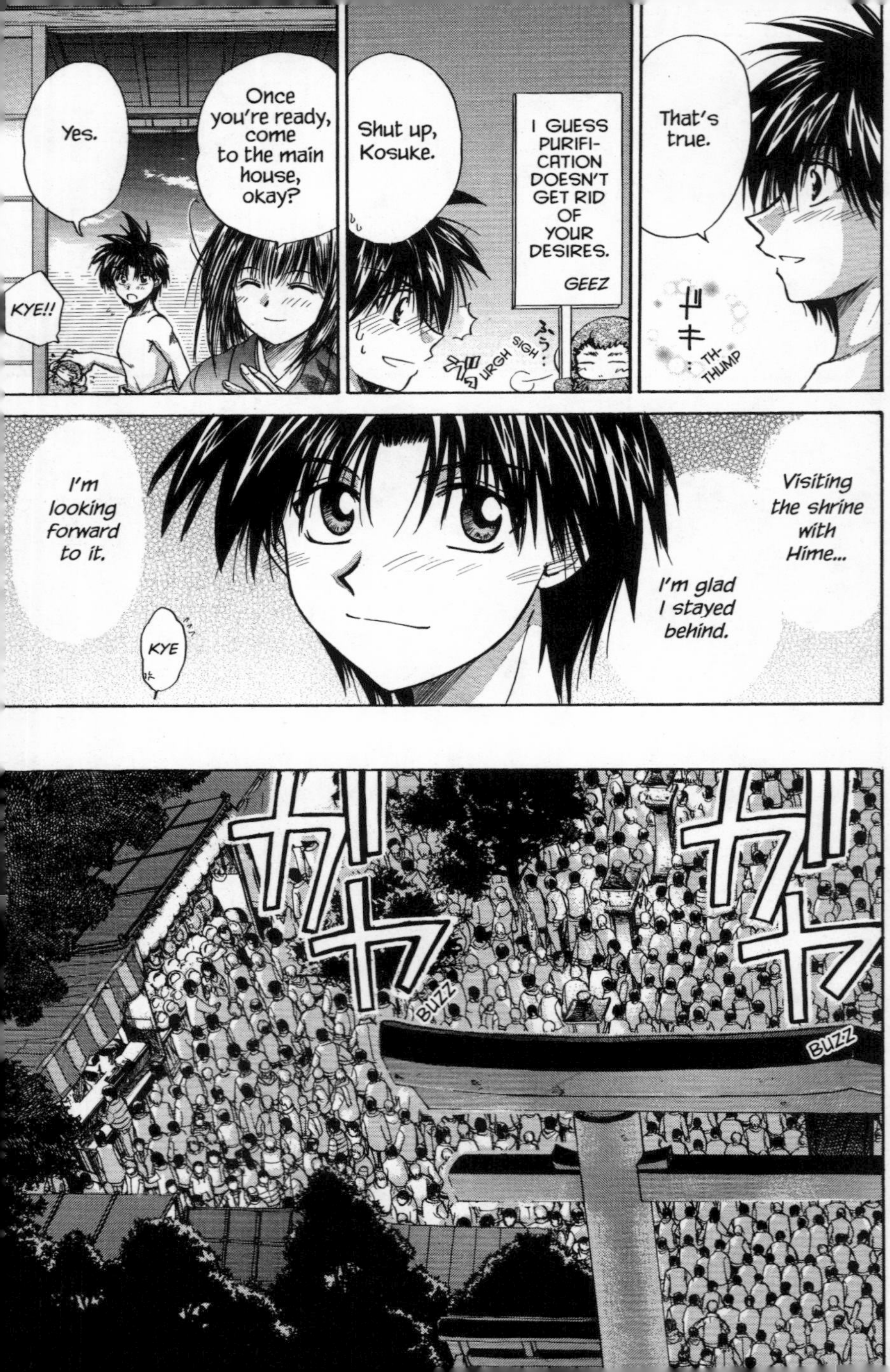

That's true.
TH-THUMP
I GUESS PURIFICATION DOESN'T GET RID OF YOUR DESIRES.
GEEZ
SIGH
Shut up, Kosuke.
URGH
Once you're ready, come to the main house, okay?
Yes.
KYE!!
Visiting the shrine with Hime...
I'm glad I stayed behind.
I'm looking forward to it.
KYE
BUZZ
BUZZ

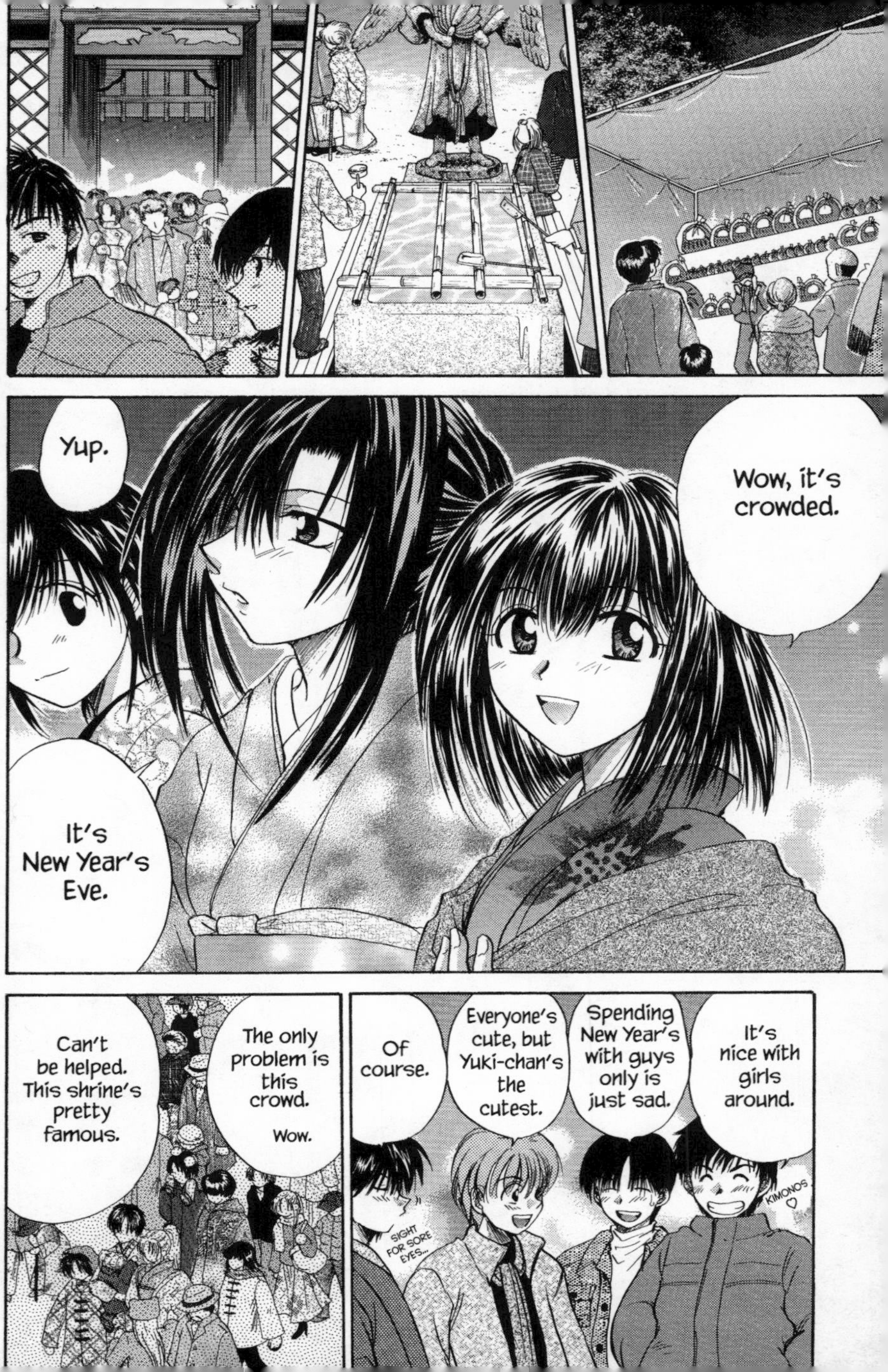
Wow, it's crowded.
Yup.
It's New Year's Eve.
It's nice with girls around.
KIMONOS ♡
Spending New Year's with guys only is just sad.
Everyone's cute, but Yuki-chan's the cutest.
SIGHT FOR SORE EYES...
Of course.
The only problem is this crowd.
Wow.
Can't be helped. This shrine's pretty famous.

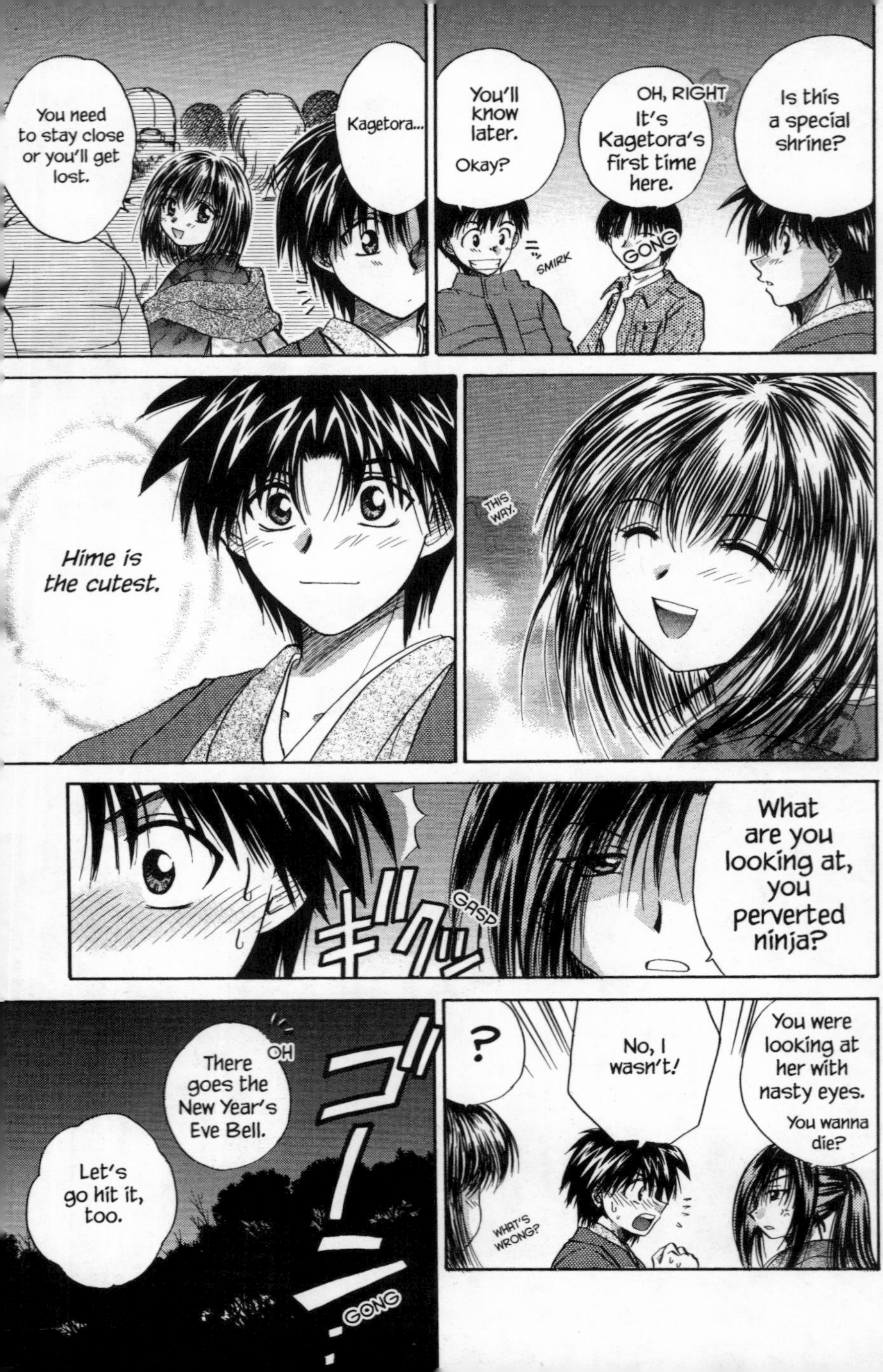
Is this a special shrine?
OH, RIGHT
It's Kagetora's first time here.
GONG
You'll know later.
Okay?
SMIRK
Kagetora...
You need to stay close or you'll get lost.
THIS WAY.
Hime is the cutest.
What are you looking at, you perverted ninja?
GASP
ギクッ
You were looking at her with nasty eyes.
You wanna die?
No, I wasn't!
?
WHAT'S WRONG?
OH
There goes the New Year's Eve Bell.
Let's go hit it, too.
GONG

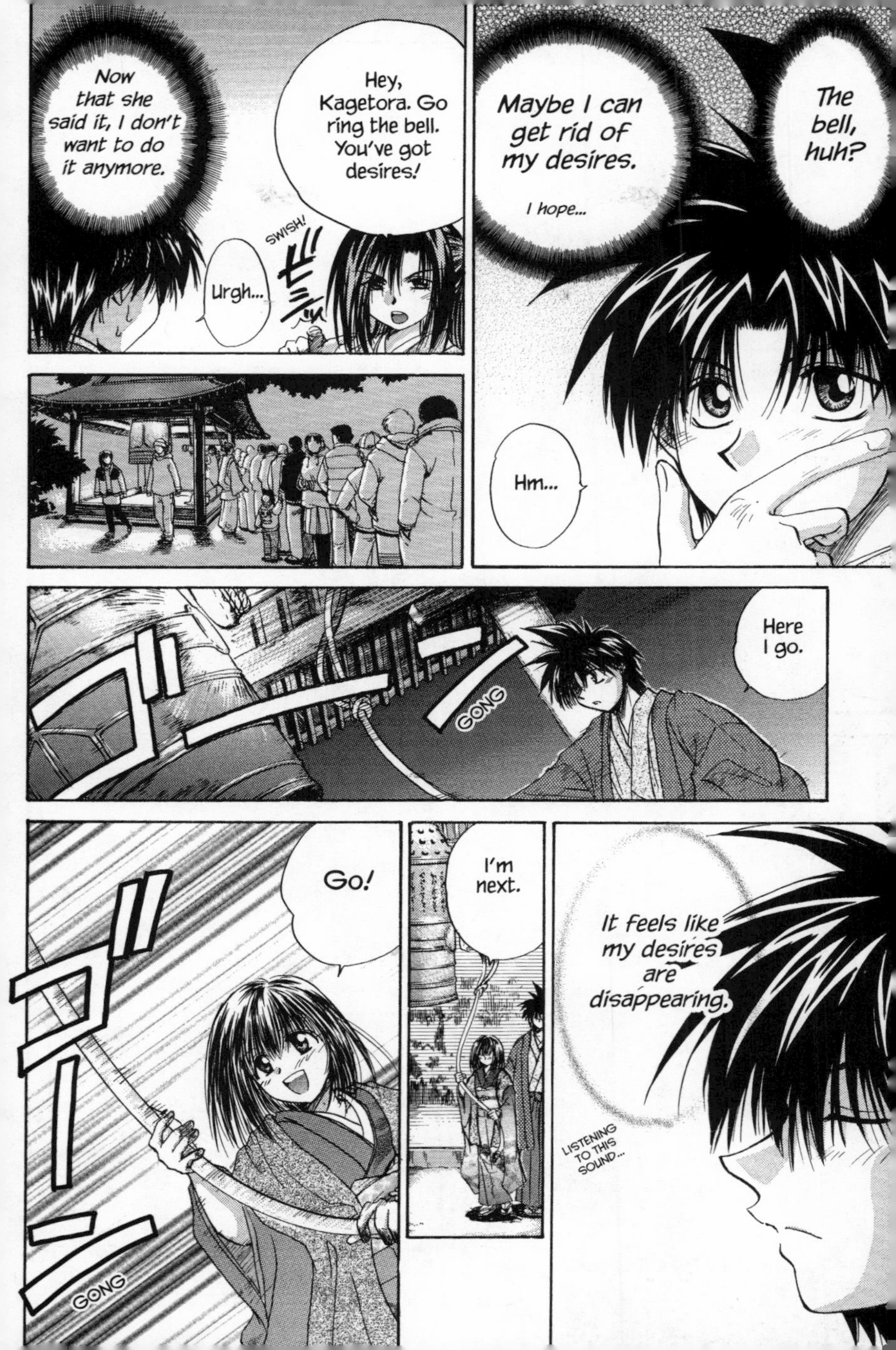
The bell, huh?
Maybe I can get rid of my desires.
I hope...
Hm...
Hey, Kagetora. Go ring the bell. You've got desires!
Now that she said it, I don't want to do it anymore.
SWISH!
Urgh...
Here I go.
GONG
It feels like my desires are disappearing.
LISTENING TO THIS SOUND...
I'm next.
Go!
GONG

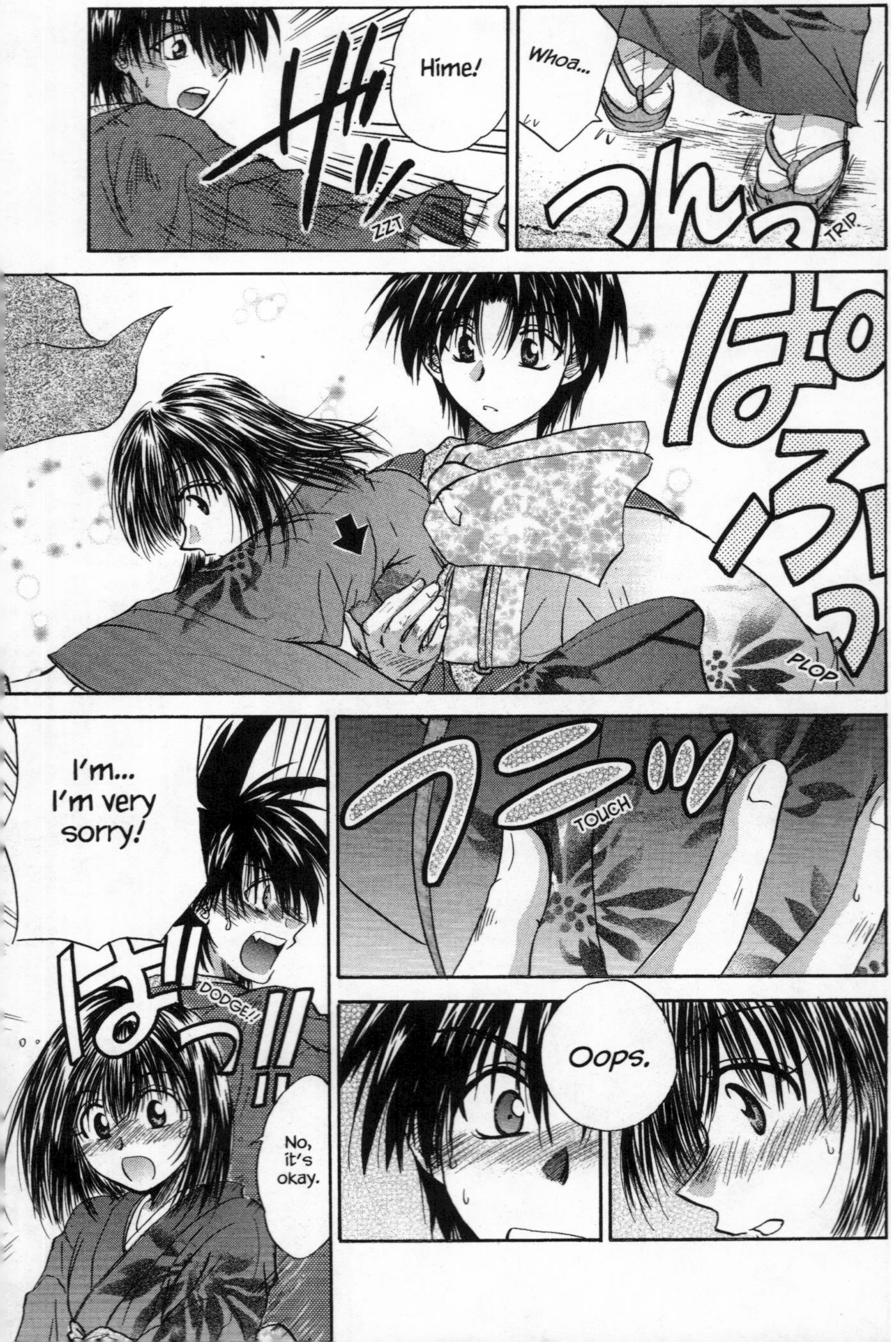

Whoa...
つんっ
TRIP
Hime!
ザッ
ZZT
ぽろっ
PLOP
TOUCH
Oops.
I'm... I'm very sorry!
はっ!!
DODGE!!
No, it's okay.

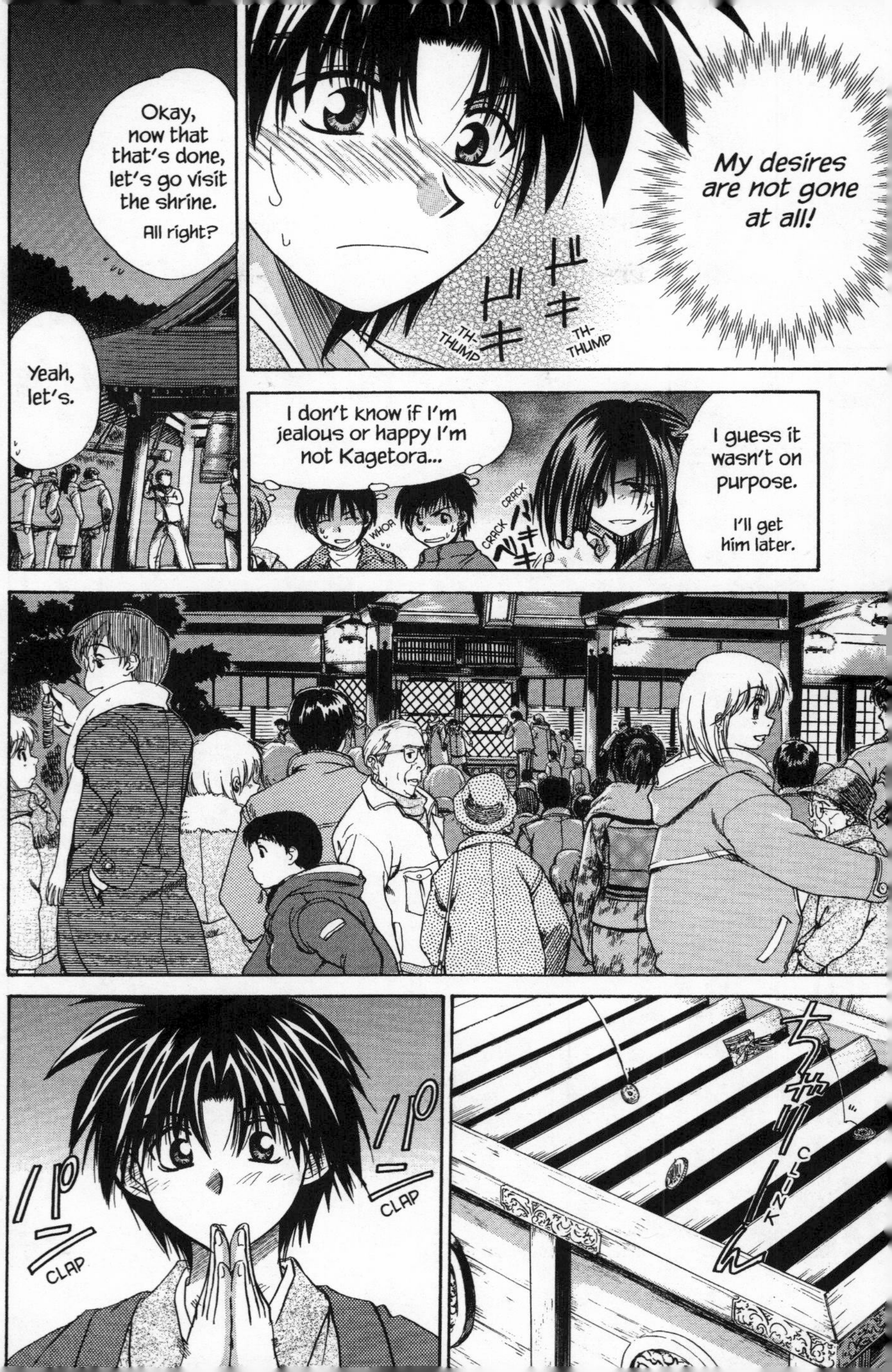
My desires are not gone at all!
TH-THUMP
TH-THUMP
I guess it wasn't on purpose.
I'll get him later.
CRACK
CRACK
WHOA
I don't know if I'm jealous or happy I'm not Kagetora...
Okay, now that that's done, let's go visit the shrine.
All right?
Yeah, let's.
CLINK
CLAP
CLAP

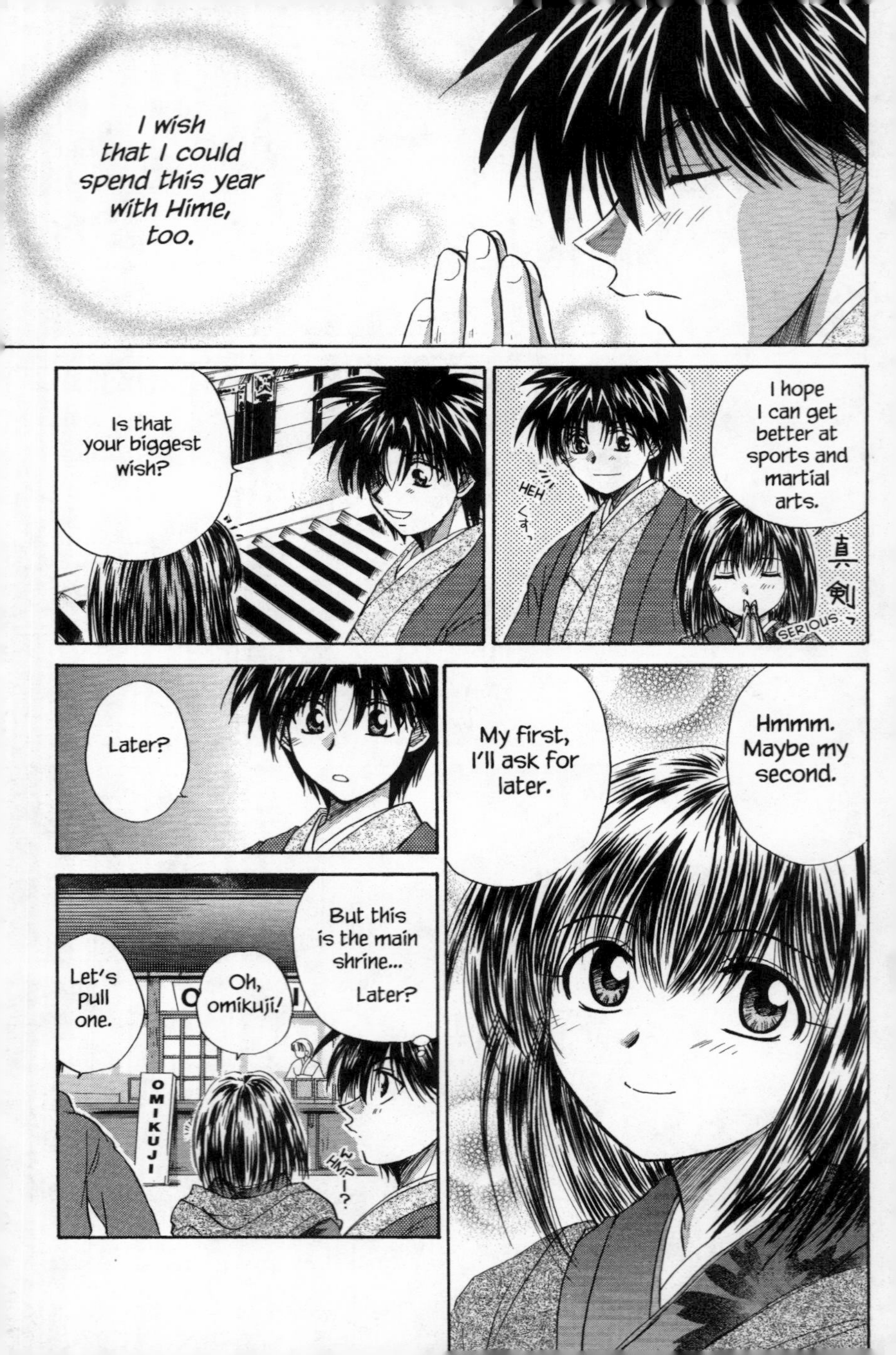
I wish that I could spend this year with Hime, too.
I hope I can get better at sports and martial arts.
HEH
くす
真剣
SERIOUS
Is that your biggest wish?
Hmmm. Maybe my second.
My first, I'll ask for later.
Later?
But this is the main shrine... Later?
Oh, omikuji!
Let's pull one.
OMIKUJI
HM?

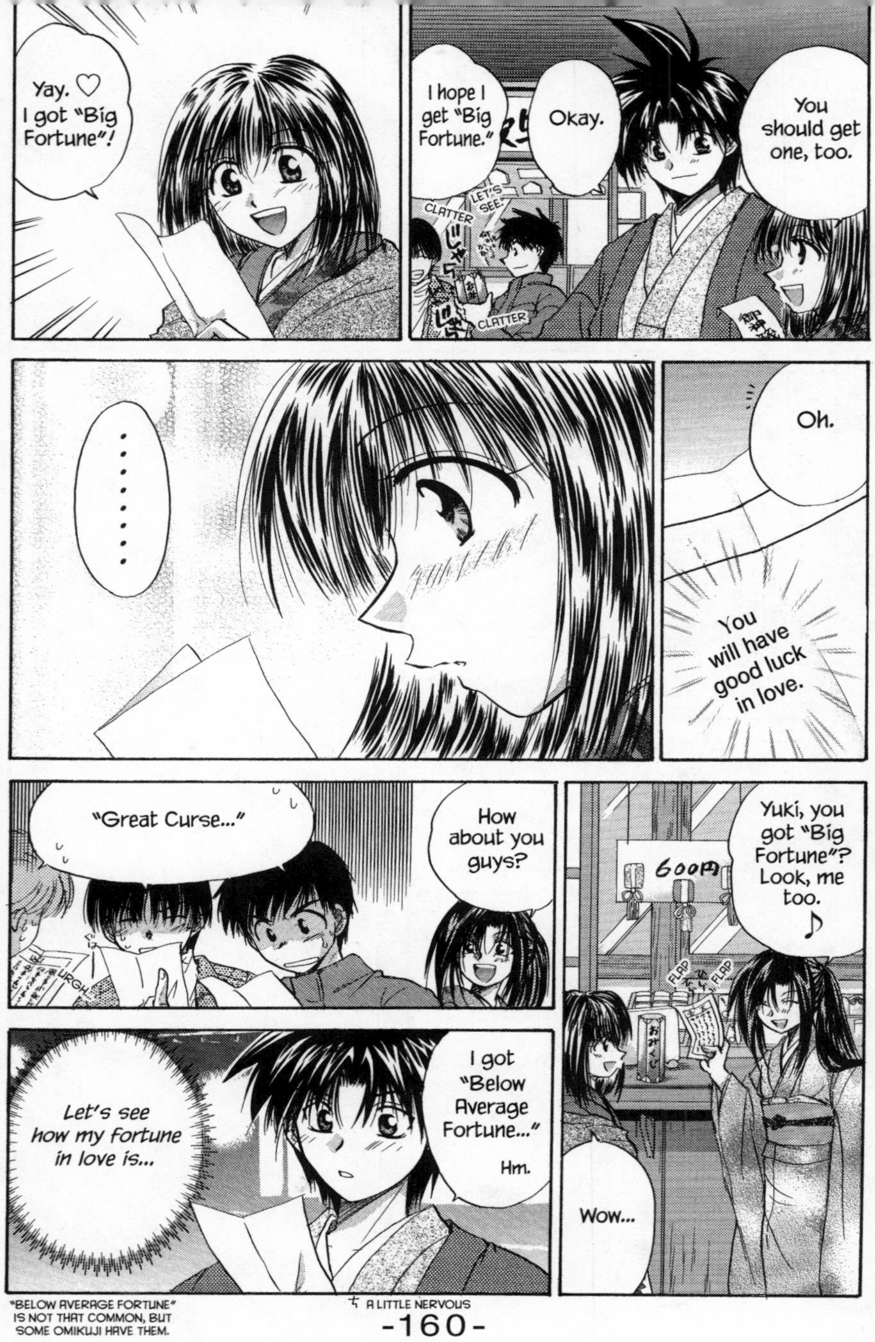
You should get one, too.
Okay.
I hope I get "Big Fortune."
LET'S SEE.
CLATTER
CLATTER
Yay. ♡ I got "Big Fortune"!
Oh.
You will have good luck in love.
....
Yuki, you got "Big Fortune"? Look, me too. ♪
FLAP
FLAP
600円
Wow...
How about you guys?
"Great Curse..."
URGH.
I got "Below Average Fortune..."
Hm.
Let's see how my fortune in love is...

"BELOW AVERAGE FORTUNE" IS NOT THAT COMMON, BUT SOME OMIKUJI HAVE THEM.

ち A LITTLE NERVOUS

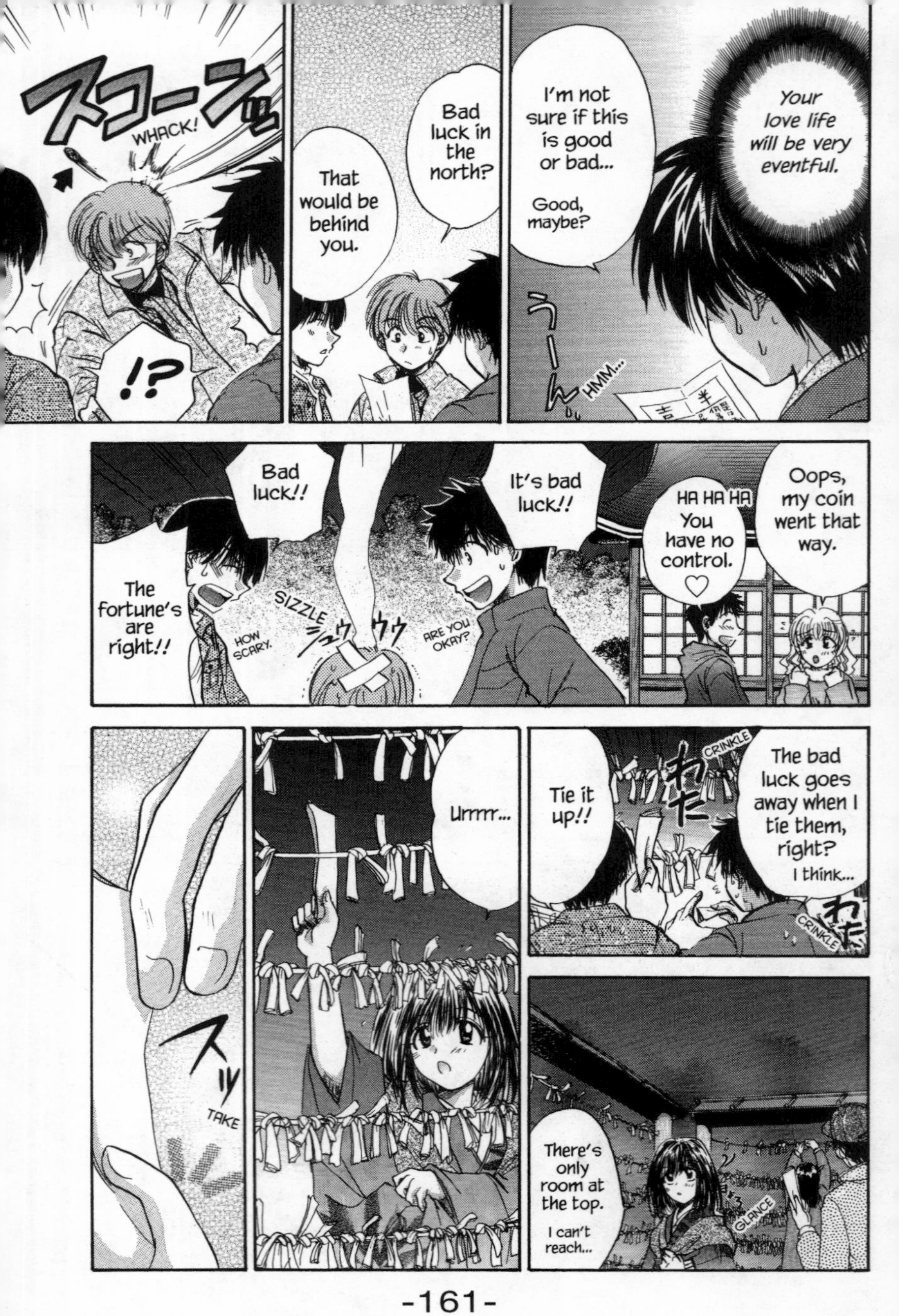
Your love life will be very eventful.
I'm not sure if this is good or bad...
Good, maybe?
うーん
HMM...
Bad luck in the north?
That would be behind you.
スコーン
WHACK!
!?
Oops, my coin went that way.
HA HA HA
You have no control. ♡
It's bad luck!!
ARE YOU OKAY?
SIZZLE
HOW SCARY.
Bad luck!!
The fortune's are right!!
The bad luck goes away when I tie them, right?
I think...
わた
CRINKLE
Tie it up!!
わた
CRINKLE
There's only room at the top.
I can't reach...
GLANCE
Urrrrr...
スッ
TAKE

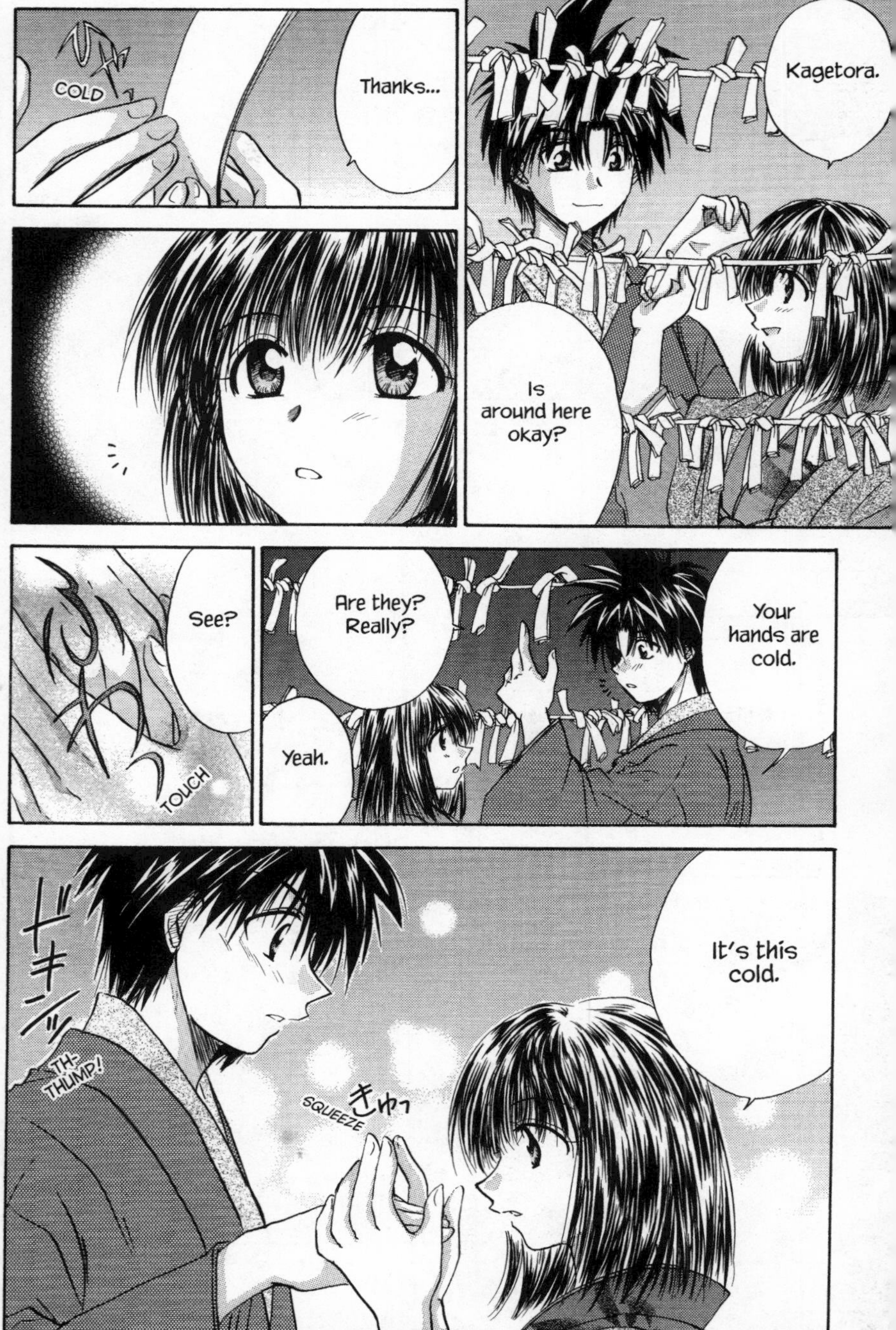
Kagetora.
Is around here okay?
COLD
Thanks...
Your hands are cold.
Are they? Really?
Yeah.
See?
TOUCH
It's this cold.
SQUEEZE
きゅっ
TH-THUMP!

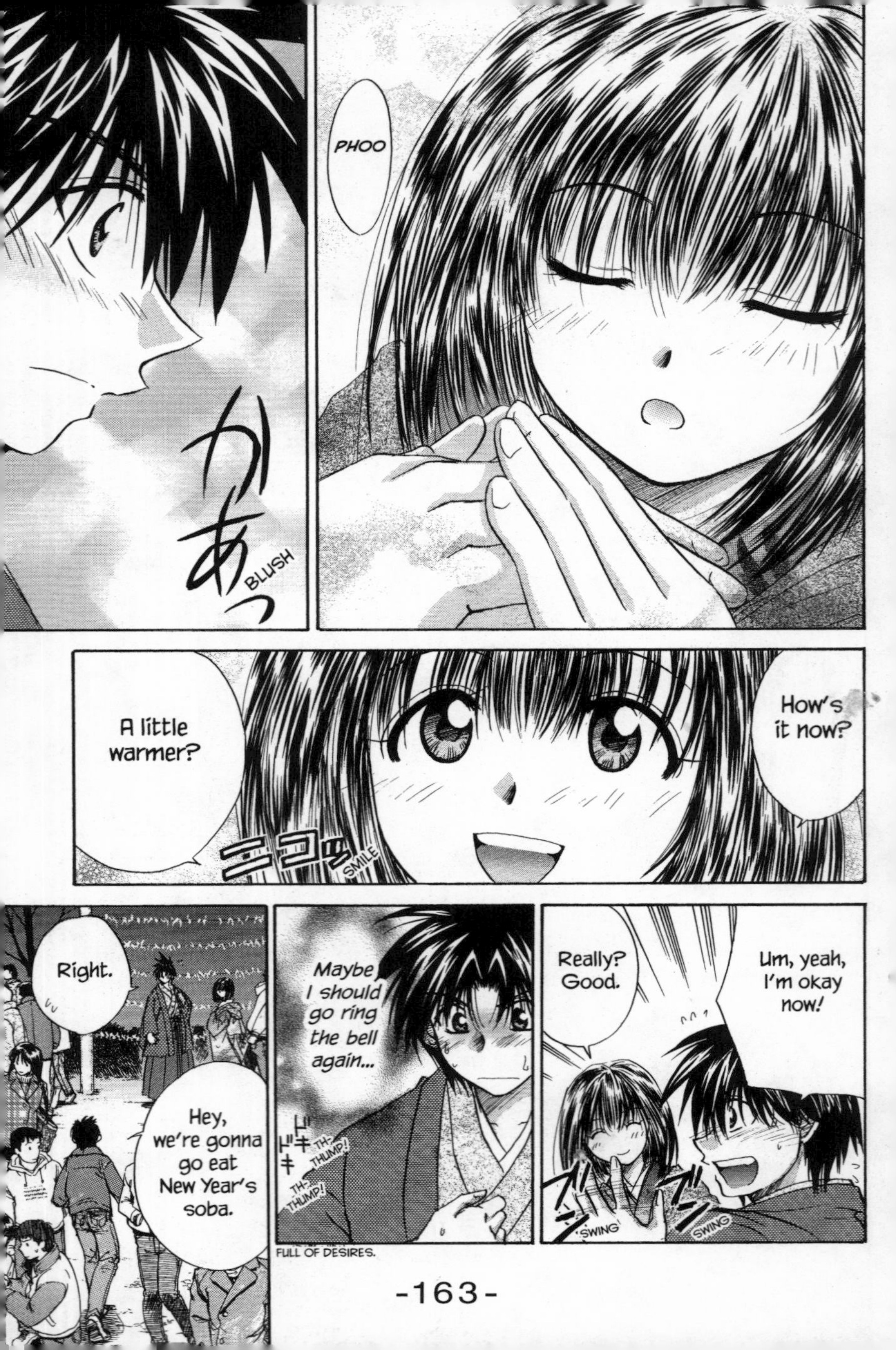
PHOO
かあっ
BLUSH
How's it now?
A little warmer?
ニコッ
SMILE
Um, yeah, I'm okay now!
Really? Good.
SWING
SWING
Maybe I should go ring the bell again...
ドキ
TH-THUMP!
ドキ
TH-THUMP!
Right.
Hey, we're gonna go eat New Year's soba.
FULL OF DESIRES.

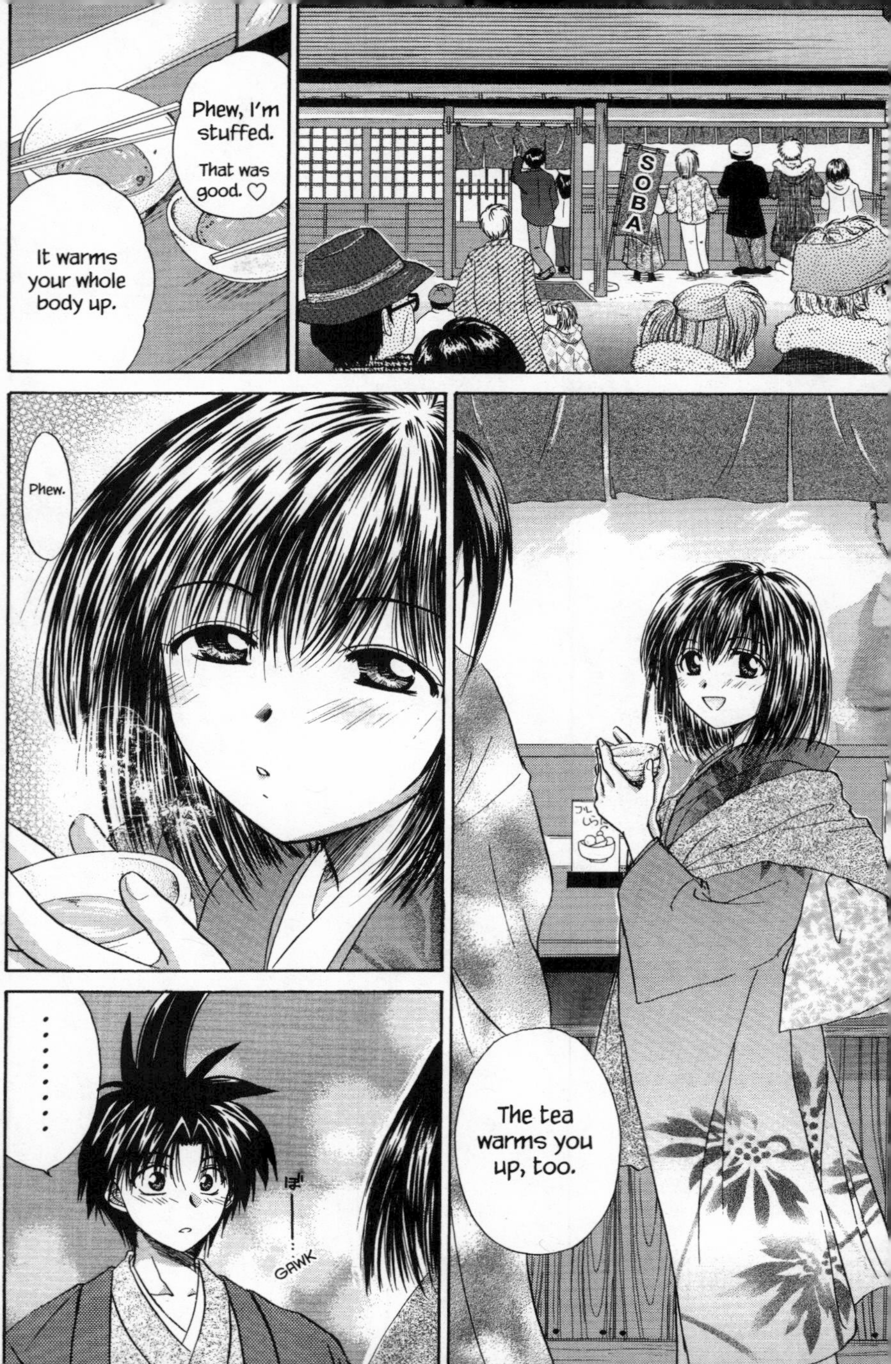
SOBA
Phew, I'm stuffed.
That was good. ♡
It warms your whole body up.
The tea warms you up, too.
Phew.
......
GAWK

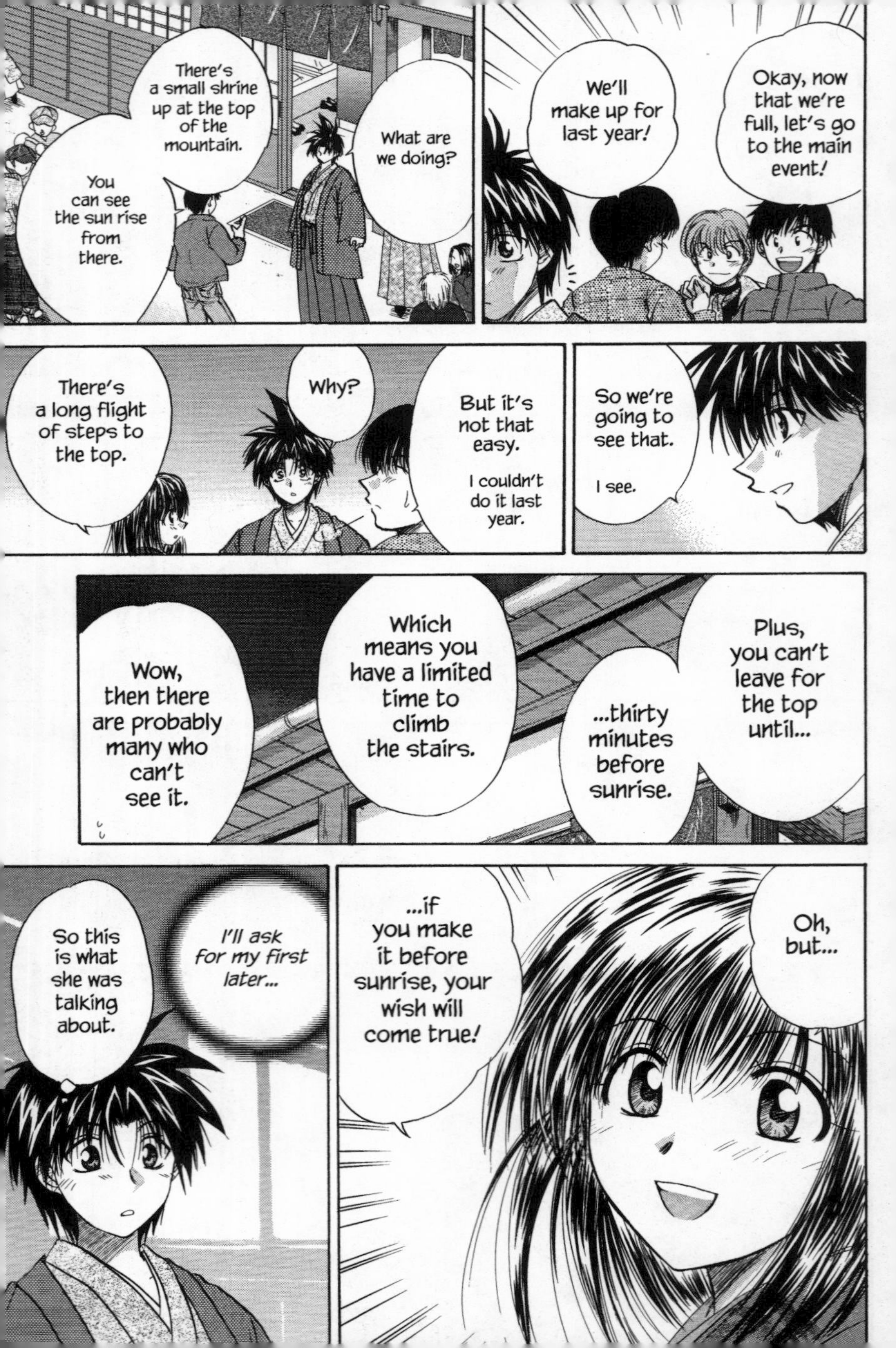

Okay, now that we're full, let's go to the main event!
We'll make up for last year!
What are we doing?
There's a small shrine up at the top of the mountain.
You can see the sun rise from there.
So we're going to see that.
I see.
But it's not that easy.
I couldn't do it last year.
Why?
There's a long flight of steps to the top.
Plus, you can't leave for the top until...
...thirty minutes before sunrise.
Which means you have a limited time to climb the stairs.
Wow, then there are probably many who can't see it.
Oh, but...
...if you make it before sunrise, your wish will come true!
I'll ask for my first later...
So this is what she was talking about.

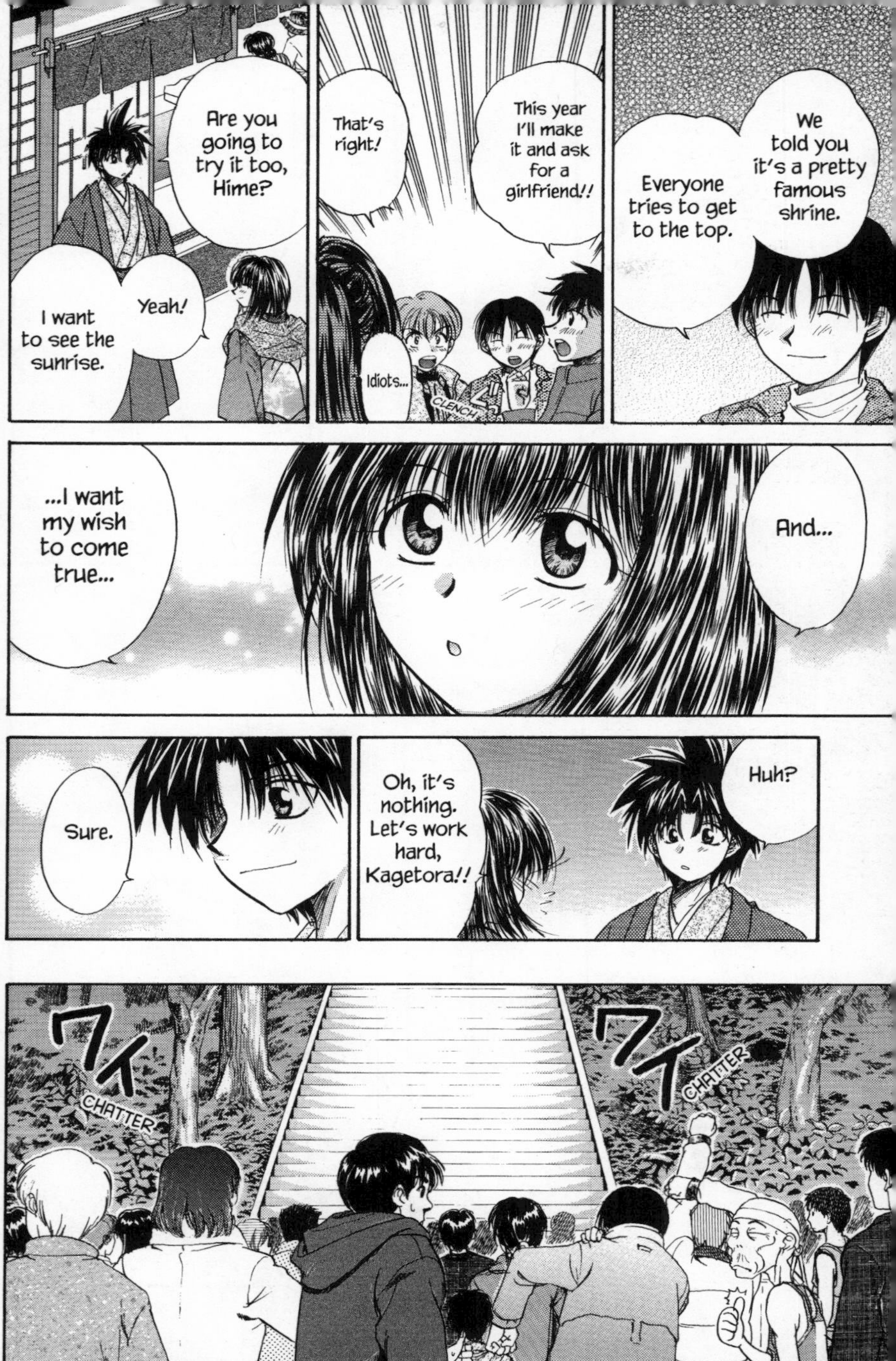
We told you it's a pretty famous shrine.
Everyone tries to get to the top.
This year I'll make it and ask for a girlfriend!!
That's right!
Idiots...
CLENCH
Are you going to try it too, Hime?
Yeah!
I want to see the sunrise.
And...
...I want my wish to come true...
Huh?
Oh, it's nothing. Let's work hard, Kagetora!!
Sure.
ワイ
CHATTER
ワイ
CHATTER

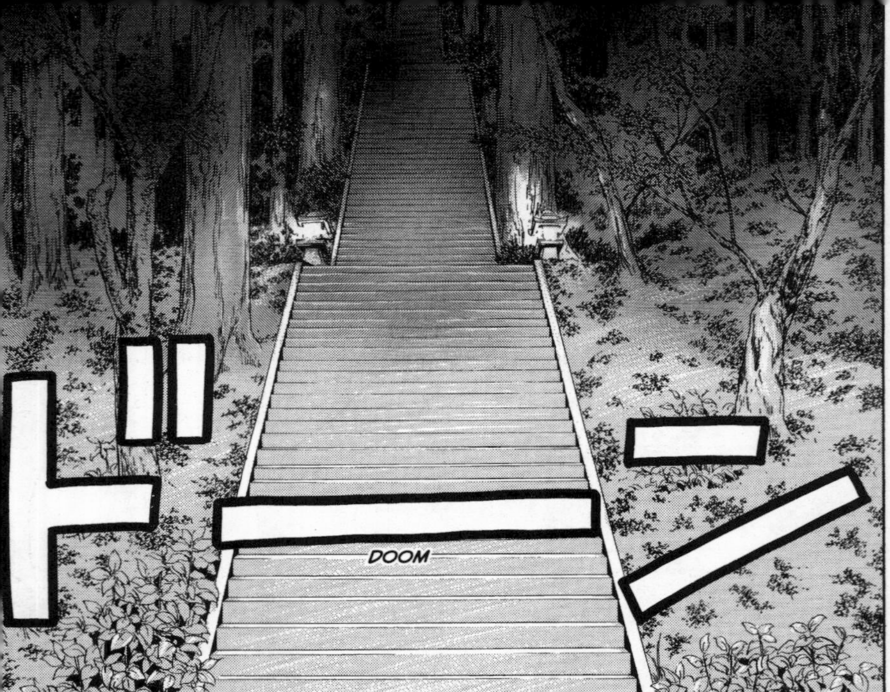
DOOM

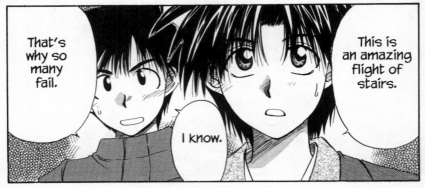

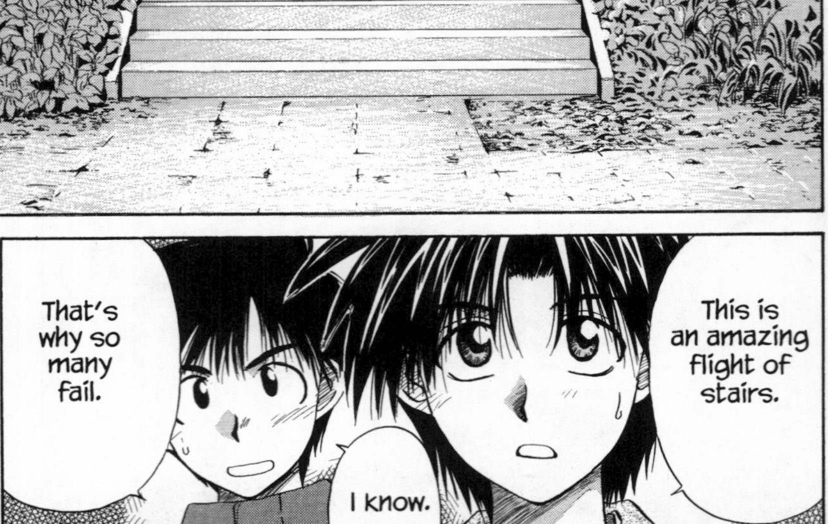
This is an amazing flight of stairs.
I know.
That's why so many fail.

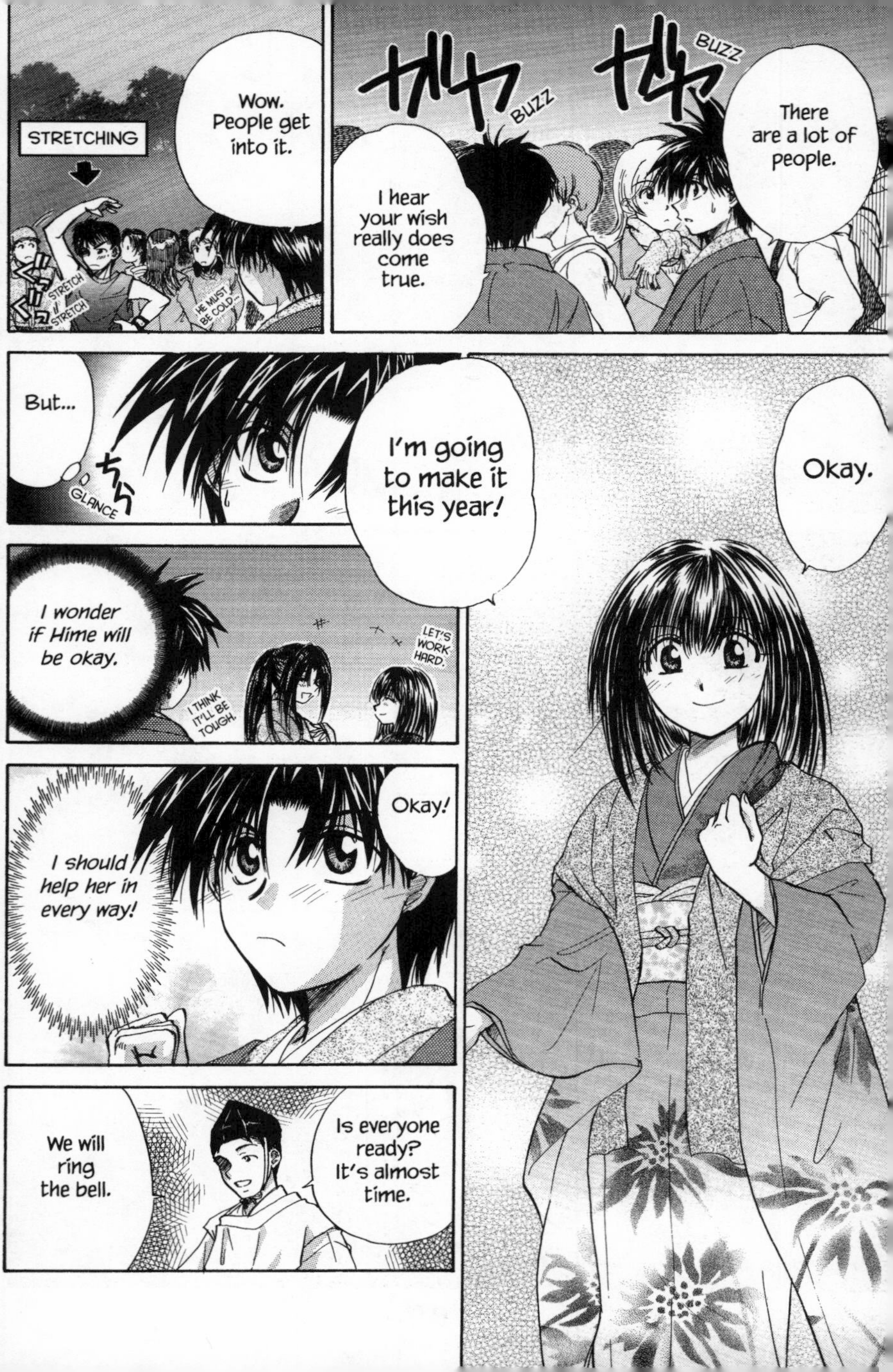
BUZZ
BUZZ
There are a lot of people.
I hear your wish really does come true.
Wow. People get into it.
STRETCHING
STRETCH STRETCH
HE MUST BE COLD...
I'm going to make it this year!
Okay.
But...
GLANCE
I wonder if Hime will be okay.
LET'S WORK HARD.
I THINK IT'LL BE TOUGH.
Okay!
I should help her in every way!
Is everyone ready? It's almost time.
We will ring the bell.

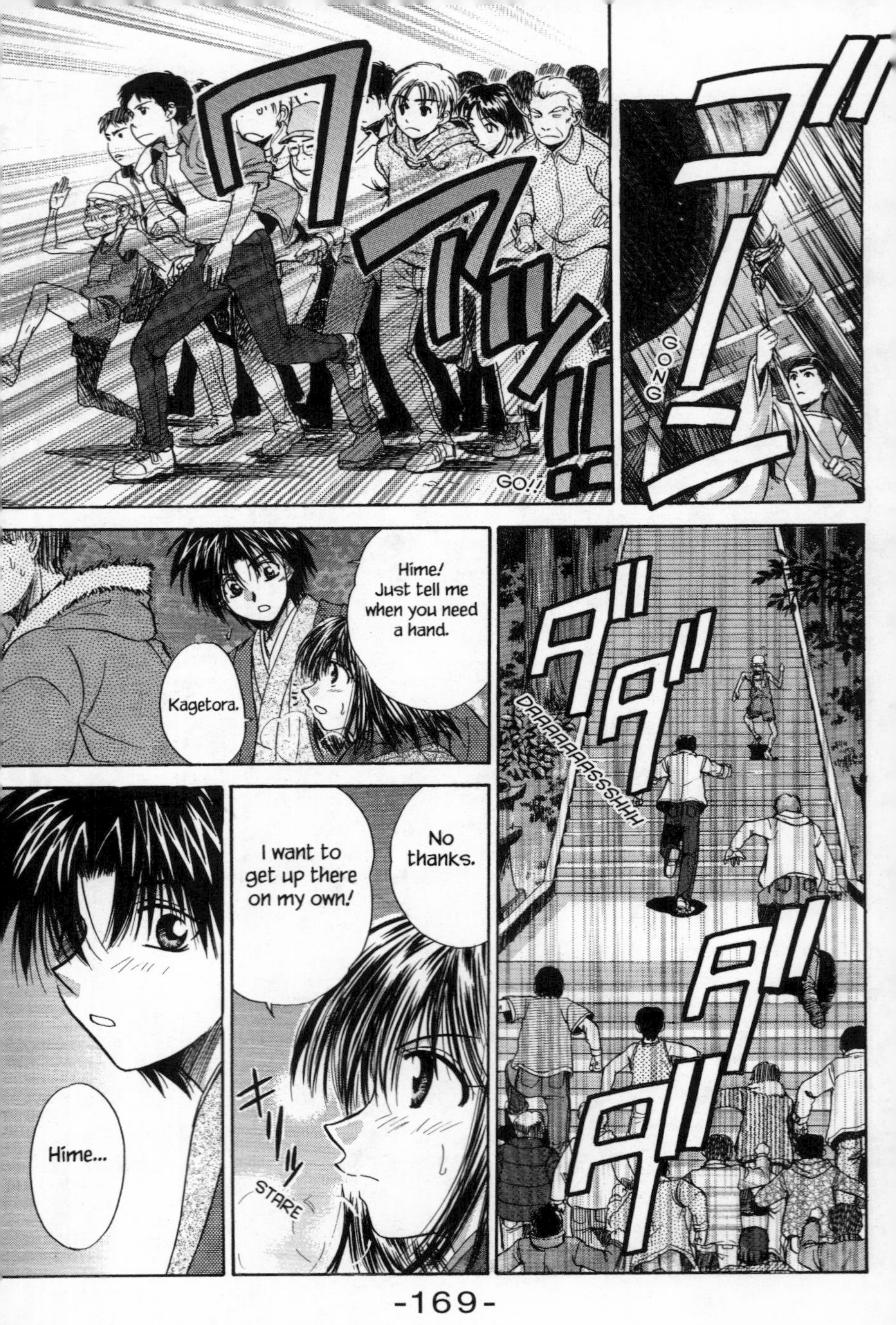
GONG
GO!!
DAAAAAAAASSSHHH
Hime! Just tell me when you need a hand.
Kagetora.
No thanks.
I want to get up there on my own!
STARE
Hime...

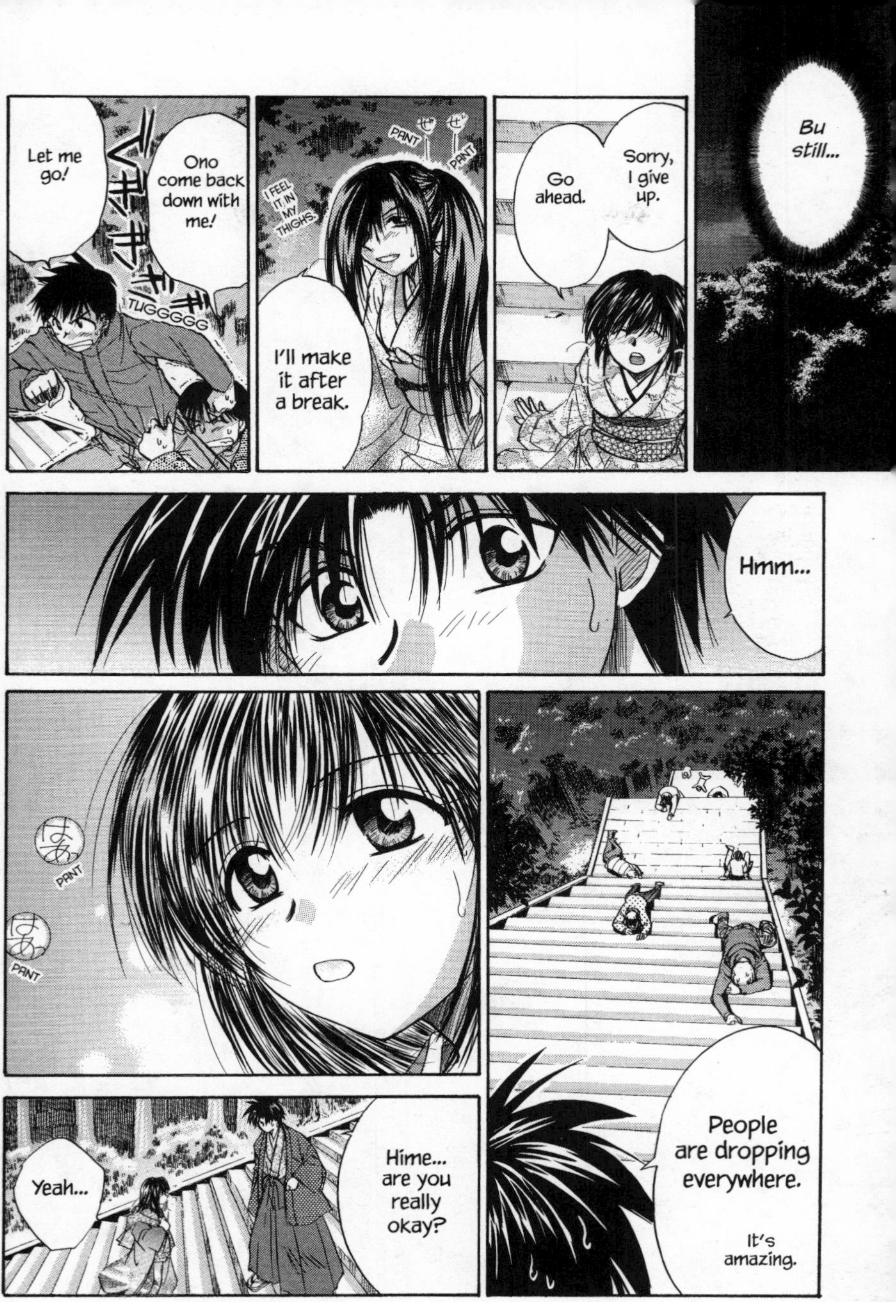
Bu still...
Sorry, I give up.
Go ahead.
PANT
PANT
I FEEL IT IN MY THIGHS.
I'll make it after a break.
Ono come back down with me!
Let me go!
TUGGGGG
Hmm...
People are dropping everywhere.
It's amazing.
はあ
PANT
はあ
PANT
Hime... are you really okay?
Yeah...

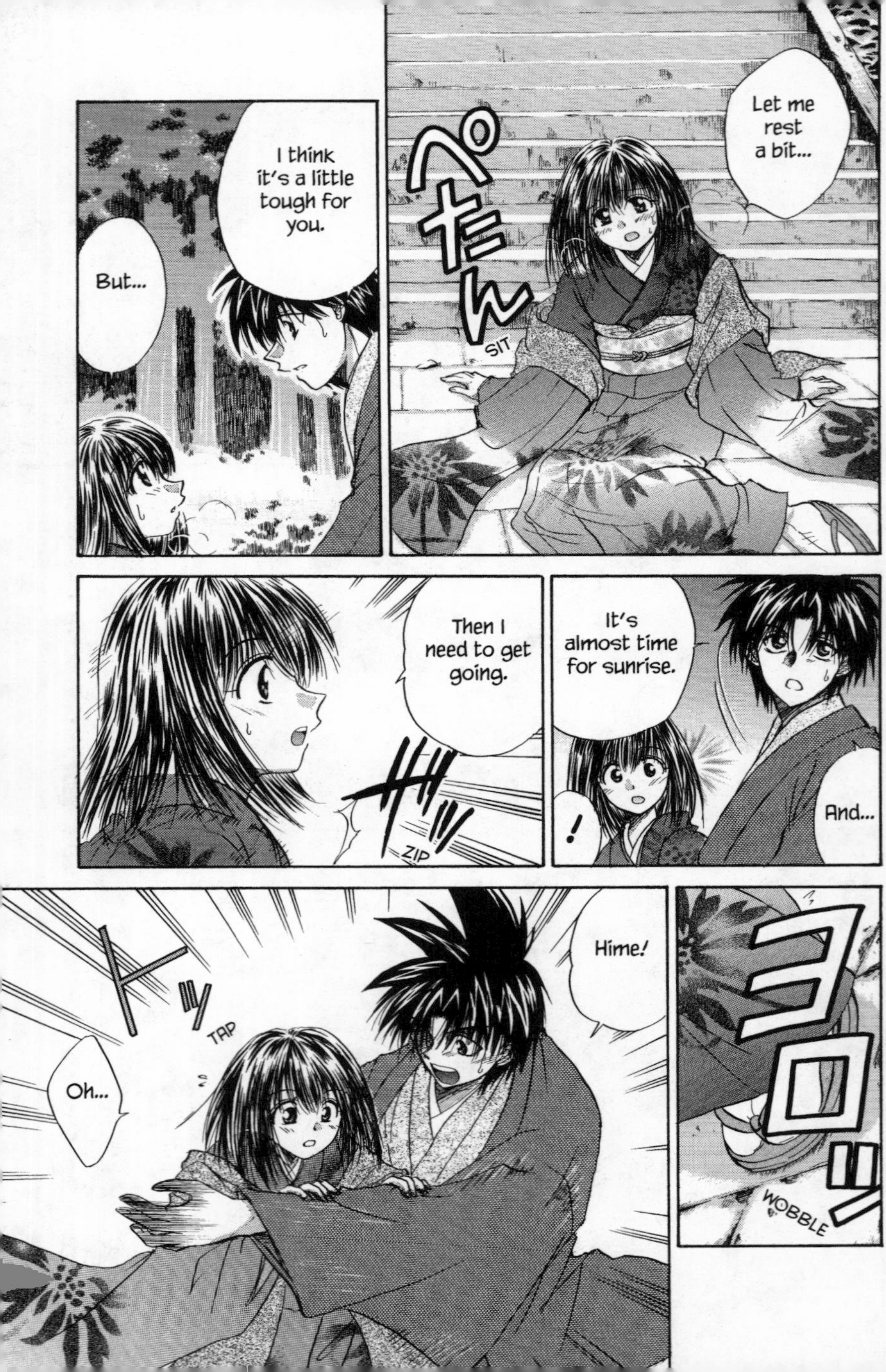
Let me rest a bit...
ぺたん
SIT
I think it's a little tough for you.
But...
It's almost time for sunrise.
And...
!
Then I need to get going.
ZIP
ヨロッ
WOBBLE
Hime!
トッ
TAP
Oh...

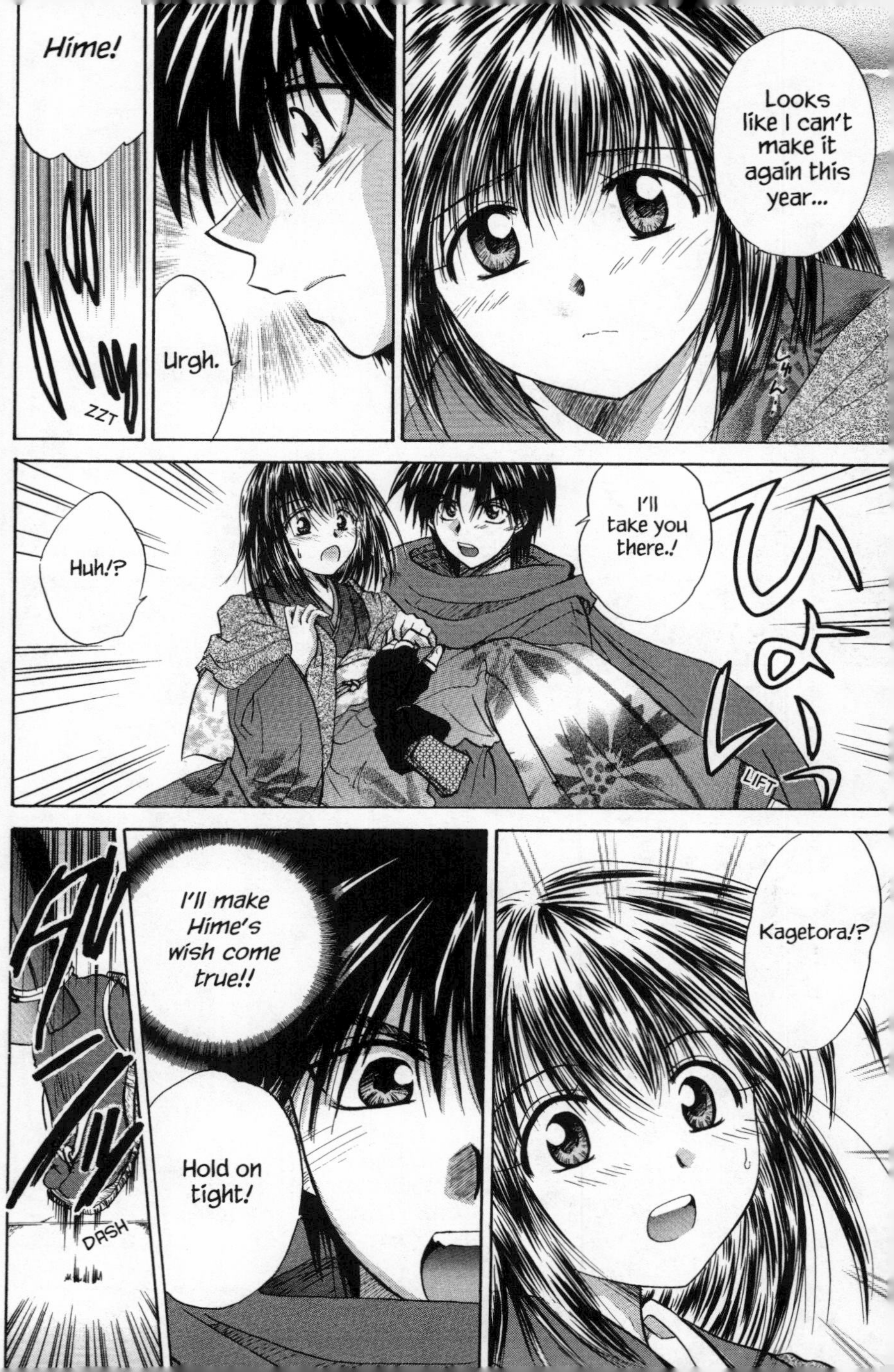
Looks like I can't make it again this year...
Urgh.
Hime!
ZZT
I'll take you there.!
LIFT
Huh!?
Kagetora!?
I'll make Hime's wish come true!!
Hold on tight!
DASH

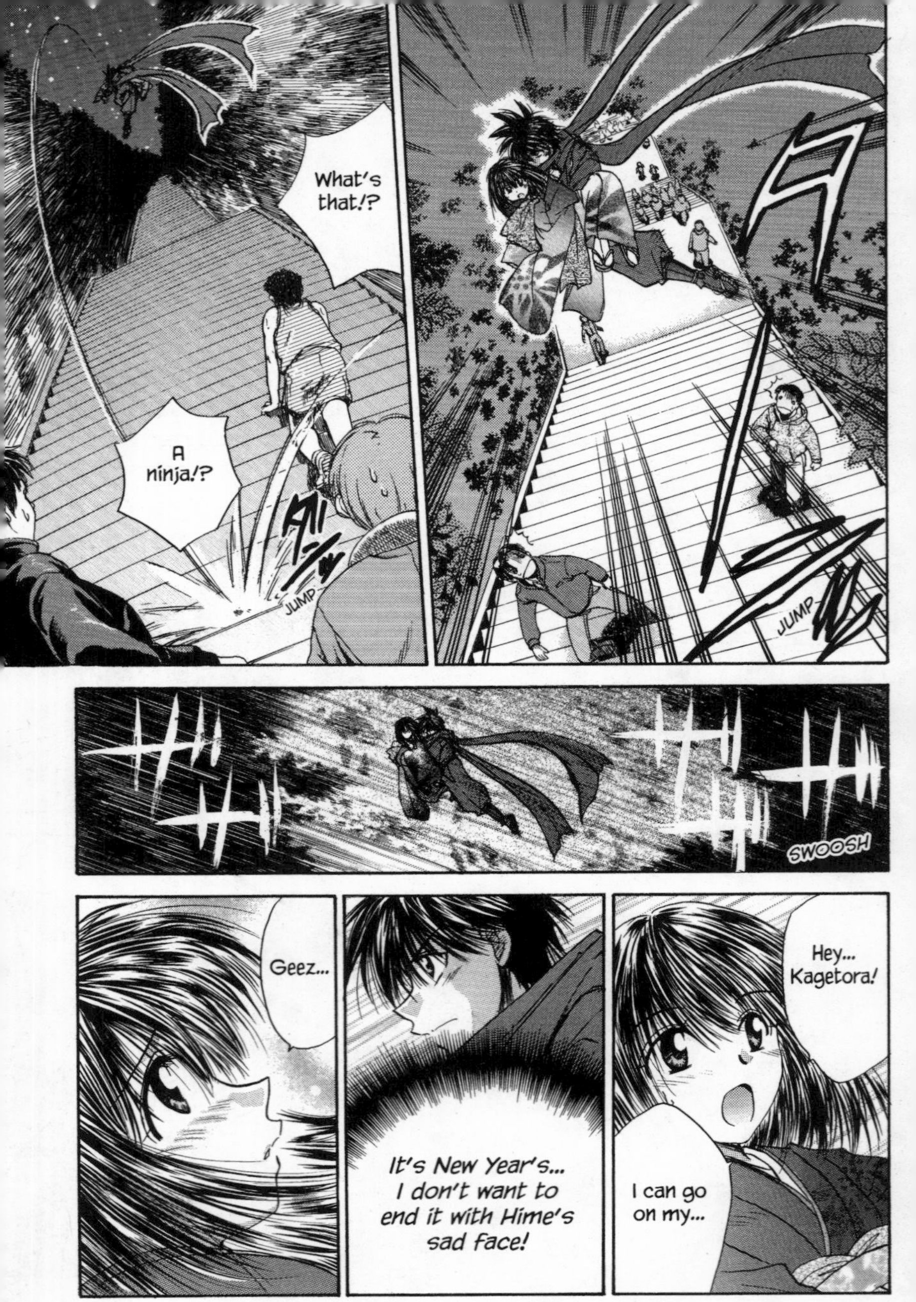
JUMP
What's that!?
A ninja!?
JUMP
SWOOSH
Hey... Kagetora!
I can go on my...
It's New Year's... I don't want to end it with Hime's sad face!
Geez...

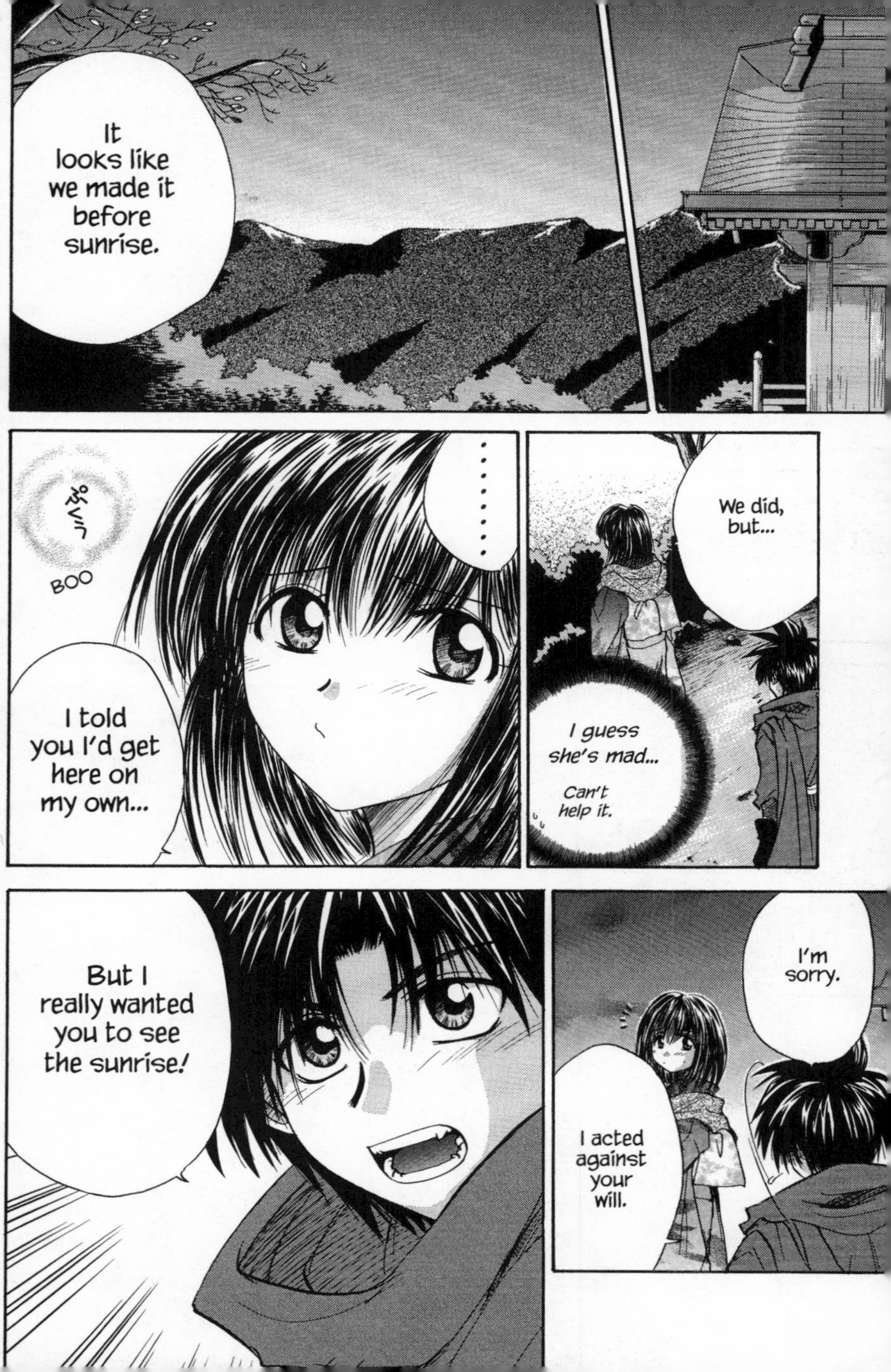

It looks like we made it before sunrise.
We did, but...
I guess she's mad...
Can't help it.
....
BOO
I told you I'd get here on my own...
I'm sorry.
I acted against your will.
But I really wanted you to see the sunrise!

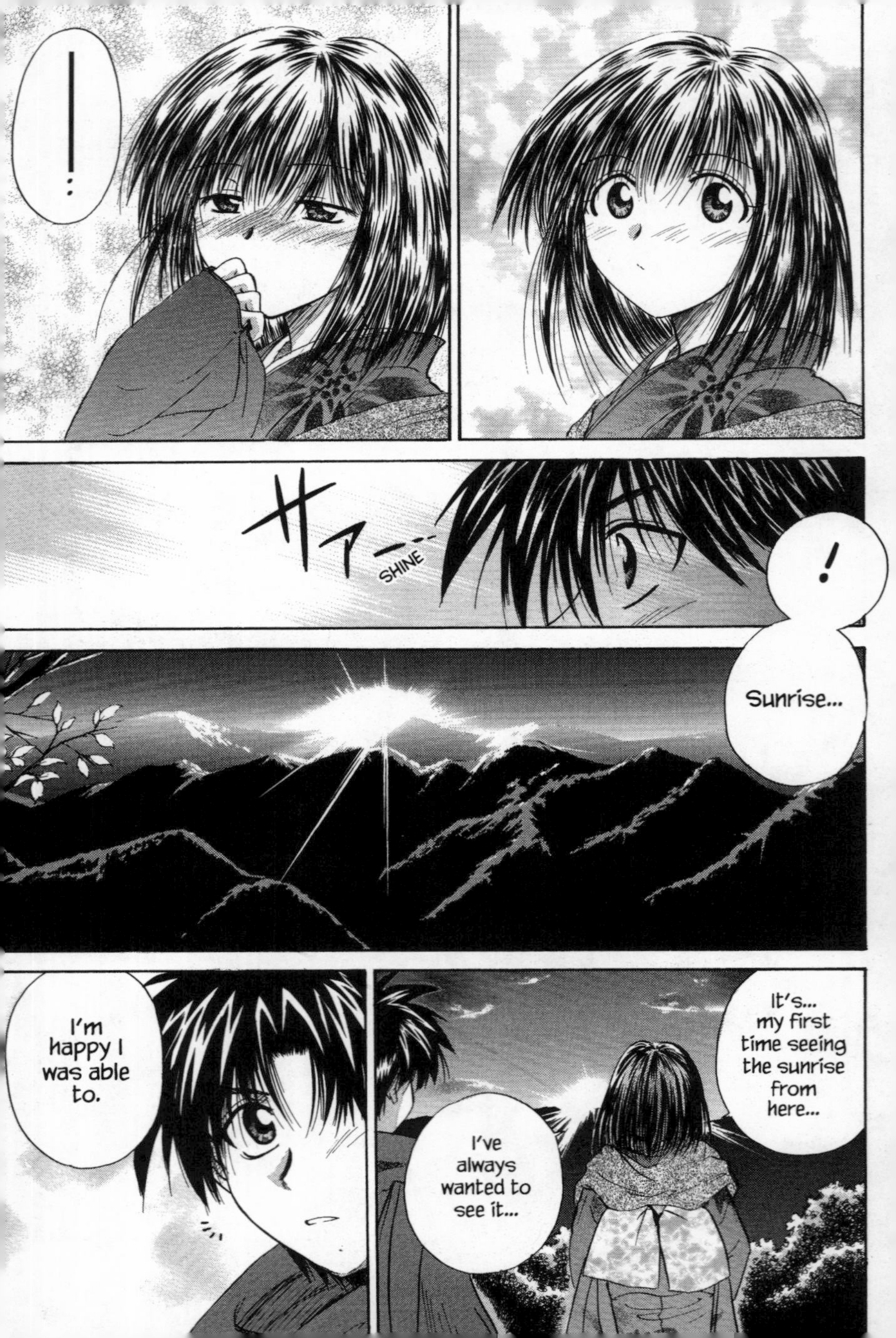

…!
サァーー
SHINE
!
Sunrise...
It's... my first time seeing the sunrise from here...
I've always wanted to see it...
I'm happy I was able to.

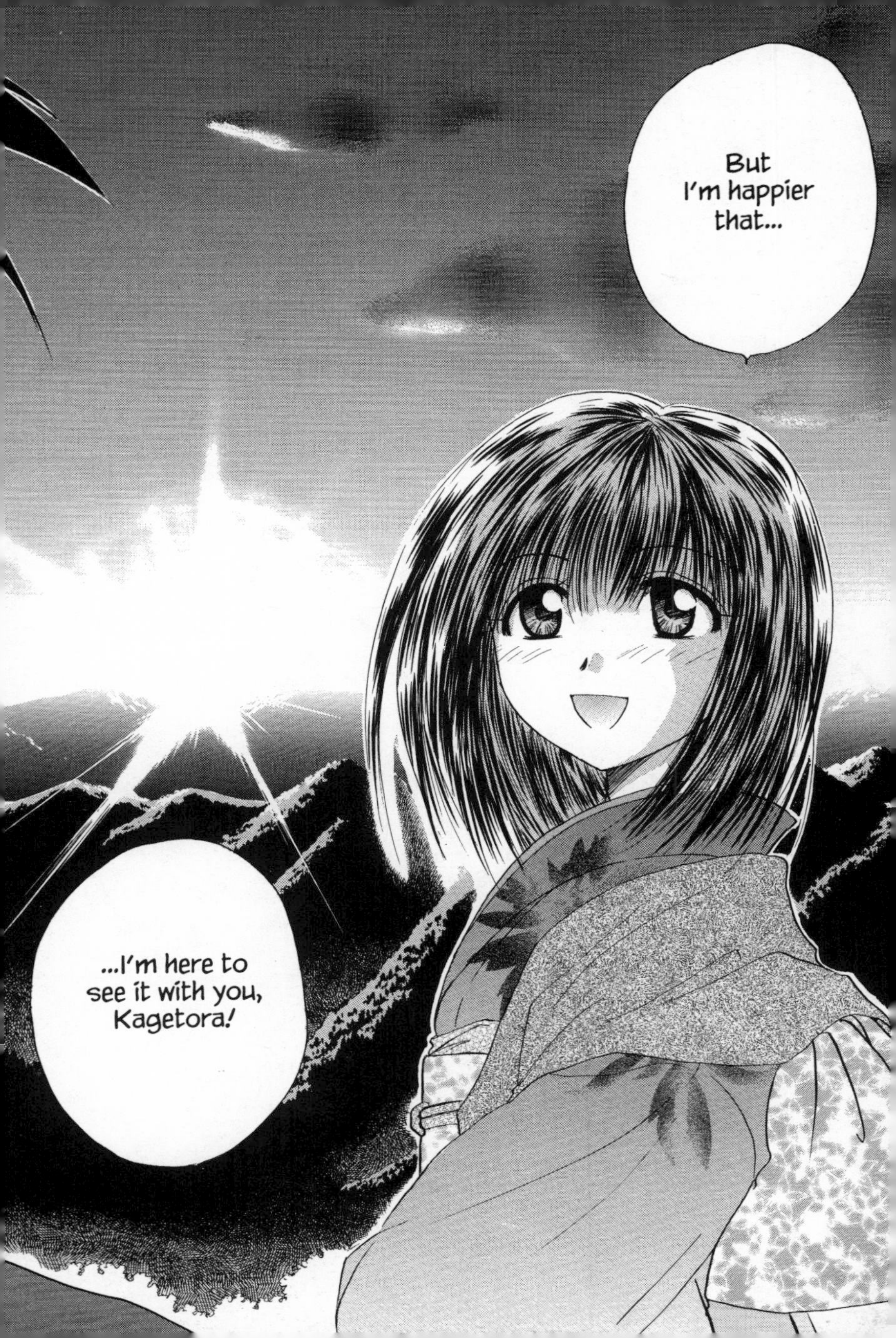
But I'm happier that...
...I'm here to see it with you, Kagetora!

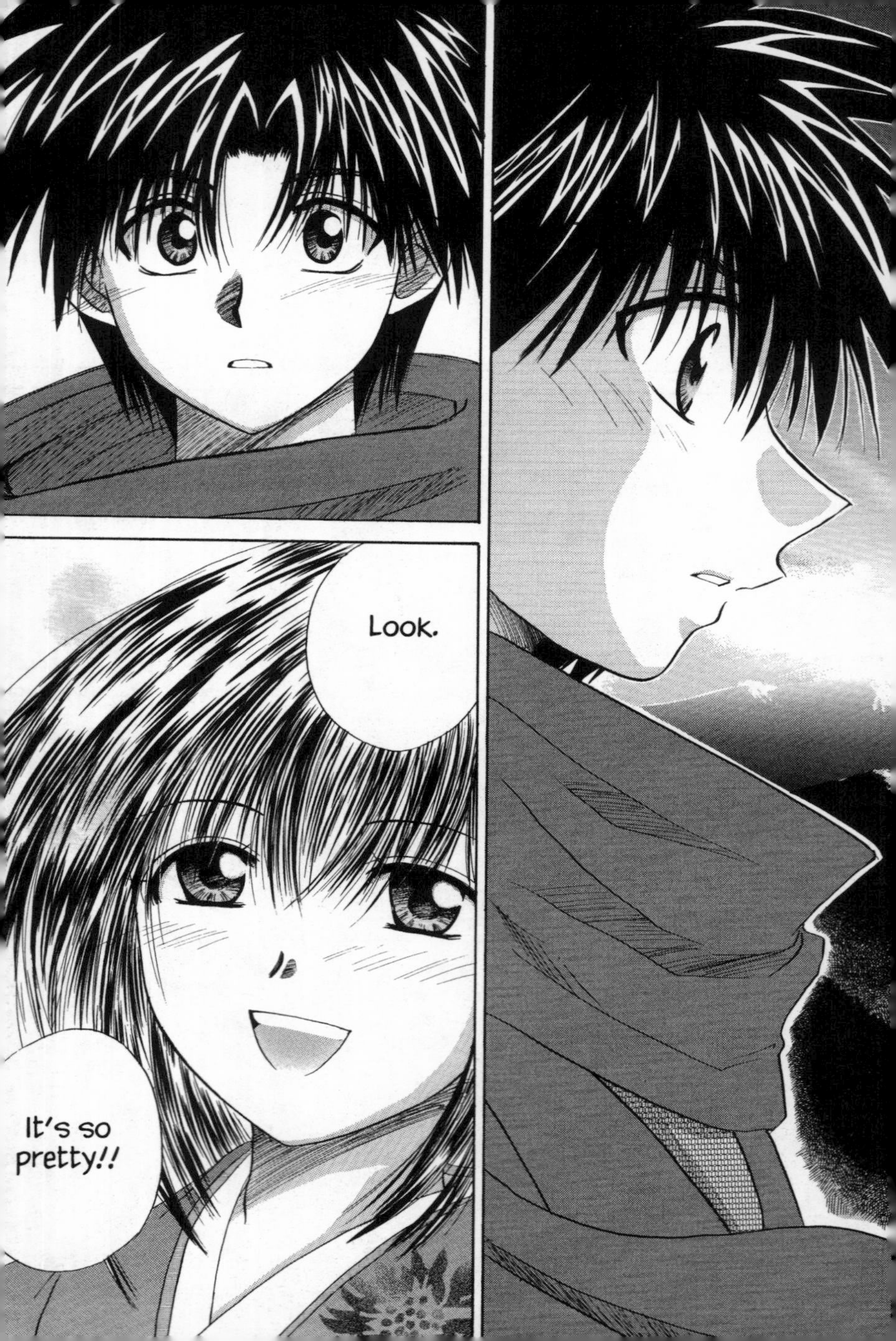
Look.
It's so pretty!!

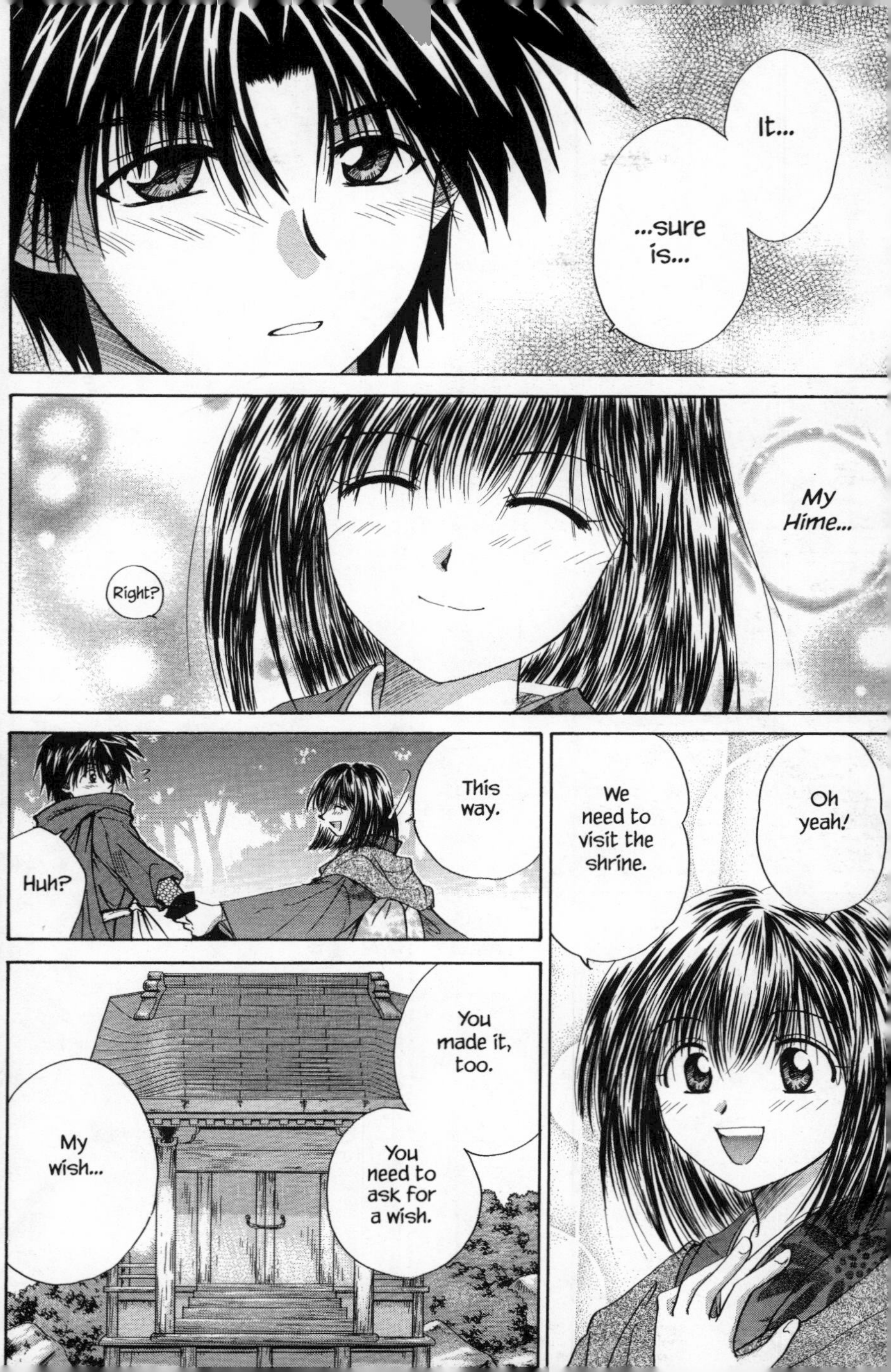
It...
...sure is...
My Hime...
Right?
Oh yeah!
We need to visit the shrine.
This way.
Huh?
You made it, too.
You need to ask for a wish.
My wish...

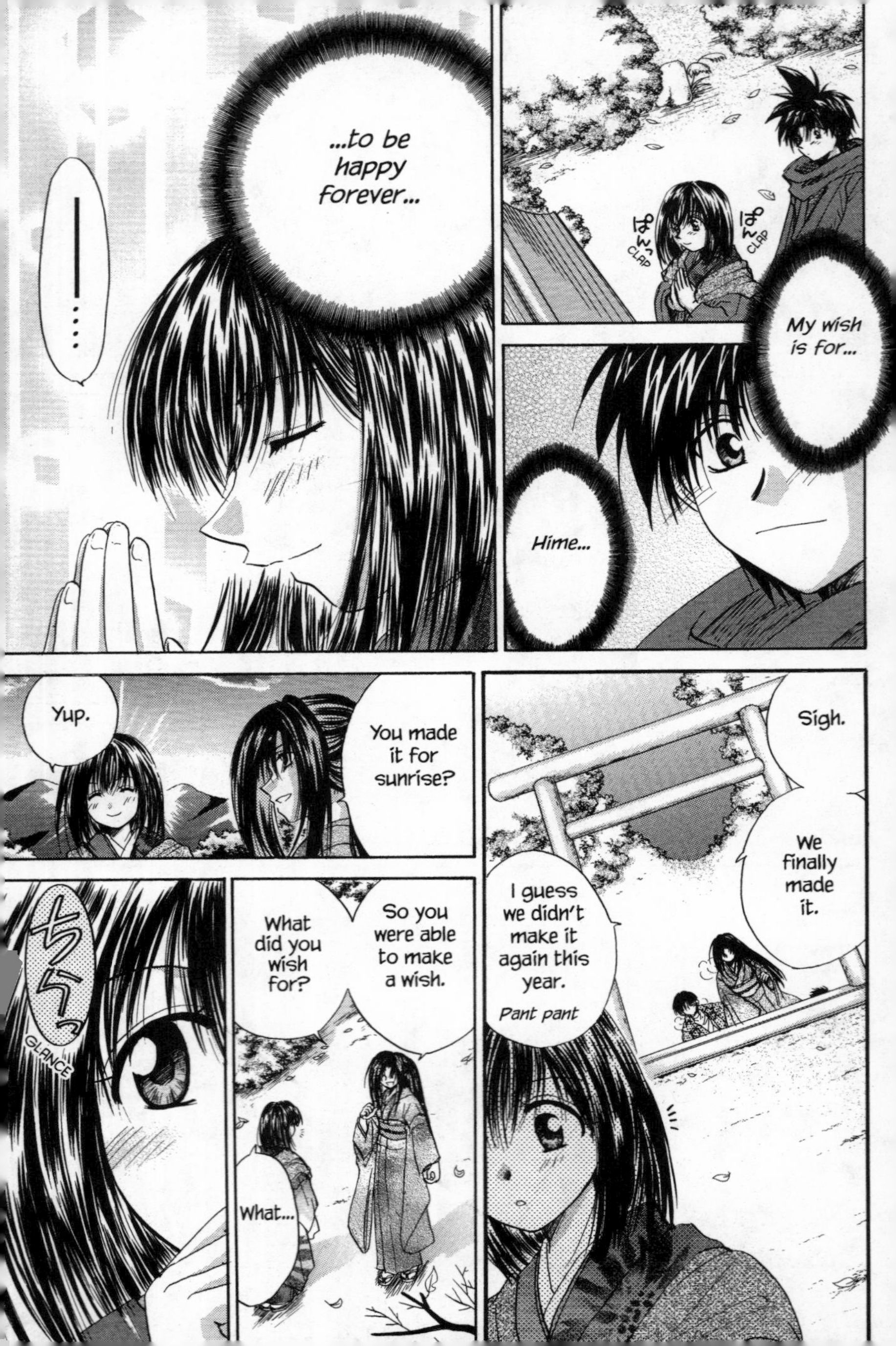

ぱんっ CLAP
ぱんっ CLAP
My wish is for...
Hime...
...to be happy forever...
—......
Sigh.
We finally made it.
I guess we didn't make it again this year.
Pant pant
You made it for sunrise?
Yup.
So you were able to make a wish.
What did you wish for?
What...
ちらっ GLANCE

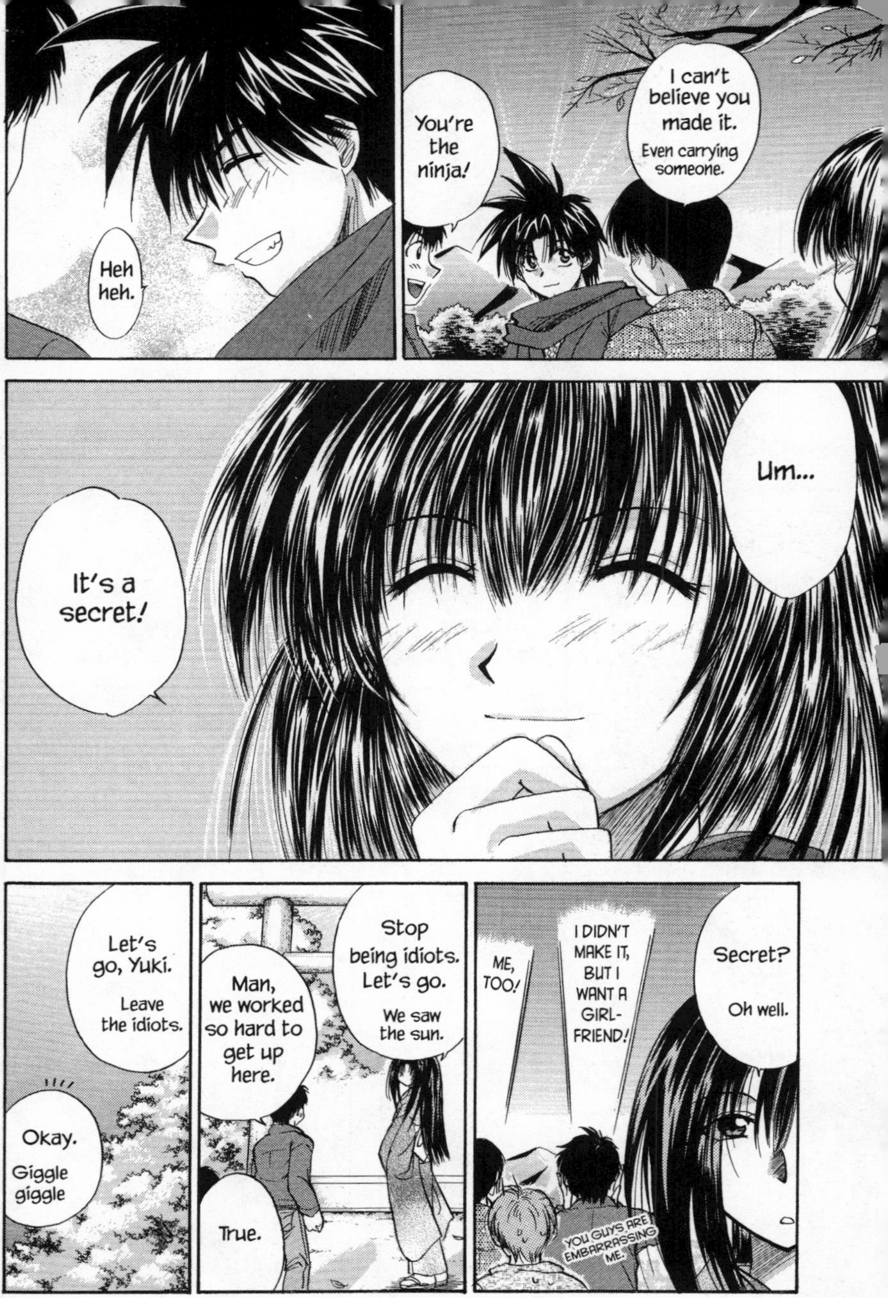

I can't believe you made it.
Even carrying someone.
You're the ninja!
Heh heh.
Um...
It's a secret!
Secret?
Oh well.
I DIDN'T MAKE IT, BUT I WANT A GIRLFRIEND!
ME, TOO!
YOU GUYS ARE EMBARRASSING ME.
Stop being idiots. Let's go.
We saw the sun.
Man, we worked so hard to get up here.
True.
Let's go, Yuki.
Leave the idiots.
Okay.
Giggle giggle

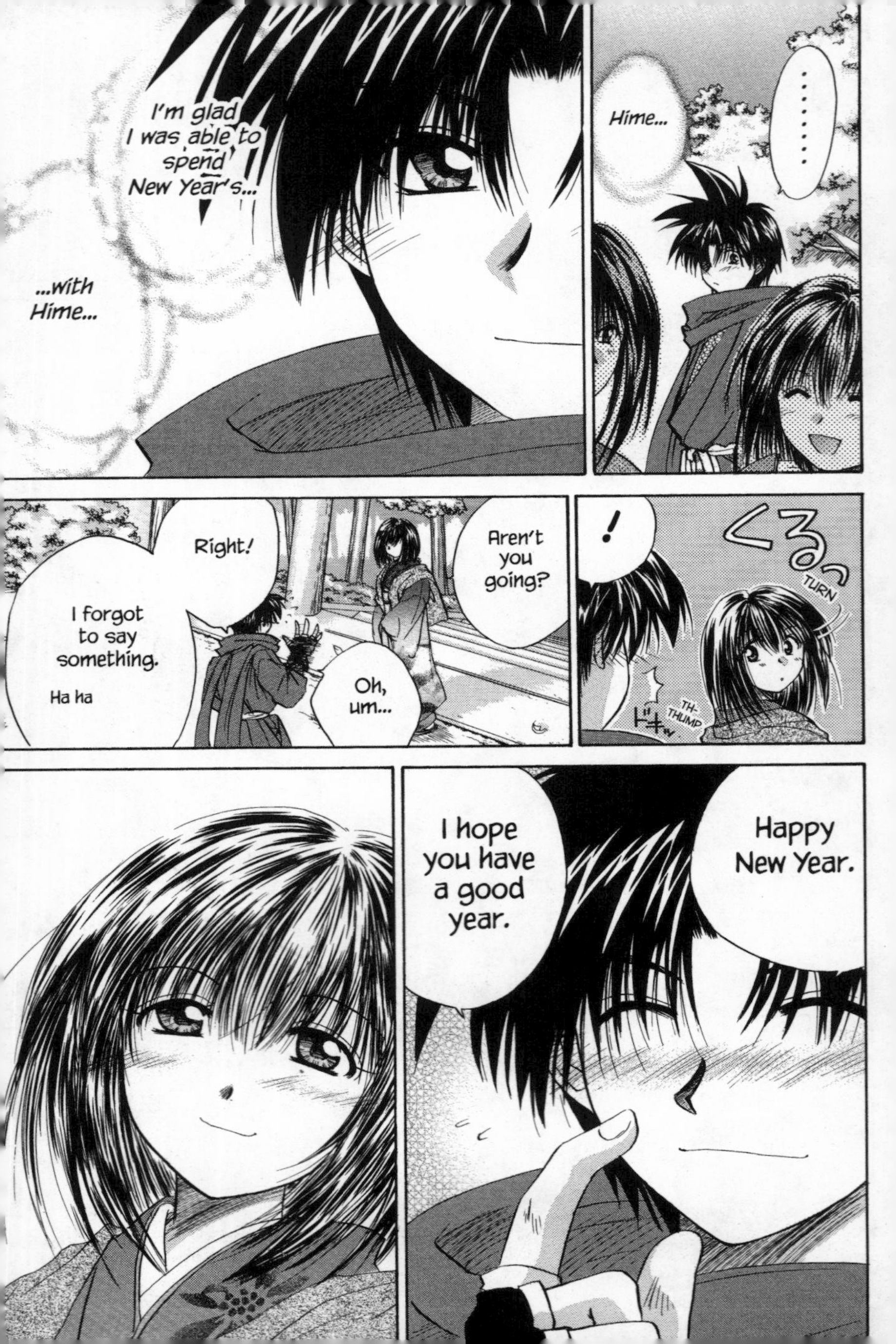

......
Hime...
I'm glad I was able to spend New Year's...
...with Hime...
!
くるっ
TURN
TH-THUMP
ドキ
Aren't you going?
Oh, um...
Right!
I forgot to say something.
Ha ha
Happy New Year.
I hope you have a good year.

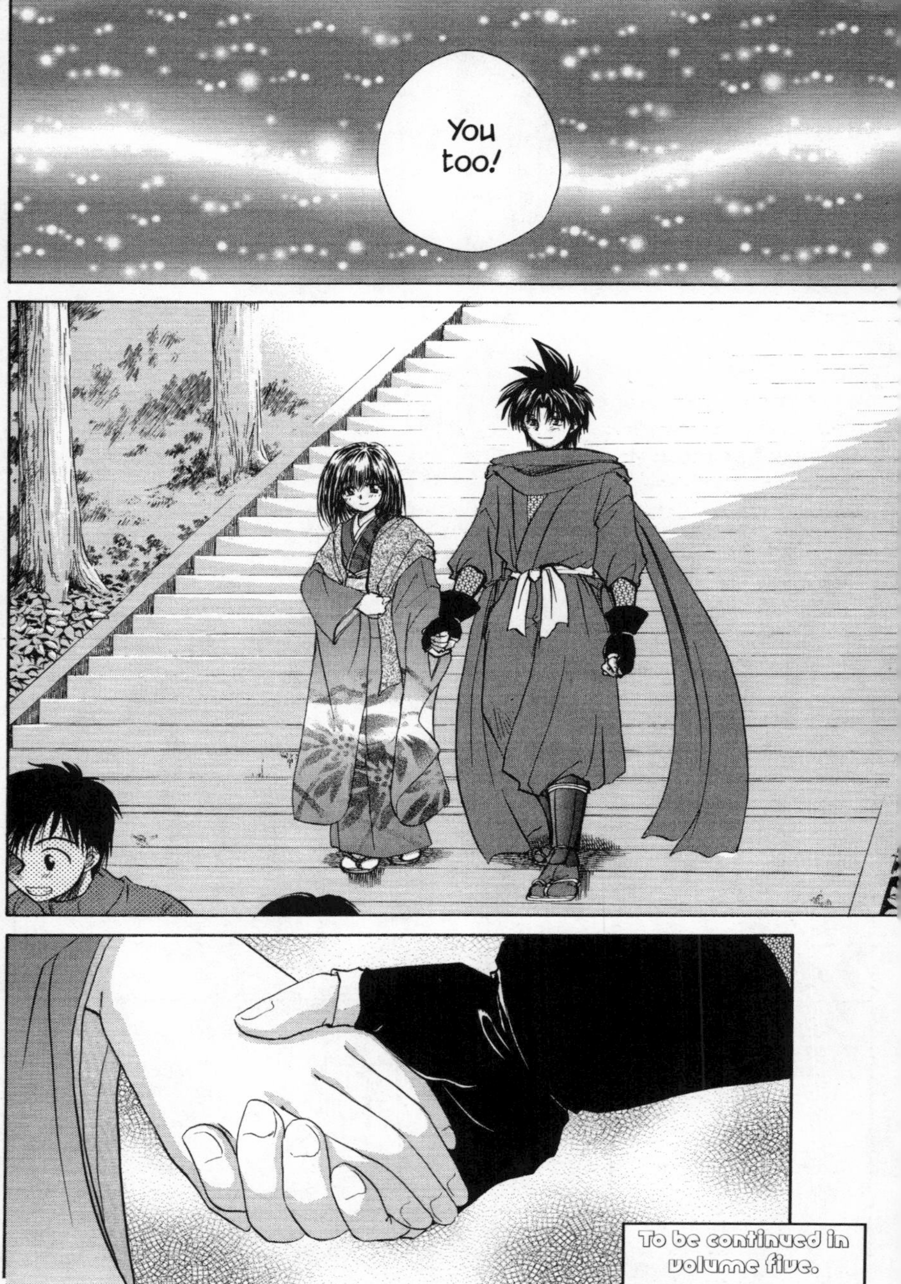
You too!
To be continued in volume five.

Bonus Page

This is **Segami**. Thanks to you, we are at Volume 4. This time the Bonus Page is only one page, so there are no 4-panel comics. *(laugh)* I'll just talk about random stuff.

About Ninjas- Part 4

I went to Togakushi. I went up the flight of stairs and was tired by the time I got to the Kid's Ninja Village. There were no kids... But I did get to see the mechanic house and stuff. It must've been a weird sight to see a grown-up play. It's okay because there weren't that many people. *(laugh)* I also went to other places related to ninjas. And of course, I worked at night at the hotel. I wonder why I work so hard to travel...

About Traveling

I went to Kanazawa... There was a lot of snow. Of course I visited the Ninja Temple, but my main purpose for traveling was crab. I ate it. I ate so much. I think I won't have crab for a while...When I returned from Kanazawa I went to Kyoto. (This was for gathering pictures). I went to the Movie Village and met some actors. It looks like they are in a famous drama series. Even if they are only in it to be killed off. When I watch it, I should look out for them. *(laugh)*

About Weapons - Part 2

My weapon collection has increased. Of course, they are important materials necessary for my work. But the problem is where to put all of it... Currently it is spread out in my workspace. My work area is looking more and more fishy...

About Traveling, my excuse

Writing about the places I go makes it look like I'm out and about playing around. But really, it's mostly for work!! I take many pictures to use as resources! I don't take any pictures of myself! Although that sounds sad, too... Maybe next time I should take at least one of myself.

Thanks

Thank you for all your letters. It takes a while but I do write back. So for those of you waiting, please watch out for it! By the way, S-san... thank you for the very cute card. I know raising a child is tough, but please continue to work hard! I am rooting for you! Other people... I know work and studying are tough, but please keep at it!! I will work hard, too!... Even if I take breaks to go travel.

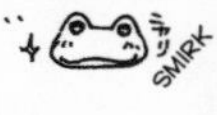
SMIRK

Special Thanks

アシスタント・・田中くん・大島ちゃん
Assistants: Tanaka-kun, Oshima-chan
担当・・森田氏
Editor: Morita-san
コミック担当・・法土さん
Comic Editor: Houdou-san

瀬上あきら
Akira Segami

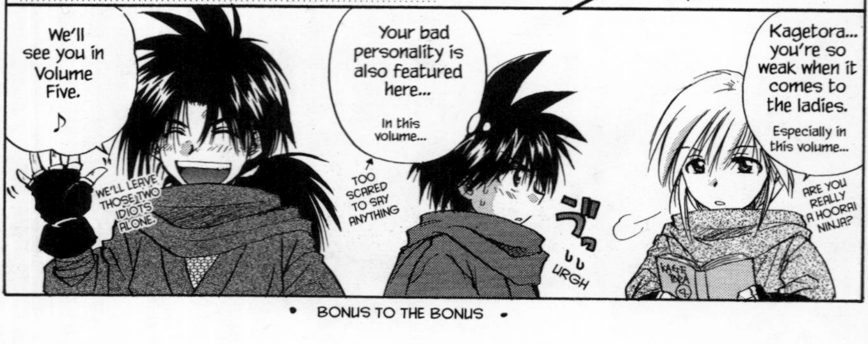
Kagetora... you're so weak when it comes to the ladies.
Especially in this volume...
ARE YOU REALLY A HOORAI NINJA?
Your bad personality is also featured here...
In this volume...
TOO SCARED TO SAY ANYTHING
URGH
We'll see you in Volume Five. ♪
WE'LL LEAVE THOSE TWO IDIOTS ALONE.

• BONUS TO THE BONUS •

About the Author

Segami's first manga was published by Shogakukan in 1996. He went on to do a few other small projects, including two short stories entitled "Kagetora" in 2001 and 2002. The character proved to be popular with fans, so Segami began his first ongoing series, *Kagetora*, with Kodansha in 2003. The series continues to run today.

Translation Notes

Japanese is a tricky language for most Westerners, and translation is often more art than science. For your edification and reading pleasure, here are notes on some of the places where we could have gone in a different direction in our translation of the work, or where a Japanese cultural reference is used.

Sake, author note

Although known in the United States as a Japanese rice wine commonly ordered at sushi restaurants, the Japanese use the term "sake" for anything that is alcoholic. The rice wine is properly known as "Nihonshu" or "Ponshu" for slang. ("Pon" is from "Nippon," which is one way to pronounce "Japan" in Japanese.)

Watermelon Cracking, page 14

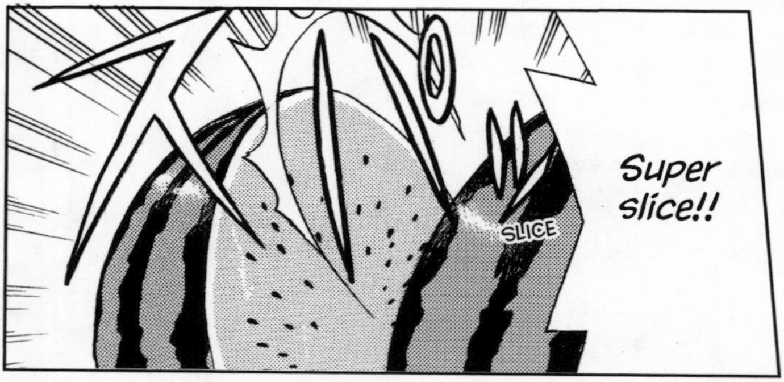
Super slice!!
SLICE

Watermelon Cracking is a popular game the Japanese play at the beach. As with a piñata, a person is blindfolded and tries to hit the watermelon. After someone successfully cracks the watermelon, they are supposed to eat it. But usually the watermelon gets sandy, so people who intend to eat it put a plastic sheet underneath.

Cavalry Battle, Page 22

Cavalry Battle used to be a common event at Japanese schools during Field Day. Because of the difficulty of the event, it is usually done by fifth graders and older. It is a game where three or four people make a horse, and the lightest person becomes the warrior on the horse. The warriors are divided into two groups, and they battle each other. The group with the most warriors still standing at the end wins. The rules vary, but in younger grades, kids fight to take the hat a warrior is wearing. Due to the potential danger of this event, Japanese schools rarely have it anymore. But before all the lawsuits, this event was highly popular and usually held toward the end of Field Day.

***Fireworks,* Page 33**

In Japan, people can play with fireworks any day during the summer. This is why Kagetora and his friends can play with fireworks at the resort. Fireworks are also sold virtually anywhere, such as department stores, supermarkets, and convenience stores.

***Mouse Tail Fireworks,* Page 33**

Mouse tail fireworks act the same way as the American firework, Ground Spinners. They are named as such because the Japanese versions are shaped like a mouse tail—unlike the Ground Spinners, which are cylindrical in shape.

***Tamaya,* Page 33**

Japanese people say *Tamaya* when a big firework goes up. This is a tradition originating from the Edo Period when two firework makers known as Tamaya and Kagiya competed to make the best fireworks. The two would set off fireworks and yell out their names *Tamaya!* and *Kagiya!* every time their work went up.

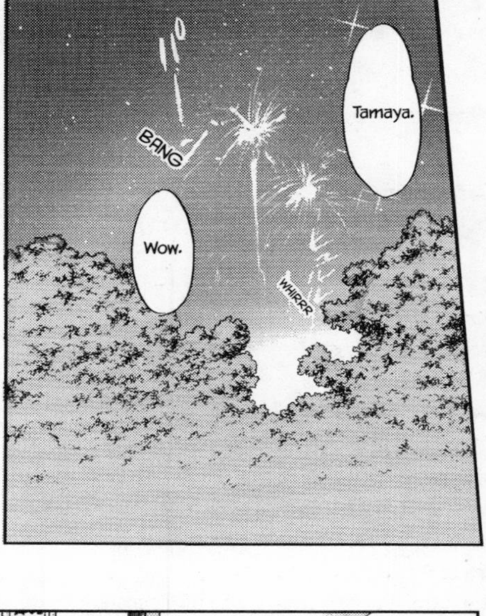
Tamaya.
BANG
Wow.
WHIRRR

***Dedicated Weapons,* Page 40**

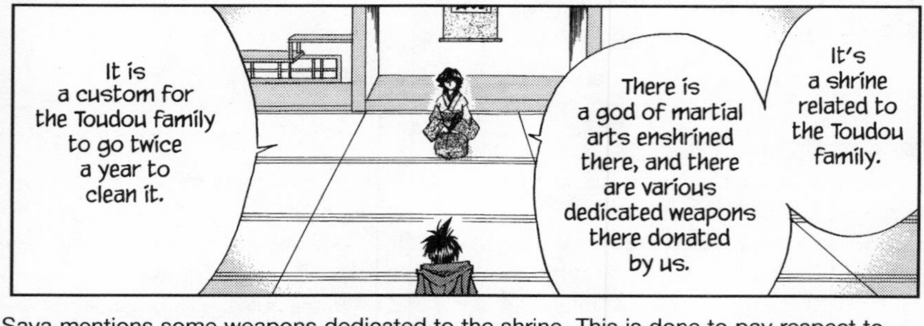
It's a shrine related to the Toudou family.
There is a god of martial arts enshrined there, and there are various dedicated weapons there donated by us.
It is a custom for the Toudou family to go twice a year to clean it.

Saya mentions some weapons dedicated to the shrine. This is done to pay respect to the gods, or to amuse them. Usually a weapon of a famous warrior (i.e. an important general) is dedicated.

Miko, Page 41

Yuki is wearing a *Miko* outfit. A *miko* is a shrine maiden. Modern miko perform ceremonial dances or assist priests in wedding ceremonies.

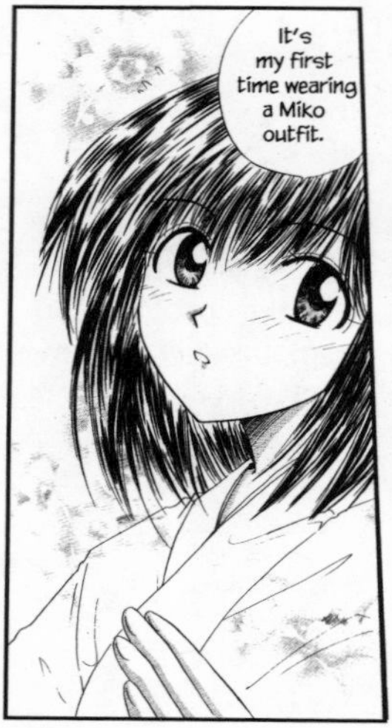
It's my first time wearing a Miko outfit.

Drinking Age, Page 48

In Japan, the legal drinking age is 20.

Aiki Jujitsu, Page 81

Aiki Jujitsu is a Japanese martial art, in which artists use the attacker's force and redirect it against them.

Ohagi, Page 123

Ohagi is a Japanese sweet dish made with sweet rice and covered with red beans. It is also known as *botamochi,* but the Japanese call it *botamochi* when it is eaten in the spring. *Ohagi* is the name for this dish when it is eaten in the fall.

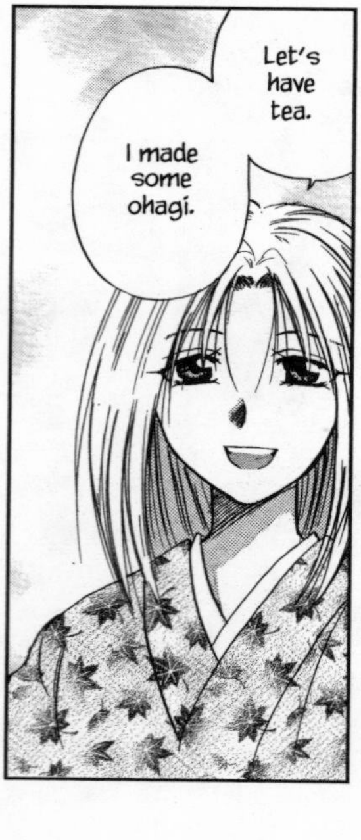
Let's have tea.
I made some ohagi.

***Purification*, Page 149**

Purification is usually done in the river or the ocean to wash off the impurities and sins. This allows them to literally flow away. But since going into the river or ocean is not practical, Yuki and Kagetora are doing it with plain water.

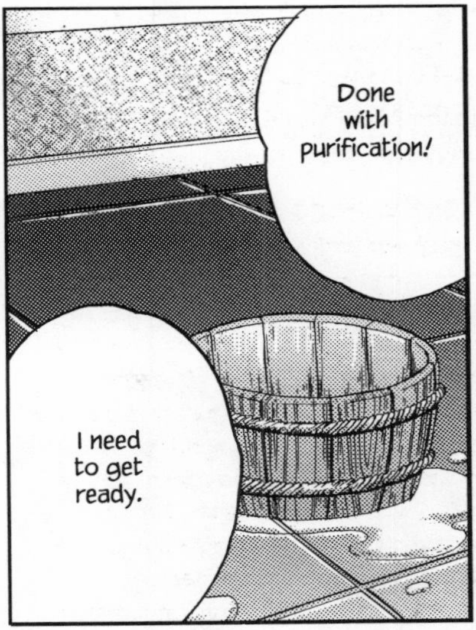
Done with purification!
I need to get ready.

***New Year's*, Page 151**

During the New Year, people will typically go home to spend time with their family. Kagetora is supposed to go home to his Hoorai house, but instead he decides to stay in Tokyo with Yuki. The New Year is celebrated from New Year's Eve until the third day of the New Year.

***Visiting Twice*, Page 152**

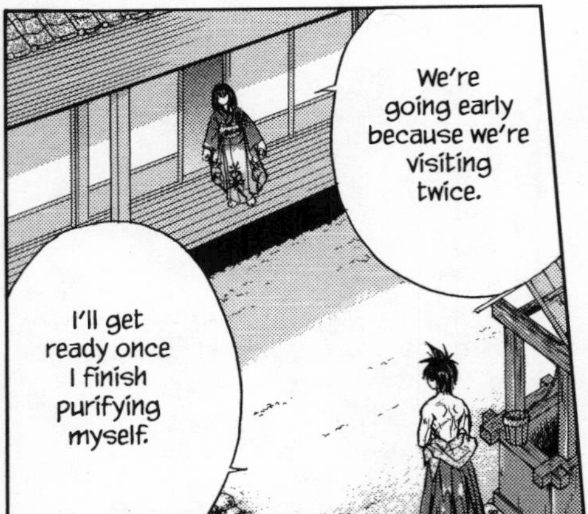
We're going early because we're visiting twice.
I'll get ready once I finish purifying myself.

Yuki here is referring to *ninen-mairi,* which is the act of visiting the shrine before and after the New Year. They will pay a visit once before midnight, and then again when the New Year begins. Young people or people who don't have kids are typically the ones who will do this. Families will usually wait until the morning of the New Year to visit the shrine. Either way, famous shrines will be crowded with people.

New Year's Eve Bell, Page 155

On New Year's Eve, the shrines ring the bell 108 times. This comes from a Buddhist belief that man has 108 desires, and by listening to the calm sound of the bell, we can get rid of them.

Omikuji, Page 160

Omikuji are fortunes written on thin strips of paper. They are sold at temples and shrines. Japanese people will usually buy one on New Year's Day to see what kind of fortune they will have for the year. Ono is shaking something in the background, which is a container of bamboo sticks. One will come out of the hole in the container, which will have a number on it. You take a slip of paper from one of the drawers with your number. *Omikuji* fortunes range from Good to Bad in six to seven levels.

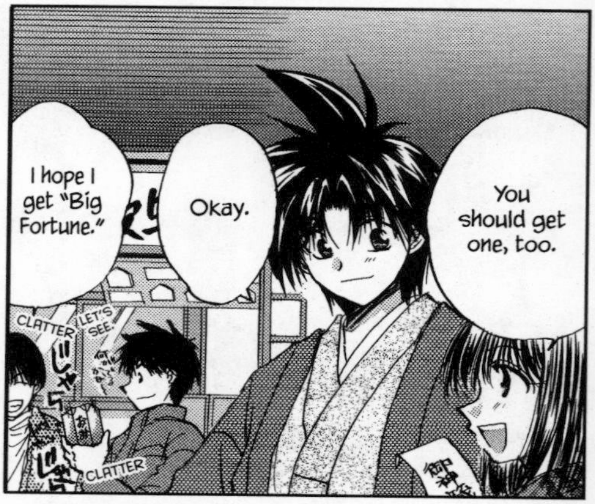
You should get one, too.
Okay.
I hope I get "Big Fortune."
LET'S SEE.
CLATTER
CLATTER

New Year's Soba, Page 163

Japanese people eat soba, or buckwheat noodles, on New Year's Eve. Buckwheat noodles are very long and thin, which has led to the belief that if one eats these noodles they will have a long and prosperous life.

Togakushi, Page 183

Togakushi is an area in Japan with a famous ninja village. They have a museum and the mechanical house Segami talks about.

Kanazawa, Page 183

Kanazawa is located in the western region of Japan. The Ninja Temple Segami talks about is properly known as Myoryuji Temple. There are escape routes, hidden chambers, secret tunnels, and trick doors.

Kyoto, Page 183

Kyoto is the former capital of Japan, located in the western region. The Movie Village Segami talks about is a movie set open to the public. (Think of it like Universal Studios.) Toei, one of Japan's top film production companies, runs it.

Preview of Volume 5

We are pleased to present you a preview from volume 5. This volume is available in English now!

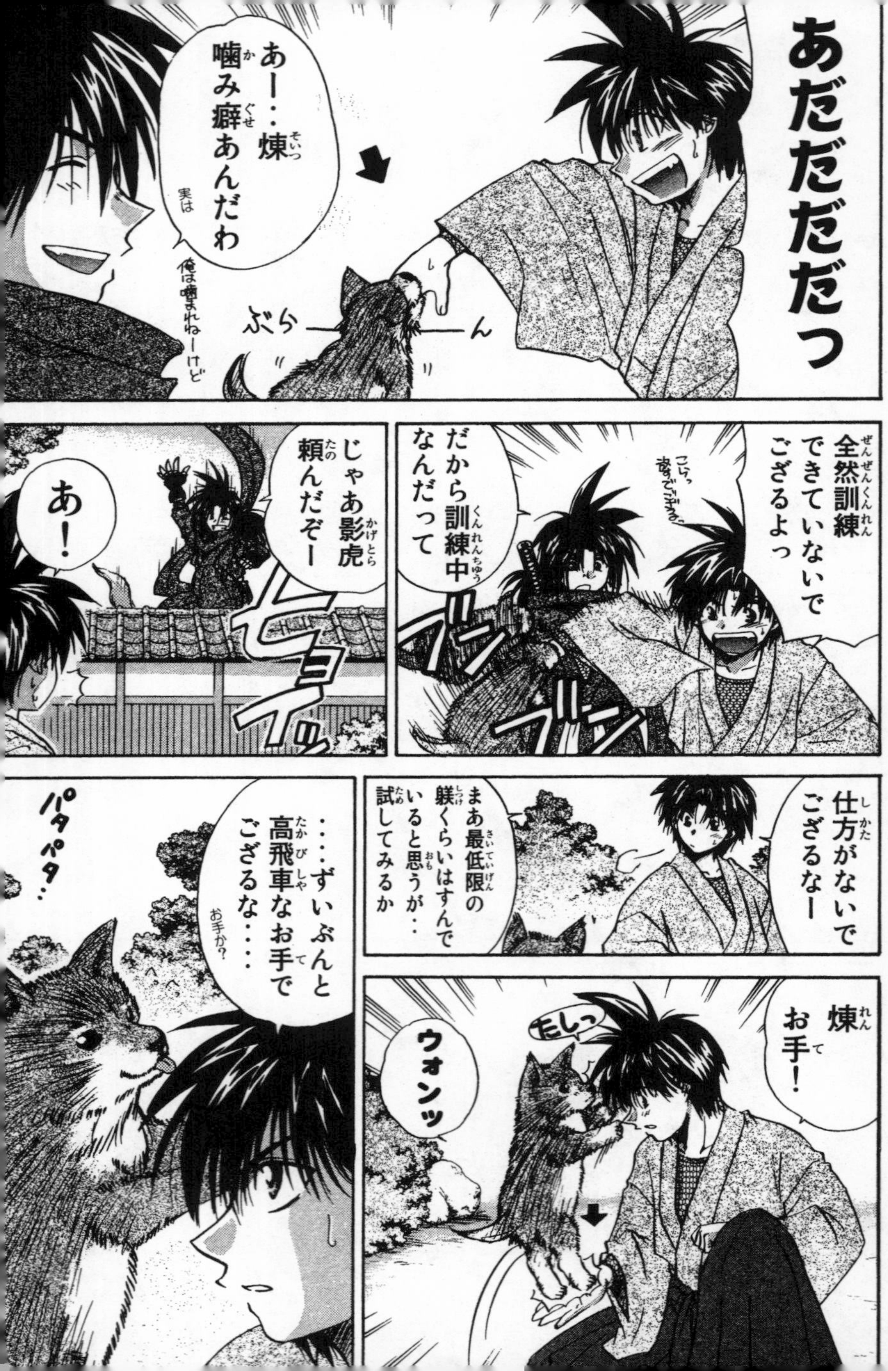

あだだだだっ
ぶら――ん
あー・・煉噛み癖あんだわ
実は
俺は噛まれねーけど
全然訓練できていないでござるよっ
こらっ 放すでござるっ
だから訓練中なんだって
じゃあ影虎頼んだぞー
ヒョイッ
あー!
仕方がないでござるなー
まあ最低限の躾くらいはすんでいると思うが・・試してみるか
煉お手!
たしっ
ウォンッ
・・・・ずいぶんと高飛車なお手でござるな・・・・
お手か?
パタパタ・・

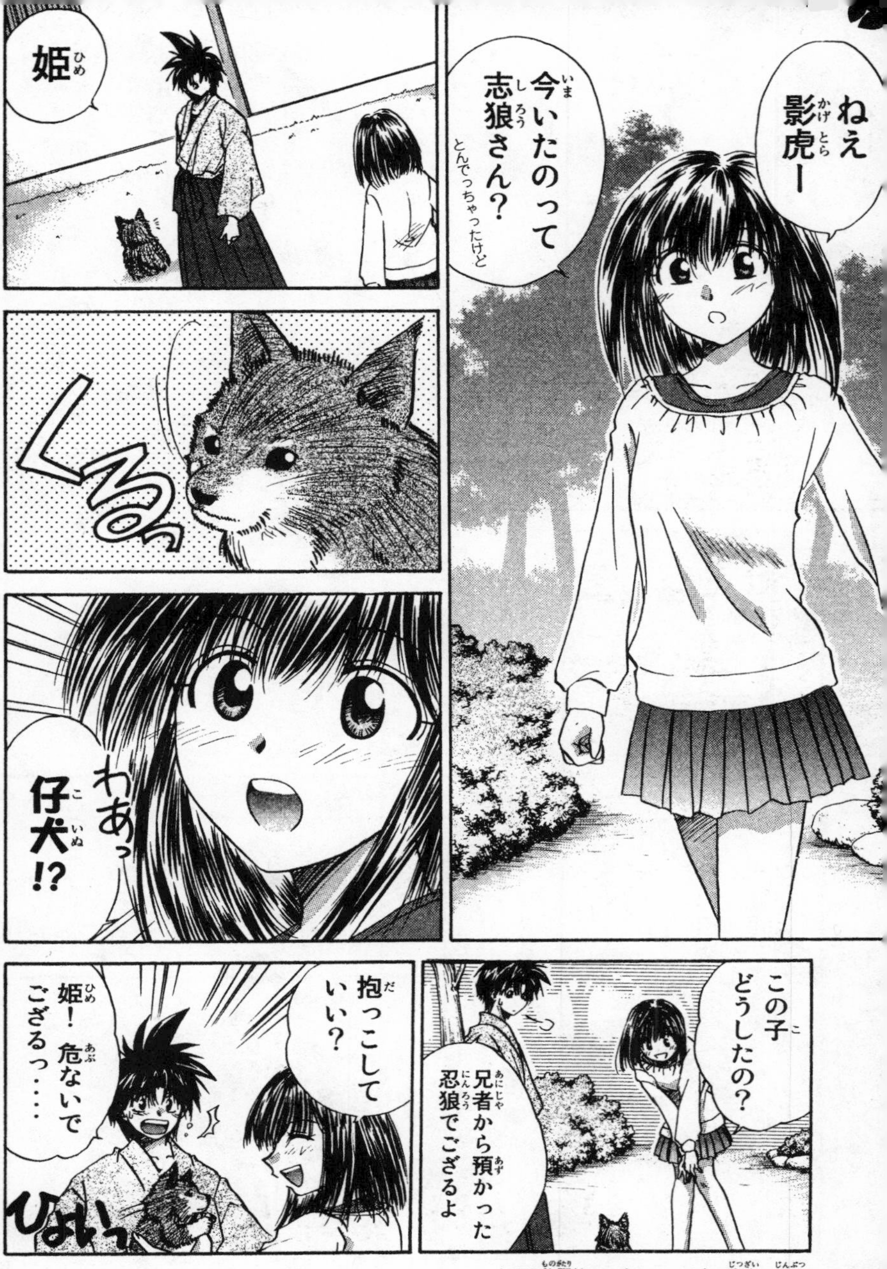
ねえ影虎ー
今いたのって志狼さん？
とんでっちゃったけど
姫
くるっ
わあっ
仔犬!?
この子どうしたの？
兄者から預かった忍狼でござるよ
抱っこしていい？
姫！ 危ないでござるっ‥‥
ひょいっ

★この物語はフィクションです。実在の人物、団体名等とは関係ありません。

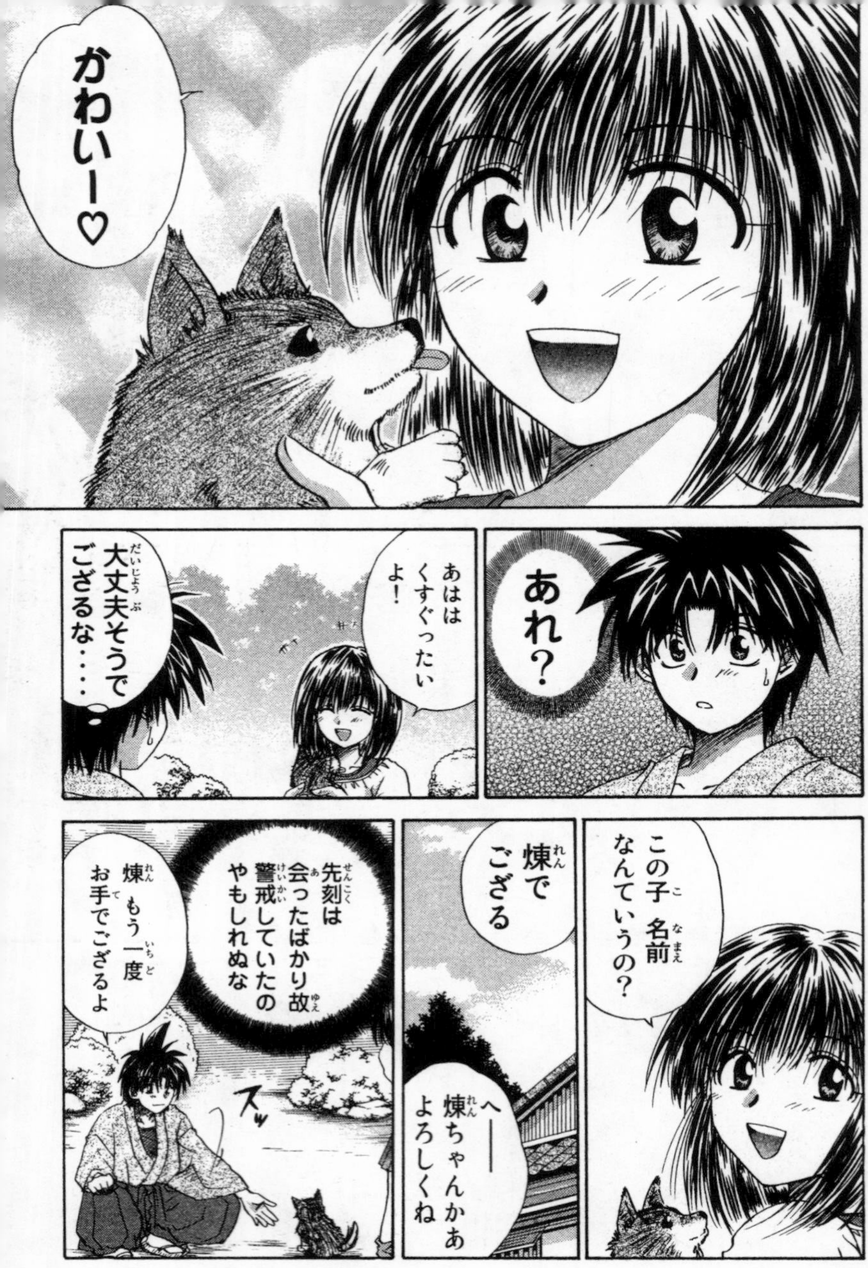
かわいー♡
あれ？
あははくすぐったいよ！
大丈夫そうでござるな‥‥
この子名前なんていうの？
煉でござる
へー煉ちゃんかぁよろしくね
先刻は会ったばかり故警戒していたのやもしれぬな
煉もう一度お手でござるよ
ズッ

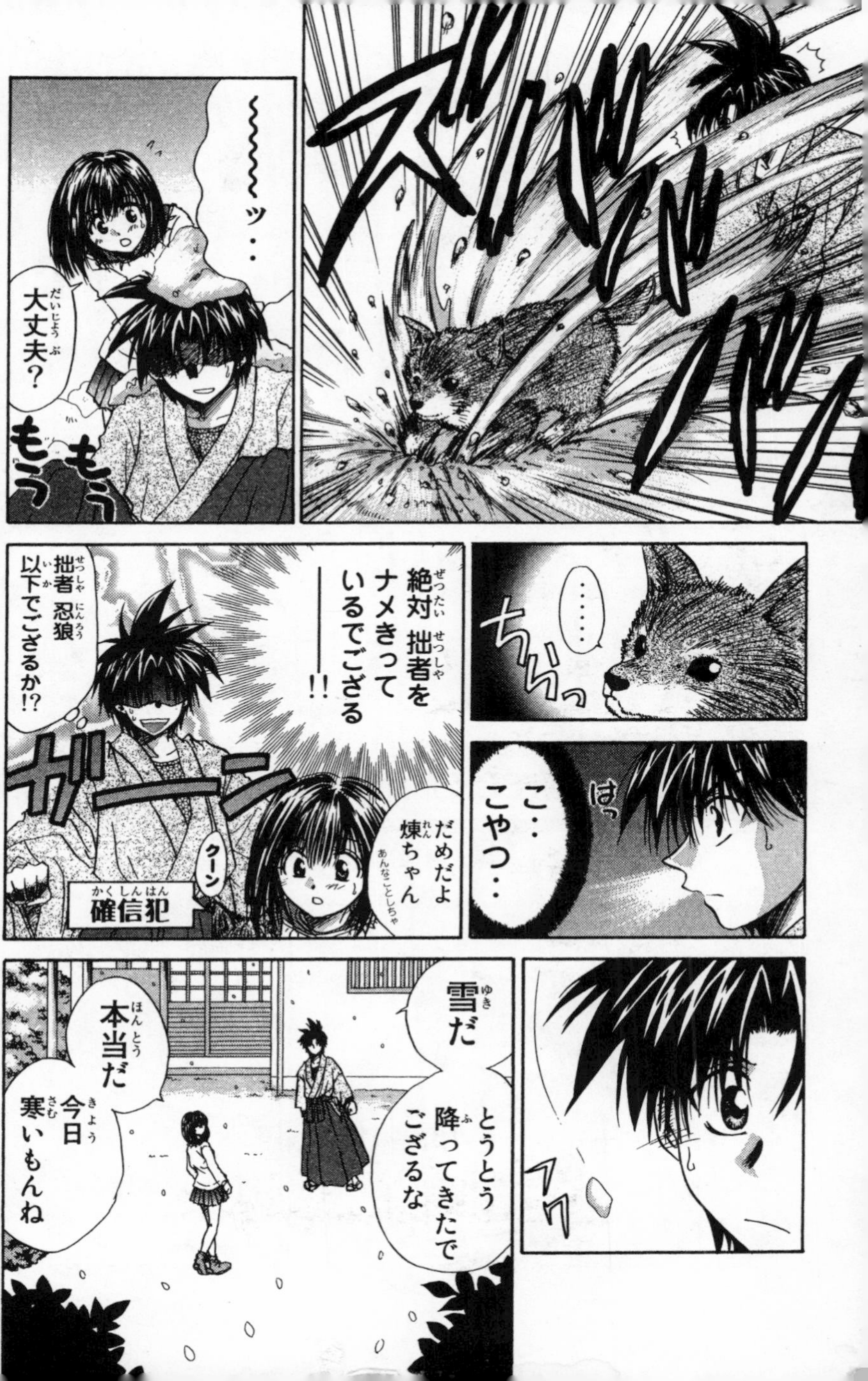
～～～～ッ・・
大丈夫？
……
ちらっ
はっ
こ・・こやつ・・
絶対拙者をナメきっているでござる――!!
拙者 忍狼以下でござるか!?
だめだよ煉ちゃん
あんなことしちゃ
クーン
確信犯
雪だ
とうとう降ってきたでござるな
本当だ 今日寒いもんね

You are going the wrong way!

Manga is a completely different
type of reading experience.

To start at the *beginning*, go to the *end!*

That's right! Authentic manga is read the traditional Japanese
way—from right to left. Exactly the *opposite* of how American
books are read. It's easy to follow: just go to the other end of
the book, a͟n͟d͟ ͟r͟e͟a͟d͟ ͟e͟a͟c͟h͟ ͟p͟a͟g͟e͟—͟a͟n͟d͟ ͟e͟a͟c͟h͟ ͟p͟a͟n͟e͟l͟—from right side
to left side, starting at the top right. Now you're experiencing
manga as it was meant to be.